THE HIDDEN CIVIL WAR

The Story of the Copperheads

The Hidden Civil War

The Story of the Copperheads

BY

WOOD GRAY

Associate Professor of American History, The George Washington University

1942

Published by The Viking Press · New York

TO DOROTHEA

In Appreciation

Contents

Maps

Illustrations

ACKNOWLEDGMENTS

Every book is a co-operative work, and in the years that have gone into the making of this one a debt of gratitude has been contracted that can be only partially acknowledged here. Historical research in America is made pleasant by the almost universal disposition of those in charge of its records and repositories to be helpful and considerate beyond the requirements of their positions. Among such I wish especially to thank Dr. St. George L. Sioussat, Dr. Thomas P. Martin, John J. De Porry, Vincent L. Eaton, and Donald M. Mugridge of the Manuscript Division of the Library of Congress, Donald G. Patterson, Frank E. Louraine, Leland D. Norton, Stewart Dickson, Edward H. Preston, John E. Alden, and Joy R. Blanchard of the Reading Rooms staff, and Dallas D. Irvine, Elbert E. Huber, and Jerome Thomases of the National Archives. Also Paul M. Angle, Miss Margaret A. Flint, and Miss Ruth Parker of the Illinois State Historical Library, Mrs. Alice Daly O'Connor, formerly of the Chicago Historical Society Library, Dr. Herbert A. Kellar and Miss Lorraine C. Weber of the McCormick Historical Association, Dr. Theodore C. Pease and Miss Marguerite Jenison of the Illinois Survey, Mrs. Hazel W. Hopper and Miss Marguerite Anderson of the Indiana State Library, Miss Caroline Dunn of the Indiana State Historical Society Library, Miss Mary V. Gorgas of the Indianapolis Public Library, Dr. Harlow Lindley of the Ohio State Archaeological and Historical Society, and Dr. Milo M. Quaife, Miss Anne Louise Kavanagh and Miss G. B. Krum of the Burton Collection of the Detroit Public Library. Mr. R. G. Hainsworth of the Bureau of Agricultural Economics of the United States Department of Agriculture has been most generous in providing a set of rare base maps of 1860. Mr. Frank Boyce was of valued assistance in the preparation of the original maps in this book.

Professor Avery Craven of the University of Chicago has aided this work at every stage in ways that make any expression of gratitude inadequate. It has benefited, too, from the criticisms of Professors William T. Hutchinson of the University of Chicago and Charles Ray Wilson of Colgate University. The most valued by-product of the study has been the friendship that has grown up with each of these men.

A cycle of typists has shown endless patience with an atrociously interlineated manuscript and skill in deciphering a crabbed handwriting. They have included Mrs. Vivian Franklyn Payne, Miss Beatrice Hackstaff, Miss Frances Lackey, Mrs. Elizabeth Owens Sheehy, Mrs. Mary Ellen Forlines, Mrs. Margaret Gamble, and Mrs. Barbara Younger.

11

Finally, much is due to my birthplace, the small Middle Western community of Petersburg (once New Salem), Illinois, as it existed two decades and more ago. Here the floods of Southern and Eastern immigration had met and left their marks. Aging "boys in blue" were full of reminiscences which made the era of the sixties seem as real and as recent to their hearers as they were to those who told them. There were surviving Copperheads from "Secesh Lane," too. Around the village square, at the annual "threshing run," in the smoke-filled offices of the court-house where the vote was received on election nights there were to be encountered all the types that peopled the old Middle West.

In short, I have known the men in this book, or their counterparts. I learned early something of their beliefs and prejudices, their naïveté and shrewd good sense, their hidden weaknesses and their elemental power for the common good.

CHAPTER I

Background for Defeatism:

THE MIDDLE WEST OF 1860

ONE day in the black winter of 1862 Senator Sumner called at the White House. Afterward he wrote to his friend Professor Francis Lieber, "These are dark hours. . . . The President tells me that he now fears 'the fire in the rear'—meaning the Democracy, especially at the Northwest—more than our military chances." [1] Behind this statement there is a story that is not to be found, except incidentally and incompletely, in all the mountain of books on the Civil War.

A month had gone by since the bloody repulse of the Army of the Potomac at Fredericksburg and loyal men of the North were in despair, while opponents of the war were enjoying a spiteful triumph in the apparent bearing out of their prophecies. The administration was confronted by a problem which would today be called defeatism. The term would not come into use until the World War of 1914–18 had brought the recognition that in war morale is as vital as strategy or materiel, but even in Lincoln's day it was no new phenomenon. During the Revolution there had been Tories and "sunshine patriots"; the War of 1812 had had its "Blue Light" Federalists who refused to support "Mr. Madison's War" and dabbled in secession plots; and in 1846 there had been Abolitionists and "Conscience Whigs" who urged the Mexicans to welcome American soldiers to "hospitable graves." [2] Almost every country has known the problem in some form, particularly since the French Revolution introduced to modern times the concept of the nation-in-arms that makes it necessary for a people at war to throw into a conflict their entire resources, including the economic and the psychological. Experience has shown that defeatist leadership generally comes from men who have from the outset been openly or secretly opposed to the war and its objectives, but when such a movement is at its height the greater danger may arise from those who desire victory but who have become discouraged by prolonged fighting and mounting costs. To this danger the United States, sprawling and heterogeneous and with a tradition of the sacred right of minority dissent, has been particularly susceptible.

The subject is not wholly historical. In any future crisis this nation may almost certainly expect to be once more face to face with some aspect of defeatism. Men inspired by political ambition, or sympathetic with the philosophy of the enemy, or blinded by petty hatreds will probably play the role that their fellows have in the past. They can expect to be assisted by those who so much dread any disturbance of their accustomed existence that they will close their eyes and insist that there is no need for action and sacrifice. These elements will unite in denouncing anyone who may attempt to arouse the nation to a sense of danger, vehemently charging that person with having manufactured the danger or even insisting that he is himself more to be feared than the enemy. All these things have been characteristic of such times in the past, and if anyone doubts that the materials for such opposition exist today he has not read his daily newspaper thoughtfully enough in recent years. The story here is told only in terms of itself and against the background of the 1860's, but implicitly and inescapably there are parallels which point to the future as well as to an earlier past. A wise people learns from such experiences.

The belief that the North would not fight wholeheartedly, if it fought at all, was one of the three chief factors that the South had counted on to insure the success of secession. It was a hope that persisted even after the others were gone. One expectation, that of foreign aid, was fading by the end of 1862. After Gettysburg and Vicksburg it had completely disappeared; and also it was by that time no longer possible to hope for a strictly military victory—on the basis of superior leadership, natural fighting qualities, and advantageous geography—against the numbers and resources of the North. The Confederacy was reduced to fighting a stubborn, slowly yielding defensive action that could have but one result—if the North were sufficiently determined upon victory to pay the cost. It may not be too much to say that the last half of the Civil War turned upon this last condition. In the end, of course, the South was herself engulfed in defeatism, and one of the most faithful servants of the Confederacy would later admit that "we failed because too many of our people were not determined to win." [3] But that is another story, and one that has already been told. [4]

Primarily the South was looking to the Middle West, a section which in spite of internal variations had a basic unity of outlook, make-up, and interests that set it off from other parts of the nation. There would be opposition to the war in the Northeast, the border slave states, Kansas, and the Far West, but in none of those other areas would defeatism seriously endanger the Union cause. They would have their own problems and points of view, arising from the distinctive character of their environment, population, and history. This study is concentrated upon the defeatist movement in the region where it had its greatest strength, the Midwest. Bound by many ties to the states that formed the Confederacy, many of its people were opposed to war as a means of restoring the Union, although after April 1861 no other course of action could accomplish that end. Only a few of the opponents of the war would have actual dealings with agents of the Confederacy, but all, whatever their intentions, would to the extent of their activities serve its purposes as certainly as though members of a formal alliance.

All opponents of the war had at least one thing in common: they were human beings acting from human motives. These motives grew out of a complex of forces—geographic, economic, racial, political, and personal—some of them the result of events of the immediate past while others had their roots in an antiquity measurable only in millenniums and millions of years. Most of them were the reflection in one way or another of a rural civilization, product of a land that, rising in foothills along the Ohio River, swept back to the north and west in timbered valleys and rolling prairies to include an area four times as large as Great Britain.

More than half of its people were directly employed in agricultural pursuits, the vast majority small farmers engaged in the production of foodstuffs—wheat, corn, oats, and livestock. Nature had endowed the region with all things needed for agricultural prosperity, but it had not equally favored every part of it. Ages before, the glaciers had pushed down from eastern Canada and carried

AGRICULTURAL WEALTH, 1860. Black counties—per capita value of land
and improvements below average for the state.

along the topsoil of the lands from which they came, mixing it with
rock fragments that were pulverized by mechanical action—thus
retaining elements of fertility that would have been lost in slower
methods of disintegration—and then had spread the resulting material in a thick blanket over the section. One of the finest seed
beds on the earth's surface was thus created. But only one of the
succession of glacial expansions reached the southern parts of Illinois, Indiana, and Ohio, while a strip of land along the Ohio River
lay entirely beyond the limits of the ice sheets. A portion of central
Wisconsin was also left unglaciated by a split in the ice flow, and
the middle section of Michigan suffered in another fashion, the
topsoil being swept off and replaced by a deposit of undigested

rocks and sand. In 1860, consequently, the northern third of the
Middle West, being generally infertile and with potentialities for
lumbering and mining rather than agriculture, was still thinly
populated, the central third had the best agricultural endowment,
while the people of the less favored southern third tended to be
envious of their more fortunate neighbors to the north. Here at the
outset was a line of division within the section as old in the world
as the tillage of the soil.[5]

By 1860 the frontiersman's ax had cleared away much of the
original forest, but much still remained as evidence of another factor that had shaped the early development of the section and fostered its internal divisions. Rainfall, although everywhere adequate
for full utilization of the soil, had varied sufficiently, in combination with the range of temperature, to divide the original garment
of vegetation into three roughly wedge-shaped regions converging
near the southeastern corner of Lake Michigan: the western wedge
grassland, the northeastern coniferous forest, and the southeastern
deciduous forest. Since the earlier or true type of frontiersman from
the South needed timber close at hand for his isolated, self-sufficing
existence, he had been restricted to the latter two regions. Settlement of the prairies had lagged behind, awaiting a man-made system
of transportation that would bring in lumber from a distance, re-
served for later comers from another direction, the east.

The outstanding economic requirement of the Middle West was
facilities to carry its surplus foodstuffs to market in the urbanized
industrial sections of the northeastern United States and northwestern Europe. Indeed, the development of transportation in the
nation as a whole in the half-century preceding the Civil War had
been in large part shaped by this need. By 1860 the problem had
been solved in its major aspects by the construction of railways,
much of the ten thousand miles of trackage in the country having
been laid to connect the farms and trade centers of the Midwest
with the cities of the north Atlantic seaboard. From Boston, New
York, and Philadelphia the lines stretched to the Mississippi River
and half-way across Iowa. Of the Midwestern states only Minnesota
had yet no trackage within its borders and it was served by a line
that tapped its system of river transport near the southeast corner
of the state. Illinois had the greatest railway mileage of any state in

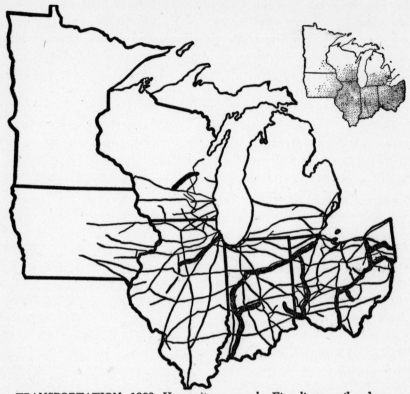

TRANSPORTATION, 1860. Heavy lines—canals. Fine lines—railroads.
AGRICULTURE, 1860 (Insert). Each dot—25,000 acres of improved land.

the Union. Although efforts had been made by cities of the Southeast to intercept the trade of the section north of the Ohio River
with rival lines, they had fallen far short of their objectives, and it
was noteworthy that only at Washington, D.C., and Louisville,
Kentucky, were there connections between the otherwise independent railway systems of the North and South. Iron bands a thousand
miles long bound East and West together in a commercial network
in which the South had little part. Alongside the railroads ran the
telegraph lines carrying business orders, news, and the interchange
of ideas. These, too, served to bind the Midwest to the Northeast
more closely than to the South.[6]

But in viewing the commercial connections of the section it must

be remembered that the railways were largely a development of
the 1850's. The story had been a very different one in earlier decades. In the beginning trade had depended chiefly upon natural
waterway systems. Of these there were two, neither entirely satisfactory. The far-flung Mississippi River system was tortuous and
subject to many navigation hazards, and it gave access to markets
other than those of the South and the West Indies by an extremely
roundabout course; on the other hand, the Great Lakes lacked
navigable feeder streams and natural harbors and were separated
from the ocean by falls and the jurisdiction of an alien power. Until
man succeeded in correcting and supplementing nature, the Mississippi in spite of its shortcomings possessed the advantage. Before
the close of the eighteenth century, flatboats and keel boats were
already bearing cargoes from the old Northwest Territory to New
Orleans. After 1812 the steamboat offered a new means of river
trade, and a decade or two later nearly a thousand steamboatloads
of goods from the upper valley were being unloaded each year at
the wharves of the delta metropolis. Innumerable flatboats supplemented that traffic and also peddled supplies from village to village
and plantation to plantation along the great river and its tribu-
taries.[7] By negotiations that opened the British West Indies in 1830
to a larger sale of Midwestern products, Jacksonian diplomacy ushered in the golden age of the river. In all this period the trading
ties of the Midwest were primarily with the South. The most feasible connections with the Northeast were either by a circuitous
route down the river to the Gulf of Mexico and then by coastal
vessels to the north Atlantic ports, or else by pack animals along the
forest trails crossing the Appalachians, in either case impractical
for the free movement of bulky or perishable commodities.

The completion of the Erie Canal inaugurated a revolution in
trade routes. The Great Lakes gained an outlet that avoided Niagara Falls and ran entirely within the territory of the United States.
The natural lack of navigable rivers to bring goods to the lakeshore
was overcome by the construction of other canals that tapped the
Mississippi system at strategic points; five major projects of this
character were completed between 1832 and 1856. Lake Erie was
linked with the Ohio River by way of the Scioto, Miami, and Wabash rivers, and Lake Michigan was connected with the Mississippi

by way of the Illinois and Wisconsin rivers. Lake harbors were constructed or improved with appropriations from the federal government, and roads were built to supplement the main trunks of the waterway system, many of them being surfaced with planks, a practice originally developed on the soggy plains of eastern Europe and introduced to North America by a governor-general of Canada who had traveled in Russia. Even regions once tributary to New Orleans now began to send their produce northward. Although most of the merchants and citizens of the river metropolis were slow to sense this change, since the loss was balanced by the continued development of the lower Mississippi region, the keener observers perceived that a revolution was taking place.[8] To no one were the implications more alarmingly clear than to James Dunwoody Brownson De Bow, a native of Charleston who was then a resident of New Orleans. De Bow, a master of statistics, was the editor of the federal census of 1850 and of *De Bow's Review of the Southern and Western States,* both publications which are still indispensable to any student of the period. Speaking in the legislative hall in Nashville in 1851 he lamented:

. . . What is New Orleans now? Where are her dreams of greatness and of glory? . . . Whilst she slept, an enemy has sowed tares in her most prolific fields. Armed with energy, enterprise, and an indomitable spirit, that enemy, by a series of bold, vigorous, and sustained efforts, has succeeded in reversing the very laws of nature and of nature's God —rolled back the mighty tide of the Mississippi and its ten thousand tributary streams, until their mouth, practically and commercially is more at New York or Boston than at New Orleans. . . .[9]

The change brought about by the canals was climaxed by the building of railroads, and meanwhile the expanding demands of the manufacturing areas had come to dwarf the markets offered by the Gulf Coast and the West Indies. New Orleans, once the focus of the exported resources of the great central valley of the continent, was by 1860 largely a port for its own immediate hinterland and had all but ceased to be a factor in the commerce of the Northwest. Local trade with the South, although still flourishing in certain districts, was greatly overshadowed by the volume of business transacted with the Northeast. But the change had been too recent for its meaning to be fully understood. A belief that im-

portant economic considerations bound South and Midwest together was deeply imbedded in the assumptions of the latter
section. The average Midwesterner, no close scanner of current statistics, was still thinking to a large degree in terms of the old lines
of trade. In his economic motivation past tradition was almost as
important as contemporary fact.

Blood as well as trade bound the Midwest to the South. It is impossible to know just what proportion of the nearly 8,000,000 Midwesterners, one-fourth of the population of the nation, were of
Southern descent in 1860. The census of that year reveals that seven
per cent had been born in the slave states (as compared with eleven
per cent in 1850), by far the greatest proportion of them living in
the lower tier of states, where they constituted eleven per cent of
the inhabitants of Indiana, ten per cent in Illinois, and five per
cent in Ohio. Unfortunately the published records do not give the
statistics by counties, and to obtain such information would involve
the herculean task of retabulating the millions of original returns
in the Bureau of the Census. No record was made of parents' birthplace, but it is reasonable to assume that more than one-half of the
fifty-seven per cent born in the Midwest were of Southern origin.
Perhaps about forty per cent of the Midwesterners of 1860 were of
Southern blood, forty per cent Northeastern, and twenty per cent
of foreign birth or parentage. From other records we know that in
certain districts the Southern elements especially predominated. In
Ohio there were three such areas: one, in the southeastern part
of the state east of the Muskingum River, known as the "Seven
Ranges"; a second, the "Virginia Military Tract," between the
Scioto and Miami rivers; and the third, a northwestward extension
of the second toward the Indiana and Michigan boundaries. The
same was true of southern Indiana and southern Illinois, of that
portion of western Illinois that lay along the Illinois and Mississippi
rivers, and in Iowa along the Mississippi and in a strip about two
counties wide along the border of the state of Missouri.

The process of settlement had closely paralleled the development
of means of transport and to a considerable extent was governed
by it, immigration from the South being overwhelmingly predomi-
nant in the earlier period, only to be in time outnumbered by
Northeastern immigration. The path of Southern migration can

be traced back to Pennsylvania, which as a British colony had gained such an excellent reputation for economic opportunities and political and religious liberty that during the eighteenth century the port of Philadelphia became a veritable funnel of immigration through which flowed a stream of English, Scotch-Irish, and Germans seeking to better themselves in the New World. Swelling rapidly, this stream covered the most attractive lands of the colony and, turned southward by the Appalachian system, spread into the piedmont belt from Maryland to Georgia. In this back-country region, joined by migrants from the tidewater South but otherwise largely shut off from contact with the lowlands by the fall lines in the rivers, these folk developed a distinct way of life, indigenous and self-sufficient, to become the first authentic American frontiersmen. By the third quarter of the eighteenth century this reservoir of population began to overflow across the Appalachian barrier. Its people were driven to seek new homes by a number of factors, including the natural increase of population, the exhaustion of lands by "soil butchery," confusion in land titles, the economic depressions that followed the American Revolution and the Napoleonic wars, reaction to the advance of the plantation system, and political disagreement with the tidewater sections. Beyond the mountains were rivers and Indian trails leading them to the Ohio River; and a decade before the much heralded first settlement of New Englanders at Marietta men of this stock had staked out "tomahawk claims" on the right bank of the Ohio. The early group settlements of the New Englanders on the Ohio and in the Western Reserve along Lake Erie were more spectacular and would receive more attention from later historians, but in respect to the numbers involved they were much less significant than the prosaic, individualistic, and continuing migration from the South.

The families from the Southern uplands had adjusted themselves to a type of life which demanded two essentials, timber and navigable streams. The forest supplied logs for their rough cabins and the material for turning out crude household utensils and farm tools. It fed the voracious open fireplaces at which their food was cooked and which were their only means of holding back the bitter cold of winter. Creeks and rivers permitted a minimum of trade in guns, ammunition, knives, ax blades, needles, and a few other

articles without which even the frontiersman could not subsist.
Where such conditions were to be found these people settled, avoid-
ing the unsuitable treeless prairies. Until after the Civil War this
area was to be the stronghold of the Southern stock in the Middle
West.

Among these people the views and prejudices of the immigrant
generation tended to persist and to be transmitted to their descendants. Many had brought with them a hatred of slavery and the
plantation system which seemed to give an unfair economic advantage to wealthier men. But also—and failure to grasp this fact
has led to much misunderstanding of the attitude of the Midwest
toward sectional issues of the 1840's and '50's—this hatred extended
with equal or greater fervor to the Negro himself, and it was coupled
with the ever-present fear that any weakening of his bondage would
permit him to migrate northward. Later arrivals in communities
founded by Southerners quite naturally tended, whatever their
origins, to fall in with the habits and views already established
there. The sense of blood ties with the South was a factor to be
reckoned with. The strain was a distinct and persistent type—narrow, prejudiced, combative, easy-going but intolerant, fiercely individualistic and equalitarian yet capable of persistent loyalty to
leaders and concepts that succeeded in winning its allegiance. It
did not quickly or easily give up its identity or convictions.[10]

Until the natural obstacles to communication between the Northeast and Midwest were disposed of, Eastern settlement was comparatively meager, such early movements as those of the New Englanders to Marietta and the Western Reserve being isolated ven-
tures rather than indicative of a general movement of population. Up to the third decade of the nineteenth century the Northeastern surplus of people generally sought out still unoccupied
lands in Vermont, New Hampshire, and Maine, or went to northern
Pennsylvania or the central and western portions of New York.
New England colonies in the Ohio Valley remained small islands
in a sea of Southern folk, while the lack of outlets to market and
the scarcity of timber in much of the Great Lakes region made that
section, to which Northeasterners would naturally have turned, one
that had little appeal for the prospective settler. As late as 1821 it
was reported that there was not a single white inhabitant in the

prairie district reaching from Chicago to Peoria, and four years later there were still less than 1300 people in the whole northern half of Illinois.[11]

But with the completion of the Erie Canal and the subsequent development of artificial waterways and the railway systems there came a tremendous change. An easy means of reaching the land around the Great Lakes was now available. Even more important was the fact that the new transportation answered the riddle of prairie farming, since cheap transportation eliminated the self-sufficient stage of pioneering and made lack of timber no longer a deterrent to settlement. At the same time the last of the remaining good lands around the borders of the Northeast itself were being taken up, leaving an unaccommodated surplus agricultural population eager for a new outlet. To such the Midwest offered unrivaled attractions. Not only were its lands fertile and easily obtainable, but its abundant crops could be conveniently and cheaply sent to market. And behind the invitation to migrate was a growing threat. The increasing competition of Western products in Eastern markets placed before those who farmed worn-out acres a three-way choice: to remain and sink into deepening poverty, to seek a place in the rising industrial system of the cities, or to take the route to the newly opened country. For thousands the last was the most acceptable choice. The northern portions of Ohio and Indiana and the northern and eastern parts of Illinois began to fill rapidly with the evidences of civilization, and the new states of Michigan, Wisconsin, Iowa, and Minnesota were brought into being. To this movement central and western New York had the relationship that the Southern piedmont had borne to the earlier migration. In three decades the one-time dominance of upland Southerners in the Midwest was strongly diluted and blood ties with the South were matched by connections with the Northeast.[12]

The change did not come about without friction, for Southerners and Yankees viewed each other with distrust. In many respects their temperaments were strikingly dissimilar. The Easterners were acquisitive and disposed to respect education and to adhere rigidly to the social proprieties. The earlier settlers seemed to them shiftless, ignorant, rough, and quarrelsome, while they were in turn regarded as cold, grasping, sanctimonious, and hypocritical. The Southerners were accustomed to the apocalyptic evangelism of the camp meeting and valued ministers who, in Lincoln's expressive simile, preached as though fighting bumblebees. They were repelled by the cold piety of the Yankees. Thus suspicion repaid suspicion with interest compounded. A persistent group cleavage and repeated clashes of personalities marked the contact of the two elements in spite of contrary forces that tended to effect a merging of interests and outlook.

Besides these two native American elements there were three sizable groups of the foreign-born who had a hand in building the Midwest as it existed in 1860. They were, in the order of their numbers and importance, the Germans, Irish, and natives of Great Britain and the English-speaking provinces of Canada. At the outbreak of the war they totaled more than one-sixth of the population. As a rule they came in by the same routes as the Northeasterners and settled in the same districts. In Germany, particularly in the Rhine Valley, a number of expulsive influences had been at work: the spread of the Industrial Revolution had disrupted the economic life of regions in which handicraft manufactures had flourished, and acute suffering accompanied the process of readjustment; crop failures and other problems had depressed agriculture; there was a resurgence of governmental efforts to enforce religious conformity; and the blighting of the hopes of political liberals in the abortive uprisings of 1830 and 1848 drove many in central Europe to despair of the possibility of reform at home. To all such classes reports of the economic attractions and the hospitable democracy of the United States carried a tempting invitation. Those who first ventured across the ocean generally wrote back glowing accounts of the fulfillment of their hopes, and these "American letters" stirred hosts of others to follow. Thrifty peasants, land-hungry for generations, were drawn in great numbers to the rich agricultural areas of the West, where they added a strong German strain to the northern prairies and to the Illinois counties that lay across the Mississippi River from St. Louis. Others found that their skills in shoemaking, wood and cabinet work, brewing, and many other pursuits were greatly in demand in the rising new cities of the West and remained in these urban centers as artisans and tradesmen. In such places as Chicago, Cincinnati, St. Louis, and Milwaukee the Germans comprised from one-fifth to one-third of the total inhabitants. Both their foreign speech and their tendency to cluster together in compact communities of their own served to set them apart. They consequently tended to react as a body on public questions.[13]

Crop failures, an oppressive land system, and suppressed aspirations for national independence had scourged the Irish from their old homes. A smaller proportion than of the Germans succeeded in reaching the Midwest. Most of them arrived in America possessed of little but hatred of Britain and the ability to do manual labor. In the East industry offered them opportunities for employment, while their scanty resources could ill afford the cost of a journey to the interior immediately after an ocean voyage. But in time many did go West, often being recruited as laborers in constructing canals and railroads, and then in many instances when such tasks were completed they settled down along the routes their hands had built. Thus they came into the great commercial centers and to such way-points as Joliet, Illinois, where an Irish colony brought in for the digging of the Illinois Canal dominated local politics for years. Their unhappy late experiences with farming in the old country, added to their proverbial gregariousness, turned most of the Irish to the larger cities. They were most numerous in Chicago, where in 1860 nearly one-fifth of the inhabitants were of Irish birth, and least so in Milwaukee, being there but one-twentieth of the total. All told, natives of Ireland residing in the Middle West in 1860 amounted to some 320,000 persons, as compared to 585,000 Germans. Set apart by their Roman Catholic religion and their humble social status they, like the Germans, tended to stand together in their political reactions. Concentration in settlement and natural aptitude for human contacts made them an element of no mean power in politics.[14]

The foreign-born from Great Britain and British America were more numerous than is generally known, for they totaled some 290,000. Since neither language nor religion constituted a bar between them and the mass of native population they quickly merged in the general pattern, almost without ever having been regarded as "foreigners." They tended to merge more readily with the New Englanders than with any other group, settling where that element did and sharing its attitudes, including hostility toward the institution of slavery. Alien elements other than these three were too few and scattered to have any particular influence in determining the section's attitudes.

In the election of 1860 the Republican party not only carried each of the seven states for Lincoln but elected each of its candidates for governor as well. But against this was the fact that in the section as a whole the Republican margin of victory was the narrow one of eight to seven and that until but a few years before the Democratic party had been entrenched in power. Politics in the three or four decades preceding the war had reflected the forces already considered—population origins, commercial affiliations, and economic status—perhaps in about that order of importance. In the process new animosities and divisions had been created. Until the 1850's the Democratic was the dominant party, basically representing in its creation by Jefferson and its realignment under Jackson an alliance between Southern and Western views. The preponderance of Southerners in the early settlement, mostly men of the back-country type that had rallied to the Democratic standard in the old home, gave that party an initial and powerful advantage. Other factors operating in the same direction were the belief that the commercial relationship of the Midwest could best be served by the economic program favored by that party and the frontier tendency to be dubious of the Whigs as tinged with aristocratic and plutocratic pretensions. With the infiltration of the foreign-born an added support accrued to the party of Old Hickory and his successors. The Germans and Irish sensed a certain condescension and hostility in the more prosperous Whig elements, and working upon this foundation the proselyting cleverness of the superior Democratic machine was able to garner the greater part of their votes. During this period the Whig party was unable to compete with the Democrats on anything like equal terms, except possibly in Ohio. In that state the Yankees of the Western Reserve and the Marietta district were able to ally themselves with Southerners who had brought with them a strong Federalist and Whig inheritance, an element numerous in the Virginia Military Tract and represented by such leaders as Thomas Corwin, Thomas Ewing, and William Henry Harrison.

In time the alliance with the South under the Democratic banner

began to weaken. During the administration of President Polk a
conviction developed in the West that the national leadership of
the party was concerning itself exclusively with Southern interests.
In the presidential election campaign of 1844 the Democrats had
promised the "reoccupation of Oregon"—to which Midwesterners
were already migrating—all the way to Alaska. Polk's betrayal of
this commitment by accepting a compromise boundary at the 49th
parallel while adding all New Mexico to the "reannexation of
Texas" may have been directed by common sense, but it rankled in
Western memories. His veto of the Rivers and Harbors Bill of 1846
was an even more direct blow to the section that stood most in need
of such legislation. A protest convention of representative Westerners of both parties that met in Chicago in the following year
indicated a reshaping of political affiliations. And more funda-
mentally the growth of Northeastern settlement and the transport
revolution were preparing the way for a major change.

In 1854 the Kansas-Nebraska Act precipitated a far-reaching
party realignment. In its economic program the new Republican
party represented in Western eyes a sectional bargain with the industrial Northeast. It was expected that in return for limited concessions to the East in regard to protective tariffs and increased
banking facilities the West would secure transportation subsidies,
perhaps culminating in a transcontinental railway, and a homestead policy that would quickly fill out the prairie frontier and
bring the profits of unearned increment and expanded commerce.
To cap this program and set it off, the question of slavery would
serve a double purpose to which the two sections could equally
agree. The proposal for checking the spread of that institution into
the territories would offer a high moral appeal to those who were
responsive to a sentimental issue; at the same time it would serve
as a formula for preventing the increase of the plantation interest's
voting strength in Congress, thus thwarting the common enemy of
the Western farmer and Eastern manufacturer. Righteousness and
practical considerations could be yoked ingeniously together.

In the process a beginning, at least, was made toward winning
over the German vote. The small group of educated political liberals among them, represented by such men as Carl Schurz, Franz
Sigel, and Gustave Koerner, welcomed the idealism of the new

movement and urged their fellows to join them in the Republican alliance. By 1860 they had made marked inroads among the formerly Democratic Germans, although the tradition (originating with the natural tendency of those like Schurz to overestimate their own influence and later perpetuated by the comfort it gave to racial pride) that this group held the balance of power in the Midwest and was therefore decisive in the success of the new party seems not to be borne out by the available evidence. The mass of Germans were conservative and slow moving in their political thought, but with the solid establishment of the Republican organization the majority tended gradually and eventually to shift over to the new allegiance. A contributing factor may have been the fact that many of them had never been entirely happy in party association with the Irish, for whom they had a long-standing antipathy. Furthermore, the effort of certain Southern senators to attach an amendment to the Kansas-Nebraska Act (the Clayton Amendment) excluding unnaturalized foreigners from political rights in these territories seemed, even though unsuccessful, to foreshadow an abandonment by the Democratic party of its earlier friendliness toward the foreign-born.[15]

In the election of 1856 all the Midwestern states but Indiana and Illinois were found in the Republican presidential column, and in 1860 the choice of a candidate to suit the tastes of these two states resulted in the carrying of the Midwest as a block for Abraham Lincoln. The intersectional viewpoint of the Middle West had undergone a fundamental transformation in the three decades preceding the outbreak of the war. But there still remained many strong ties with the South. The large number of Southern origin or descent had not generally abandoned their earlier sentiments. The Irish remained stanchly faithful to the Democratic party, both valuing the past favors which it had accorded them and afraid that any meddling with the slavery question might result in the freeing of the Negroes, who would then come north to be the economic competitors and even the social equals of the laboring Irish. A large German block, especially among those who were Roman Catholics, was still suspicious of the Republicans, eying askance the large Know Nothing element which they had taken over in many of the states; and many of the German radicals who had crossed the party line on an anti-slavery plank were temperamental and egotistical to a degree that limited their dependability. Commercial ties with the South continued to be important, and, as a matter of fact, newly constructed railroads running south from Louisville and Columbus, Kentucky, and east from Memphis and Vicksburg were opening regional markets for Midwestern products. The river trade held a strong appeal for the imagination of the section and influenced its thinking more than cold statistics would warrant. There remained upon the statute books of Illinois and Indiana prohibitions of the immigration of free Negroes into those states, evidence of the persistence of a prejudice that would not be easily cast aside. In the campaign of 1860 Lincoln's campaign managers had found it advisable to play down even his moderate anti-slavery attitude; and in the end 700,000 voters in the Middle West still opposed the 800,000 voters who supported him. It was self-evident that the East-West alliance, with its various associated policies, was by no means universally accepted.

So stood the Midwest on the threshold of the supreme crisis of nationality in the United States. A section divided within itself would be called upon to turn its back upon many of the loyalties and traditions of its past. Upon one thing there was nearly complete agreement among its people, that the preservation of the Union, in which it had ties with all sections, was of vital importance to its interests. It was equally certain that without its endorsement the preservation of the nation by the use of force would be impossible; but it was not at all certain that it would consent to such an endorsement. It was a question, perhaps transcending all others, on which would turn the future of the Union.

CHAPTER II

The Period of Indecision

(December 20, 1860–April 12, 1861)

THE ballots of the presidential election had hardly been counted before events a thousand miles away began to move in a direction that would put the traditional attitudes and internal antagonisms of the Midwest to the supreme test. When it became certain that a "Black Republican" would succeed the "dough-faced" Buchanan in the White House, the legislature of South Carolina summoned to Charleston a sovereign convention to reconsider the state's connection with the Union. On December 20 the convention unanimously declared all ties between South Carolina and the other United States to be dissolved. A blunt fact had been thrown among the delicately adjusted constitutional theories of three-quarters of a century.

In spite of a generation and more of sectional quarrels and threats the Midwest was as little prepared for the fact of secession as for an invasion from the moon. Threats of secession had been so recklessly made in connection with every dispute of consequence since the adoption of the Constitution that they had come to be looked upon as a conventional form of bluff, a move in recognized political stategy, rather than as notification of serious intention. The cry of "Wolf!" had lost its power to warn. Consequently, when the febrile Carolinians converted a debated theory into an awful reality the first reaction of the Northern people was one of incredulous amazement followed by consternation.

The electoral campaign had been reassuring. Republican spokesmen, apparently sincere, had industriously fostered the view that Southern threats were nothing but another attempt to frighten "old women of both sexes." [1] In mid-autumn the ever-omniscient Chicago *Tribune* had explained to its readers:

ELECTION OF 1860. Black counties—50% or more against Lincoln.

Our friends may now expect a concerted howl of disunion from Texas to Maine. This is the only card left to our adversaries, and they will assuredly play it with desperate energy. We shall have a flood of letters from valiant Democratic Boabdils setting forth the imminent peril of the Union . . . public meetings in the slaveholding States passing resolves against the inauguration of a constitutionally elected President —correspondence between the Governors of slaveholding States recommending the calling together of the Legislatures of their respective States upon the election of Lincoln—and last, if not least of all, a call for a Southern Convention which will never be held, or, if held at all, will not be productive of anything more serious than a few fire-eating speeches, and a few blood-and-thunder resolutions. . . . There will be no disunion. . . .[2]

The Democrats, who might have been expected to play up the issue whether or not they took it seriously, evidently thought that it was too stale to do service.[3] After the campaign was over, one of their newspapers confessed editorially, "During the election we had looked upon the threats of the South and taunts of the North as electioneering clap-traps, incident upon overexcitement, unrestrained enthusiasm and impulsiveness."[4] Even Breckinridge newspapers in the Middle West paid little attention to the possibility that secession might be a consequence of Lincoln's election,[5] and when one Democratic editor racked his brain to discover thirty reasons why Lincoln should be defeated he completely overlooked this argument.[6] Late in the canvass disturbing reports of the state of feeling in the South convinced some of the Democratic leaders that the danger was real, and during the last week or ten days before the election the Cincinnati *Enquirer,* the Indianapolis *State Sentinel,* Detroit *Free Press,* Columbus *Ohio Statesman,* and Chicago *Times and Herald* began to sound the alarm.[7] But it was too late. The editors might as well have tried to cause water to run back uphill. Even in the six-week period between the election and the adoption of the South Carolina ordinance most people believed that only a very small and noisy minority of Southerners were advocating secession and that the great majority were lovers of the Union who would in due time assert themselves and prevent harm from being done.[8]

When South Carolina took action without waiting for the rest of the South and her example was followed by the Gulf states, wishful thinking finally became an impossibility, and the people of the North were forced to admit the existence of a distasteful reality. What, then, should be done about it? Almost as a matter of course the average citizen expected the national leaders to work out an acceptable program of compromise, the method that in the past had been unfailingly successful in resolving sectional disputes. In the flood of correspondence that poured in upon the men regarded as best able to draw up such measures,[9] in the resolutions of nonpartisan mass meetings,[10] in individual gaugings of public opinion,[11] and in the varied but significant reactions of politicians there was impressive evidence of the strength of the popular current in this direction. Had any of the major proposals for compromise which were advanced in the winter of 1860–61 been submitted to a popular referendum, it would probably have been ratified by a large majority in every state of the section.

But the force of public opinion, powerful though it may be, is limited in the possibilities of its application under a representative form of government. An election had just been held, and those who had been put into power would have the responsibility for taking action according to their own best judgments during their stated terms of office. The choice of accepting or rejecting such a type of solution would therefore rest not with the people at large but with men who were politicians, constrained to consult not only the welfare of the nation and the demands of public sentiment but also the realistic interests of their party.

Since the Republicans were shortly to take over the presidency and were in possession of most of the Northern state governments, the initiative in dealing with the situation obviously lay with them. Like the people, however, their leaders were at first uncertain and then divided as to the most advisable course of action. When the reality of secession became clear most of them began to move to one of three positions. Some took the view that secession might as well be acquiesced in, others tried to find a satisfactory basis for compromise, while the third group insisted that secession was simply rebellion and as such could only be answered with military force.

For a while there were some indications that the Union might be permitted to go by default. "Whenever any considerable section of this Union shall really insist on getting out of it, we shall insist that they be allowed to go," [12] said the New York *Tribune*, the weekly edition of which had such a wide circulation and influence among the New England element in the Great Lakes area that it could almost be called a leading Midwestern newspaper, adding that "if the Cotton States shall have become satisfied that they can do better out of the Union than in it, we shall insist on letting them go in peace." [13] A few newspapers published in the Middle West cautiously endorsed such sentiments, and many stanch Republicans at least believed that disunion would be preferable to any action that would tend to extend slavery.[14] Some even found satisfaction in the reflection that a purification of the Union would result from the departure of its sinful members.[15] The Rockford *Register* voiced the attitude of a community in the heart of an intensely Abolitionist region in Illinois:

The probability is that a rupture is at hand. Well, we are not sure but this is the best thing that can be done in the long run. It certainly is the best, unless some means could be adopted for the gradual, but certain extinction of slavery in the nation, or at least its absolute confinement to the States where it exists.[16]

A larger group, unable to take consolation from any such reasoning, nevertheless disapproved of any attempt to use military force to prevent secession on the grounds of impracticality. According to such people, even in the unlikely event of its being possible to restore federal authority by an appalling expenditure of lives and material resources there would remain the necessity of holding a rebellious people in perpetual subjection. A vast standing army would become a permanent burden upon the country, and the whole basis and character of the government would be transformed.[17] In the important state of Ohio the most powerful Republican papers, led by the Columbus *Ohio State Journal* and the Cincinnati *Commercial,* seemed for a time to be leaning toward this view,[18] and so strong was the trend that even the militant Chicago *Tribune* was momentarily forced to agree that

. . . the drift of opinion seems to be that, if peaceable secession is possible, the retiring States will be assisted to go, that this needless and bitter controversy may be brought to an end. If the Union is to be dissolved, a bloodless separation is by all means to be coveted. . . .[19]

But if the first round went to those who were willing to permit secession, the next belonged to the group that favored compromise. Supported by tradition, they could hope to provide common ground for those who rejected the use of force and those who would fall back upon it as a final resort. The real leaders of this group were two Easterners, William H. Seward, soon to be Secretary of State and a much better-known party figure than Lincoln, and Thurlow Weed, the quasi-boss of the New York Republican machine.[20] But several Midwestern Republicans could be counted in the supporting cast, among them the principal heirs of the old Whig organization in Ohio, Thomas Corwin, his close friend Thomas Ewing, and their protégé John Sherman.[21] All three men were characterized by a sensitivity to public opinion that made them at any time first-rate weathervanes. This was attested by their remarkable political longevity. Corwin had been state legislator, governor, congressman, United States senator, Secretary of the Treasury under Fillmore, and would round out his career as Lincoln's minister to Mexico; Ewing had likewise been senator, had served in the cabinets of both Harrison and Taylor, and was the patriarch of a remarkably far-reaching family hierarchy of politicians; Sherman was the brother of William Tecumseh Sherman (who was Ewing's son-in-law) and would have one of the longest unbroken careers in the history of American politics as congressman, senator, Secretary of the Treasury under Hayes, and Secretary of State in McKinley's cabinet. Another Midwestern member of the group inclined toward compromise was the shrewd and affable Schuyler Colfax of Indiana, a member of the House from 1855 to 1869 who would be Speaker after 1863 and then as Vice-President suffer political ruin in the Crédit Mobilier scandals. As late as January 12 Colfax was urging his Republican colleagues in Congress to make some effort toward compromise if only to be in a stronger position to appeal to public confidence should war come.[22] The strength of this group lay in its evident concordance with the general trend of popular opinion, but its fatal weakness would prove to be the congenital reluctance of its leaders to go very far in publicly advocating specific compromise measures until there had been some official pronouncement by the party. When, however, Congressman William B. Kellogg of Illinois, recognized as an intimate and counselor of the President-elect, proposed a series of compromise resolutions on February 8 similar to the measures earlier introduced into the Senate by John J. Crittenden of Kentucky, it seemed for a moment that the party leadership might be committing itself to conciliation.[23]

But in the end neither renunciation of the Union nor proposals for compromise received the stamp of official Republican approval. A third group, more penetrating and realistic in its analyses, saw that the adoption of either a policy of separation or of concession would not only fail, in all probability, to obtain the results hoped for by its advocates but would almost certainly lead to the disruption and overthrow of the Republican party. Perhaps the first clear exposition of this point of view came from Oliver P. Morton, governor-elect of Indiana, whose Bismarckian figure would dominate the affairs of his state during the Civil War period as his statue today dominates the approach to its capitol. (The statue of his chief Democratic opponent, Thomas A. Hendricks, is appropriately relegated to a corner of the State House grounds.) In a powerful address delivered at Indianapolis on November 22 Morton pointed out that compromise or acquiescence in disunion would be equally fatal to American nationality. The first would mean the abandonment of the only principle upon which a republic can operate, that of majority rule; the latter would tend to dissolve the obligations binding together even the remaining states and lead eventually to a number of weak confederacies as the ignoble successors of a once glorious union.[24] The logic of this argument, inherent in the structure of the republic, was bound to impress all who were not blinded by prejudice or made insensible by fear.

More than the application of constitutional logic gave support to this view. Anti-slavery sentiment played a part. Some members of this faction were at first inclined to welcome secession as a means of dissociating themselves from a hated institution, but in the end nearly all could see that in war there would be a unique opportunity for the total destruction of slavery.[25] Outright Abolitionists might seem an inconsequential minority in the Republican organization, but their qualities of mind were such that they formed a stubborn nucleus and rallying point during the brief but critical period in which many of the party leaders seemed to be overwhelmed by events.

Another consideration was even more compelling. To many Republicans it was increasingly clear that to retreat from the party position of opposing slavery in the territories—certainly the minimum price that would be demanded by the South in agreeing to any compromise—would mean the abandonment of their only common principle. The heterogeneous factions that had been brought together by so much careful effort but which were not yet fused into a solid and disciplined organization might fly apart again. To acquiesce in secession, on the other hand, would leave the party open to the fatal accusation of having both occasioned and permitted the disruption of the Union. In either case the newly won victory at the polls would turn to dust in their hands, and years of planning and construction would go for nothing. Viewing this prospect, Senator Salmon P. Chase of Ohio, shortly to be designated Secretary of the Treasury, confessed, "I am sick at heart. Our first victory will not be lost, I trust, utterly; but the organization which we have built up with so much pains to make the victory available to higher progress is almost certain to be broken up." [26] Others determined to prevent such a result if possible. When the Washington Peace Conference in February gave momentary promise of success, Senator Zachariah Chandler urged Governor Austin Blair of Michigan to send delegates who would aid in blocking any agreement, reporting:

. . . Ohio, Indiana and Rhode Island *are caving in,* and there is *danger* of Illinois, and now they beg us for God's sake to *come to their rescue, and save the Republican party from rupture.* I hope you will send *stiff-backed* men or none. . . . Some of the manufacturing States think that a *fight* would be AWFUL. *Without a little blood-letting this Union will not, in my estimation, be worth a rush.*[27]

It was reported that a block of Republican congressmen had taken shape to prevent approval by the government of any concessions. Former Congressman Joshua Giddings informed his son that

I left Washington yesterday . . . I know that you will feel anxious from the public press, for the safety of the republican party and I write to say that cowardice the stock in trade so long used by northern dough-faces has sadly fallen off within a few days and is now a drug in the market. Seventeen Senators and fifty eight representatives stand firm in Washington as they assure me. And if they continue to do so, the others will yield and Seward's effort to disband our organization will prove fruitless. The feeling in the Country is up to the fighting point and we are ready to *fight,* but not compromise. Tell our friends to thank God and take courage.[28]

This was not solely a decision of the party chiefs. Local organization workers were so ravenous for the fruits of victory—appointments to office and contracts for public printing—that they were driving Lincoln to distraction and causing even such a veteran politician as Congressman George W. Julian of Indiana to flee from

home to escape their ceaseless importunities.[29] These men had no
wish to see the party lose its ability to reward them in the future
and they flooded their leaders with reports based on intimate contacts with the people of hundreds of communities. Nearly all bore
the same message: a popular reaction was rising against the Republican party. With steadfastness, however, it might be ridden out, but
weakness and retreat would turn it into an engulfing flood.[30] Wrote
one:

. . . I hope from the bottom of my soul that no pro-slavery concessions
will be made. It will ruin the Republican Party if they do. Even Civil
War would be better than to degrade ourselves by yielding an iota of
our principles. . . .[31]

And another warned, "Should Mr. Lincoln . . . favor Com-
promise—that is, any of the plans now before the Country, as the
Crittenden, or Guthrie, or Border State, or *any amendment to the
Constitution* giving Slavery further guarantees, privileges and
immunities—he would *fall, never to rise again,* and the Republican
Party, as a Party, would be *smashed into a thousand fragments!*" [32]

In the final analysis, however, it was the President-elect who set
the party machinery in motion to reject compromise and meet secession head on. Although issuing no public statements he had many
effective channels through which to make his views known throughout the Republican organization. Besides his private correspondence and personal interviews with those who hurried to Springfield
to discuss appointments, he made use of Governor Yates and other
local associates as intermediaries, while the editorial columns of the
Illinois State Journal (widely reprinted by other Republican newspapers and known to be acting as his spokesman) enabled him to
reach the party rank-and-file. Through all these media he urged the
logical impossibility of any other course of action than dealing with
secession as rebellion against legal authority.[33] "Stand Firm—Be
True," the *Journal* commanded. "We feel indignant . . . when we
hear timid Republicans counseling an abandonment, in part, of
Republican ground. We are asking for nothing that is not clearly
right. We have done nothing wrong—we have nothing to apologize
for—nothing to take back, as a party." [34] At the first report of secession this paper flatly informed South Carolina that such action

meant war, in which the Republican party must feel bound to use every resource at its command to enforce the full authority of the laws.[35]

Under such compulsions the party ranks stiffened. An interlocking network of correspondence made it known that the party line called for no retreat from the Republican platform on which victory had been won.[36] A rising newspaper chorus confirmed this attitude.[37] Any member who continued to waver was likely to be solemnly advised that he was in danger of being marked as politically untrustworthy.[38] Compromise measures lost any chance of succeeding. The Crittenden proposals, most promising of the lot, broke down in Congress. When Virginia called a peace convention presided over by former President John Tyler that met in Washington from February 4 to 27, Wisconsin, Michigan, and Minnesota refused even to send delegates, and other Midwestern states took part without any desire for its success. Illinois appointed delegates only after the matter had gone so far that to refuse would have prejudiced the position of Lincoln, who had at first advised Governor Yates to boycott the undertaking and declared that "he would rather be hung by the neck till he was dead on the steps of the Capitol, before he would buy a peaceful inauguration." [39] Governor Morton required the Indiana delegates to pledge opposition to any concessions before he would certify their appointment.[40] Having insured the rejection of compromise, the next efforts of the party were toward strengthening the militia establishments of their states [41] and appealing to the Democrats for promises of support when the anticipated war should come.[42]

In this fashion the Republican party during that momentous winter took the road to war. But obviously the Union could not be restored by force without the support of the greater part of the Democrats. Like the Republican leaders those responsible for determining the policy of that party were at first aghast, then confused and divided, and finally brought into general conformity to a central line of action. After the first shock had passed, remembering Andrew Jackson, one group called for a strong hand in suppressing rebellion, a second held disunion to be preferable to war, while a third favored an earnest effort to compromise before committing themselves upon the ultimate decision.

Those Democrats who from the outset were unequivocally willing to support the position adopted by the Republicans were an almost invisible minority. Certain Midwesterners such as Congressmen William Allen of Ohio, William S. Holman of Indiana, and John A. McClernand of Illinois had in some degree made known their opinions to this effect, but among the letters received by the leaders from their followers during the winter only a few, a very few, urged the taking of a stern and indignant course toward the South.[43] A handful of Democratic newspapers, including the Columbus *Ohio Statesman*,[44] Cleveland *Plain Dealer*,[45] and Chicago *Post*,[46] gave some support to this attitude.

Far more were disposed to disclaim any obligation on the part of the Democrats to support the national government, holding that the major blame for the crisis lay with their Northern opponents rather than with the South. In their chagrin over political defeat some got a vengeful satisfaction from the situation. "The republicans here are not so jubilant over the election as was expected," commented the Cairo (Illinois) *City Gazette*. "They already begin to taste the fruits of their heresies—in the news from South Carolina—and don't feel exactly like shouting." [47] There was some defense of secession as a constitutional right, or at least morally justified as an act of revolution by repeated Northern assaults on Southern institutions. The Belleville (Illinois) *Democrat* declared that

. . . it is not worth while to try to conceal the fact, *that the North is hopelessly abolitionized.* To *submit* then, or *secede*, is forced upon the South. That their rights have been long disregarded, and now defiantly trampled under foot, by the North, is true, and a tame submission under it, with the threat of repetitions still more aggravated, or, an abrupt withdrawal, to abide the consequences, is now the only alternate.[48]

Another southern Illinois journal reported that "the sympathies of our people are mainly with the South. 'If South Carolina, or any other state wants to secede,' say our people, 'let her in God's name go peaceably.' " [49] The Chillicothe (Ohio) *Advertiser* maintained that "the right of secession is an inherent attribute of the confederate form of government," [50] and the Kenosha (Wisconsin) *Democrat* argued:

. . . The right of secession inheres to people of every sovereign state. . . . South Carolina voted herself into the Union; she can vote herself out. . . . [The framers of the Constitution] expected a time to come when one or more of the States should determine to secede. The[y] refused to incorporate a clause into the Constitution enabling Congress or the President to use force against a seceding State. They declared any state had an inherent right to secede at pleasure, and a forcible union would be an invasion of that right. . . . This accounts for the lack of constitutional prohibition of secession.[51]

After full consideration most Democrats, regardless of the precise nature of their views, were able to agree upon a common program, that of giving wholehearted support to any compromise measure. Everything in their traditions recommended such a course. The party had long stressed the policy of attempting to find common denominators for conflicting sectional interests within the nation, and, since a maximum of state autonomy was looked upon as a basic constitutional principle inherited from Thomas Jefferson, it was not embarrassed by the thought that to make concessions in the face of secession would weaken the national authority and prestige. And, of course, all Democrats were aware that if they could successfully sponsor a compromise arrangement acceptable to the South they would bring off a political coup of almost staggering value. They saw clearly the Republican dilemma and hoped that the organization of their enemies might break up far more rapidly than it had been constructed, leaving the field free for Democrats to enjoy the fruits of political success which they had so long possessed. It was a tempting prospect, and every effort was made to give it realization. The support of the Northern Democrats was thrown unitedly behind the compromise proposals in Congress and elsewhere,[52] and meanwhile there was deprecation of any action from either side, but especially from the North, that might further embitter the relations of the sections. Politicians and the party press unceasingly urged the repeal of the "Personal Liberty" laws that had been passed by various states to impede the enforcement of the Fugitive Slave Law of 1850, and some advised the abandonment of Fort Pickens and Fort Sumter.[53] A solid front was presented against Republican efforts to strengthen the militia organizations in the Midwest on the grounds that any such action would discourage

CLEMENT L. VALLANDIGHAM

further negotiation and tend to drive the border states into the Confederacy. Only one Democratic vote was cast for such a measure in the Ohio senate, the Democratic members of the Indiana legislature served notice of their intention of preventing a quorum for the consideration of a bill of this nature, and determined obstructionist tactics likewise prevented action by the state of Illinois.[54] When the Republicans in turn were able to block compromise efforts in Congress and in the border state peace convention, the Democrats began to demand the calling of a national convention of delegates from all the states and concentrated their efforts on this object until the outbreak of hostilities.[55]

But the crux of the issue lay one step farther on. Since the Republicans had determined that there would be no compromise, the real question was what Democrats would do when confronted by a choice between preserving the Union through war or maintaining peace at the cost of separation. Some had already pledged themselves to the former alternative, both from motives of patriotism and from the conviction expressed by Congressman McClernand of Illinois, *"If we become entangled with disunionism we will be lost as a party."* [56] Stephen A. Douglas, idol of the Midwestern Democracy, although publicly threatening to withhold his support from coercion as a tactical maneuver intended to bluff the opponents of compromise, was privately committed to the proposition, *"We can never acknowledge the right of a State to secede and cut us off from the Ocean and the world, without our consent."* [57]

There was no certainty, however, that the majority would follow Douglas. Senator George E. Pugh and Representative Clement L. Vallandigham notified a bipartisan caucus of the Ohio members of Congress in December that they would never under any circumstances accept coercion, and they were understood to threaten war in the North if it should be attempted.[58] In speeches delivered in the House Vallandigham and George H. Pendleton denied that there was any right in the national government to use force against any ordained action of a state.[59] Allen G. Thurman, another Ohio Democratic leader, although withholding endorsement from this constitutional theory, arrived at the same point by insisting that the practical obstacles to coercion were insurmountable.[60] In Chicago a local Democratic convention announced that "we regard civil war between the States as the most terrible of calamities, to be prevented by every honorable concession, and that, in the event of the failure of all efforts to compromise, and thereby confirm the allegiance of the seceding States, it would be unwise and impolitic to seek by war to compel an unwilling Union; and that, in the opinion of this meeting, it would be greatly preferable that the consent of the other States should be given to their peaceable separation from the Confederacy, upon fair and just terms if demanded." [61]

Frequently heard was the assertion that the Union as it had previously existed was one that could only be perpetuated through a voluntary association of the states. Reaper-manufacturer Cyrus H. McCormick's Chicago *Times and Herald* held, "When the hearts of the people of any great section are permanently alienated, the Union is already practically dissolved, and the forms of dissolution will soon follow. The Union is valuable only so long as its services to the people make it dear to them." [62] There was a widespread fear that even in a successful war the nation would fall prey to a military dictatorship in which its birthright of self-government would be forever lost. A gloomy and forbidding vision arose:

. . . A war of conquest would end in a military despotism, and leave all, not only impoverished in purse and ruined in honor, but our liberties would be sacrificed in the wreck. The fate of a free people depends upon their ability to withstand the blandishments of military glory—once yield to this and despots will seize the whole and trample country and people in the dust. The North has more to dread from such military movement than the South. We shall have the expenses to bear—we shall have the army to fill up, and if successful or unsuccessful, we shall come out of the conflict of arms, broken in spirits and exhausted in energies, with a standing army on our hands, and with military leaders that will have all the power in their own control, and the people unable to wrench it from them. [63]

A divided nation would be preferable, and there was the consolation that by rejecting the use of force it might be possible to retain the border slave states which might, after an interval in which passions would cool, serve as magnets to draw the estranged states back into the union. [64] As these people saw it:

With the madness of the hour will come a long season of sober reason, and when we get through raving and ranting and tearing things up, we shall feel better, talk more soberly, act more discreetly. . . . Time, the healer of a thousand troubles, will come to our aid; the absurdity of taking each other's lives will expose itself; the impossibility of living in enmity will work out a speedy revolution—and those who seek their fortunes in revolution and riots, in blood and carnage, in thefts and robberies from sacked cities and desolated farms and plantations, will starve out on expectation and shrink to their common haunts, as food for the police.[65]

Against the view that eventual reunion was to be expected, others argued that the disruption of the Union was only the natural and inevitable result of having attempted to extend a single political jurisdiction over too large and diverse an area. That raised the question, if disunion were to be accepted as permanent what should be the relationship of the Middle West to the reconstituted alignment of the states? In the section that still regarded the Ohio River as its vital artery of trade a movement began for extending the boundaries of the Confederacy to include the southern parts of Ohio, Indiana, and Illinois.[66] Public meetings in Perry County, Ohio,[67] and Pope County, Illinois,[68] endorsed such proposals. In Southern Illinois Congressman John A. Logan and Legislators W. H. Green and A. J. Kuykendall were rumored to be backing the movement. The editor of the Chicago *Tribune,* Charles H. Ray, wrote on January 16 to Senator Trumbull, "I believe, upon my soul, that if the Union is divided on the line of the Ohio, we shall be compelled to struggle to maintain the territorial integrity of this state."

But more generally discussed was the proposal to organize a separate Northwest Confederacy. This, it was expected, would be allied with or stand in very friendly connection with the Southern Confederacy. In some proposals it was to be extended to include the Far Western and even the Middle Atlantic states, but it would certainly exclude New England—hopelessly committed to anti-slavery agitation, and, of course, given obstinately to voting the Republican ticket. A contemporary survey of Illinois newspapers listed the Joliet *Signal,* Carthage *Republican* (Democratic), Macomb *Eagle,* Quincy *Herald* (mouthpiece of Congressman William Richardson), Cairo *Gazette,* and Lewistown *Fulton Ledger* among those giving the proposal at least an open-minded hearing. A mass meeting at Nashville, Brown County, Indiana, resolved that "if the North fail to make just concessions to the South by proper guarantees, or the South reject them when made, whereby the Union is dissolved, or the Gulf States shall set up a separate Confederacy, we are in favor of forming a central Republic composed of the middle and conservative States as a necessary brake-water against the ultraisms of the extremes." [69] As a corollary but necessary part of this move-ment there was a concerted Democratic press campaign to stir up all the latent distrust of Yankees by recounting examples of New Eng-land hypocrisy, intolerance, and disloyalty to the Union, while heaping praise on the aims, Constitution, and President of the Confederacy.[70]

A peace-at-any-price demand for the appeasement of the South did not necessarily carry with it an unwillingness to resort to force in dealing with the problems before the country. On the contrary, many threats were made to take up arms if necessary to thwart the coercionist plans of the Republicans. When the proposal to enlarge the militia was before the Illinois legislature State Representative William H. Green of Massac County warned his Republican col-leagues that "if the North were marched upon the South, her forces would be met on the prairies and made to march over the dead bodies of the men who people them," [71] and the Joliet *Signal* grum-bled:

. . . We learn that the Black Republican artillery company at Plain-field are drilling for service. They are making ready to go down South to subdue the Southern people. Well, let them go—but in their journey they should avoid passing through this city for fear that they and their cannon might be tumbled into the river.[72]

The sentiments of a large number of people living in the southern part of Ohio were apparently voiced by a correspondent of the Cin-cinnati *Enquirer* when he wrote:

Has it yet occurred to the Abolition fanatics of Ohio . . . in the event of a complete separation of the South from the North . . . that there is now existent in our State limits, a power that will be sure, in the mad hour when *coercion and civil war* shall be attempted by Mr. Lincoln's sectional Administration . . . to start up in serried column to command the peace . . . that will say to their brethren of the South, "Stay at home; no Abolition horde shall pass *our* border into yours, to compel your submission to the aggressive policy upon your rights of a sectionally elected and sectionally conducted Administration . . . unless they first pass our lines, and before doing that they will make the discovery that if we cannot command the peace, we can *compel* it, and will surely do so." [73]

The editorial columns of that paper a few days later added a veiled warning that the calling of the militia might "become dangerous to those in authority." [74] Henry M. Rice of Minnesota told the United States Senate that they must not expect any of the Northwestern states ever to vote a dollar or a man for war. To Governor Ramsey he wrote that "there are thousands of brave men who will never draw the sword. They will look to our State." [75] From Wisconsin came the promise of the Green Bay *Advocate* that men who did not intend to let their regular business activities and personal interests suffer because of "a fuss about a paltry stone fort" or "the moral condition of the niggers at the South" would, if war should come, turn without mercy upon those within their own state whom they would hold responsible.[76] In the Michigan legislature State Senator Brownell threatened revolution at home in case of war with the South,[77] and the Detroit *Free Press* spoke out most bluntly of all, threatening that

. . . if troops shall be raised in the North to march against the people of the South, *a fire in the rear will be opened upon such troops which will either stop their march altogether, or wonderfully accelerate it.* . . . if . . . war shall be waged, *that war will be fought in the North* . . . here in Michigan, and here in Detroit, and in every Northern State . . .[78] there are some sixty-five thousand able-bodied men, voters at the late election, citizens of this State, who will interpose themselves between any troops that may be raised in Michigan and the people of the South.[79]

Making full allowance for the individual nature of such statements, the emotional stress under which they may have been made, and the obvious Democratic strategy of using bluff to force the Republicans to support some program of compromise, there still remained a residue of true intent, ominous in import. Behind these scattered samplings of opinion stood the resolutions adopted by fully representative conventions of the Democratic party called to three state capitals, Columbus, Indianapolis, and Springfield, during the month of January to consider the national crisis. The Ohio gathering, presided over by Hugh Jewett, who would be the party's nominee for governor a few months later, voted almost unanimously that "when the people of the North shall have fulfilled their duties to the Constitution and the South—then, and not till then, will it be proper for them to take into consideration the question of the right and propriety of coercion." [80] The Indiana convention, meeting under the sponsorship of the Democratic State Central Committee, urged that the "Union be preserved, if at all, by the cultivation of fraternal affection among the people of the different sections" and added that "if civil war shall result from the aggressive policy of the Republican party, the rash councils of Southern statesmen, or by the impolitic and unwise exercise of coercive power on the part of the Federal Government, it would become the duty of Indiana, bound, as her citizens are to the North and the South by ties of consanguinity and commerce, to act with other conservative States, as a mediator between the contending factions." [81] And it was resolved by the Illinois convention that "we distinctly deny that the federal government has any constitutional power to call out the militia to execute those laws within the limits and jurisdiction of any state, except in aid of the civil authorities." [82] It was little wonder that the South was confident of a hopeless division of Northern opinion.

As spring came on there were indications that large numbers of the voters who had no fixed party allegiance were swinging over to the Democrats. Municipal elections in general revealed a marked falling off of Republican strength as compared with the vote of the previous autumn. Cleveland, Cincinnati, Columbus, Sandusky, Toledo, Chicago, and many a smaller city witnessed setbacks for the Republicans that in some cases bordered on routs.[83] The charge that they had provoked secession by their agitation of the slavery question and then had, for partisan reasons, prevented the working out of a reasonable compromise was taking a serious toll. "It is the first party that I have any knowledge of that was broken . . . before it *had* hardly been inaugurated," gloated a correspondent of Senator Douglas.[84] On the other hand the breach in the Democratic ranks that had grown out of the quarrel between Douglas and President Buchanan in 1857—but which in the Midwest had never been so much a matter of principle as of patronage—had virtually disappeared. A united and aggressive Democratic party was ready to take full advantage of its rival's weakness.

Would the strengthened Democrats direct their power to checkmating the Republican policy of reunion by force? Men in Washington and Charleston would soon put this question in a way that would require an answer. On the surface everything suggested the correctness of Southern hopes and expectations in regard to the Middle West.

But almost imperceptibly another sentiment was taking shape that would invalidate such predictions—an undefined impatience with unproductive discussion and chimerical panaceas. While politicians had been occupying the center of the stage a development in popular psychology of deep significance had been taking place. The mass of people, at first fearful at the thought of war, had been growing constantly more exasperated at the failure of their leaders to enter upon a course of action. Humiliation at the apparent impotence of the North, as one after another of the Southern states withdrew from the Union, begot a rising anger and demands for some solution that would bring to an end the harrowing uncertainty. In such a frying pan the idea of a leap into the fire began to have its appeal. A young man who would soon put on the uniform of a soldier expressed a sentiment which thousands had come to share:

. . . I have grown impatient to see the power of the Government and the loyalty of the people put to the test. . . . If we have to lose the Government, I had rather lose it by action, than by inaction. And I had rather see the old ship go down with the flag flying, amid the roar of its own and its enemy's cannon, than to see her grow into disuse and contempt while rotting idly at the wharf.[85]

A spell seemed to have been cast over the federal government, paralyzing its faculties. Let it be broken, was the demand. Make some kind of decision! Take some action! Human nerves could no longer bear a situation in which no policy was determined upon and nothing was done. "Let this intolerable suspense and uncertainty cease!" demanded the formerly pacifistic New York *Tribune*. "If we are to fight, so be it." [86] A Democratic editor ruefully observed that the state of the public mind had come to approximate that of the man who expressed the wish "that his sick wife would get well or something." [87] Here, then, is an explanation for the reaction to the firing on Fort Sumter. The great popular uprising that was to follow the opening of hostilities may on the surface have been an outburst of indignation that "the Secessionists had fired on the emblem of national authority flying over the walls of a national fortress," [88] but deeper than that it represented a catharsis for the highly wrought emotional condition of a people.

CHAPTER III

The Period of Impatience

(April 12, 1861–February 6, 1862)

THE reign of uncertainty and divided councils which had prevailed in the North since South Carolina's ordinance of secession was brought abruptly to an end by the news that Confederate batteries in Charleston harbor had opened fire on Fort Sumter. Hesitancy and doubt gave way to indignant demands for the prompt suppression of rebellion, and a psychological revolution of sweeping implications took place. Four racking months filled with a sense of futility and helplessness while the Union appeared to be slipping away had drawn popular feelings taut; thirty-four hours of shock, outrage, humiliation, and mounting fury as the wires brought reports of the progress of the bombardment to crowds that never left the telegraph and newspaper offices climaxed the strain. The cord of forbearance snapped.

Old divisions and recriminations were forgotten in an overwhelming urge to act. President Lincoln's call for volunteers, coming close upon the fort's surrender, offered a channel in which emotions could find release. It would be useless to try to give a complete picture of the days that followed in the Midwest and throughout the North, for the men before whom the scene was unfolding would attempt in the columns of hundreds of newspapers and in countless private letters to describe what they had seen and would end by confessing the inadequacy of words. But they remembered it to the end of their lives. In city, town, and hamlet, and at remote crossroads there was a confusion of flags, fifes and drums, banners inscribed with patriotic declarations, bunting-draped platforms shared by Republicans and Democrats, and little groups of excited men suddenly forming to exhort one another to still greater excitement. Men volunteered, and their neighbors saw for the first time

51

that they were heroes, and more volunteered. County boards and city councils met to appropriate funds for the subsistence of the recruits until state or federal authorities could assume the responsibility, and voted money too for the families of those whose enlistment might cause hardship. Railroads were placed at the disposal of the authorities, bankers offered emergency loans to the state, citizens subscribed funds to equip newly formed companies, and farmers furnished teams and wagons to hastily organized commissariats. Uniforms were made at home according to specifications carried in the newspapers, and there too knapsacks were fitted out —sometimes filled with articles that would have escaped even the nightmares of a regular army sergeant. The worship in maidens' eyes heightened the appeal of volunteering, and the charge with which the village belle presented a homemade flag sent each company off to the mustering depot with high resolves. "The telegraph news presents a wonderful sight," marveled an anti-war paper, "the whole North seems to be in a flame of excitement"; [1] and from each community the report was to the same effect.

The *war* feeling runs high here—all party sentiment is merged in the higher sentiment of *preserving the Union,* against a set of hotheaded *rebels* at the South, who seem determined to "rule or ruin," to destroy our government, or be *wiped out* from the face of God's earth, & driven into the Gulf of Mexico, as I hope they will be.[2]

With the fervor of the Fourth of July celebration, political rally, and camp meeting revival, the people's decision blazed across the section. Months later George Bancroft, the historian, could record the judgment, "There has never been anything greater than the uprising of the people in April last." [3]

The initial leadership and direction of this mass upheaval were provided most notably by the state governors, each of those in the Midwest a Republican and, since the creation of a new party had demanded such qualities, a man of ability and determination. The governor of Ohio was William Dennison, a successful lawyer and business man, formerly a Whig leader in the state senate. In 1864 he became Postmaster-General and chairman of the Republican National Committee and might have been carried even higher by his undoubted talents had they not been obscured by a cold exterior that impeded personal popularity. Oliver Perry Morton (originally Throckmorton) of Indiana, a product of Miami University and the law school of Cincinnati College, had been elected lieutenant-governor in 1860 in an arrangement by which the governor-elect was immediately elevated to the United States Senate. A solid man possessed of a stalwart physique which fitted his indomitable personality, he became the virtual dictator of his state during the Civil War period. When his work there was done he moved on to the Senate in 1867, and until his death ten years later was one of the national leaders of the party in spite of being struck down by paralysis. Richard Yates, governor of Illinois, was a native of Kentucky and the first graduate of Illinois College in Jacksonville. A Democrat until breaking with the party over the slavery question, he served in the legislature from 1842 to 1850 and was a member of the United States House of Representatives from 1851 to 1855 and of the Senate from 1865 to 1871. Of statesmanlike mien, capable, energetic, and warm-hearted, he was also temperamental, and this quality was augmented in his later years by periods of alcoholic intemperance which he himself keenly regretted. Austin Blair, the Michigan governor, was a New Yorker whose lean face mirrored New England backgrounds. He was a graduate of Union College, was by turns Whig and Free Soiler, and a founder of the Republican party. After his governorship he sat in Congress from 1867 to 1873. Another New Yorker was Alexander W. Randall of Wisconsin, a lawyer by profession and an anti-slavery Democrat in politics before being elected governor in 1857. With the expiration of his term in 1861 he was appointed minister to Rome, returning in 1863 to become Assistant Postmaster-General and chief dispenser of the patronage. Under Johnson he was Postmaster-General. Samuel Jordan Kirkwood was a native of Maryland who began his political career in Ohio before moving to Iowa in 1855. After one term in the legislature of the latter state he won the governorship in 1861, was re-elected in 1863, and served again from 1875 to 1877. He was United States senator in 1866–67 and from 1877 to 1881, and was Secretary of the Interior in 1881–82. Alexander Ramsey, governor of the new state of Minnesota, had had a considerable political career as a member of Congress and chairman of the Whig Central Committee in Pennsylvania before being appointed the first territorial governor of Minnesota. After Minnesota became a state he served as governor from 1859 to 1863, was United States senator from 1863 to 1875, and Secretary of War under Hayes. Since Ramsey was frequently absent from the state, much of the burden of office fell on the colorful Ignatius Donnelly, who had become lieutenant-governor at the age of twenty-eight. Elected to Congress in 1863, Donnelly broke with his party in 1869 and thereafter was an inveterate leader of third parties, from Liberal Republican to Populist. He also wrote a number of bizarre but widely popular books, including *Atlantis* (which ran through twenty-one American and several European editions), *The Great Cryptogram,* which attempted to establish Francis Bacon as the author of Shakespeare's plays, and three novels of which *Caesar's Column* had the greatest popular success.

The hearty, confident responses of these men to Lincoln's call for troops must have given new courage to the anxious President. It was a thundering chorus that answered the roll-call of the states: "What portion of the 75,000 militia you call for do you give to Ohio? We will furnish the largest number you will receive." "On behalf of the State of Indiana I tender to you for the defense of the nation and to uphold the authority of the Government 10,000 men." "The Governor's call was published on yesterday and he has already received the tender of forty companies. . . . Illinois is a unit." "I am enabled to say that the people of Michigan respond with the utmost enthusiasm. . . . Michigan will send another regiment at the same time if the War Department at Washington desires it." "Let the President call for 100,000 more men. We have no parties now. The people [of Wisconsin] will not be content to furnish one regiment alone." "Please assure the President that the people and the Executive of Iowa will stand by him unflinchingly. Ten days ago we had two parties in this State; today we have but one, and that one is for the Constitution and Union unconditionally." "Minnesota regiment ready in ten days." [4] And their optimistic reports had basis. From all sides offers of volunteer companies and regiments poured in; everywhere fear was expressed that this company or that would not be accepted under the quota. Pressure, political and personal, was brought to bear on officials to favor the acceptance of certain organizations. Men stood for hours in long lines before recruiting stations fearful that the quota would be filled before their names could be enrolled.[5] The governors appeared more able than the federal administration to sense the extent of the task that faced the North. By April 19 one of Ohio's famous "Fighting McCooks" (fourteen members of one family that served in the war) was en route for Washington in command of two regiments for the defense of the capital, and two days later a Chicago regiment was sent to guard the strategic city of Cairo, Illinois.[6] By letter, telegram, representations through members of Congress, and even personal trips to Washington the governors tried to secure permission to accept all the offers of troops with which they were deluged. In vain they warned Secretary Cameron, the complacent party spoilsman at the head of the War Department, that to cool the ardor of the people by discouraging their efforts to volunteer might later be regretted, that the first upsurge of patriotic enthusiasm could never be recaptured.[7]

In virtually all reports of the great uprising the fact was stressed that Democrats were vying with Republicans in support of the administration's policy. In view of the attitudes and threats of the winter and spring this was a pivotal consideration. At war rallies spokesmen of both parties proclaimed the adjournment of politics for the duration of hostilities.[8] Democratic newspapers called for a solid front against the challenge to nationality. "Let every man drop all issues and rally to the support of the government," was typical advice. "It is no time now to discuss what has or what has not been done, or what might or might not have been done." [9] In the Ohio legislature Democratic opposition to a bill for strengthening the militia and rendering it capable of aiding the federal government was suddenly changed into an eager co-operation that hurried through its enactment with but one dissenting vote.[10]

Just how had this transformation been effected? Many had, no doubt, come around to the conclusion that had motivated Lincoln's course, that to permit secession or grant concessions in the face of secession would be to dissolve the binding power of the Union. The conviction was widespread and had its roots deep in the American mind that the

. . . cause of Republican government—of Free Democracy—stands or falls with the preservation of this Union. This cause has long been deemed at stake on what men call the "American Experiment"; this nation had a sacred origin; it has had the most favorable auspices . . . if it falls to pieces, it will be because of the inherent weakness of popular government . . . and liberty-looking men in all lands will mourn over so great a calamity should it come; a calamity whose influence will reach to the utmost boundaries of the civilized world.[11]

Many, no doubt, had all along determined that this would be their course of action once fighting should have begun. But stronger still was the force of the popular current, too strong to be resisted. The people had accepted the challenge with few misgivings. Untutored in the sufferings of war, they were looking for a struggle of short duration, a sort of summer outing from which the young men would return in the autumn covered with honor and glory. The volunteers themselves saw a promise of adventure, relief from the monotonous drudgery of the narrow world of farm and shop, comparatively good pay, and just enough danger to add spice to the prospect.[12] In this situation the leaders must follow, or cease to be leaders. Several of the Ohio legislators frankly explained their change of position on the militia question on this basis.[13] Republicans expressed to one another their feeling of relief that the dilemma which had confronted their party had been resolved. "Administration stock has risen very high," commented one,[14] and another added, "It's all right now—and has turned just as I expected —certainly as I *hoped,* and as I, together with a number of others here, *all the while contended.*" [15]

But not all was unity and acquiescence. Some Democratic politicians were not in attendance at the war meetings, and the most enthusiastic reports admitted that in nearly every community there were "a few skulking traitors" not caught up in the general enthusiasm.[16] A considerable number of newspapers were unreconciled, among them in Ohio the Ashland *Union,* Cambridge *Guernsey Jeffersonian,* Canton *Stark County Democrat,* Circleville *Watchman,* Coshocton *Democrat,* St. Clairsville *Gazette and Citizen*, Dayton *Empire* (spokesman for Congressman Vallandigham), and the Columbus *Crisis,* the Kenosha *Democrat* in Wisconsin, and the Council Bluffs *Bugle* in Iowa. Others, such as the Detroit *Free Press* and Indianapolis *Sentinel,* gave at best a sullen and grudging support to the war, and the great Cincinnati *Enquirer,* most powerful organ of the party in the Middle West, pursued a wavering course.[17] A leading Democrat of Wisconsin, Frederick W. Horn, three times speaker of the state senate, announced his opposition to the continuation of a Union in which the Midwest was plundered for the benefit of "Pennsylvania Iron mongers and the New England manufacturers" and resigned his captaincy in the militia rather than serve in a war which he believed had been provoked by the President to "rescue a sectional party from utter destruction."[18] Cyrus H. McCormick, reaper-manufacturer, owner of the Chicago *Times and Herald,* and money-bags of the party in Illinois, refused to give countenance to the effort to coerce the section from which he had sprung,[19] and a number of the congressmen from southern Indiana and from western and southern Illinois, including Daniel W. Voorhees (spellbinding orator known as "the Tall Sycamore of the Wabash"), James C. Robinson (Democratic nominee for governor of Illinois in 1864), John A. Logan, and William A. Richardson (elected senator in 1862), were understood to be withholding their support.[20] Most conspicuous of all was Congressman Clement L. Vallandigham, who refused to retreat an inch from his formerly expressed views. In an open letter to the Cincinnati *Enquirer* he announced:

My position in regard to this civil war, which the Lincoln Administration has inaugurated, was long since taken, is well known, and *will be adhered to to the end.* . . . I know that I am right, and that in a little while "the sober second thought of the people" will dissipate the present sudden and fleeting public madness, and will demand to know why thirty millions of people are butchering each other in civil war, and will arrest it speedily.[21]

Sorest spot of disaffection seemed to be "Egypt," the triangle of southern Illinois. There the Jonesboro *Gazette* and Cairo *City Gazette* announced an unchanged attitude toward coercive action, the latter stating:

Our Position—1st. We are opposed to organizing and arming the militia except for home defense.

2nd. We are opposed to our Legislature voting one cent to aid in equipping troops to be sent out of the State for the purpose of prosecuting the unnecessary war inaugurated by the present administration.

3rd. We call upon the people of Southern Illinois to stand unitedly as mediators between the North and South.

4th. We solemnly and earnestly protest against the occupation of our city or any part of Southern Illinois by troops from either section.[22]

Gatherings at Marion, on April 15, and at Carbondale demanded the recognition of Southern independence, protested Governor Yates's proclamation calling for troops for "subjugating the people of the South," and stated that if the border states seceded, southern Illinois should attach itself to the Confederacy.[23] While every other district of Illinois was oversubscribing its troop quotas, places in the regiment assigned to "Egypt" went begging, and, instead, men were reported to be going south by hundreds to enlist in the Confederate forces, with the encouragement, it was said, of William J. Allen, soon to be elected a member of Congress.[24] There were dark whisperings that Congressman John A. Logan was discouraging volunteering for the Union army and even considering the raising of a regiment for the service of the Confederacy.[25]

At this point Senator Stephen A. Douglas, possessed perhaps of the largest and most devoted personal following in the political history of the Middle West, intervened. Having since 1856 undergone a transition from an able politician into a patriot rising above narrow partisanship, he was now to give his "last full measure of devotion" to the nation. A conference at the White House with his old friend and long-time rival, the President, found the two men in agreement that the evidences of continued disaffection in the Midwest required immediate attention. Douglas informed his followers of his position by telegrams, open letters, and newspaper statements, and as soon as possible set out on a trip across the doubtful areas. After a brief speech at Bellaire, Ohio, and an address before the Ohio legislature, he arrived in Indianapolis. Here an immense gathering, undeterred by a heavy shower of rain, hung on every word as he spoke from the balcony of the Bates House. The Indiana legislature met in a session marked by transports of sentiment and expressions of unity: The officers earlier elected by the Republican majority resigned and were replaced by a unanimously chosen bipartisan slate, patriotic songs were sung, huzzas "three times three" were given, and the entire membership then adjourned and marched behind a band to Camp Morton to hear Douglas deliver another address before the Indiana volunteers. On April 25 he was in Springfield and appeared before the legislature to urge undivided support of the war. That body, up to then wrangling over the militia bill, stopped its bickering and quickly passed the measures needed to put the state on a war footing. Just before adjournment its members took an oath to defend the flag and adopted the gesture of enlisting as a company of militia, subject to call by the governor. On May 1 Douglas delivered in Chicago his last, and perhaps greatest, address. In a republic, he declared, there could be no justification of resort to the sword by a party or section defeated at the ballot box, and he left to his followers a motto, "There can be no neutrals in this war, *only patriots—or traitors.*" [26] A few days more and he was gone, worn out by exertions that the state of his health could not support. With his passing the future of the defeatist movement was given an opportunity which might have been denied to it had he lived through the war. But he had fended off an immediate danger.

Opposition to the coercive policy now almost wholly disappeared. Journals formerly defiant or lukewarm admitted the futility of further thoughts of compromise and called for the most vigorous possible prosecution of the war.[27] C. H. McCormick and Congressman Richardson pledged unqualified support, and McCormick sold his newspaper to Wilbur Storey, former owner of the Detroit *Free Press.*[28] From southern Illinois came reports that Douglas's campaign had stamped out the secession movement there, and heavy enlistments began that would make the district throughout the remainder of the war the banner recruiting area of the state.[29]

The weeks that followed the return of Douglas to the West were of all periods of the war those which saw the greatest unity in public opinion. Such papers as the Chicago *Times* and Cincinnati *Enquirer* were enrolled among the stanchest supporters of the administration, approving its measures, commending the capacities of its personnel, and attempting to protect it against the radical anti-slavery group within the Republican party. The *Enquirer* answered Lincoln's critics:

For our own part we freely say that, considering all the circumstances of the case, in our opinion, the Administration has been very efficient. The Secretary of the Treasury has been very successful in raising money to carry on the war. The Secretary of War has done as much as any inexperienced Secretary could have done within the time he has been operating. And the Secretary of the Navy has done almost magical work with the means at his command. We think these Republicans expect too much and grumble too much.[30]

The *Crisis,* it is true, still refused to approve of the war and served notice of its purpose of continuing to urge a peaceable settlement, but it called upon the legislature and people to spare no efforts meanwhile to raise, equip, and supply the army.[31] Congressman Logan wrote to his wife on July 4 that he was ready to abandon "standing out against the storm," and somewhat later resigned from Congress to return home and recruit a regiment for the Northern army.[32] Vallandigham was almost the only public man of any prominence who still avowed his recalcitrance, and even he announced in Congress on July 12 that he would now vote for as much money and as many men as might be necessary "to protect and defend the Federal Government." [33]

The reverse at Bull Run seemed only to intensify the unity and determination of the section and led to demands for a more vigorous and ruthless prosecution of the war. Mass meetings were once again the order of the day. "The defeat of our army has created another Fort Sumter rising of the people in their might," reported one observer. "Now let our Government use the topmost wave of their response & show itself *In Earnest!*" [34] Volunteering, with somewhat less demonstrativeness, was even heavier than in April and May. Although the initial enthusiasm could not be entirely recaptured, the incentives to enlistment were still strong. Bounties were beginning to be offered, accentuating the appeal of army service to those in the humdrum and low-paid occupations of civilian life (where the average farm wage was only "fourteen dollars a month, board and washing," as against a remuneration of from $20 a month for privates to $218 for colonels, in addition to bounties). The return of the frolicking three-month volunteers from patrol duty at Cairo and other points, well pleased with their quasi-military experiences, gave a strong impetus to further enlistments in their communities.

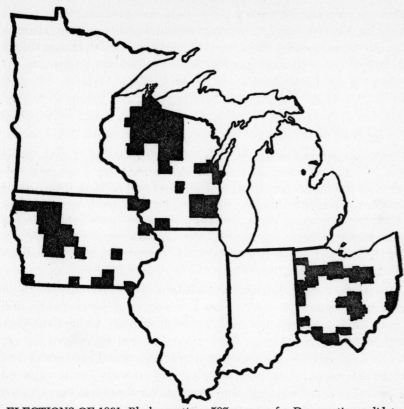

ELECTIONS OF 1861. Black counties—50% or more for Democratic candidates for governor in three states.

The Ottawa (Illinois) *Free Trader* stated, "The return of the three months boys from Cairo a week ago, in fine health and spirits, with their pockets full of rocks, and a large proportion of them so well pleased with their service that they expressed their purpose after a brief splurge to re-enter the service for the war, has given an immense impulse to the recruiting business in these parts during the past week." [35] The report of the Secretary of War on December 1, 1861, showed that volunteering in the Midwest had far outstripped that of the rest of the nation—the states of this section having furnished nearly three-fourths as many troops as the rest of the North combined. With a population only slightly larger than that of Massachusetts, Indiana had raised twice as many men for the war, and

Ohio alone, with Illinois not far behind, had provided more troops than all New England.[36] Democrats had volunteered as freely as Republicans, swelling the total and tending to dissolve any lingering attitude that the war was the responsibility of a party. The appointment of such Democrats as McClellan, Halleck, Hooker, Grant, Rosecrans, Dix, Butler, McClernand, and Logan to leading positions in the military forces had been helpful. Senator Trumbull was apprised of the reaction in "Egypt" by one of his constituents:

> You ask me how the war spirit is here! When our first Comp. under Geo. Abbott—all German Republicans enlisted for 3 months—left our town the Democrats hissed and throwed [sic] rocks at them, saying that they wished all this [sic] dam [sic] black Republicans would be killed, but as soon as W. R. Morrison [later for many years a Democratic leader in Congress] received the Commission as Colonel of the 49th Regt. every thing changed; strong secessionists joined his Regt. and no more was said about this horribel [sic], unjust war.[37]

The various state election campaigns of the fall were listless, with few issues, and were marked by a cessation of partisanship that would have appeared impossible a year before. They clearly established the general disposition toward united support of the administration above all other considerations. Local conventions of the Democrats in many cases adopted as their keynote the vigorous prosecution of the war and even warned that there was no place for freedom of speech "in the mere spirit of party or of factious opposition to the Government." [38] Many Democrats were disposed to leave their old affiliations for some kind of party merger. In Ohio the Republicans invited them to join in a new organization to be known as the Union party, with the single-plank platform of preservation of the Union, and put forward a former Democrat, David Tod, as candidate for governor; but in Iowa the Republicans were strong enough to insist that the coalition be made under the old party name. The Democratic nominee for the lieutenant-governorship in Ohio refused to make the race on the ground that it was not a time for the existence of a party in any respect opposed to the federal administration, and two men rejected the nomination for the governorship on the Democratic ticket in Iowa before a third, who had previously turned down a nomination as lieutenant-governor, was finally prevailed upon to accept it. In the voting Gov-

ernor Kirkwood was re-elected in Iowa, the Union Republican
ticket headed by Edward Salomon carried Wisconsin, and in Ohio
Tod triumphed over Jewett, the Democratic candidate, by a four-
to-three majority. In the newly elected Ohio senate twenty-six
Union members (twenty-one former Republicans and five former
Democrats) overshadowed the eight Democrats, and seventy-three
Unionists (forty-four of Republican and twenty-nine of Democratic
antecedents) faced twenty-four Democrats in the House.[39]

But this era of harmony was not to last much longer. Many Democrats had probably never been altogether sincere in their profes-
sions of support of the war policy. They had, it would seem, merely
bowed before the weight of public feeling and threats of mob action or had been prevailed upon by the arguments and example of
Douglas, perhaps privately resolving to throw off such pretensions
as soon as the public temper had somewhat subsided. The overwhelming victories of the supporters of the administration in the
fall elections had been in themselves stimuli to the re-emergence of
dissent. Partisan affiliations and interests, around which so much of
the activity of the section had revolved for three or four decades,
could not be discarded easily, and Democratic politicians and newspapers were beginning to be deeply concerned for the future of
their organizations and for their own careers. Only a few months
past it had seemed that their opponents' party was on the road to disintegration; now their own appeared threatened with extinction.
The Cincinnati *Enquirer* bitterly observed that the popular cry
of "No More Party" seemed in effect to mean "No More Democratic Party." Self-preservation therefore, demanded the fostering
of discontent. It was an easy step from the belief that the war had
rescued the Republican party from destruction to the supposition
that it had been inaugurated primarily for that purpose, and from
there not difficult to reach the conclusion that Democrats were in
consequence not bound to support it. As the autumn progressed,
Democratic editors, spurred on by the sight of their Republican
competitors enjoying the postmasterships and public printing that
constituted choice plums of the political spoils system, entered
upon a concerted campaign to call the voters of the party back to
the fold. This made it necessary to find issues upon which the Republicans might be worsted.[40] Appeals to three prejudices that were

deep-seated in a large section of the population—first, dislike and jealousy of New England; second, fear of governmental centralism; and, third, anxiety over the consequences of a possible freeing of the slaves—offered promising approaches to the accomplishment of this design. The failure of New England to furnish troops in numbers proportionate to those enlisted in the Middle West was played up and coupled with reminders of that section's own earlier gestures toward nullification and secession. She was pictured as maneuvering to put the burden of taxation on the West, already suffering from the loss of Southern markets, while she managed to reap huge profits from war contracts and the new protective tariffs, and it was charged too that she had provoked secession by her Abolition fanaticism and insatiable grasping for pampering economic legislation and yet was contributing almost nothing to the war that she had brought about, using it merely as a means of sucking the lifeblood of the West.[41]

Equally effective as an appeal to those who had been nurtured in the doctrine that governmental power ought to be distributed toward the periphery of the body politic instead of concentrated at the center was the charge that the federal authorities were usurping unconstitutional prerogatives. Doctrinaire Democrats were quick to take alarm at any suggestion that there were inherent in the position of the President certain "war powers" not to be found in his peacetime functions. The Constitution, it was insisted, "is an instrument whose powers can not be enlarged or abridged to meet supposed exigencies at the caprice or will of the officers under it. . . . Exigencies and necessities will always arise in the minds of ambitious men, anxious to usurp power—they are the tyrants' pleas, by which liberty and constitutional law, in all ages, have been overthrown." [42] That meant in effect that the administration had the right to save the Union only by means which hair-splitting strict constructionists among the Democrats would approve; otherwise Democrats would be free to consider themselves absolved from any further support of the war.[43] Many and dire were the predictions that this sort of situation might soon be expected. To forestall this, if possible, the Democratic press must be untrammeled in its right to criticize and oppose any phase of the war policy. "People have as much right to oppose a war as they have to oppose a National Bank,

Tariff, or any other policy they think wrong. There is nothing particularly sacred in a war that it can not be discussed with perfect freedom." [44]

Another latent fear to which an effective appeal could be made was that Republican policy was gradually being directed toward using the war to free the slaves. This was a topic of deep concern, not merely to those—mostly of Southern descent or connections—who approved of slavery *per se*, but to small farmers and city laborers generally. The release of the Southern slaves might be expected to set loose a flood of Negro migration into the Middle West to enter into an intolerable economic and social competition with the humbler strata of whites.[45] One element particularly quick to be aroused on this issue was the Irish, then generally constituting the bottom level of society in the larger cities and most likely to feel the effects of competitive Negro immigration. In Milwaukee, where they were turbulent and politically powerful, as the aftermath of an altercation between an Irishman and a Negro a mob broke into the jail and hanged the Negro amid cries of "Kill the damned niggers!" and "Damn the niggers and Abolitionists!"—an indication of the fertile soil for an opposition movement playing up the issue.[46] In this field, too, the editorial attitude of the Democratic newspapers gave notice that action by the administration contrary to the wishes of the Democrats would be regarded as releasing them from any pledge of support to the war program.[47]

That the press campaign to regenerate the Democratic party as an opposition group, war or no war, was having success was indicated by the large number of county conventions that met during the fall and winter to redefine the principles of the party and agree upon a set attitude toward the conflict. Typical was the decision of the Putnam County, Indiana, Democracy:

. . . We will therefore vote for men and money to suppress rebellion . . . but when perverted so as to interfere with the Constitutional rights of any of the people of the several States, we will then vote against men and money and the prosecution of the war.[48]

Republicans were not blameless in the cooling of the Democratic attitude toward the war. It was a difficult task at best for strongly partisan Democrats to acquiesce in a reversal of their earlier policy, and many of their rivals were not disposed to make the process any easier or less humiliating. Republican office seekers were forever attempting to brand Democratic incumbents of postmasterships and other appointive positions as disloyal in order to procure their dismissal. The Republican press was equally relentless. Instead of manifesting a conciliatory disposition toward reluctant and eleventh-hour converts to the war policy many editors were apparently intent above all else upon party gains and the destruction of their journalistic competitors. Rather than trying to consolidate support of the administration, they seemed determined to maneuver their rivals into positions where they could be denounced as being at heart opposed to the war and as harboring treasonable designs. To this end they employed misrepresentations, gibes, and every other conceivable type of provocation. Thus in Cincinnati the *Enquirer* was kept under a galling, three-cornered crossfire from the Republican *Commercial, Gazette,* and *Times* and, quite as might have been expected, was provoked into irritated and indiscreet rejoinders. Accused of having come to support the war policy only by reason of being overawed by the mass uprising of the people, of secretly continuing to believe that the South could not be conquered, and even of not desiring the war to succeed, it fell back to its earlier retorts that the war had been brought about only because of the soulless refusal of the Republicans to preserve national unity through the Crittenden measures. The fact that its misgivings about the constitutionality of certain administration actions were represented as willingness to see the Union destroyed rather than to have it restored through any measures of doubtful legality aroused a countersuspicion that the Republicans were plotting a deliberate flouting of the Constitution. At last it broke forth in rage:

The Republican papers are great on treason. . . . It is treason to circulate petitions for a compromise or peaceful readjustment of our national troubles . . . to question the constitutional power of the President to increase the standing army without authority of law . . . to object to squads of military visiting private houses, and . . . make search and seizure . . . to question the infallibility of the President, and treason not to concur with him in all his recommendations. It is treason to talk of hard times . . . to say that this war might have been avoided had the Crittenden Compromise been adopted and not spit upon by the Republican leaders. In fine, it is treason to be truthful and faithful to the Constitution and the people. . . .[49]

In fine, one might suppose, it was an honorable thing to favor policies that might cause the Republicans to accuse one of treasonable designs.

Comparable duels were carried on between the *Journal* and the *Sentinel* in Indianapolis, the *Journal* and the *Register* in Springfield, and their counterparts in other cities and county seats throughout the section. Democratic newspapers declared that a united support of the administration was something that the Republican press, for its own reasons, was evidently seeking to prevent.[50] All too often the game succeeded in arousing Democratic editors to defiant retorts and in strengthening their determination to remain adamant in opposition. The proprietor of the Circleville (Ohio) *Watchman* broke into a lather of fury, declaring:

The nameless boobies who write editorials for the Cincinnati Commercial are very profuse in the use of the word "tory." All who do not shout hosannas to Abe Lincoln and indorse his unconstitutional and unholy war upon the people of the South are denounced as tories. The contemptible jobbernowls who blather about tories do not know the definition of the word. . . . In America during the revolution those who favored the claims of Great Britain and justified the Government in all its usurpations under the pretense of enforcing the laws, just as the abolitionists are doing now, were called tories. Those who refused to sustain a government which was administered by tyrants for the oppression of the people were called rebels. The word "tory" . . . when applied to the men who oppose this damnable abolition war and the unconstitutional and outrageous acts of a would-be military despotism which have destroyed this Union . . . has just as much meaning and sense as we generally find in the fanatical cant of such blockheads and filthy blackguards as preside over the columns of the Cincinnati Commercial and other treasonable abolition sheets.[51]

Here was a man working himself into a frame of mind in which rebellion against the administration would seem to be the higher patriotism.

More provocative still was a disposition on the part of supporters of the war to use violence or threats of violence against those who were thought to be less enthusiastic in the cause. In the reaction to Sumter there had been much talk and some action in this direction which played a part, certainly, in achieving the appearance of comparative unity of opinion at that time.[52] During the summer, when unity had been more substantially achieved, this tendency had generally subsided, although leaving rankling memories in its wake. Even then a number of men in various localities had been beaten up for indiscreet or angry rejoinders, usually growing out of political arguments, and a man in Ogle County, Illinois, was hanged by a mob on the suspicion of being a Confederate sympathizer and of having resorted to arson against his enemies.[53] With the reappearance of political dissent the mob spirit rose again. In the late summer and autumn some Democratic rallies were forcibly broken up, an instance occurring in strongly Republican Wayne County, Indiana, where Governor Morton had his home.[54] In a number of places leading Democrats were humiliatingly forced to take public oaths of loyalty, the editor of the Indianapolis *Sentinel* being among those subjected to this indignity.[55] The Canton (Ohio) *Stark County Democrat* in late August and the Terre Haute, Indiana, *Journal and Herald* in October had their offices gutted by mobs, and the St. Clairsville *Gazette*, Bellefontaine *Gazette*, Jackson *Iron Valley Express* and Marion *Mirror*, all in Ohio, were the objects of unsuccessful attempts or of threats.[56] Often those who were attacked were guilty of no worse offense than the expression of doubts concerning a coercive policy or even mere criticism of the administration.

Democratic anger over such outrages was heightened by the observation that spokesmen of the opposite party in many instances refused to disclaim them. Some Republicans openly asserted that those who maintained attitudes implying sympathy with the South had divorced themselves from the protection of the laws. The Burlington *Daily Hawk-Eye,* speaking for the Republicans of Iowa, issued a warning "To Whom It May Concern":

It may be as well, perhaps, to come to a definite understanding. This community, as well as many others, has for some time past tolerated a few individuals whose conversation has been such as to give reason to doubt their loyalty. . . . If they really sympathize with the rebellion they should go where they belong, to the rebel states. . . . We have no disposition to draw down upon any man, or class of men, public indignation or violence. But we only give expression to the general feeling when we say that no man's personal safety can be assured for one moment after the conclusion shall have been clearly arrived at that he is a traitor.[57]

The inevitable result was to unite the Democrats, whether or not basically opposed to the war, in the common conviction that their opponents were seeking to destroy them by any means at hand. Pro-war Democratic papers and politicians came to the support of anti-war Democrats on the basis of the right of free speech, and the peace advocates were thus emboldened to assume a position of more open opposition coupled with threats that any further violence directed at them would result in "a worse revolution in the North than that going on in the South." [58] As to the reaction of the individuals who had been mistreated or annoyed by threats, it is quite understandable that many who had not been actually opposed to the war might easily have been converted to such a position by their experiences. In this connection the following newspaper item is revealing:

A gentleman who is engaged in buying horses was talking to some persons, expressing his views mildly, we are told, when an individual . . . stepped up, drew a pistol, and called the stranger a traitor. . . . The moral effect of this . . . was seen at once. The man who conceived himself to have been ordered to shut his mouth at the point of a pistol was provoked to utter the most extreme views, and to dare his antagonist to attempt to intimidate him.[59]

The subject of personal rights was likewise involved in the practice of arbitrary arrests. On an order from Secretary Seward a former Democratic senator from Iowa, George Wallace Jones, was imprisoned.[60] While minister to Colombia he had, during the previous winter and spring, written to his college mate Jefferson Davis and others expressing sympathy for the South, although urging the preservation of the Union. Solely on the basis of these intercepted letters he was arrested on December 20 after his return to the United States and was held at Fort Lafayette in New York until February 22, 1862. Also conducive to anxiety was the expulsion from the United States Senate of Democratic Senator Bright of Indiana for having in March 1861 addressed a letter to Davis as "President of the Confederate States of America." This action, the only actual expulsion in senatorial history, has been generally credited to partisan motives and occurred on February 5, 1862, after an angry debate of twenty days. Bright, a Buchanan adherent, unpopular with many Democrats, had been a member of the legislature, lieutenant-governor, and senator since 1845.[61] Even war Democrats were alarmed as they saw individual rights and constitutional guarantees flouted, and the Douglas and Buchanan factions began to draw together in a common defensive unity.[62] Actual opponents of the war were confirmed in their belief that it had been fashioned as a screen for the destruction of their party. Many began to threaten resistance to illegal actions of officials and to consider reprisals against the violence and threatened violence of mobs.[63]

At first largely as a means of self-protection and to some extent for revenge there began in this period the development of those secret anti-war organizations that were in time to assume such extreme proportions. Those who had been or who expected to be objects of arbitrary arrest or victims of patriotic mobs had already at hand an organization suited to their purpose. About 1854 a Dr. George W. L. Bickley, one-time citizen of Cincinnati, had organized a filibustering society under the name of the Knights of the Golden Circle. Its military branch, the American Legion, proposed to invade Mexico as the first step in adding to the United States a great tropical slave plantation area surrounding the Gulf of Mexico (hence "Golden Circle"). Insignificant in the pursuit of its original purpose, it had in 1860 shifted front to promote secession and had played a small part in the success of that movement in the Gulf states, and in the spring of 1861 had been to some extent utilized in organizing secession sentiment in the border slave states.[64] Now came its real opportunity. Its secrecy would serve to conceal a movement likely to be suspect by law and by public opinion, its high-sounding ritual salved uneasy consciences, and its oaths and pledges of mutual assistance rendered assurance to the fearful. In April 1861 a chapter was said to be organized in Williamson County, Illinois. By late summer there were reports, generally denied by the Democratic press, of the existence of lodges of the order in several counties in the three Ohio River states and in Iowa. In the Cincinnati area, southern Illinois—especially in Jefferson and its neighboring counties—and the section along the Illinois River such activities appeared by the end of autumn to be particularly rife. The existence of groups as far north as Floyd County, Iowa, and Detroit, Michigan, was rumored. In October four leading citizens of Marion, Ohio, including the editor of the *Mirror,* were arrested on charges of membership, and grand juries in Franklin and Seneca counties conducted inquiries.[65]

Although originally organized as leagues of mutual self-defense against mob outrages, many of the secret lodges soon turned to more mischievous activities. In southern Illinois the Knights were thought to be aiding men to go south to join the Confederate army; the United States marshal at Des Moines received evidence that members of the order were engaged in transporting military supplies to the insurrectionists in Missouri; Governor Morton claimed the uncovering of a plot to burn bridges over which troops were being transported; loyal citizens in southern Illinois began to suffer from undercover depredations; and in the strongly Democratic Irish mining section around Dubuque, Iowa, it was asserted that men were having their homes burned for enlisting in the Union army.[66] In a number of communities expressions of open sympathy with the South began to be heard. One of these was in Chicago, where a nucleus of people of Southern origin, a large Irish contingent whose Roman Catholic Bishop Duggan made little show of support for the Union cause, and an influx of gamblers whom the war had driven from their usual haunts on the floating palaces of the lower Mississippi combined to make the city a place where it was commonplace to hear boasted hopes for the Confederacy. Rebel officers captured at Forts Henry and Donelson were, to the indignation of the Republican mayor, feted at the hotels upon their arrival in the city.[67]

In this setting there began a revival of agitation for a peaceful solution of the national difficulties. Papers of the stripe of the Indianapolis *Sentinel,* Cincinnati *Enquirer,* and Columbus *Crisis* started in rather cautiously to discredit the war. The *Enquirer,* which at the beginning of July had editorially pledged its support to the war policy of the administration without regard to its earlier attitude, had by the end of that same month once more reverted to the view that it would be better to allow the Confederacy its independence than to continue a war which, won or lost, would surely leave a dictatorship in its wake, for

. . . when hate and vengeance possess a people, they are ready for a conqueror; and the trained military chieftain and his pretorians will rush into the first interval of exhaustion, and like a new Philip, lord it over us all . . . we ought not to continue the waste of life and treasure. We must not hazard the overthrow of our liberties by the permanent intrusion of force into the administration of our system. And Ohio has the right, and it is her duty, as the proprietor of one-tenth part in the confederation . . . to speak early and speak continually . . . in favor of peace at the earliest moment, and for such an adjustment of the issue as will banish the presence of force; and restore, if we can . . . the Federal Constitution and the Union for which it provides. If we can not attain that glorious object, then we can propose what other scheme will be entertained for peaceable and permanent reconciliation of the belligerent States. It is apparent that no appeal to the cannon's mouth will give us back our old relations; and that all settlements of that kind which subjugate States and destroy our bravest and best, and fill the land with weeping and desolation, can only be barren as well as disastrous.[68]

Such frankness, however, was unusual even in the editorial columns of this paper. Generally, indirection was resorted to, such as giving prominence to correspondence from contributors, front-paging extracts from such extremist New York publications as the *Journal of Commerce, Banner of Freedom,* and *Freeman's Journal,* and reprinting extracts from Douglas's earlier speeches in opposition to war while ignoring his later ones supporting it. The first was a particularly effective method. Largely anonymous and increasingly vituperative, these correspondents maligned officials, denounced every act designed to render more effective the waging of the war, and in many cases demanded that independence be accorded the Southern states.[69] In late July Congressman S. S. ("Sunset") Cox of Ohio gave comfort to the movement by introducing into the House a resolution outlining a further effort at peace. Cox proposed the amending of the Constitution in an effort to assuage Southern grievances and suggested the appointment of seven prominent Northern conservatives—Martin Van Buren, Millard Fillmore, Franklin Pierce, Thomas Ewing (Ohio), Reverdy Johnson (Maryland), Edward Everett (Massachusetts), and James Guthrie (Kentucky)—to confer with a similar group of spokesmen which it was hoped would be commissioned by the South. In view of the fact that there was nothing to warrant the assumption that the South could be persuaded to return to the Union under any terms, such a proposal was fit only to dull the edge of a single-minded public support of the war. Though rejected, the proposal received forty-five votes against eighty-five and suggested that many flies might be caught with poisoned honey.[70]

All these things added up to an indication that a movement was getting under way to commit the Democratic party to an anti-war policy, reoccupying the position that it had generally held before fighting began. In the autumn political campaign, which on the surface had constituted a strong endorsement of the war policy, there had been signs pointing in this direction. The Democratic platform in Ohio, while rejecting disunion under any circumstances, had still clung to advocacy of a national conference to try to win back the South by concessions. It had stipulated that Democratic support was pledged only to a war aimed at the restoration of "the Union as it was," likely to become in time an important qualification. Suggestive, too, was the selection of Samuel Medary, editor of the *Crisis* and unreconstructed opponent of the war, as presiding officer of the nominating convention and chairman of the Democratic State Central Committee. Medary, born to a Quaker family in Montgomery County, Pennsylvania, had moved to Ohio in 1825 and a year later founded the *Ohio Sun* at Bethel to support Andrew Jackson's presidential candidacy. From 1834 to 1837 he was a member of the legislature and then for a decade held the position of state printer and published the Columbus *Ohio Statesman,* organ of the Democratic party in the capital city. Appointed territorial governor of Minnesota by Buchanan in 1857 and later holding the same office in Kansas, he returned to Columbus in January 1861 to establish the *Crisis.* This weekly publication because of its singleness of purpose and its industry in reprinting items pertaining to the subject clipped from other papers of the section became virtually a journalistic clearing house of the anti-war movement in the Midwest.[71] The resolutions on party policy adopted by many of the county conventions in Ohio, Indiana, and Illinois revealed strong doubts as to the efficacy of war as a Union restorative, sharp fears of official despotism, and still persistent faith in the possibilities of compromise. Several flatly opposed the war. Vallandigham seemed to have retained the support of the party organization in his district, and in endorsing his position the Butler County Democrats had declared that "a war forcing upon the sovereign people of a State even the *best* form of government, is neither wise, just, constitutional or practicable; that we solemnly protest against its further continuance for so fatuous a purpose." [72] In Iowa the party's gubernatorial nominee, Charles Mason, had announced his belief that a "severance of the Union . . . would . . . be a thousand times preferable to the establishment of a government by force." [73]

Paralleling the Democratic shift away from the war policy was a growing disapproval of the administration by a powerful segment of the Republican party. An aggressive minority had from the beginning hoped that the conflict would somehow result in the extinction of slavery and had persisted in that intention in spite of the Johnson-Crittenden resolutions. Adopted by a nearly unanimous vote in Congress the day after Bull Run, these resolutions defined the purpose of the war as purely the preservation of the Union without any intent of imperiling the rights or institutions of the South. Representative Crittenden of Kentucky and Senator Andrew Johnson of Tennessee were the authors. Lincoln's hesitancy to move in the direction of overthrowing the controversial institution for fear of alienating conservative supporters of the war and his conciliatory policy toward the border states aroused the impatience and irritation of this group. "For the last three months Kentucky has been the government," complained one critic to Senator Trumbull. "We are paying to [sic] much for Kentucky. . . . I hope Mr. Lincoln can leave Washington without making Buchanan's administration respectable." [74] The more extreme were even saying that if slavery were not to be destroyed they saw no point in attempting to continue the war. [75] The President's repudiation of General Fremont's confiscation proclamation had brought this division on policy into the open. Particularly resentful were numbers of the German element, a group much needed for continued Republican ascendancy in the Midwest. [76] Intra-party disagreements were sharpened by patronage squabbles. The Illinois group which had taken a leading part in maneuvering Lincoln's nomination had built up extravagant hopes as to the spoils of victory that would fall to them. Governor Yates and other State House officials in Springfield seemed particularly put out when they were not consulted on appointments to the degree that they had anticipated, and they were so placed as to be able both to hamper needed state and national co-operation and to endanger Lincoln's position as party leader.[77]

Underlying much of this dissatisfaction was the feeling that the administration had revealed shortcomings in both intelligence and vigor, that it had placed in high positions Democratic generals of doubtful trustworthiness and ability and neglected Republican officers, and that it was unbearably slow in achieving measurable results with the forces that the efforts of the people had put into its hands. At the inception of the conflict there had been an unjustified but confident assumption, common to nearly all wars, that the rebellion could and would be crushed by a single concerted effort which would take a few weeks, or a few months at most, to complete. Impatience had been manifest from the outset. "For God's sake get Mr Lincoln to *quit telling* anecdotes—and to go to work in earnest," Secretary Chase was advised. "Richmond, Va. should be in possession of the Government by 1st June at farthest!" [78] Bull Run gave a temporary setback to such naïve hopes for a quick victory, but the construction of a powerful, well-drilled, and well-equipped army in the late summer and early autumn soon revived them. The great movement was generally expected to get under way and to have substantially attained its objective by the end of 1861.[79] When the army of the Potomac and the western contingent on the Mississippi failed to move before winter closed down, exasperation and impatience returned with redoubled force. Discouragement settled over the North. At the beginning of the new year it was reported by a leading Republican of German origin that the Midwest was in the grip of despondency. Recruiting, he said, was at "a dead standstill," the Germans were morose and resentful, the government appeared bereft of leadership, inaction was sapping the public spirit, the foreign outlook threatened war with Britain and France, and over at Benton Barracks in St. Louis a "half-crazy" fellow named W. T. Sherman was driving 10,000 recruits to mutiny by his tyranny. Unless decisive victories should be won within the next sixty days, foreign intervention and internal lethargy would combine to make the contest hopeless.[80]

There were indications sufficient to convince the most optimistic that the earlier enthusiasm for volunteering was almost completely spent. Local authorities were no longer so open-handed in making appropriations for war purposes.[81] Even from the volunteer army itself were coming rumors of discontent. Under the best of conditions it would not have been easy to effect a transfer from civil to military life of men so little accustomed to mass discipline and authoritarian restrictions, and conditions in 1861 were far from ideal. In the confusion of mustering hundreds of thousands of men in a country without a previous extensive military establishment, the system of supplies and pay in the hastily created encampments often broke down, leading to charges of inefficiency, neglect, and corruption and the souring of the outlook of the volunteer. Inexperienced and in many cases unfit officers chosen in the haste and confusion of the time furnished added grounds for disgruntlement. As the complaints of the soldiers reached the public a damper was put upon further enlistment. Worse still, many were deserting.[82]

Officials feared that dangerous subversive forces were at work. At first under Secretary of State Seward and then under Edwin M. Stanton, the new Secretary of War, steps were taken to check them. Agents were stationed at Detroit to ferret out a suspected clandestine trade between the South and the outside world by way of Canada; a number of residents of southern Illinois, Cincinnati, and Lapeer County, Michigan, were arrested on executive order; and a watch was placed upon newspapers regarded as having disloyal aims.[83] These measures not only suggested the existence of undesirable conditions but in themselves created disturbance and ill feeling.

As 1862 opened, the high enthusiasm of the previous spring and the stanch determination of the summer had given way to gloom and grim forebodings, and the portents offered little hope for betterment. In the House of Representatives on January 29 John A. Gurley of Ohio, a Republican, delivered a speech that constituted a virtual motion of lack of confidence in the administration.[84] With

Congress prompt as ever to challenge executive authority, serious mischief might be done. Elements opposed to continuation of the war had been provided with a focus in the convening on January 7 of the constitutional convention in Illinois which Republican in-attention had allowed to be dominated by the Democrats. Turning aside from its appointed function the convention showed itself bent upon providing a means of expression for all elements of grievance and discontent. "Should the General Government be weakened by any reverse of fortune," a Republican state official prophesied, "I think they will then make the attempt to take the State out of the Union." [85] All the efforts, the enthusiasm, and the sacrifices of the past year appeared to have been in vain. The futility and hope-lessness of the previous winter had returned, and the energies of the North seemed to be frozen into glacial immobility.

CHAPTER IV

The Period of Confidence

(February 6–August 30, 1862)

DEJECTION and impatience were quickly dispelled by the forward movement of the spring of 1862. Early in February Grant's dramatic capture of Forts Henry and Donelson served to open the Mississippi as far as Vicksburg and, followed shortly by Farragut's taking of New Orleans and by successes in Missouri, set off throughout the North an almost delirious reaction. The legislature of Maine dispatched expressions of gratitude to the governors of all the Midwestern states.[1] From the army of the Potomac came the report, "The whole army is wild with delight & egear [sic] to try their own hand in the fight," and the promise, "When the roads are better this army will move on to South and victory." [2] An unknown New Englander was inspired to express in verse the feelings of his section:

O gales that dash the Atlantic's swell
Along our rocky shores
Whose thunders diapason well
New England's glad hurrahs,

Bear to the prairies of the West
The echoes of our joy,
The prayer that springs in every breast,
"God bless thee, Illinois!"

. . . .

In vain thy rampart, Donelson,
The living torrent bars,
It leaps the wall, the fort is won,
Up go the Stripes and Stars.

Thy proudest mother's eyelids fill,
As dares her gallant boy,
And Plymouth Rock and Bunker Hill
Yearn to thee, Illinois.[3]

The people of the Midwest, closest to these signal triumphs, were particularly buoyed up in spirit. "The recent victories in various quarters seems [*sic*] to be restoring the confidence & courage of the nation," [4] it was observed.

Republican criticism of Lincoln subsided. "Things look a little more encouraging," Senator Trumbull wrote to Governor Yates. "The President at last seems to be waking up." [5] Abolitionist congressmen who had been most critical a short time before began to counsel their like-minded constituents to have patience with Lincoln and to trust the natural course of events to lead to slavery's extinction. One malcontent, still disposed to stir up the embers of dissatisfaction by the circulation of a petition calling for more vigorous and ruthless prosecution of the war, wrote disgustedly to Congressman Julian of Indiana that he could arouse no interest among his neighbors, who had "decided that hereafter they would put their trust in the Lord and Abe Lincoln, specially the latter. They were satisfied and would sign a petition for nothing whatever." His particular local *bête noire* was a Methodist minister, and he concluded, "These Methodist preachers give me more trouble than anybody else in my work of managing mankind. The Lord have mercy on them." [6] Super-patriots temporarily left off heckling the administration and turned their attention to projects for the stern punishment of those who were responsible for the supposedly tottering rebellion. One man proposed that all rebel officers be given life sentences at hard labor and used to build a railway to the Pacific,[7] and another wished the whole of South Carolina to be confiscated and turned over to the Negroes.[8]

Democratic opposition became noticeably mollified. Most members of the party joined in the general rejoicing, sharing the confident belief of the Republicans that Grant's double-edged stroke in Tennessee had broken the back of the Confederacy in the West.[9] Peace organs showed in their own way recognition of the political significance of the changed military situation by belittling the victory and emphasizing the losses entailed in the taking of Donelson. As the tide of success ran ever stronger, even they were forced to abandon this position to join war Democrats in agreeing that the military power of the Confederacy was on the verge of certain collapse.[10] "We have only conquered the South," the *Crisis* thought on May 7, "not reconciled it." Moderates in the party now took the lead in laying out a line of policy in which for the time being a limited support would be accorded the Lincoln administration as a buffer against the Radical wing of the Republican party. The way would thus be prepared for the Democrats in the next presidential election to capitalize upon McClellan's military reputation and the usual post-war reaction against the party in power.[11] Some Republicans, sensing the possibilities in such strategy, did not entirely welcome this about-face. The *Illinois State Journal* warned its readers:

DANGER AHEAD FOR LOYAL PEOPLE

. . . Democrats were for peace on any terms, and urged a compromise that should make the great North get down on its knees and humbly beg the pardon of the Slave Power for having expressed its choice at the ballot-box in a Constitutional way, for a President of the United States. . . . Time passed on, and at length the power of the government was felt. Port Royal was taken—Zollicoffer's army was defeated—Roanoke fell before our arms—Fort Henry fell into our hands—Fort Donelson was ours—we captured the rebel fleet in Croatan Sound—we again occupied Springfield, Mo.; Price's son and aids were captured—Bowling Green was evacuated—one thousand more prisoners were captured at Fort Donelson—Clarksville was taken—and, in all this time, not a single reverse to our arms. Rebeldom is in terror, and predicts the failure of treason. Northern Democracy now turns about in favor of the Union! And now the danger to loyal men stares them in the face. Democracy gets up meetings to glorify over Union victories. Democracy votes money in an unauthorized way to aid the noble men who were wounded in the cause of our beloved country, and Democracy claims to be *par excellence* the special patron of this war and the friend of the Union! . . .[12]

But danger of obstructionism on the part of the Democrats was temporarily removed. The constitutional convention in Illinois, which had shortly before appeared so ominous, lost its power to harm. Republicans confidently predicted that its proposals would be rejected by the voters, thus disposing of the gerrymanders, provisions for ousting the incumbent state administration by a new election in the fall of 1862, and other features obnoxious to the party in power.[13] A special committee of the convention had earlier been constituted under the chairmanship of James W. Singleton, an anti-war spokesman, to investigate the welfare of the Illinois volunteers, obviously to provide a sounding board for the discontent and grumbling which might be found among still unseasoned troops. Now it became a boomerang. The volunteer officers, including such Democrats as U. S. Grant and John A. Logan, were almost unanimous in their commendation of the work of Governor Yates.[14] One major, apparently without guile, reported that the only thing lacking in his regiment was a flag and that he would be glad to have the committee send him one.[15] But the committee's come-uppance was had from a certain cavalry officer who responded:

Your circular, dated January 23, 1862, enclosing a resolution of the Illinois State Constitutional Convention, came to hand to day. Should I give you the information the resolution calls for I should make as great an ass of myself as the Convention has of you by asking you to attend to that which is none of your business, and what is not the business of the convention.

If I am rightly informed, you were elected to make a constitution for the State of Illinois. Why in the hell don't you do it?

Comparing the furniture of the Soldiers of the several states has no more to do with your duties than my duties permit me to inquire into the sanity of the members of the convention.

. . . .

If the committee on Military affairs is so very anxious to exhibit its ability in inquiring into war matters I would suggest—as the resolution permits me to make suggestions—that it inquire into the history of the Mormon War, in which its venerable chairman played so conspicuous a part.[16]

This impish epistle, delightedly published by the Republican press, set the state to laughing—at the expense of the convention.

With the Mississippi open except for the stretch from Vicksburg to Port Gibson, with Kentucky virtually cleared of Confederate forces, and Tennessee apparently about to be reclaimed, the promise of an early victory seemed beyond question. Edwin M. Stanton's appointment to succeed Simon Cameron pleased all factions and suggested that the War Department would acquire new energy and efficiency.[17] From the camps where the Confederate prisoners seized in the recent victories were being kept came reports that many were seeking permission to enter the Union army, believing their own cause hopeless.[18] As McClellan's seemingly irresistible army began its advance up the Yorktown Peninsula toward Richmond there developed in the North a spirit of complacent assurance as unwarranted as had been the gloom of the winter.[19] After the evacuation of Yorktown by the Confederates, the Democratic Detroit *Free Press* on May 8 declared, "THE DAY IS WON. The fate of the rebellion sealed." Such overconfidence held disturbing possibilities in the reaction sure to take place among the people at large if any setback in the military situation should occur. But the most serious immediate consequence was that, being shared by high-ranking federal officials, it led the new Secretary of War into one of the most egregious blunders of the entire conflict. On April 3, 1862, at a time when expectations of approaching victory were making volunteers readily obtainable, Stanton gave orders for the disbanding of the recruiting service. Officers detailed to it were to return to their regiments. Recruiting offices were closed and their furnishings sold.[20] As a result of this incredible error not only was the country deprived of troops that were to be needed desperately within a few weeks and with which the Confederacy might have been overwhelmed in spite of setbacks, but it assured the people of the North that the administration considered the war to be virtually over and that no additional forces would be needed for the completion of the task.[21]

In May, "Stonewall" Jackson came whirling down the Shenandoah Valley to end this fool's dream. McClellan's plans were disrupted and fears were entertained for the safety of Washington. In a state of panic which he quickly communicated to the country at large, Stanton frantically telegraphed to the governors of the Northern states that the enemy was marching on the national capital in great numbers and that all possible reinforcements should be rushed to its defense.[22] The fruits of the order of April 3 were at once apparent. Illinois and Ohio reported that from a month to six weeks might be required for either of them to muster a regiment; Governor Salomon of Wisconsin observed that the disbanding of the recruiting service had led the people to turn "their minds to other pursuits"; and Governor Morton of Indiana feared that conscription might be required to obtain the needed troops.[23] Fortunately, such expectations proved overpessimistic. Arrangements were made for replacing troops on guard duty with newly enlisted three-month volunteers, and these with additional recruits were hurried to the front.[24] On June 6, 1862, the War Department issued orders for the re-establishment of the recruiting service.[25] By the end of that month McClellan's now precarious position in Virginia, combined with the fact that the drive in the West to complete the opening of the Mississippi had been permitted to come to a standstill, made it patent that an enlarged military force was required. In view of the anxious state of public feeling and of earlier assurances that no further enlistment would be necessary, federal leaders feared that a call for new troops might cause a panic. It was accordingly arranged to have the governors "request" Lincoln to issue such a call in order without delay to complete the overthrow of the Confederacy. In response the President signed a proclamation asking for 300,000 volunteers. On August 4 he supplemented this with an additional call for 300,000 militia to be mustered into the federal service for a period of nine months. Any deficiencies in the quotas assigned to each state were to be filled, after August 15, by conscription.[26]

The response of the people to these sudden and tremendous levies proved that their determination for victory had not abated. The troop calls were taken as an indication that the administration was at last fully awake to the need of marshaling every resource for an irresistible movement. There was little tendency to doubt that one concerted effort would be sufficient to effect the speedy and victorious conclusion of the war. As late as June 2 Stanton assured the governor of Ohio, "The appearances now are that if recruits can be had rapidly enough to allow all the drilled force to be put into the field the war can be finished up in three months." [27] To the informed it should have been apparent early in July that the offensives of the spring had lost their force, but the mass of people, at least in the West, seemed to be unaware of the true significance of the military situation until Pope's defeat at the second Battle of Bull Run on August 30. Lincoln had assured the governors that with

50,000 additional men it would be possible to conclude the war in two weeks; [28] and Confederate prisoners in numbers were still desirous of enlisting in the Union army.[29]

A singular unity of purpose and determination was manifest. Democrats formerly or soon to be identified with the peace faction were as active as Republicans in encouraging volunteering. William Allen of Ohio gave effective speeches at war meetings; [30] Ex-Senator George E. Pugh offered to raise a regiment of infantry in Hamilton County, Ohio, a peace stronghold during a large part of the war, and promised to complete the work within ten days,[31] while Vallandigham rendered passive assistance by publicly urging those subject to conscription not to resist or in any way attempt to evade their constitutional obligations, declaring:

> Whoever shall be drafted, should a draft be ordered according to Constitution and law, is in duty bound, no matter what he thinks of the war, to either go, or find a substitute, or pay the fine which the law imposes. He has no right to resist; and none to run away.[32]

Local governing bodies helped the work along by pledging assistance to families of those enlisting and by offering bounties, commonly around $60, to each volunteer. A bounty offered by the federal government of $25 per man, in addition to local and state funds, helped to swell the financial inducements, and funds donated by individuals and private organizations added to the total.[33] The Chicago Board of Trade, for example, subscribed a bounty fund of $30,000, recruited a battery of artillery, and set about the enlistment of a full regiment; the employees in the Aurora shops of the Chicago, Burlington, and Quincy Railroad set up a fund for the families of those of their own number entering the army; and throughout the section evidences multiplied of the energetic determination of the people of all classes and affiliations to fill the ranks of the army to saturation.[34]

Over all hung the threat of drafting for any deficiencies in state quotas. Regarded as a disgrace to both the individual and the community that might require such compulsion, it served as a compelling stimulus to volunteering.[35] The press of both parties constantly warned that those who did not volunteer before the deadline might expect to be forced into service by the degrading agency of a draft.

One paper warned that "although volunteering is progressing all over the country and with commendable rapidity in many sections, yet so important is it that reenforcements be put in the field within the next few weeks, that drafting will undoubtedly be resorted to . . . before the close of the present month if volunteers are not immediately forthcoming." [36] "Prepare to Shoulder Your Muskets Whether You Will or No," warned another. "The government wants soldiers and must have them, and if they do not volunteer they will be compelled to go, willing or unwilling and without a dollar of bounty pay. Let all liable to do military duty remember this fact and act accordingly." [37] Such a combination of reward and compulsion was, under the circumstances, certain to be productive of volunteers in great numbers. "The people here have all at once become loyal in the highest degree," wrote a somewhat ironic correspondent of the *Prairie Farmer* from southern Illinois, "that is, if a willingness to volunteer is an evidence. But this spirit has been awakened since the call for the last 300,000 by draft. As many as 2,000 came into Jonesboro last Saturday, cursing the Republicans, and wanted to volunteer—to volunteer for nine months and get the bounty." [38]

Everywhere rousing war meetings, comparable to those of the previous summer, were held.[39] Secretary Stanton authorized several of the Northwestern governors to draw on the federal treasury for $1000 each, "to be expended at your discretion in employing speakers, or in such other secret manner as you may deem advisable." [40] Every state reported volunteers flocking in, particularly after the crops were harvested.[41] Of the 509,053 new enlistments under the calls of July 1 and August 4, two-fifths were obtained from the Middle West.[42] All the states of the Midwest did well. Particularly remarkable was the response of Illinois, which next to New York furnished the largest number of recruits from any state, 58,689 men in all, a feat that was officially recognized in the final report of the provost marshal general at the end of the war as the greatest single example of volunteering in the entire struggle.[43] In that state the early ripening of the wheat crop and the failure of the stand of corn induced thousands of farmers to enlist in order to get proffered bounties and good pay (especially in comparison with farm wages in the off season), in full confidence that the war would be over in time for the spring plowing.[44] A misunderstanding as to the state's quota also played its part by leading to the supposition that a larger number must be raised than was actually the case.[45] One rural county, Winnebago, in the northern part of the state, reported a full thousand enlisted in twenty days, and in a burst of enthusiasm a local paper observed:

The spirit of '76 abroad in every house and hamlet of this glorious County. Men by scores and hundreds are leaving field, workshop and office and rushing into the ranks in defense of their country. In Rockford nothing is heard from morning till night but the sound of the fife and drum and the measured tramp of military companies. . . . Large four-horse teams, loaded with volunteers and bearing aloft the stars and stripes, frequently pass our office from different directions—and barring the want of uniforms and the sheen of the muskets, our city for days has presented all the bustle and activity of a camp.[46]

Some newspapers, including the Alton *Telegraph* and the Canton *Register,* had to discontinue because their entire working forces enlisted.[47] The state outstripped even Ohio, with a considerably larger population, in the total mustered. No wonder that the War Department was moved to send a special message of congratulation to Governor Yates,[48] or that citizens of the state felt leave to boast:

. . . in the space of a few weeks, in the busiest time of the year, Illinois has marshalled fifty thousand of her brave sons who are now ready to take part in the battle for the Union and the Constitution. And her broad prairies are yet in a blaze of patriotic excitement; and, if need be, she can and will double the vast army already sent out from her workshops, farms, factories, and the various vocations and fields of labor.[49]

A heartening example of the ability of a democracy to function in a crisis had been furnished by that summer's recruiting. It could not be overlooked, however, that it had rested on the twin supports of inter-party unity of effort and confidence in a victory only momentarily delayed. The Confederates had in the meantime been given a new commander before Richmond who would soon bring bitter disillusionment in regard to the latter expectation, and in the Middle West, even in the midst of prevailing good feeling and confidence, there were factors operating to widen the chasm of distrust separating Democrats and Republicans.

For one thing, Democrats were increasingly aroused to exasperation and apprehension by the continuation of arbitrary arrests. During 1861 much criticism of this practice had been expressed, but it was limited by the awareness that strong secession movements in the border slave states, to which its application had been largely confined, required drastic repressive measures. There was reassurance, furthermore, in an "Executive Order, Number I, Relating to Political Prisoners," of February 14, 1862, that, the danger from civil treason in this quarter having passed, all those previously arrested would now be freed.[50] But it soon appeared that many were not being released and that in fact military arrests of civilians were being made with increased frequency in the Midwest itself. It was in Illinois that this extension of the practice began first to be apparent on a considerable scale. For this David L. Phillips, United States marshal for the Southern District of Illinois, was in large part responsible. On February 23 he dispatched to the Department of State a detailed report of investigations which he had been carrying on for some time in southern Illinois and urged the arrest of certain individuals of Marion, Mount Vernon, and McLeansboro, all men of local prominence who seemed particularly active in opposing the war and interfering with its prosecution. From the War Department, which had now displaced the Department of State in jurisdiction over the matter, came on the 27th orders to arrest these individuals and to convey them to Fort Lafayette in New York harbor.[51] On August 8 Secretary Stanton issued a blanket order to all law enforcement officers authorizing the arrest for trial before a military commission of anyone seeking to discourage volunteering, giving aid and comfort to the enemy, or, through writing, speech, or act, engaging in any disloyal practice.[52] In Illinois a number of men of prominence were thereupon taken into custody, including William Joshua Allen of Marion, recently elected to fill a vacancy in Congress, Judge Andrew D. Duff of Benton, Judge John H. Mulkey of Cairo, State's Attorney John M. Clemerson of Marion, the editors of the Paris *Democratic Standard*, M. Mehaffey and F. Odell, and Madison Y. Johnson and David Sheean, attorneys of Galena.[53] Most of these, and many smaller fry, were imprisoned without trial, in Fort Lafayette, Fort Delaware, or the Old Capitol Prison in Washington.[54] This latter place of confinement was in the very shadow of the capitol and had served as a temporary meeting place for Congress after the British arson. One of the prisoners incarcerated there noted the presence of some twenty-five citizens of Illinois among its inmates within a period of a few weeks. In other Midwestern states those arrested, usually on charges of interfering with enlistment or similar activities, included Dennis A. Mahoney, editor of the Dubuque (Iowa) *Herald,* Dana Sheward, editor of the Fairfield (Iowa) *Constitution and Union,* and Dr. Edson B. Olds, a prominent and respected citizen of Lancaster, Ohio.[55] Briefly held in custody were two eccentric characters, Henry Clay Dean, homespun orator of Iowa, sometimes known as "Dirty Shirt" Dean, confined for two weeks in jail at Keokuk,[56] and John W. Kees of Ohio, editor of the Circleville *Watchman.* The latter was a critic of the war and all its associated policies and personalities who might well have contested the title of the most vituperative journalist in a day given to unrestrained denunciation. In the spring of 1862 he had paid his respects to a Republican postmaster supposed to have sent copies of the *Watchman* to Washington with recommendation for the editor's arrest:

We . . . did not know that such a vile and dirty reptile ever disgraced the face of God's green earth, by existing upon it. . . . He is a dirty, contemptible, negro-thieving scoundrel, and a perjured wretch! What a fit subject for a *pimp,* the dirty fiend and libel upon humanity that he is! He would not only steal negroes—he would steal horses—he would steal chickens—he would rob the widow and orphan—and the devil himself would refuse such an infamous wretch admission into hell. He is a tory, a traitor, a thief, to the extent of his very limited brains, and if he has any of that article, they are the brains of the slimy viper!

. . . If the vile animal called a hyena is to have an existence after death, it should be with Samuel Hill, in some pollution far beneath the bottomless pit.[57]

Noting that those arrested were almost without exception Democrats, and frequently men of local and even state importance in the party, many Democratic adherents began to fear that the ultimate objective of such arrests was the silencing of all criticism of the administration policies. A new wave of mob actions, including the destruction of the offices of the *Democratic Citizen* of Lebanon, Ohio, and in Illinois of the Bloomington *Times*,[58] tended to confirm this deduction. Both authorized and irresponsible measures of this nature tended to stiffen the attitude of the peace advocates, deepening their conviction that the war was aimed primarily at the destruction of their party rather than the restoration of the Union. Sympathy was aroused for the victims of such actions among even those not in agreement with their views, serving to draw the opposition factions closer together, alienating supporters from the administration, and generally strengthening the position of the anti-war elements.[59]

Other factors—including the threat of conscription, latent Southern sympathies, fears of Negro emancipation, and general endangerment of the Democratic party—were also leading considerable numbers in the Northwest to opposition to the government at the very time when co-operation seemed most effective. The prospect of draft in August was so disturbing as to prompt hundreds of able-bodied men to attempt to escape to Canada or the Far West, or to go into hiding in the more remote rural sections, as a result of which Secretary Stanton ordered the arrest of anyone liable to the draft who might attempt to leave the county of his residence,[60] a system of passes being arranged shortly thereafter to permit necessary and legitimate travel.[61] In some localities there were threats to resist any attempt at conscription,[62] and in at least one Wisconsin township there was so general and persistent a refusal of the inhabitants to submit to enrollment of those liable to service as to cause the federal authorities to decide to "let them slide" for the time.[63]

"Southern sympathy," a quality hard to define in the Middle West during the war, was doubtless often exaggerated by those who stood to gain by discrediting individuals or groups of Southern derivation,[64] but that such an attitude played a part in the situation can hardly be doubted. Men such as Cyrus H. McCormick, whose Virginia birth caused him to try to remain neutral during the conflict,[65] at least withheld their active support from the Union cause. Others exercised their sympathies more actively and were in many cases instrumental in aiding the escape of Confederate prisoners. The officials of Illinois believed that there were so many people of doubtful loyalty in even the state capital that it would be unsafe to attempt to keep prisoners there.[66] As early as June 1862 there were serious fears that a plot was on foot in one of the largest of the military prisons, on Johnson's Island in Lake Erie, for an insurrection of the inmates with help from sympathizers outside.[67]

Leaders of the opposition continued to find Midwestern fears of Abolition a string upon which they might play effectively. In a speech in the national House of Representatives on June 3, 1862, Samuel S. Cox of Ohio painted a fearful picture of the flooding of the section with the freed Negroes of the South if the radical Republicans should triumph in their aims, and asked, "Is there a member here who dare [*sic*] say that Ohio troops will fight successfully or fight at all, if the result shall be the flight and movement of the black race by millions northward to their own State?" [68] The Democratic press never tired of stressing the labor competition to be anticipated by white laborers from free Negroes, or of giving maximum notoriety to reports of Negro outrages against whites—especially of one or two cases of rape that occurred in the Midwest in this period, or of publishing the statements of the growing insolence and indolence of "niggers" since they had been encouraged by a Republican administration to believe themselves as good as white people.[69] Many were the evidences of the strength of any appeal on such grounds. The Ohio legislature was said to be deluged by petitions asking that measures be taken to avert the immigration of free Negroes into the state, and in Illinois the electorate, in turning down the proposed new constitution in July, in a separate vote expressed approval, by a margin of more than 100,000, of a section forbidding Negro immigration.[70] No effort was spared by the anti-administrationists to tar the Republican party with the charge of Abolition intentions. Besides general accusations they pointed toward proposals by Governor Yates and many other Republican officials for the recruiting of Negro troops as evidences of a disposition to lift the blacks to a position of equality, and called attention to the accumulating indications that the radicals were forcing President Lincoln toward their position—a view which some of those radicals, among them Horace Greeley, were coming to share.[71]

Nor could Democrats forget, even in wartime, that theirs was a political party, whose views and success required the defeat of the Republicans. As they saw their victorious opponents putting through a homestead policy in Congress, embracing the protective tariff principle at levels ever higher, passing legislation that granted immense favors to bankers, and extending the functions of the federal government through such measures as the creation of a Department of Agriculture—all activities anathema to the historic policies of their own party—they were genuinely alarmed.[72] Unity in support of the war administration entailed, it appeared, tacit support for all these measures as well. Was not the price too great to pay? And would it be possible to oppose the civilian program of the administration without engaging in obstruction of the war policy as well?

One direction in which the growing sentiment of opposition was taking form was revealed by increasing testimony to the spread and augmenting strength of the Knights of the Golden Circle and of other secret, semi-treasonable organizations of similar methods and objectives. Disturbing reports came from southern Illinois, where lodges of the order were reported to exist in a number of counties. In this section open admission of sympathy with the Confederacy was occasionally heard. An early summer picnic party at Carlinville was reported to have given cheers for Jefferson Davis and groans for Lincoln, and in both Charleston and Vandalia groups of men dared to ride through the streets hurrahing for Jefferson Davis and for General John Morgan, the Confederate raider. Western Illinois, in the vicinity of Quincy, was also believed to have been penetrated by anti-war organizations.[73] The Detroit *Tribune* likewise found that branches of the K.G.C. were established in many parts of Michigan.[74] Some of the state executives of the Northwest became so alarmed for the security of their own section that they urged the formation of a home guard force for emergency service. Governor Tod of Ohio believed that detachments of this reserve might be required in Indiana, Illinois, and his own state.[75] Morton of Indiana in the latter part of June dispatched to Stanton a full and confidential report of the existence of a secret political organization in Indiana of an estimated strength of 10,000 members, whose ascertainable purposes included the obstruction of recruiting, opposition to the collecting of taxes for war purposes, and in general the fostering of distrust of the constituted authorities. As a defense he recommended that the Indiana Legion, already organized in the Ohio River counties as a protection from sudden raids across the river, be made a state-wide force and equipped by the federal government with ten thousand stands of arms.[76] Democratic newspapers continued to underrate or to deny the existence of the Knights of the Golden Circle in the North and represented it as a bogey created by their opponents for political purposes.[77]

Undoubtedly there was a disposition on the part of the Republicans to exaggerate the strength and distribution of the order in an effort to identify the Democrats in general with it, but much of the evidence for the growth of the Knights manages to survive such criticism. The imminence of conscription had apparently been a particular stimulus to its development. Some of the newspapers that denied their existence tended to encourage the secret societies by giving moral sanction to the use of force against "abolitionist agitators" and by a constant impugning of the legality of the acts of the administration.[78]

The secret societies represented an extreme and, as yet, not dangerous type of opposition. A more serious threat was to be found in indications that the Democratic party in the West was being revitalized and reconstructed under leaders unenthusiastic or openly hostile toward the attempt to restore the Union by war. During the spring marked gains had been made by the party in local elections. In Chicago, Cincinnati, Dayton, and numerous smaller municipalities the election of Democratic mayors, councilmen, and other officials indicated that the current was running against the Republicans, particularly since national issues rather than local ones had been emphasized in the campaigns.[79] Democratic journals were drifting to a position increasingly unsympathetic toward the administration.[80] The *Crisis,* handicapped by being a weekly and by limited facilities for news collection but actuated by a singleness of purpose—and that purpose one that seemed rapidly to be winning new adherents—was forging ahead to a position of editorial leadership in the anti-war party. Growing in circulation and influence, it was increasing its warnings of dangers impending from Negro emancipation, corruption, the alliance between wealth and government, and official despotism if the Republicans were continued in power.[81]

The essential impulse for Democratic revival, however, came from party representatives of the Midwest in Congress who, with four exceptions, joined in signing an "Address to the Democracy of the United States" which was largely the handiwork of Clement L. Vallandigham. Proposing the question "Shall the Democratic party be now disbanded?" the manifesto returned an emphatic negative and laid down a platform for concerted action. This included principles of strict construction of the Constitution—with due regard to state rights and jealous limitations of governmental powers—and non-interference anywhere by the federal government with the institution of slavery. The group's attitude toward the war was defined in the announcement that

. . . Democrats recognize it as their duty as patriots to support the Government in all constitutional, necessary, and proper efforts to maintain its safety, integrity, and constitutional authority; but at the same time they are inflexibly opposed to waging war against any of the States or people of this Union . . . for any purpose of conquest or subjugation, or of overthrowing or interfering with the rights or established institutions of any State.[82]

The manifesto, dated May 8, was followed by addresses before the House by Richardson of Illinois, Voorhees of Indiana, and Cox of Ohio indicating that the document was intended to serve as the platform of the Western Democracy in the forthcoming congressional election.[83] Significantly, only three Eastern congressmen signed the Address. The response at home indicated that both the press and minor politicians were in thorough accord with this movement for party revival along militant lines. The effect produced on the extremist wing was suggested by a statement of the Carlinville (Illinois) *Spectator:*

We call the special attention of our readers to the address of the Democratic members of Congress from the free States. The sentiments contained in it look as if a day of redemption was approaching, and that the days of *leaden despotism* were drawing to a close. The vulgar, swaggering usurper at Washington, *who has the unblushing impudence to intimate that he,* and he alone, *is the Government of the United States,* may begin to take warning. This address comes like the peal of the tocsin and the roar of the alarm gun. The *unity of despotism* they pledge to resist, as did our fathers, *with their lives, their fortunes and their sacred honor.* Let the Democracy come bravely up to the move that promises to disenthrall the country from the *tyranny more odious than Austrian despotism.* This is a move in the right direction, and the only objection to it is that it does not go far enough.[84]

Adherence to the movement was pledged by many Democratic county conventions, including these Ohio counties: Fairfield, Holmes, Clark, Butler, Shelby, Ashland, Stark, and Hocking.[85] The state Democratic convention of Iowa meeting in Des Moines on July 17, 1862, exhibited a spirit in sharp contrast to the hesitant attitude in the previous year and adopted a platform in substantial conformity with the congressional manifesto.[86]

The indications were that the party in the West was coming under the control of men who would raise opposition to the war as an issue paramount to the saving of the Union. In making nominations partiality was in many instances shown for candidates whose loyalty to the national cause had been suspect.[87] The purpose was generally to demonstrate Democratic indignation over the arbitrary arrest of citizens, but the result might be the elevation to leadership of the men whose views were least compatible with success in restoring the Union. A popular reaction due to military reverses in conjunction with other causes for dissatisfaction might return the Democratic party to power in the national House of Representatives and the legislatures of two or more of the Western states. With an election campaign approaching, most of the Democratic leaders confined themselves to safe generalities as to what they would do if elected to office. But one man, John J. Jennings, Iowa state senator from Dubuque, expressed a view that might be held secretly by many others. Boldly he published a statement wishing success to the Confederate armies, saying:

They are Americans, and I wish to see them acquit themselves in a manner worthy of American citizens and soldiers. I wish to see them conduct themselves with such vigor, *as to compel the North to yield such compromises in the end as will secure to them their constitutional rights*. The Constitution is founded in compromise, and by compromise only can it and the Union be preserved.[88]

CHAPTER V

The Period of Disgust

(August 30–December 13, 1862)

As 1862 passed the mid-year the heat of summer could not keep a chill realization from creeping over the souls of the Northern people. In the swamps before Richmond both the Army of the Potomac and the hope of a speedy victory were bogging down. Lee stopped McClellan's advance up the Yorktown Peninsula in the Seven Days' Battles and forced him to transfer his army to the south side of the James River. For a while it was thought that this might be only a temporary check and that before long the spring offensive would be resumed. But the War Department, having lost faith in the campaign, called back the army to Washington and replaced McClellan with General John Pope, protégé of the Republicans, who had received credit for victories in the West that more properly belonged to Grant. The public then understood that the end of the war was not in sight, and consternation followed as Lee crushed Pope on August 30 at the second Battle of Bull Run and invaded Maryland while another Confederate army under President Davis's pet, Braxton Bragg, advanced into Kentucky to threaten Louisville and Cincinnati. McClellan, restored to command, succeeded in checking Lee in the battles of South Mountain and Antietam and drove him back across the Potomac River; and the Confederate western army, stalemated by Bragg's ineptitude, had to retreat into southeastern Tennessee. But the feeling of relief derived from this escape could hardly compensate for the disappointment of earlier hopes. Fault-finding became the order of the day. Among men of all parties the conviction grew that the titanic efforts of the people in lavishly supplying the government with means to conduct the war had been ill-repaid by the feeble and maladroit fashion in which those means had been used.[1] Serving as a barometer of public opinion, the rapid and continued depreciation of the United States treasury notes graphically indicated the decline of confidence in the government's ability to accomplish the enormous task which it had undertaken.[2] All signs pointed to the failure of the expectations that shortly before had appeared so bright.

At this inopportune time the Republican (or Union) party had to face congressional and state election campaigns. There were many issues for the Democrats to exploit. Basic, of course, was the universal dissatisfaction with the conduct of the war, constituting not only a major issue in itself but generating an atmosphere in which other types of discontent would flourish.

A particularly thorny issue was the question of arbitrary arrests. During the summer the government had been more industrious than ever before in hustling off to prison without regard to civil law men who were regarded as obstacles to the prosecution of the war. On September 9 Secretary of War Stanton, perhaps in recognition of the unpopularity of the policy, issued instructions to all military and civilian officials that no arrest was to be made until specifically authorized by the Secretary, a general commanding a military district, or the governor of a state,[3] but there were no indications that this marked any real change of policy. Arrests continued, although perhaps with some abatement in number.[4] Most of those already in custody were kept in prison without opportunity to hear the charges against them or to obtain possible evidence of their innocence. These arrests, often unjust and always haphazard in their application, stirred up resentment among unquestioned supporters of the war. Even if the war had been going well such measures would have been seriously questioned, but with it proceeding from bad to worse the reaction was doubly strong. The Democrats had an issue that cut deep and they drove it home with the assertion that if the administration had been as energetic in attacking the enemy as in striking down the rights of its own citizens, the war might well be drawing to an end.[5] In order to highlight the issue the Democrats put up several of the victims of the system as candidates for public office. One, Dennis Mahoney of Iowa, was nominated for Congress, and Congressman William Joshua Allen of Illinois was nominated for re-election, the latter's candidacy being successful. Such widespread indignation had been aroused by the arrest of Dr. Edson B. Olds, an elderly and respected citizen of Lancaster, Ohio, that when his neighbors sought to vindicate him by electing him to a vacancy in the legislature the Republicans did not even attempt to make a contest.[6] Just on the eve of the elections a final touch was given by the murder of J. F. Bollmeyer, editor of the Dayton *Empire* and Vallandigham's journalistic spokesman. Although it was eventually established that the affair was the result of a purely personal quarrel, the Democrats were able in the excitement of the moment to turn it to account by representing it as an indication that the Republicans were adding assassination to their practice of imprisoning outspoken Democrats.[7]

The Abolition issue reached its climax in this period. On September 22 President Lincoln, under pressure from the radical faction in his own party and needing to appeal to European public opinion, issued his preliminary annoucement of the Emancipation Proclamation. It came at an unfortunate moment. The public, irritated with the administration for its bungling of the military situation, was not for the time being disposed to respond with enthusiasm to any of its works, and since the Northern armies no longer held the offensive the document seemed the product of futility, even desperation. There was a further handicap in the fact that since its organization the Republican party had always officially insisted that its program called for no interference with slavery in the Southern states, and this had been adhered to during the war in the face of repeated Democratic charges that it was the Republican intention to discard that promise at the first opportunity. Consequently the Republican position was extremely awkward. The Democrats attacked the new policy from every direction. They scorned it as an emblem of Republican hypocrisy, charged that the issuance of the Proclamation would be outside the constitutional power of the President, predicted that its chief effect would be to drive the South to a desperate and unified resistance to being brought back into the Union, and declared that if it should be successful it would result in the disruption of the economic and social systems of the Midwest by flooding the section with freed blacks who would underbid white men in the labor market and degrade them socially by forced association. The Chicago *Times*, once well disposed toward Lincoln, stated:

The President has at last weakly yielded to the "pressure" put upon him about which he has so bitterly complained, and issued his proclamation of negro emancipation . . . he has no constitutional power to issue this proclamation—none whatever. . . .

Nobody need argue with us that he has the power under military law. Military law does not destroy the fundamental civil law. In war, as in peace, the Constitution is "the supreme law of the land."

The government, then, by the act of the President, is in rebellion, and the war is reduced to a contest for subjugation.[8]

And the *Crisis* wailed:

We have at last hit upon the lower round of our national existence. The abolition fires which have burnt to the very core of the nation's heart, have at last burst to the surface, and spread over the whole land. Sad is our fate and monstrous the depths to which we are precipitated. . . . It unites the South as one man, and throws its destructive virus into the veins of the North to inoculate every region, city, town and hamlet.[9]

The aspect of the question most disturbing to the Midwesterners was the constantly reiterated fear that the bars would be lowered for a horde of Negroes to sweep into the section. It was among the foreign-born proletariat of the cities and small farmers of Southern origin that the specter was most disturbing. The Negroes were expected to compete with the whites for unskilled urban employment and thus force wages down to disastrous levels. In agriculture the ex-slaves might be used by ambitious land-owners to set up a large-scale type of operation comparable to the plantation system that had driven many Midwesterners or their ancestors to leave their former homes in the South. The apprehension had been sharpened during the preceding months by actions of the War Department which were given wide publicity by the Democratic press. In spite of the fact that the laws of Illinois forbade the entrance of free Negroes into the state, and in the face of the overwhelming vote of the people in July in favor of a constitutional enactment to this effect, Secretary Stanton had ordered the general commanding at Cairo to colonize and to find employment for confiscated Negroes sent north by Federal armies. Industrial employers in search of cheap labor also attempted on their own initiative to introduce Negro laborers into the section, and in July this led to a serious riot among the employees of grain and produce firms in Toledo,[10] while tense situations existed in many other cities. A mass meeting of workingmen in Quincy, Illinois, expressed the reaction of the laboring class in a series of resolutions in which it was announced "that we hereby give notice to those engaged in this business of attempting to ride down and crush out the free white workingmen of Illinois, by thus seeking to bring free negro labor into competition with white labor, that we cannot and will not tolerate it; that we will seek our remedy, *first*, under the law; *second*, at the polls; and *third*, if both these fail, we will redress our wrongs in such a manner as shall seem to us most expedient and most practicable." [11] The action of the Illinois State Republican Convention in promptly and unanimously endorsing Lincoln's announcement, besides other signs of Republican acceptance of the administration's leadership in this policy, had the effect of emphasizing in the eyes of the voters of the section the clear-cut issue between the two parties on the question of emancipation.[12]

The three chief weapons which the Democrats of the West employed against their opponents in the election campaign were disgust with the handling of the war, indignation over arbitrary arrests, and fears of the consequences of setting the Negroes free, but they made effective use of other issues as well. Many variations were played upon the theme that Republican policies worked to the disadvantage of the economic interests of the Middle West. It was charged that the tariff and taxation policies adopted by the Republican majority in Congress were bleeding the Mississippi Valley region for the benefit of Eastern manufacturers and capitalists.[13] There were gloomy prophecies, too, that the cost of the war and resort to a fiat currency would lead to national bankruptcy in which the economy of the section would go down in the general debacle. Much use was also made of innuendoes that the party in power was plotting to set up a military dictatorship, that it had deliberately prevented Democratic generals from winning victories, and that it was moving toward things even less tangible and more fearsome.[14] The state of the public mind was such that the vagueness of these charges made them all the more effective in furthering distrust of the administration.

Republican difficulties were multiplied by divisions and lethargy

within the party. The split between the anti-slavery radicals and
the more moderate elements of which Lincoln was representative
had gone deep, and lasting animosities had been built up. The
radicals had become increasingly exasperated with the reluctance
of the administration to make use of the opportunity presented by
the war for the abolition of slavery.[15] Strict party men were disturbed by the appointment of Democrats to positions of command
in the army, and when military affairs went awry they were quick
to suspect treachery.[16] Some Republicans declared their indifference to the war in view of the manner in which it was being directed, Joseph Medill of the Chicago *Tribune* writing in July to
Senator Trumbull:

> There will be a feeble response to the late call for 300,000 volunteers
> to serve under proslavery generals to fight for "Union and Slavery." The
> Vallandigham Democrats don't volunteer. The "Abolitionists" have
> been "modified" and snubbed so often that they will stay at home until
> the Government declares a policy likely to put down the rebellion and
> remove its cause at the same time. Free men are reluctant to join the
> army, expose their lives and destroy their health merely to . . . guard
> rebel property.[17]

And another had predicted, "Though many will spring to arms in
response to the late call for 300,000 more men many who would
do so were the policy embodied in Gen. Hallecks order no. 3
changed and all available men and means employed by the government to speedily cripple and end the Rebellion, openly declare
they will never shoulder a musket or enter the ranks while such
practical folly marks the conduct of the war." [18] When Lincoln
went over to the emancipation policy there was naturally a sense of
elation among such men, and Senator Benjamin Franklin Wade
of Ohio could write to Congressman George Washington Julian of
Indiana, "Now, hurrah for Old Abe and the *proclamation*," [19] but
their resentments and suspicions could not be dissolved overnight.
And military reverses confirmed their belief in the general ineptitude of the administration. Senator Zachariah Chandler on September 10 asked the War Department:

> . . . Is there *any* hope for the future. Are imbecility *and treason* to be
> retained and promoted to the End of the Chapter. The loss of the Battle

& invasion of Maryland were bad enough, but under the belief that traitors in the army would be punished & the enemy yet be exterminated, the people of the North West were hopeful, but the restoration of McLelland [*sic*] Porter & Franklin to command without trial has cast a hopeless gloom over our entire community which has never before been seen. . . .[20]

That same day in a letter to Senator Lyman Trumbull of Illinois Chandler broached the proposal of a virtual *coup d'état* to force Lincoln into conformity with the policy of the radicals:

It is *treason, rank treason,* call it by what name you will, which has caused our late disasters. Jealousy & discontent at the removal of Mc-Clelland [*sic*] & promotion of Pope will be the cause assigned, but where ruin, death & the probable destruction of the Govt is the effect of disobedience of orders *treason* is the cause. I fear nothing will save us but a *demand* of the loyal Governors *backed by a threat,* that a change of *policy* & men shall *immediately* be made. . . . This seems to me the last hour. Your President is unstable as water. If he has as I suspect, been bullied by those traitor Generals, how long must it be before he will by them be set aside & a Military Dictator set up. McClelland's army is totally demoralized & made for anything but fighting. It will not fight under its present commanders. . . . For God & country's sakes, send some one to *stay* with the President who will control & hold him. I do not dispair [*sic*], but my *only* hope is in the Lord, & I don't believe he will let us be destroyed.[21]

Against such a background the preliminary announcement of emancipation was naturally regarded as a grudging and tardy concession.

Also contributing to Republican discord was the frayed state of administrative nerves as a consequence of the military reverses, and this led to some personal quarrels that added to the confusion among the party leadership. A petty misunderstanding arising from a question of authority in mustering of state troops into federal service provoked a sharp tiff between Lincoln and Governor Yates of Illinois, while Stanton offered a gross and gratuitous insult to Governor Salomon of Wisconsin in a similar misconstruction. On August 23 Lincoln had telegraphed Yates, "I am pained to hear that you reject the service of an officer we sent to assist in getting off troops. . . . If Illinois had got forward as many troops as Indiana,

Cumberland Gap would soon be relieved from its present peril. Please do not ruin us on *punctilio.*" To Yates, a warm-hearted and emotional person who was at the moment in an exalted mood of self-congratulation over the unmatched success of recruiting in Illinois in the previous weeks, this undeserved censure came as a slap in the face. His hurt disclaimer did not clear up the misunderstanding. Other officials became involved, and the quarrel continued and extended itself.[22] After this incident there was an attitude of injury in all of Yates's relations with the national administration that both hampered the vital co-operation of his state in the national cause and placed him in the ranks of the opponents of Lincoln in the Republican party, a fact of which the public soon became aware.[23] Governor Salomon, alarmed by Indian outbreaks in the state of Minnesota, had appealed insistently to the federal government for assistance and made efforts on his own responsibility to get arms with which the inhabitants of threatened regions of Wisconsin could protect themselves.[24] When news of this reached Stanton he sent an angry dispatch admonishing the governor:

You are entirely mistaken in supposing that you are the exclusive judge as to whether arms and ammunition of the General Government are to be sent to your State. The President must be judge. You have not until now stated any fact for the judgement of the President, but contented yourself with giving imperious orders. The Department has borne and will continue to bear, them patiently, and will act upon any facts you may communicate. Orders have been given to send ammunition. The arms it appears you have seized.[25]

Salomon being more even-tempered by nature than Yates, this flare-up does not appear to have had any very lasting consequences, but it constituted one more evidence of the snarling and irritations in the Republican ranks. Thoughtful Republicans recognized the danger to their electoral interests involved in their divisions, but they seemed for the time being able to do little to bring about any measure of reconciliation.[26]

In contrast to the situation of the Republicans, the Democrats were united, aggressive, and prepared to make the broadest and most effective possible appeal to the electorate. Certain in advance of the votes of peace advocates, they took care to alienate no supporters of the war who might be won over through dislike of arbitrary acts of government, disapproval of emancipation, or uneasiness about the alleged incompetence and peculation of officials. Men in the party who nursed peace-at-any-price sentiments apparently carefully avoided raising this issue in the campaign, but occasionally a chink would appear, revealing the sentiments hidden beneath the surface. In a rambling impromptu speech before the Democratic state convention at Columbus on July 4, 1862, in which for the most part he confined his attack to Abolition and violations of civil rights, Congressman Vallandigham let slip the opinion:

. . . Foreign intervention and the repeated and most serious disasters which have lately befallen our arms, will speedily force the issue of separation and Southern independence—*disunion*—or of Union by negotiation and compromise. Between these two I am—and I here publicly proclaim it—for the Union, the whole Union and nothing less, if by any possibility I can have it; if not, then for so much of it as yet can be rescued and preserved; and in any event and under all circumstances, for the Union which God ordained, of the Mississippi Valley and all which may cling to it, under the old name, the old Constitution and the old flag, with all their precious memories, with the battle fields of the past . . . with the birth place and burial place of Washington the founder and Jackson the preserver of the Constitution as it is and the Union as it was.[27]

And in speaking of the emancipation policy the Chicago *Times* stated:

The democratic party is for the war as long as it shall be prosecuted for the preservation of the Constitution and restoration of the Union.

. . . .

The democratic party resists the southern rebellion with fire-arms. As yet it resists the abolition rebellion only with arguments and ballots; we pray God that it may suppress it by these weapons and that it shall not be compelled to resist it with bullets.[28]

But for the most part the Democratic party did not permit the mask which it had adopted for the duration of the campaign to slip even to this extent. Newspaper editors and platform speakers stressed the assertion that although their party repudiated the policy of emancipation and would seek its repeal, they would continue to give undiminished support to the war.[29] Vallandigham himself, in a prepared speech accepting a renomination for Congress by the unanimous vote of his district convention, placed his candidacy on the single issue of defense of the people's liberties.[30] A short time before in a speech at Dayton that many of his followers considered his finest oratorial work he pictured himself as a symbol of the threats hanging over freedom of opinion. In a passage that revealed the essence of his personality—on one hand undoubted courage and a gift for arousing the enthusiasm of an audience with fiery words and personal magnetism and on the other narrowness of vision and omnipresent theatrical egotism—he defied the authorities to arrest him:

. . . I was born a freeman. I shall die a freeman. It is appointed to all men once to die; and death never comes too soon to one in the discharge of his duty. I have chosen my course—have pursued it—have adhered to it to this hour, and will to the end, regardless of consequences. My opinions are immovable; fire cannot melt them out of me. I scorn the mob. I defy arbitrary power. I may be imprisoned for opinion's sake— never for crime; never because false to the country of my birth, or disloyal to the Constitution which I worship. Other patriots, in other ages, have suffered before me. I may die for the cause; be it so; but the "immortal fire shall outlast the humble organ which conveys it, and the breath of liberty, like the word of the holy man, will not die with the prophet, but survive him." [31]

In Illinois the Democratic nominee for congressman-at-large, James C. Allen, whose approval of the war had long been a moot point, assured an audience in Chicago on October 10 that, although he had originally favored compromise, he had since the commencement of hostilities supported the war policy with his whole heart. Upon this issue, he declared, there was no division between the parties. Only the threat of Negro migration into the state and the question of arbitrary arrests were before the voters.[32]

Democratic party platforms were constructed to fit this moderate pattern. Whereas the Democrats of Ohio in 1861 had called for the continuation of efforts to negotiate a reunion by peaceful means, the platform of 1862 omitted any such proposal. Instead it emphasized the assertion that the Democrats had been the true and unswerving supporters of the war, while the Republicans had hindered its prosecution by fostering divisions. The latter, ambitious for party or factional advantage, had intrigued against the President and his generals, forced upon the electorate the unnecessary issue of Abolition, and had attempted to stigmatize conservative Democrats as rebel sympathizers. Radical Republicans, the Ohio platform declared, were the ones who had threatened to withhold support unless the policy of the nation were directed to their liking, in contrast to the Democrats, who had in no degree diminished their exertions in the undertaking since the emancipation announcement. The Democratic purpose was defined as winning the war, stamping out fraud and graft in the purchase of military supplies, the checking of arbitrary arrests, and the legal punishment of the leaders of the rebellion, as contrasted with the Republican purpose of a sweeping and indiscriminate confiscation of the property of a whole section. The convention resolved:

. . . That we are, as we have ever been, the devoted friends of the Constitution and the Union, and we have no sympathy with the enemies of either. . . . That every dictate of patriotism requires that, in the terrible struggle in which we are engaged for the preservation of the Government, the loyal people of the Union should present an unbroken front; and therefore all efforts to obtain or perpetuate party ascendancy by forcing party issues upon them that necessarily tend to divide and distract them, as the abolitionists are constantly doing, are hostile to the best interests of the country.[33]

The Indiana state platform was very similar in tone, and other state, district, and county conventions, and local mass meetings also followed that line.[34] A typical district convention was that of the Democrats of the first congressional district of Illinois meeting in Chicago on October 14. Its speakers stressed the fact that Democratic support of the war was *unconditional* and that the success of the war policy could best be insured by turning out the party that had not only shown a singular incapacity in its conduct but had complicated it by raising the question of Abolition and by needless attacks on the rights of Northern citizens.[35] For the time being, for political reasons, peace sentiment was kept under cover.

The autumn elections of 1862 saw Democratic strategy at its peak. Votes were solicited from every source. Conservative Republicans were invited to support the Democratic nominees with perfect confidence that all that they believed in could thus best be realized, and they were reminded that until the announcement of the emancipation policy Lincoln had been better supported by the Democrats than by the radicals of his own party. They were told that the elections of Democratic members of Congress and Democratic state officials would be the most effective means of strengthening the President against the Republicans who had been forcing his hand against his better judgment. "Which is your election?" they were asked. "Will you assist us in upholding the President in his endeavors to maintain the Constitution unimpaired, or, cling to party association, assist abolitionism to accomplish disunion?" [36] Covert signs were given to the peace Democrats, however, that they were not being ignored, but that a party victory would enable their views to be put into effect. The *Crisis* showed no lack of confidence in the intentions of the party and continued to prepare the way for a peace movement at the proper time by giving an exaggerated picture of the doleful situation of the Northern armies. After the Battle of Antietam its readers were told:

The past has been a most eventful week in the horrors of war, yet without any definite results commensurate with the number of battles fought, or the horrible destruction of human life. Were it the only purpose to depopulate the country by destroying the male portion of the human family, the success has been remarkably great on both sides. The horrors of this war on the fields of battle [in spite of the fact that one might be sure the government did not report the full losses] have no parallel in modern times. . . .

The whole country in the region of the late battles in Maryland is filled with wounded soldiers, and the graves of the dead number their thousands, if not tens of thousands. Every house, barn, stable and out building contains its full complement of maimed and dying, and still the cry of those at home is for more victims! The whole civilized world looks upon us with astonishment and cries out against such madness, as it appears to them.

The result of the bloody affray in Maryland is, that the Confederates have retreated across the Potomac toward Winchester. After taking Harper's Ferry and about 12,000 prisoners and more than a million dollars of public property, they abandoned it, and it is in possession once more of our troops. . . .

What effect the Lincoln and Seward Proclamation freeing the slaves may have on these bloody conflicts, time alone can develop. This we know: had this proclamation been issued sooner, many in the army would not have voluntarily gone. . . .[37]

In view of all these considerations it was not surprising that the Democrats registered some overwhelming triumphs in the elections of October and November. In Ohio, Indiana, and Illinois, the three most populous and powerful states of the Midwest, they carried all before them. In Ohio they elected fourteen out of nineteen members of the federal House of Representatives, in Indiana seven out of eleven, Illinois nine out of fourteen, and for good measure gained three out of six seats in Wisconsin. For the whole section there would be thirty-four Democrats among the total of sixty-four Midwestern representatives in the next Congress, a net gain of eighteen seats for the party. Majorities were won also in the legislatures of Indiana and Illinois. In Ohio and Indiana the Democratic candidates for secretary of state were victorious by majorities of 5500 and 9500, respectively, and the Republican incumbent in the race for the state treasurership in Illinois was defeated by 16,500 votes.[38] But time would reveal that, important though the gains of the Democrats were, more significant still was what they failed to gain. Republican success in Michigan, Iowa, Minnesota, New England, and the border states (the last by means that would not always have borne the light of unbiased examination) preserved a diminished administration majority in Congress. In Ohio, where alone, it was proved, the peace Democrats had leadership able and determined enough to initiate state action to bring the war to a close, fate played a trump card. By mere chance both the governor and the legislature of that state were elected in the odd-numbered years. In Illinois and Indiana it happened that the governorship ran for a four-year period and that the occupants, elected in the Republican victory of 1860, were in both cases resourceful and determined men, qualified to curb Democratic majorities in the legislatures. In view of subsequent developments it may not be too much to say that these fortuitous circumstances deserve recognition among the decisive factors in the outcome of the Civil War.

After the elections Republican politicians, sobered and made thoughtful by their reverses, engaged in a confidential exchange

ELECTIONS OF 1862. Black counties—50% or more for Democratic candidates for Congress.

of views as to the causes of their defeat.[39] The analytical quality, presumptive honesty, and general agreement of these reports make them worth studying for what they reveal as to the state of the public mind in the Middle West in the last quarter of 1862. It was agreed that military arrests and other official actions of disputed legality had alienated many. (The general release, in the month or two following the elections, of most of the victims of the arbitrary arrests who were still in custody may not have been unrelated to recognition of this fact.[40]) To a surprising extent, too, it was conceded, the people had been frightened by the belief that a Negro inundation of the Northwest would result from emancipation. Republican inability to maintain unity of organization and purpose and their failure to campaign actively were also given as reasons for defeat. A few held that the war had drawn more Republicans than Democrats into the army, thus tipping the political balance, but this contention, hardly supported by the available evidence, was advanced largely as a public face-saver. But above all, it was agreed, these reasons were subsidiary to the primary and moving cause—the disappointing military situation and the resulting conviction that the authorities had not displayed a skill in utilizing the resources granted them commensurate with the efforts of the people in providing them. As one writer expressed it,

. . . The popular reason for declining to support the administration is, that the people have furnished men and means in abundance for all purposes to conquer the enemy; but after a year and a half of trial, and a pouring out of blood and treasure, and the maiming and death of thousands, we have made no sensible progress in putting down the rebellion . . . and the people are desirous of some change, they scarcely know what.[41]

This same period saw the growth of dangers other than political, threatening to obstruct the great task of recruiting and maintaining an army in the field capable of subduing the Confederacy. From many quarters came reports of resistance to raising troops by conscription, of the augmenting strength of the secret anti-war societies, assistance given to the escape of Confederate prisoners, the carrying on of contraband trade with the South, and the desertion or surrender to the enemy of men in the service. All were evidence of a disintegration of morale under the prolongation of the war. Although not yet of dangerous proportions, they were disturbing omens for the future. It seemed that the tremendous recruiting efforts of the summer had exhausted the ability and the will of the Midwest to furnish additional troops. For a time the national administration, on the recommendation of a conference of governors held at Altoona, Pennsylvania, on September 24, weighed the advisability of a call for 100,000 additional levies to meet the crisis.[42] Such a bold step might have produced a favorable effect on public opinion by suggesting that the North was capable of still greater exertions in the face of need. But nothing materialized, and the section largely concerned itself with the organizing and equipping of men already raised and with drafting for deficiencies on earlier calls.

Unnecessary in Illinois, which had met her obligations under all calls, the draft was carried out in other states in a straggling and haphazard fashion. Originally scheduled for August 15, it could not be completed until well into October and November. The work of enrollment and drawing was left largely to state officials.[43] In spite of widely entertained fears of trouble, no great or general resistance was encountered. There were a few outbreaks, however. In Cleveland a mob destroyed a box containing the names to be drawn for service.[44] Another uprising occurred in Blackford County, Indiana, where the net result was a three-day delay in the completion of the conscription.[45] A draft officer at Rome, Henry County, Iowa, was driven out of town by four ruffians, but a squad of soldiers sufficed to restore order.[46] The worst outrages occurred in Wisconsin among the foreign-born. Early on October 10, the day scheduled for the drawing, a mob marched through the streets of Port Washington, in Ozaukee County, north of Milwaukee, bearing banners inscribed "No Draft," stormed the court-house, drove off the draft commissioner, and destroyed the enrollment records. Finding that the commissioner had escaped, the mob turned its attention to leading citizens who were firm supporters of the war. The county judge, the district attorney, the register of deeds were set upon and beaten. Then the rioters entered the homes of several public officials, venting their spite in such vandalism as they could, and ended by wrecking the plant of a local industrial concern. The governor promptly dispatched six hundred troops to the scene, apparently newly recruited men who were being prepared for the battle-front. These, under the command of a determined provost marshal, restored order, made more than fifty arrests, and carried through the draft. In Washington County a group of men tried to take the lists from the commissioner, but he escaped on horseback with his records. Between one and two hundred men, many of them armed, appeared in Green Bay to stage a protest against conscription, but, after some tenseness, contented themselves with marching. The commissioner in Kewaunee County was temporarily driven from his task by another mob.[47] The situation in Milwaukee for a time took on a threatening aspect. Having given notice on the Saturday before the scheduled conscription day of their intention to resist by parading through the Ninth Ward with music and banners inscribed with the "No Draft" slogan, the rougher elements of the city turned out in force on Monday morning. Finding no evidences of drafting activities at the court-house they moved on to the sheriff's office, where the commissioner read them a dispatch from the governor postponing the draft and resigned his job.[48] Gathering together such military forces as he could, the governor overawed the opposition and carried through the draft here and elsewhere. In all, about one hundred and fifty men were arrested in different localities and transported to the state capital, where they were held for some weeks while the authorities tried to determine the proper disposition of their cases.[49]

Generally speaking, the Democratic journals, even when disposed to regard conscription as a measure of doubtful constitutionality, counseled their readers to obey its administration. There were a few, however, which virtually invited armed resistance or insubordination and desertion. In Ohio the sullen Ashland *Union* expressed the opinion:

. . . We are inclined to the opinion that a large majority of the men will make very poor fighters for niggers. They don't believe in the programme. They think that a white man is as good as a nigger, and can see no reason why *they* should be shot for the benefit of niggers and Abolitionists. Those are their sentiments and they will stand by them, and if the *despot* Lincoln had a few hundred thousand such men in the field he would meet with the fate he deserves: hung, shot or burned—no matter which.[50]

And there were a good many hints that, though carried through this time, a more general measure of conscription in the future might meet with serious obstacles.

One effect of the conscription issue was to give a new meaning and direction to the secret anti-war society movement. As defiance of the draft took its place beside resistance to arbitrary arrest as a motive for joining a mutual protection association, there came reports that membership in such organizations was growing and that the movement was spreading to new areas. In southern Illinois it was said that many who would be subject to compulsory military service were purchasing arms and engaging in drill for organized resistance to the conscripting officers.[51] Since that state had already filled its quota, no test was made at this time of the seriousness of the situation. The spirit abroad in that region was, however, revealed in a circular distributed during the autumn, reputedly by emissaries of the Knights of the Golden Circle:

RESISTANCE TO TYRANTS IS OBEDIENCE TO GOD

To all Patriotic Men in the United States:

Whereas, the repeated violations of the Constitution of the United States by the present party in power, do most seriously threaten the liberties of the people and tend to the destruction of constitutional liberty, the great anchor of a democratic republic, we, who are hereby united in order to check these outrages upon the rights of loyal citizens, and to prevent this Government from degenerating to a military despotism, to be controlled by unscrupulous fanatics, "do pledge our lives, our property, and our sacred honor," to maintain constitutional liberty, to the extent guaranteed by our fundamental laws, and determine that no more citizens shall be illegally arrested and detained, and that we will resent such usurpation in every legal and peaceable mode, and in the event of defeat we will fall back upon that God-given right—physical resistance to despotic power.[52]

In other ways, too, the handiwork or spirit of these societies was evident. Aid was given to the escape and concealment of Confederate prisoners from the camps of the Midwest.[53] Federal officers were troubled by the shipment of arms from Illinois into Missouri destined, it was believed, either for the Confederate forces or for guerrilla bands who were Southern partisans,[54] and there were even to be noted the beginnings of guerrilla activities in parts of the Old Northwest, the counterpart of similar annoyances in Missouri and Kentucky. On solicitation of the officers of the Illinois State Agriculture Society, Governor Yates applied to Secretary Stanton for permission to raise four regiments of men over forty-five years old to operate against such bands.[55] Whispers were heard of a general rising to set up a Northwest Confederacy.[56]

Worse still were the indications that disaffection was spreading to the troops in the field. The highest officials were inclined to the belief that many Northern soldiers were permitting themselves to be captured in order that they might be sent home by the enemy under parole.[57] Some regiments that had been captured by the Confederates and released on parole to return to Columbus, Ohio, and Chicago were so mutinous and intractable that General Lew Wallace at Camp Chase asked that no more be sent to that place until he could establish discipline, and General Daniel Tyler at Camp Douglas had to fight incendiary fires set in the barracks and finally to put one whole regiment under armed guard.[58] Some of the men permitted to return home pending exchange failed to return to duty when so ordered.[59] Reports of such tendencies were so widespread that they reached the Confederate authorities and no doubt encouraged them in their hopes for victory.[60]

During the political campaign, as we have seen, most Democratic spokesmen who were opposed to the war *per se* kept their attitudes pretty much to themselves, obviously in the hope of reaping as large a harvest as possible among advocates of the war policy who were for any reason discontented with the administration. With the elections over and a greatly augmented power in the hands of their party, the members of the faction no longer felt it necessary to disguise their intentions. The Jonesboro *Gazette* of southern Illinois returned to the proposition that the South could not be conquered and held that the people of the North were coming around to a position where they would no longer be driven to the encounter. As an indirect approach to the position some papers gave considerable space to the opinions of the intensely pro-Confederate London *Post*, a paper beyond the reach of the federal authorities and therefore a suitable medium for opinions which American newspapers were not themselves ready to avow.[61] The Chicago *Times* editorially suggested that the party might soon renounce any further support of the war:

THE DEMOCRATIC POLICY

Some of the abolition newspapers are anxious as to the "policy" of the democratic party, now that it is victorious in so many of the States, with reference to the national difficulties. The democratic party will have no responsibilities and no duties with respect to our national difficulties, except to support the administration in all wise and constitutional measures for the suppression of the rebellion, until the

CAMP DOUGLAS, near Chicago,
where Confederate prisoners from the West were confined.

Legislature which has just been elected shall meet, when it will probably declare a policy which will be constitutional, wise, just, expedient, and, we trust, effective to close the war, restore the Union, establish permanent peace, and inaugurate enduring national prosperity. In this regard, the inaugural address of Gov. Seymour, of New York, will be awaited by the country with extraordinary interest.[62]

Early in December such secondary party figures as Richard T. Merrick and former Governor John Reynolds of Illinois came out openly for the abandonment of any but conciliatory means for the restoration of the Union. Speaking to the Young Men's Democratic Invincible Club of Chicago on December 11, Merrick called the war "unwise, injurious, and unnecessary," and declared that the states ought to resist arbitrary arrests with the militia and that individuals had the right to shoot down officers attempting such arrests. He declared, amidst applause, that if the President should issue his announced proclamation the war ought no longer to be supported. "With the objectives announced in this proclamation as the avowed purpose of the war, the South cannot be subdued and ought not to be subdued. These men of the South are blood of our blood and bone of our bone." If disunion were unavoidable, Merrick argued, the West should look to her own interests and so reorganize the Union as to leave New England outside.[63] In a communication to the *Crisis* from his home in Belleville, Illinois, Reynolds announced:

I am for peace under any plan or able readjustment the people will make. I think a reunion is the plan of adjustment; but, in the name of God, no more bloodshed to gratify a religious fanaticism.

. . . .

I would prefer a re-constitution of the Union and become again a friendly and united people, including the North and the South; but any amicable adjustment of the present war is better than the desolation and ruin of the country. I think the people have decided that the war must cease and peace be restored.[64]

On December 5 Vallandigham introduced into the House of Representatives a series of resolutions setting forth that, since the people had entered upon the war with the understanding that it was being waged solely to restore the Union to precisely the condition that it had had before secession, any public official attempting to change or pervert its purpose (i.e., by the introduction of the emancipation policy) would be adjudged guilty of a high crime against the Constitution.[65] Supported by fifty votes against seventy-nine for tabling, these resolutions might be viewed as the beginning of an attempt to release the Democratic party from any further support of the war. Even among the non-political mass of the people some sort of vague sentiment for peace and an expectation of the abandonment of the war seemed to be spreading. William S. McCormick wrote to his brother Cyrus, "I think it probable that the government will yield to the pressure of *the people* against this war—ere long." [66] General McClernand, after sampling the views of the people of the Northwest, wrote Stanton that unless the Mississippi River were opened in the near future the people of the section might decide to abandon the war as an economic necessity.[67] Governor Morton expressed the same view—had, perhaps, inspired McClernand's communication—and warned:

The fate of the North-West is trembling in the balance. The result of the late elections admonished all who understood their import that not an hour is to be lost. The Democratic politicians of Ohio, Indiana and Illinois assume that the rebellion will not be crushed and that the independence of the Rebel Confederacy will before many months be practically or expressly acknowledged. Starting upon this hypothesis, they ask the question: What shall be the destiny of Ohio, Indiana and Illinois? Shall they remain attached to the old Government, or shall they secede and form a new one—a North-Western Confederacy—as a preparatory step to their annexation to the Government of the South? This latter project is the programme and has been for the last twelve months. During the recent campaign it was the staple of every Democratic speech, that we of the North-West had no interests or sympathies in common with the people of the Northern and Eastern States; that New England is fattening at our expense; that the people of New England are cold, selfish, money-making, and through the medium of tariffs and railroads are pressing us to the dust; that geographically these States are a part of the Mississippi Valley and in their political association and destiny cannot be separated from the other States of that Valley; that socially and commercially their sympathies and interests are with those of the people of the Southern States rather than with people of the North and East; that the Mississippi River is the great artery and outlet of all Western Commerce; that the people of the North-West can never consent to be separated politically from the people who control the mouth of that river; that this war has been forced upon the South for the purpose of abolishing slavery and that the South had offered reasonable and proper compromises, which, if they had been accepted would have avoided the war. In some of these arguments there is much truth. Our geographical and social relations are not to be denied; but the most patent appeal is that connected with the free navigation of the Mississippi river. The importance of that river to the trade and commerce of the North-West is so potent as to impress itself with great force upon the most ignorant minds and requires only to be stated to be at once understood and accepted. And I give it here as my deliberate judgement, that should the misfortune of arms or other causes, compel us to the abandonment of this war and the concession of the independence of the Rebel States, that Ohio, Indiana and Illinois can only be prevented, if at all, from a new act of secession and annexation to those States, by a bloody and desolating Civil War. . . .[68]

Unless some striking military success should come soon to reverse the tide of Northern failures, real threats to the continuation of the war for the Union might shortly be anticipated.

CHAPTER VI

The Period of Despair

(December 13, 1862–July 4, 1863)

ECEMBER brought no victories. On the 13th, General Burnside, made desperate by responsibility, attempted to storm the bluffs of the Rappahannock at Fredericksburg, and the flower of the Army of the Potomac went down before the withering fire of Lee's veterans. In the West at the end of that month the Army of the Cumberland was checked in a costly slugging match at Murfreesboro, and Sherman's vain attempt to resume the clearing of the Mississippi River by capturing Vicksburg only proved the inadequacy of the force at his command. The conquest of the South had never seemed less possible. Democratic opponents of the war believed that the time had come to demand the restoration of peace on any terms; if any excuse were needed for the repudiation of earlier pledges it could be found in the proclamation of Negro emancipation. When a $475,000,000 army appropriation bill came before the House of Representatives on December 18, 1862, almost the entire Midwestern Democratic delegation significantly abstained from voting.

A month later Congressman Vallandigham delivered the keynote speech for the peace group. Approaching the zenith of his career at the age of forty-three, Vallandigham had inherited his name from a Flemish Huguenot ancestor who had settled in Virginia about 1690, but it was probably from a strong admixture of Scotch-Irish blood that he had derived the underlying qualities of his nature. The son of a Presbyterian minister, he had left his course of studies unfinished at Jefferson College after a dispute with its president over a point of constitutional law and had prepared himself for admission to the bar. In 1845 he became the youngest member of the Ohio legislature, was chosen speaker the next year, then for a time edited the Dayton *Empire,* and in 1858 entered Congress as a supporter of Buchanan. Once he had been almost alone as an open opponent of the war, but the voters of his district had continued to support him and only a Republican gerrymander had prevented his re-election in the campaign that had just closed. And in spite of that defeat he had emerged as the nearest approach to a major party leader that the Midwest had produced since the death of Douglas. Now his day had come. He had waited and prepared for it two long, bitter years. On January 14, before a packed, attentive House that listened for an hour and a half without interruption, the piercing-eyed, calmly arrogant Ohioan taunted supporters of the war.

Defeat, debt, taxation, sepulchres, these are your trophies. In vain the people gave you treasure, and the soldier yielded up his life. . . . The war for the Union is, in your hands, a most bloody and costly failure. The President confessed it on the 22d of September, solemnly, officially, and under the broad seal of the United States. . . . War for the Union was abandoned; war for the negro openly begun, and with stronger battalions than before. With what success? Let the dead at Fredericksburg and Vicksburg answer.

And now, sir, can this war continue? Whence the money to carry it on? Where the men? Can you borrow? From whom? Can you tax more? Will the people bear it? . . . How many millions more of "legal tender"—to-day forty-seven per cent. below the par of gold—can you float? Will men enlist now at any price? Ah, sir, it is easier to die at home. I beg pardon; but I trust I am not "discouraging enlistments."

. . . .

Sir, my judgement was made up, and expressed from the first. I learned it from Chatham: "My lords, you cannot conquer America." And you have not conquered the South. You never will. It is not in the nature of things possible; much less under your auspices. . . .

. . . .

But why speak of ways or terms of reunion now? The will is yet wanting in both sections. . . . What then? Stop fighting. Make an armistice—no formal treaty. Withdraw your army from the seceded States. Reduce both armies to a fair and sufficient peace establishment. Declare absolute free trade between the North and South. . . . Let time do his office—drying tears, dispelling sorrows, mellowing passion, and making herb and grass and tree to grow again upon the hundred battle-fields of this terrible war.

. . . It cost thirty years of desperate and most wicked patience and industry to destroy or impair the magnificent temple of this Union. Let us be content if, within three years, we shall be able to restore it.[1]

This major address was followed by other statements in which Vallandigham further defined his attitude. "I warn you now," he told his colleagues when the House was debating the conscription bill, "that whenever . . . you undertake to enforce this bill, and, like the destroying angel in Egypt, enter every house for the first-born sons of the people—remember Poland. . . . Be not encouraged by the submission of other nations." [2] And in a speech at Newark, New Jersey, on February 14 he outlined a method of forcing the administration to abandon the war. Speaking as the self-styled "representative of the peace sentiment of the Northwest," he pointed out that, since volunteering had virtually ceased and the terms of enlistment of many already in the army would soon expire, a refusal of the people to submit to conscription would give the Confederate armies such a preponderance in manpower that the North would have to make peace on terms satisfactory to the South.[3] "I am for peace," he told a New York audience on March 7, "and would be, even if the Union could not be restored, as I believe it can be; because, without peace, permitting this Administration for two years to exercise its tremendous powers, the war still existing, you will not have one remnant of civil liberty left among your-selves."[4]

A few other Democrats in Congress were bold enough to speak out in a similar vein. Senator David Turpie of Indiana, in oppos-ing a bill for the compensated abolition of slavery in Missouri, de-clared that he would not support a war for any purpose but "the restoration of the Union and the unity of the States. If the war is not waged for that purpose, I am for peace today. If it is found that that purpose is impractical or impossible, I am for cessation of hostil-ities this moment." "As dear as the Union is to Indiana," he an-nounced, ". . . it is not of more value than the rights of the States and the people." [5] Samuel Sullivan Cox, congressman from Ohio, told an audience in New York City that resentment in the Midwest was so intense that a second Civil War and the setting up of another Confederacy were likely. His manner of speaking suggested commendation of the movement in spite of the pains he took to disclaim any connection with it.[6] Most of the Midwestern Democrats in Congress, however, were inclined to lend their assent to Vallandigham's declarations through silence rather than by explicit affirmation. Leading Democratic newspapers in the Middle West, uninhibited by the occupational caution of the office holder, showed no such reticence. The Cincinnati *Enquirer,* Columbus *Crisis* (now rapidly gaining new readers), Detroit *Free Press,* Indianapolis *Sentinel,* Chicago *Times,* Davenport *Democrat and News,* and Dubuque *Herald* took the lead in coming out for peace, and were followed, with varying degrees of bluntness or ambiguity, by the smaller dailies and weekly journals of the section. The *Enquirer* announced:

> The real genuine Democracy of the country *were never at heart for the war.* . . . The idea that a voluntary Union, such as our fathers made, could be established by force was too ridiculous to find a lodgement in the brain of any reasoning Democrat. All saw its logical error and all really condemned it in their hearts. They were opposed to it in principle before the war commenced, and the fact of commencement did not change their views, but experience has confirmed and strengthened them.[7]

A drumfire of denunciation was opened on the war policy from every side. Editorials declared that there was not the remotest possibility that the North could ever be victorious, the news columns supported this contention by exaggerated accounts of the extent and significance of Union defeats and by belittling Union successes, while any other available space was filled with clippings from other anti-war papers. These included excerpts from the editorials of the London *Times* and other British newspapers that were most smugly confident of a Southern victory. Prominence was also given to letters from discouraged soldiers.[8] Another technique was to invite hostility and distrust toward the army by circulating atrocity stories, apparently emanating from Confederate propaganda sources, charging the Union army with mistreatment of the civilian population of the South. The *Crisis* loved to harp on alleged Union "barbarities" and at times must have given its readers the impression that the ravishing of Southern women was the principal diversion of Northern soldiers.[9] A variation on this theme was the playing up of reported Negro assaults on whites, both North and South, with the implication that the Emancipation Proclamation had greatly increased such outrages.[10] Further enlistments were discouraged, and there were intimations that the men in the army should consider themselves freed from any obligation of further service since the proclamation had added a new purpose to the war. The Dubuque *Herald* told them, "You perceive that it is to emancipate slaves and to enable adventurers to make money by plunder that you are used as soldiers," and asked, "Are you, as soldiers, bound by patriotism, duty or loyalty to fight in such a cause?" [11] Even revolutionary resistance to the continuation of the war was encouraged. "The people are fools to content themselves with assailing tyrants who have deprived them of their liberties," the *Herald* continued. "There is but one way to deal with arbitrary power, and that is to treat it precisely as one would do, if he had the power, with a highwayman who might undertake to rob him of his money." [12]

The more conservative Democratic papers did not stand so firmly on the anti-war position, but by continued harping on shortcomings in the conduct of the war they gave tacit assistance to the peace faction. Few attempted to reprove even the most extreme statements of that group, and virtually none made any effort to reinvigorate their readers' enthusiasm for the war.

Many of the newspapers demanding peace reprinted editorials from Southern papers which clearly rejected peace upon any terms but the independence of the Confederacy. They must have known, therefore, that a voluntary reunion would come, if at all, only after a lapse of years. Political expediency naturally caused them to avoid any emphasis of that point. Much of their talk about the possibilities of an immediate reunion by negotiation must have been intended merely to mislead the gullible, to provide a sugar coating for the unpalatable reality that permanent disunion was the price of immediate peace.

The views of Vallandigham and the anti-war editors were underwritten by scores of local mass meetings and county conventions of the party, some called especially to discuss the issue and others called primarily to make nominations for the spring elections. Some of these contented themselves with merely denouncing emancipation and arbitrary acts of government, but a very large number took more extreme positions, ranging all the way from demands for the calling of a national convention to consider the possibilities of compromise to outright rejection of the continuation of the war under any circumstances. The Democrats of Auglaize County, Ohio, declared that "an experience of two years has taught us, that the Union can never be restored by force of arms"; [13] those of Putnam County, Illinois, were sure that the further prosecution of the war would not only be fruitless but would undermine free institutions in the North; [14] and a meeting in Wayne County, Indiana, called for "a cessation of hostilities for a sufficient time to cool the excited minds and passions of both sections of the country," to be followed at the proper time by a "peace convention." [15] Agreeing upon "an armistice and a national convention as the only means by which our present national difficulties can be adjusted," the Van Buren County, Michigan, Democrats resolved that "since the war has been converted from its original purpose of a restoration of the Union under the Constitution, we are opposed to furnishing means or men on the basis of the abolition of slavery by executive or military power." [16] In Logan County, Illinois, a meeting threatened resistance to conscription as a form of "French despotism" and argued that the soldiers already in the army had been recruited by fraud, because the real purpose of the war had been hidden from them.[17] In Iowa an assembly in Mahaska County announced that "we regard the Conscription Bill as unconstitutional, uncalled for, and that we are under no legal obligations to submit to its effect," [18] and another in Wapello County determined to "deliberately and firmly pledge ourselves, one to another, that we will not render support to the present Administration in carrying on its wicked abolition crusade against the South; that we will *resist* to the *death* all attempts to draft any of our citizens into the army." [19] In many other counties up and down and across the section expressions just as forthright were adopted. The only state in which this was not true was Minnesota, where the party was weak and largely confined its criticisms to the effectiveness of the administration in carrying on the war rather than its objectives. It appeared that the local Democratic organizations almost everywhere else were willing to see their party committed to a movement for peace. A state convention held in Detroit on February 11 to nominate candidates for the Michigan judiciary election also endorsed the proposal for a national convention to arrange terms of peace, holding that "in case of differences and conflicts between the States and the Federal government, too powerful for adjustment by the civil departments of the government, the appeal is not to the sword by the States or by the general government, but to the people, peacefully assembled by their representatives in convention." [20]

The adoption by the national government of any type of proposal for the cessation of hostilities would have meant in effect—whatever may have been said to the contrary—the eventual recognition of southern independence. It is inconceivable from either a military or a psychological point of view that the North could under any circumstances have effectively renewed the struggle after having agreed to an armistice. Nor was there any basis for believing that the South, then or later, could have been brought back into the Union by anything short of complete conquest. Northern Democrats who held hopes to the contrary were either self-deluded or consciously attempting to mislead the people. Among the leaders it seems probable that the latter situation predominated. From occasional frank statements, significant ambiguities, and careful avoidance of the subject a pattern appears that suggests that a great many of the peace advocates knew that they were in fact advocates of disunion. Some thought the military situation hopeless in any case. Others were convinced, as a result of the narrow and unrealistic nature of most political theory in the United States in the first half of the nineteenth century, that despotism was the only alternative to an absolutely voluntary association of the states. Many were apparently reckless as to the eventual result if only they could have the immediate satisfaction of seeing the Republican party discredited and driven from power. None seemed to grasp the simple fact that majority rule is the foundation of republican government.

A recurring note in the defeatist chorus was the suggestion of an eventual new confederacy of the Western states, a project dor-nant since 1861.[21] Numerous editorials [22] and the resolutions of several conventions gave it endorsement. A Democratic meeting in Douglas County, Illinois, announced that "we regard the emancipation proclamation . . . as the entering wedge which will ultimately divide the middle and northwestern States from our mischiefmaking, puritanical, fanatical New England brethren, and finally culminate in the formation of a Democratic republic out of the middle, northwestern and southern States. And for this we are thankful." [23] In Brown County, Indiana, a similar gathering agreed that "our interests and our inclinations will demand of us a withdrawal from political association in a common government with the New England States, who have contributed so much to every innovation upon the constitution, to our present calamity of civil war, and whose tariff legislation must ever prove oppressive to our agricultural and commercial pursuits." [24] The Columbus *Crisis* probably had this in mind when it asked, *"Shall we sink down as serfs to the heartless, speculative Yankee for all time to come—swindled by his tariffs, robbed by his taxes, skinned by his railroad monopolies?"* and answered its own question, "The West will demand a Convention of the States, with delegates elected by the people themselves, without intervention of *bayonets,* and if other States refuse to meet her, she will, through her delegates, consult her own interests." [25] The Democrats of the Middle West at last seemed to be fulfilling Southern expectations.

Demoralization meanwhile threatened the Midwestern Republicans. The seeming inability of their armies to win victories had left them bewildered and angry; Democratic desertion of the Union cause brought uncertainty and peril close to home. Nowhere on the horizon could they find any promise that conditions were likely to improve. Many sank into a state of passive dejection or quarreled bitterly with one another in an effort to assess blame for the situation. Leaders in Washington received the gloomiest of reports from their informants in the West. Confidence in the administration, they were told, had disappeared and its supporters were everywhere disheartened, while the advocates of peace were active, bold, and menacing. Only a major victory, it was agreed, could do much to revive morale. "Is it not possible," it was asked, "to make enough of a million men in the field to gain one important battle?" [26] Certainly another large-scale defeat could not be borne. Congressman Washburne of Illinois was told:

. . . The minds of all *our friends* are filled with forebodings and gloomy apprehensions . . . all confidence is lost in the Administration, and a disaster to our Armies now at Vicksburg, in Tennessee, or on the Potomac, will disintegrate this whole Country—Treason is everywhere bold, defiant—& active, *with impunity!* In case of Disaster The Administration will be face to face with it, here in the North, & failing to meet it & overcome it, we are *lost.*—Do not fancy this to be my own feelings—for I assure you we all *here,* participate in them—Men whose cool judgement I know you would respect . . . if we cannot *speedily* secure victories by our arms—peace *must* be made to secure us anything!" [27]

There were real fears of armed outbreaks. On the basis of numerous alarming reports from southern Illinois, officials of the state asked permission to raise four regiments for emergency service. Letters received from the section gave information that considerable bands of men were arming and drilling to defy conscription, were openly cheering for Jeff Davis and singing Confederate songs, and threatening to murder or "burn out" Union men. Unless action were taken at once open rebellion might, it was declared, sweep the state within thirty days. [28] Governor Morton was so apprehensive over the prospect in Indiana that he asked Lincoln to meet him for a conference at Harrisburg, Pennsylvania, a request that the President was forced to deny for fear that it would add to the public alarm. [29] Everywhere men had visions of savage fighting in familiar streets, of assassins' bullets staining the cobblestones with neighbors' blood, of a peaceful countryside turned into a vale of horror and the pleasant fields into places of human butchery. [30]

A complicating factor in the situation was the existence of widespread dissatisfaction with economic policies adopted by Congress which were looked upon as benefiting the East at the expense of the West. Skyrocketing protective tariffs, the national banking policy, and the issuance by the Treasury of enormous amounts of irredeemable paper currency were measures regarded as particularly inimical to the section. The last aroused the hostility of both the working classes and the creditor groups, since it raised the cost of living for one and brought about a decline in the value of the fixed investments of the other. Only Eastern speculators, it was thought, were in a position to profit from the situation, and in the end all classes might go down together in financial chaos.[31] Greatest concern, however, was aroused by mounting transportation charges. Eastern railway magnates were suspected of taking a monopolistic advantage of the opportunities afforded by the cutting off of the Mississippi River as an alternative route to market and of forcing up the rates at the expense of the producing West. Such a belief, it was recognized, was an underlying factor in the demands of peace advocates for the setting up of an independent Northwest which could negotiate with the South for a reopening of the river. A leading Chicago business man wrote to a New York capitalist with extensive Midwestern interests:

Our state is in very much more of a political ferment than people at the East seem to be aware of. The extraordinary and unreasonable toll levied on all products by the Rail Roads and the Erie Canal management, is producing bad fruit creating a feeling which however senseless it may be is nevertheless a very passionate one and may result in much evil— An union with a Southern Confederacy—is openly talked of by even moderate men. Practically we cannot reach the sea board either by the Mississippi or via the East—and it is ruin to our farmers.[32]

Other fears were thus conditioned by a spreading sense of economic insecurity.

In this disintegration of Republican morale there were overtones of hysteria. Some wondered if emancipation had not after all been a mistake, perhaps a fatal one,[33] while others felt that what was most wanting was audacity. Because many Democrats at home were turning against a continuation of the war, certain Republicans were suspicious of those in the army and argued that all Democratic officers ought to be dismissed from positions in which they would be able to betray the cause. There were demands for the sternest measures of repression against all groups and individuals of doubtful loyalty, and for the use of the army in a *coup d'état* to checkmate Democratic gains in the elections. An astonishingly prevalent idea was that the proper man to put in charge of a program of dictatorship was that oily chameleon, General Benjamin F. Butler, who had supported Jefferson Davis for the Democratic presidential nomination in 1860 but who within a few months had become the darling of the anti-slavery Republican radicals. One man advised Secretary Chase that the army might win a battle for a change if each man were given a sufficient quantity of intoxicating liquor to raise his courage just before going into the fight, but another wrote to Senator John Sherman that drink was the key to all the failures of the past (evidently the Confederates were all teetotalers) and that a stringent law should be passed for the severe punishment of any officer or soldier who so much as touched hard cider.[34] Confidence in all leadership was shaken. Congressman Washburne of Illinois was troubled by doubts of his protégé, General Grant. To Secretary Chase he forwarded a letter from his brother, General Washburn (the family disagreed on the spelling of the name), containing a disturbing picture of conditions in Grant's camp. Chase was given permission to show the letter to the President if he thought best.[35] In the East the editor of the New York *Tribune,* whose shallow mentality under the stress of the war was assuming an eccentricity of attitude approaching the bizarre, was up to new mischief. Hating Lincoln since the President had bested him in the exchange of letters in the summer of 1862 beginning with Greeley's "Prayer of Twenty Millions" and always a sentimental pacifist at heart, he had become firmly set on peace at any price. He was carrying on some sort of communication with Vallandigham and other opponents of the war, had approached the French ambassador to urge foreign intervention that would "drive Lincoln into it," and was even inclined to hope for additional Union defeats to speed peace. In the West, Joseph Medill, joint owner of the Chicago *Tribune,* was also willing to concede the inability of the North to win a complete victory. On January 14 he wrote a long letter to Congressman Washburne outlining a scheme for withdrawing all of the army from the Eastern front except a force large enough to defend the line of the Potomac and then concentrating all efforts on clearing Tennessee and reopening the Mississippi River. After this he proposed that an armistice be agreed to with the hope that in about ten years it might be possible to renew the war and conquer the remaining Confederate states. Said he:

. . . The Treasury is about on its last legs. The currency of the country is deteriorating fearfully fast, and if the Com. [mittee] of W. [ays] and

M. [eans] issues two or three hundred millions more the bottom will tumble out. . . . Next April and May the period of enlistment of all nine months men expires, also the two year men. No more volunteers can be obtained to fill up the ranks nor can men be had by drafting. . . .

I can understand the awful reluctance with which you can be brought to contemplate a divided union. But there is no help for it. The war has assumed such proportions—the situation is so desperate and stubborn, our finances are so deranged and exhausted, the democratic party is so hostile and threatening that complete success has become a moral impossibility. The war has been conducted so long by "central imbecility," Seward intrigue . . . proslavery half secesh generals, that the day of grace is past. But I see no prospect of reform worth anything. Halleck and his gang are still being retained. Lincoln is only half awake, and never will do much better than he has done. He will do the right thing always too late, and just when it does no good.[36]

As a practical plan of action this document was obviously based on hazy thinking and unwarranted assumptions, but it clearly indicated the bankruptcy of ideas that had been reached by much of the Republican leadership.

In this atmosphere a fratricidal strife was threatened between the radical and conservative wings of the party. Each was disposed to blame the other for the reverses suffered and to believe, therefore, that for its own group to gain control was a necessity outranking almost any other consideration. In December a determined attempt of the congressional radicals to make Secretary Seward resign was thwarted by Lincoln's clever tactics in forcing the resignation of Chase—friend of the malcontents—and then asking both men to remain. But this failure only increased the determination of the radicals to bring about the entire reconstruction of the cabinet in such a way as to tie Lincoln's hands and make him their puppet.[37] Some of the conservatives, on the other hand, were so bitter that they discussed the feasibility of forming a new party.[38] Nothing except continued military failure could be more dangerous or contribute more to insuring the success of the schemes of the peace Democrats. Even a revolutionary uprising might have some possibility of success if this factional warfare continued. It was no wonder that as a visitor to Washington at the beginning of the new year Benjamin R. Curtis, former associate justice of the Supreme

Court who was best remembered for his dissenting opinion in the Dred Scott case, should report:

> . . . It is painful to be here, because the ruin of the country & its cause & progress are meeting you at every turn. I know of no man of sense here who has any hope for the restoration of the union. I have seen a good many prominent men today, (Newyears being a festival, when everybody goes to see everybody & his wife,) & I have not seen one who does not say the country is ruined & that its ruin is attributable largely to the utter incompetence of the Prest. . . . He is shattered, dazed & utterly foolish. It would not surprise me if he were to destroy himself. There are no longer any elements of safety, but in the State governments. . . . I suppose Mas^tts [Massachusetts] will be as self sufficient and self willed as ever. . . . It is quite certain that a very unfriendly feeling towards her now exists in the West & N. West, & a western member of the cabinet told me decidedly that if a division of the country should take place, it would not be an East & West line. He evidently had little hope. . . . This is but a gloomy picture: but it is the best I can find, as the country & its affairs are seen from this place. . . .[39]

All things considered, it was appropriate that the President on March 30 should set a day for national humiliation, fasting, and prayer.[40]

Democratic threats and Republican fears were not sufficient in themselves to turn the course of the war, but there were a number of points where they might be translated into decisive action. As the new year opened, attention was centered on the legislatures of Indiana and Illinois, where Democratic control had resulted from the elections of the previous autumn. In Indianapolis and Springfield as the members of the legislatures came to town, accompanied by a number of other political figures and a host of satellites and retainers, the atmosphere became supercharged. Union men discerned auguries that suggested Paris on the eve of the Revolution. Secret Democratic caucuses, sidewalk rumors, and saloon oratory hinted of dark schemes afoot, and the usual comings and goings of small-time politicos making the most of their temporary importance took on the appearance of plottings of unfathomable purport. Out of a welter of conflicting rumors there came a widely credited report that the troops of both states, and possibly those of New York as well, would be called home from the battle-lines

until revocation of the Emancipation Proclamation; other observers were sure that plans were on foot to take over the state
arsenals, use them to equip the Knights of the Golden Circle, and
summarily expel the Republican governors from office. There were
indications, certainly, that many of the rank-and-file Democrats
were in a mood to support extreme measures. On the evening of
January 5 a Democratic mass meeting was held in the hall of the
House of Representatives in Springfield. The principal speakers
were the party's candidates for the United States senatorship, and
each one, as the crowd expressed enthusiastic approval of the most
daring pronouncements, sought to outdo his predecessors in boldness. At the climax resolutions were carried demanding the negotiation of an armistice and the calling of a national peace convention to work out a program of reunion without coercion.[41] On
January 14 a motion was introduced into the Indiana legislature
declaring that, until the Emancipation Proclamation should be
withdrawn, "Indiana will never voluntarily contribute another
man or another dollar" to the prosecution of the war, and on the
27th and 29th resolutions calling for a six-month armistice were
brought before the two houses and quickly passed by the lower
chamber. A number of other anti-war resolutions were taken under consideration and the Democratic majorities set to work on a
scheme to take the control of the militia out of the hands of Governor Morton.[42] The Illinois House of Representatives, in which
the Democrats held a majority of fifty-six to twenty-nine, adopted
by a vote of fifty-two to twenty-eight proposals for the appointment
of delegates to a peace convention, with the declaration:

Whereas, The Constitution cannot be maintained, nor the Union
preserved, in opposition to public feeling, by the mere exercise of coercive powers confided to the General Government, and that in case of
differences and conflicts between the State and the federal Government,
too powerful for adjustment by the civil departments of the government, the appeal is not to the sword by the State or by the general
government, but to the people, peaceably assembled by their representatives in convention. . . .

. . . .

Resolved, That we believe the further prosecution of the present war
cannot result in the restoration of the Union and the preservation of

the Constitution as our fathers made it, unless the President's Emancipation Proclamation is withdrawn.

. . . .

. . . We are in favor of the assembling of a national convention of all the States to so adjust our national difficulties, that the States may hereafter live in harmony, each being secured to the rights guaranteed respectively to all by our fathers; and which convention we recommend shall convene at Louisville, Ky., or such other place as shall be determined upon by Congress or the several States, at the earliest practical period.

Resolved further, therefore, That to attain the objects of the foregoing resolution, we hereby memorialize the Congress of the United States, the Administration at Washington, and the executives and legislatures of the several States to take such immediate action as shall secure an armistice . . . for such a length of time as may be necessary to enable the people to meet in convention aforesaid. . . .[43]

Close behind this threat of political action that might make it impossible to continue the war, there was the other danger that the war might be lost by the disintegration of the armies through desertion and the breakdown of further recruiting. Desertion was increasing at an alarming rate,[44] accelerated by emancipation and discouragement over the military outlook. To his brother in the Senate General Sherman reported that the failure of his expedition against Vicksburg had been due primarily to the fact that absenteeism, malingering, and failure to obtain reinforcements had reduced his force below the level of effectiveness;[45] and voluntary capture in the hope of being sent home on parole had become so prevalent that Grant ordered the court-martialing of all paroled men and officers who had been captured while straggling.[46] General John A. Logan, commander of the 17th Corps and himself a Democrat, found it necessary to issue a proclamation urging his men not to permit themselves to be misled into forgetting their duties as soldiers and patriots.[47] Men paroled by the Confederates and sent to rendezvous camps in the North showed a disposition to be sullen, unmanageable, and mutinous and were determined to leave for their homes with or without permission.[48] The colonel of a Wisconsin regiment with the Army of the Potomac wrote to a member of his family:

I think that I have expressed before to you my conviction that the army generally were most heartily tired of the war, & would be willing to accept peace on most any terms—I think it is so still & I think the *fight* is out of the men. As a general thing they do not fight well—thousands skulk every battle field, and those who go in do not stand up to the rack. . . .—I am sorry I have cause to think all this—but I must believe what I *see*—

A very great deal of the discouragement comes from the North—from Northern papers & from Northern speakers—who to save their own selfish ends would sacrifice all things— Scarcely do we read a good hopeful encouraging article in any of our papers, but nothing but howling against the Administration—against our Generals—detailing all the North *has not* accomplished—instead of what it has. . . .[49]

Open justification of desertion by certain Democratic newspapers on the grounds that volunteers had been deceived as to the purpose of the war and that the oaths of enlistment which they had taken were tacitly dissolved by the issuance of the proclamation was an important factor in the situation.[50] Other papers got the same result by sly expressions of gratification in reporting cases of desertion or the failure of efforts of the authorities to apprehend those who had fled from service.[51] A direct and powerful influence was the tone of letters to the soldiers from disaffected relatives or friends at home, many of the arguments of peace orators and editors behind the lines being thus transmitted to the men in the field. A number of these letters were intercepted, in several cases because of the fact that the addressees had already deserted. One father wrote to his son, "I am sorry that you are engaged in this war, which has no other purpose but to free the negroes and enslave the whites; to overrun the free States with a negro population and place us all, who labor for a living, on an equality with d—d negroes sent on us by abolitionists, who alone are in favor of prosecuting this unholy, unconstitutional and hellish war." [52] Another soldier was advised to "come home, if you have to desert, you will be protected—the people are so enraged that you need not be alarmed if you hear of the whole of our Northwest killing off the abolitionists. I will send you some resolutions which we received with joy. . . ." [53] These desertions inflicted compound injury on the Union cause. Armies planning crucial movements were deprived of desperately needed men; other forces had to be detached or kept back in the home districts in an endeavor to apprehend the miscreants; and every deserter who reached home carried with him wildly exaggerated tales of the hardships of campaigning, the harshness of military discipline, and the carnage of battle, thus serving to dry up the springs of further volunteering in his community.

As these deserters increased in numbers they in many instances formed bands for self-protection and general marauding, attacking in particular the persons and property of citizens known to be supporters of the war. In some areas they set up reigns of terror designed to drive out Union sympathizers and to make whole districts untenable for agents of the government.[54] It was natural for individual deserters and outlaw bands to join the anti-war secret societies as a further safeguard against apprehension, and being desperate men accustomed to fighting and bloodshed they tended to give those bodies a more revolutionary character than they had previously had. Another indication that such organizations were growing in strength and increasing in their disposition to hinder the prosecution of the war was to be found in reports from many parts of Ohio, Indiana, Illinois, and Iowa of an extensive traffic in guns and ammunition and of considerable armed drill and military maneuvers by the members of such organizations.[55] On March 19 General H. G. Wright, commanding the Department of Ohio, sought to check this by forbidding the sale of arms except on permits issued by the nearest military commander, but adequate means of enforcement were lacking.[56] Colonel Henry B. Carrington, in charge of recruiting in Indiana, and H. M. Hoxie, United States marshal for Iowa, attempted surveys of the activities of the Knights of the Golden Circle and kindred organizations in those states. Their reports were based mainly on vague rumors and hearsay plus a limited and hasty use of spies and informers. Furthermore, as men unaccustomed to dealing with conspiratorial intrigues, they lacked qualifications for intrepreting their information and no doubt they sought to gain attention for themselves and to provide political capital for the Republican party—motives particularly evident in the activities of Carrington. Nevertheless, after a liberal discount on these grounds, their reports revealed that the membership in the secret societies was numerous, widespread, and ready for concerted action if the opportunity should arise. The discouragement of volunteering, the abetting of desertion, and the prevention of conscription were certainly among their immediate objectives, and their ultimate aims might include plans for a general uprising.[57] During the spring a number of violent incidents occurred in various parts of the Midwest, including resistance to the arrest of deserters, armed parades and demonstrations against continuation of the war, and even the murder of Union men and of soldiers home on furlough—although in some of these latter cases it was not always possible to separate political from personal motives. Among the counties involved were Edgar, Union, White, Jackson, and Williamson in Illinois; Rush, Morgan, Brown, Decatur, Wayne, Boone, and Sullivan in Indiana; and Madison County in Iowa.[58] None of these incidents was in itself of more than local importance, but taken together they expressed a spirit of unrest with unpredictable potentialities. In southern Illinois there was a growth of guerrilla organizations that might in time prove especially serious. The arrest of a former sheriff of Williamson County on suspicion of leadership in the Knights of the Golden Circle led to confessions disclosing the operations of two bands of guerrillas in that county,[59] and it was said that these and similar bands in neighboring counties were in touch with Confederate partisans and regular troops in Missouri.[60]

A parallel type of violence, and one that might serve as an introduction to more general disorder, was directed against Negroes. In Illinois, where in spite of laws to the contrary, numbers of "contrabands" had filtered in, several employers of these Negroes were forced by threats, mob action, arson, or other means to discharge such laborers.[61] A worse outbreak, however, occurred in Detroit. On March 6, 1863, a mob attempted to lynch a Negro who had been convicted and sentenced to life imprisonment for the rape of a nine-year-old white girl, and when it was thwarted by a provost guard that inflicted one death and wounded others it vented its fury on the Negro section of the city. Some thirty-five houses were fired and many Negroes beaten, and the mob was finally suppressed only after military units had been called in from neighboring towns.[62]

It was a serious question whether, against such a background, recruiting could still be carried on with any success. Democrats were contending that the Emancipation Proclamation had absolved them from any obligation to give further assistance to the war; Republicans seemed disposed to sink into despondent inaction, and such attempted makeshifts as the recruiting of Negro freedmen not only failed but further aroused the hostility of the Democrats.[63] In February Governor Tod advised the War Department that volunteering was about played out in Ohio,[64] and elsewhere indications supported the conclusion by the provost marshal general at the end of the war that "volunteering had stopped, and would not have been again started without the spur of the draft." [65]

At this juncture there came a turning point in the war on the home front. In spite of a torrent of condemnation from Democratic politicians and press,[66] the Republican majority in Congress had the courage to recognize the necessity for a thoroughgoing system of conscription—directed by national rather than state officials, as in the previous summer. An act to that effect received the President's approval on March 3, 1863.[67] Fortunately the law carried with it suitable machinery for enforcement in the Bureau of the Provost Marshal General of the United States, under the War Department. Fortunately, also, the personnel of the bureau came to be composed of men of a generally high order of ability and judgment. Although in existence in a partial fashion since July 31, 1862, the real activity of the bureau commenced on March 17, 1863, with the appointment of Colonel James B. Fry as provost marshal general.[68] Fry, himself a native of southern Illinois and the son of a general, had graduated from West Point in 1847, served in the Mexican War, and had experience in this type of work as adjutant to General McDowell and as chief-of-staff under General Buell. On April 21 Stanton issued detailed regulations for the organization and functioning of the bureau, and four days later Colonel Fry announced the appointment of acting assistant provost marshals general, each of whom was to be responsible for a particular state and charged with supervising enlistments, checking enemies of the government, and keeping Fry informed at all times of conditions in his area. Though not to be responsible in any sense to the governors of the states, they were instructed to co-operate with them in every possible way. For each congressional district there was to be a provost marshal, who would in turn appoint a deputy provost marshal for each county (except in the headquarters county) and such other subordinates as were required. Military assistance needed in the administration of their duties was to be furnished to these officials by the commanders of the military departments and by bodies of invalided veterans whose formation was authorized on April 28, 1863.[69] This pervasive machinery at last gave the federal government effective contact with every locality. The system was henceforth perhaps the most important institutional factor in the non-political situation within the North. The energy and discretion of its personnel would largely decide whether the human resources needed to win the war would be forthcoming.

On June 8, 1863, instructions were issued for the enrollment of all men between the ages of twenty and forty-five.[70] Although this was to be only a preliminary to actual drafting, it encountered armed opposition in four of the seven states of the Middle West. In this the members of the secret societies played a role difficult to separate from actions that were individually motivated. The chief resistance in Ohio was encountered in an area in the north central portion of the state, centering in Mansfield, troops having to be sent into Morrow, Crawford, and Knox counties to enable the completion of the enrollment.[71] Much more serious problems developed in Indiana. On June 11, while carrying out his duties, the deputy provost marshal for Rush County was assassinated and his assistant wounded by two men concealed in a wheat field,[72] and another enrollment officer was murdered in Sullivan County on June 18. In this latter instance the crime was attributed to an organized group—presumably members of the K.G.C., who had been for some time holding military drill and had made public threats that had succeeded in intimidating everyone but the murdered man. Because no one else had been willing to face the danger, he had taken over the enrolling of two townships instead of one as was generally the rule. In reporting on the affair the provost marshal for the area estimated that in this and the adjoining congressional district in Illinois there were at least twelve hundred men secretly under arms, for the most part ignorant men dominated by a few desperate characters who had so filled them with wild tales as to the government's purpose that they might actually be led into full-fledged rebellion.[73] Also in Johnson, Fulton, Putnam, Owen, and Clay counties there were personal assaults and thefts of enrollment records, and in Boone County a group of women threw eggs at an enrollment official. In every case, however, small details of troops sufficed to carry through the enrollments and to permit the arrest of those attempting interference.[74] In Illinois there had been reports that the Copperheads were arming and drilling in preparation for resistance in Christian, Sangamon, Douglas, and other counties in central Illinois. Actual trouble, however, developed only in Cook and Fulton counties. In Chicago on June 25 a mob of some three to four hundred men and women, mostly Irish, attacked a deputy United States marshal and three assistants after they had arrested two men for refusing to give their names to the registration officials. One of the officers was struck by a brick which fractured his skull and caused doubts for a time of his recovery.[75] The scene of disorders in Fulton County was in its southern townships, a wild region, difficult of access, lying along the Illinois River. Several enrollers there were temporarily prevented from carrying out their duties, but the mediation of moderate Democrats helped to quiet the situation so that the lists could be completed. A special investigation made by the Illinois acting assistant provost marshal general disclosed that deserters were the backbone of the resistance, misleading gullible and easily inflamed followers.[76] In Dodge County, Wisconsin, an enrolling officer was murdered, and for a time an ugly situation threatened in Milwaukee, where a turbulent population, largely German and Irish, had repeatedly rioted during the preceding decade and now seemed disposed to have a showdown with the whole paraphernalia of conscription. On May 30 an official engaged in the registration in Milwaukee was knocked down and badly mangled, causing the provost marshal for the district to fear the imminence of a general uprising in the city. In spite of this apprehension, the local police force, backed by General John Pope, now commander of the Department of the Northwest (who on this occasion exhibited a coolness and good judgment in marked contrast to the rashness that had contributed to his defeat at the second Battle of Bull Run), was able to give all the assistance needed for carrying through the enrollment. In other parts of the state about the only violence encountered was at the hands of women and children endeavoring to conceal the whereabouts of their menfolk who had gone into hiding.[77] Michigan reported no trouble,[78] and there was an absence of untoward incidents in connection with the registration in Iowa and Minnesota.

In view of the tense state of affairs prevailing at the time in the Middle West it was surprising that there was not more opposition. An important factor in preventing disorder was undoubtedly the thorough organization of the provost marshal service, together with the combination of discretion and determination exhibited by most of the personnel of the service and by army commanders charged with the responsibility of furnishing them with military support. Care was exercised to avoid the unnecessary arousing of resentment, but at the same time it was made clear that no amount of resistance would be permitted to prevent its completion. Provost Marshal General Fry particularly commended his subordinate, Colonel Conrad Baker, for his vigilance and good judgment in handling the difficult situation in Indiana.[79]

Much had been due also to the pacific counsels of responsible Democrats. It had to be remembered, however, that this enrollment did not involve the pressing of men into service. The story might be different when actual drafting began. One Fulton County paper told its followers:

> Taking our names down on paper, and our bodies down to Dixie, are so very different that we unhesitatingly advise peace men to submit to the first most cheerfully, and to resist the last most defiantly. In any event peace men have nothing to lose by the enrollment. We may some-day need to know about the military status of the North, and then we shall be very glad to use the information gained from these Black Republican lists. Another thing: The hour is not yet come.[80]

Some of the peace spokesmen still contended that conscription by the federal authorities was unconstitutional, holding that such power remained exclusively in the states and that there was an inherent right in our system of government for the people to resist unconstitutional actions by force of arms. Vallandigham so advised audiences at Dayton, Ohio, on March 13, and at Hamilton, Ohio, on March 21, 1863. In the latter speech, as a satiric rejoinder to a statement in General Order No. 15, recently issued at Indianapolis by Colonel Carrington, that "the habit of carrying arms upon the person has greatly increased," the congressman said, "Well, so it has, and in times of threats and danger like these, it ought to, and in spite of all 'orders,' it will increase." [81] Friends of the government had reason for the apprehension of much greater trouble to follow. Provost Marshal General Fry, preparing for the worst, instructed his subordinates if necessary to use the troops at their disposal to draft in one district at a time,[82] a device which, though certain to result in a slowing down of the process of reinforcing the armies in the field, might become the only course of safety.

As the spring of 1863 wore on, it saw the recession of many of the fears that had ushered in that despairing winter. On all sides there were signs of returning morale and the decrease of formerly exaggerated apprehensions. For one thing, with no particular change taking place in the military situation as the troops of both sides remained in winter quarters, the earlier mood of fright naturally brought its opposite reaction. It began to be understood that the prevailing despondency had overshot the mark as much as had the overconfidence of the spring of 1862. Union rallies were held. One in the Masonic Hall at Indianapolis on January 14 was typical. Governor Morton and other speakers presented the case for the Emancipation Proclamation as a war measure (playing down the humanitarian aspect) and denounced the Democrats who had won election on pledges of support of the war which they now stood ready to repudiate.[83] Rallies elsewhere heard the peace men assigned to a place in history beside the Tories of the Revolution and the "Blue Lights" of New England of the War of 1812 (so called from their reputed method of signaling from shore to British squadrons operating off our coasts), and warnings were issued that for every conspiring Copperhead there was a tree or a lamppost from which, if need be, he could be hanged.[84]

The peace Democrats had themselves made a special kind of contribution to morale. By their frankness in revealing their aims they permitted themselves to be made whipping boys on whom supporters of the war could vent the feelings generated by frustration on the battlefield. Thus they got squarely in the way of one of the most effective epithets in American history—"Copperhead." The first use of the term is still uncertain (it appeared in the New York

THE COPPERHEAD PLAN FOR SUBJUGATING THE SOUTH

War and Argument—Cold Steel and Cool Reason—having failed to restore the Union, it is supposed that the South may be *bored* into coming back.

Our Picture represents the successful operation of this exceedingly humane and ingenious device.

From Harper's Weekly, *Oct. 22, 1864*

SHUTTING UP SHOP

UNCLE SAMUEL. "What! shutting up shop, eh!"

MANAGING MAN OF THE COPPERHEAD HOUSE. "Yes! 'taint no use. Sence the news from Ohio and Pennsylvania, we haint seen a customer, and the boss says to shut up quickly before New York ruins us outright."

From Harper's Weekly, *Nov. 7, 1863*

Tribune as early as July 20, 1861), and it had in fact been used as a general term of opprobrium long before the war. Apparently it grew out of a comparison with the supposed habit of the poisonous copperhead snake of striking without warning from concealment, but it may have been definitely fixed on the peace Democrats by the practice some of them followed at one time of wearing the head of Liberty cut out of a copper penny as a protest against the arbitrary arrests of the government. Since it was purely an epithet, it never had any definite range of application, being sometimes used to refer only to those believed to be actively in sympathy with the Confederates but on other occasions fixed on the Democratic party as a whole. "Tory" was employed earlier in the war, but it lacked spontaneity. Also used was the term "Butternut," a contemptuous reference to the home-dyed clothing of the ignorant rustics of Southern origin who so loyally supported the Democratic standard, but Democrats considered it a badge of honor, since they boasted that theirs was the party of the common people. Some even wore emblems made by cutting out a cross-section of a butternut to show two hearts joined together—those of the Northern and Southern people. But "Copperhead" stung like a lash.

Definitely a factor in heartening the war supporters at home was the indignation of the soldiers at the front against the "peace sneaks." Officers and men of Midwestern regiments in numerous instances adopted formal resolutions denouncing politicians and newspapers that were urging or insinuating the necessity of abandoning the war, sometimes accompanying their protests with threats of retribution on their return home.[85] The sentiment behind such resolutions was contained in the letter sent home by a Michigan volunteer:

We are having the dullest of all dull times now . . . nothing to do . . . so that our time is pretty much taken up with eating, sleeping smoking, and bragging about the fighting we have done and would do if we had a chance, and how we would "clean out" the Northern Copperheads if we could get home. The Illinois soldiers all that I have seen or heard of *are* down on the traitors in their State and Legislature. . . .[86]

That such denunciations were not intended to be limited to verbal censures was demonstrated on February 19, when some seventy-five convalescent soldiers from a near-by military hospital in mid-afternoon entered the office of the Keokuk (Iowa) *Constitution,* wrecked the presses, dumped the type out the window, and created havoc generally.[87] However much to be deprecated from the viewpoint of law and order, it was evident that this violent sort of demonstration as well as the more conventional expressions of soldier attitude had an effect of heartening civilian support of the war.[88] One citizen reported that

. . . there is a different atmosphere here & I feel more encouraged. I have no doubt the army is all right & if the boys ever come home we will make these home traitors regret they were enemies to their country. . . . I intend to make all the Union men around here speak out and that is not all If in the course of human events it should become necessary I mean to have them fight & that in earnest— There is nothing like being ready & get the first shot.[89]

Also encouraging was the failure of the peace Democrats to utilize their political strength for any appreciable advancement toward their objective. The Ohio legislature, elected in 1861, was under Republican control and not only was in a position to smother any proposals from the minority side but even formally censured one member of the lower house, a Mr. Dresel, who introduced resolutions condemning the acts of the federal administration.[90] In Illinois the Republicans for a time boycotted the meetings of the state senate in order to prevent a quorum for the passage of the peace resolutions, and the Democratic majority lacked the nerve to refuse to vote men and money for the war. Finally, in June, Governor Yates seized upon a technicality—the failure of the two houses to agree upon a date for adjournment—to prorogue them, subject to recall only at his discretion.[91] Any further peace overtures from this source were thus made impossible. A similar relationship of governor and legislature in Indiana permitted the Republican minority in the senate to stalemate proceedings by staging a permanent bolt to prevent a quorum, leaving Governor Morton as virtually the government of the state for nearly two years. Without legislative appropriations Morton raised money to conduct the war by loans and other expedients that only a bold man would have dared to employ.[92] With these coups the supporters of the war took heart and lost some of the fears that had obsessed them when these bodies had first convened, while the peace men were demoralized by their demonstrated lack of ability to formulate and carry out a program. It was apparent that the peace Democrats had not only failed to attain their objectives but had by their extremism alienated many of the conservatives, even of their own party, who had supported them the previous fall as a protest against Abolition and arbitrary acts of government.[93] Regaining their self-confidence, the Republicans were able to make effective use of the argument that the people must choose between a peace with union by force of arms or a peace with disunion by negotiation, using the assertions of Confederate spokesmen and newspapers as evidence to bolster the contention that there was no third choice.[94] As the great body of people were not yet ready to pay so high a price for peace, the contention served to direct middle-of-the-roaders back to support of the existing administration.

Both evidencing and aiding the return of confidence was the spread of an organization, formed in the previous summer but now enjoying a sudden rise in membership as the situation created a need for it, known as the Union League of America or Loyal League. Apparently it developed in several states of the North at about the same time. One of the first local units (possibly the first) was organized in Pekin, Illinois, on June 25, 1862, by a group that included a man who had been a pro-Union man in east Tennessee earlier in the war, and was modeled after a similar Southern society. Possessing a ritual and oaths of secrecy and of loyalty to the government, it was a perfect antidote and counterbalance to the Knights of the Golden Circle. By September 25, 1862, the Illinois League had spread widely enough for a state council meeting at Bloomington to draw representatives from twelve counties. The activities of the peace men and fears for the adequacy of the normal machinery of government in the winter of 1862–63 caused Union men to embrace it with eagerness. Some 50,000 were credited to Illinois alone. In other states there was a parallel development, with Republican officials giving it hearty support.[95] On May 20 and 21, 1863, a convention at Cleveland created a national organization to be administered by a grand council in Washington. Not only did it offer a promise of defense against any movement of violence on the part

of the anti-war societies, thus reassuring the timid and those ab-
horing involvement in disorder, but it also served as a means of
relief for the mortification resulting from military defeat. Although
no longer fully confident of their ability to subdue the Confederate
armies, loyal men felt that they might undertake with some success
the chastisement of Northern allies of the South. Members boasted
that if there were to be any "fire in the rear" it would be met by a
counterfire. One wrote:

Matters look somewhat better in Illinois. The union men are organized in nearly every County in the State. We are *about ready* and
able to take care of home troubles in *any event.*

I see militia Co.s are organizing—three co.s in Springfield are full—
two in Alton forming. Traitors are being informed that this *Government must and shall be preserved!*

We had a glorious meeting in Alton *such as was never before seen*
—to sustain our State and National Government and ratify the Prest.s
Proclamation. These meetings and organizations, are producing *peace*
in Illinois.

. . . .

Alton is *ready* and Madison Co. is getting fast into shape. Such an
earnest zeal was never before seen among Union men.

It may be as well to distroy [*sic*] this letter we desire that matters
may develope in a quiet manner.[96]

Set up to encourage enlistments, disseminate Union propaganda,
and support the war administrations, federal and state, as well as to
be ready to meet force with force, the Union League was a notable
factor in the rebirth of confidence. A member at Galena, Illinois,
wrote to his fellow-townsman Congressman Washburne, "We all
feel that our National affairs are mending. Only give us a few decided victories & everything will be right." [97]

It must be remembered, however, that the duration of such re-
born hopefulness was largely dependent upon the military situation. Should Grant fail to take Vicksburg or disaster overtake the
Army of the Potomac, despair could be expected to return with redoubled force. Desertion had not been appreciably checked. The
beginning of actual conscription might precipitate a much more
formidable resistance than had met the enrollment. Should it become necessary to reconvene the legislatures of Indiana and Illinois,

the tempers of those bodies might be found to have grown more defiant. Most definite of all was the question involved in the approaching autumn elections, when the peace advocates could hope to win the governorship and legislature of Ohio and possibly of Iowa as well. In Ohio the peace leadership was most able and determined. Victory here might revive the movement for a peace convention and provide the fulcrum by which the three Ohio River states of the section could be pried out of the Union, at least to the extent of preventing any effective further assistance to the war.

This danger was brought to a sharp focus by the action of General Ambrose E. Burnside, who after having so critically endangered the Union cause at Fredericksburg had recently been appointed commander of the Department of Ohio. Incensed by the strictures of Copperhead leaders against the administration of the war, the General on April 13 on his own responsibility ordered the arrest of anyone guilty of seditious utterances likely to obstruct recruiting. This was followed by the arrest, trial before a military court, conviction, and sentence to imprisonment until the end of the war of former Congressman Vallandigham.[98] Angry protests issued from Democratic sources,[99] and the President, embarrassed by Burnside's action but feeling unable to repudiate it entirely, commuted the sentence to expulsion to the Confederacy.[100] But the most important result was the complete surrender of the Democratic party in Ohio to the peace faction. Carried along by the indignation of the moment, its state convention without a dissenting vote chose Vallandigham as its candidate for governor. The platform advocated, though cautiously, the opening of negotiations with the Southern states.[101] General Burnside had unwittingly converted the gubernatorial race into a showdown between continuation of the war and peace at any price. Who could doubt that Vallandigham as governor, with his previous statements of attitude and the demonstrated inflexibility of his determination, would do all in his power to withdraw the support of Ohio from the war? By the middle of June, Vallandigham had succeeded, with the co-operation of the Confederate authorities, in making his way to Canada. Here, able to keep closely in touch with affairs in his own state and the other states of the Middle West, his exile was the most powerful argument for his candidacy.[102]

State conventions of the Democrats in Indiana, Illinois, and Iowa saw the party taking more outright positions in favor of peace. The twenty-third resolution adopted by the Illinois convention declared:

That the further offensive prosecution of this war tends to subvert the Constitution and the government, and entail upon this nation all the disastrous consequences of misrule and anarchy. That we are in favor of peace upon the basis of a restoration of the Union, and for the accomplishment of which we propose a National Convention to settle upon terms of peace, which shall have in view the restoration of the Union as it was, and the securing by Constitutional amendments, such rights to the several States and the people thereof, as honor and justice demand.[103]

The Iowa state convention, nominating Charles Mason for the governorship, resolved, "That our Union was formed in peace, and can *never be perpetuated by force of arms,* and that a republican government held together by the sword becomes a military despotism." [104]

As the summer of 1863 opened there were many evidences that a crisis was approaching. Local elections in the Midwest during the spring had indicated that the tide of public sentiment was still running toward the Democrats.[105] Encouragement for the peace movement was developing in the East. The Democrats of Connecticut had nominated a peace man, Colonel Thomas H. Seymour, as their candidate for governor and announced in their platform

That while we denounce the heresy of secession, as undefended and unwarranted by the Constitution, we as confidently assert, that whatever may heretofore have been the opinion of our countrymen, the time has now arrived when all true lovers of the Constitution are ready to abandon the *"monstrous fallacy"* that the Union can be restored by the armed hand alone; and we are anxious to inaugurate such action, honorable alike to the contending sections, as will stop the ravages of war, avert universal bankruptcy, and unite all the States upon terms of equality as members of one Confederacy.[106]

In New York City on June 3 a huge mass meeting, under the auspices of former Mayor Fernando Wood, overflowed Cooper Union, calling for immediate peace and urging Democrats every-

where to repudiate the war. Citing the Virginia and Kentucky resolutions as a text, one of the resolutions adopted argued:

> Now, if, as is thus proven, the States, as such, are sovereign, and that
> the Federal Government is simply a compact between the parties, with
> authority exceedingly restricted and definitely limited, can this feeble
> authority make war upon the States? . . .
> . . . Therefore, this war of the General Government against the
> South is illegal, being unconstitutional, and should not be sustained if
> we are to regard the Constitution as still binding and in force. It is a
> violation of the great American *Magna Charta* which secures the in-
> dependent sovereignty of the States of the Union.[107]

The Southern people, having hoped for such a development from
the beginning, were encouraged to new efforts to establish their
independence by reports of growing disaffection in the North.[108]
In Europe the anticipation of Confederate victory was heightened
by news of disaffection in the North, contributing to a renewal by
Southern sympathizers in England and France of demands for intervention.[109] With Lee invading Pennsylvania in the definite hope of
promoting defeatism in the North, Grant not yet successful in reducing Vicksburg, Unionists fearful, and Copperheads hopeful of
Confederate success, the fate of the Union at the end of June 1863
seemed to hang upon the military fortunes of the next few days.[110]

CHAPTER VII

The Period of Renewed Hope

(July 4, 1863–June 3, 1864)

THE first week of July 1863 ended a year of Union defeats. A year of victories followed. When Pickett's charge crumpled at the stone wall on Cemetery Ridge, and Lee had to lead his battered army south from Gettysburg, the tense anxiety that had gripped the North at the end of June was eased. The fall of Vicksburg meant even more. The Mississippi was open now, and it need no longer be feared that the end of the war would leave the rivers of the Middle West cut off from the sea. There was a promise in the air that the Confederacy would in time be subdued. Not since the surrender of Fort Donelson, a year and a half before, had there been such an occasion for celebration. Bonfires, bands, parades, and booming cannon bespoke relief and regenerated confidence. To a jubilant mass meeting of his old neighbors in Springfield President Lincoln sent a message that expressed, as only he could express it, the people's sense of thanksgiving and hope:

The signs look better. The Father of Waters again goes unvexed to the sea. Thanks to the great Northwest for it. . . .

Peace does not appear so distant as it did. I hope it will come soon, and come to stay; and so come as to be worth the keeping in all future time. It will then have been proved that, among free men, there can be no successful appeal from the ballot to the bullet; and that they who take such appeal are sure to lose their case, and pay the cost . . . while, I fear, there will be some . . . unable to forget that, with malignant heart and deceitful speech, they have strove to hinder it.[1]

Everything wore a new face. Doubters were discredited. Republicans who had been utterly discouraged a few weeks back were now convinced that the backbone of the rebellion had been broken.[2] Democrats too, even those of pro-Southern leanings, shared in the prevalent impression. "Vicksburg taken . . . ," William McCormick, grandfather of the present publisher of the Chicago *Tribune,* wrote sadly to brother Cyrus. "It would seem that by numbers and brute force the South must be crushed." [3] Radicals lately critical of the national leadership began to speak of Lincoln's renomination and re-election as both probable and desirable. A letter received by Senator Trumbull contained a confession of faith to which a large part of the Republican following could have subscribed:

In the early stages of the war, as you are aware, I did not like *some* things that were done, and many things that *were not done,* by the present Administration. Like every body else, pretty nearly, as among earnest, loyal men, I too was a grumbler, because, as we thought, the Gov't. moved *too slow.* But now, looking at it in the light of History, and . . . taking into view too, the educational process through which the public mind has [been] made to pass to sustain and give efficiency to what *has* been done; I say taking all these things into the account, we are not *now* disposed to be sensorious [*sic*] to the "powers that be," even among *ourselves.* On the contrary, it is now pretty generally conceded, that, all things considered, Mr. Lincoln's Administration has done well. I think I am not mistaken, Judge, in saying this is the general sentiment out of Copperhead Circles, and to such reptiles we don't propose to cater. . . .

. . . We have tried [Lincoln] . . . know what he is; that he is both honest and patriotic; that if he don't go forward as *fast* as some of us like, *he never goes backwards.* . . . Very many say "as we are involved in the war, and as the questions growing out of it cannot be settled for years to come, if the war *itself* can be, we can't risk a change of Administrators." Some go so far as to say, "this re-election is a political necessity." I would . . . say, if the war is so conducted as to satisfy the reasonable expectations of the friends of the war, it would seem to be the dictate of prudence to continue him four years more. [4]

Among civilians at home and soldiers in the field there was a sense of having turned a corner in the war. [5] Neither the inactivity of the Army of the Potomac nor anxious days for the Army of the Cumberland in the remaining months of the year would seriously disturb the conviction that the career of the Confederacy was drawing to an end. And when in November the Southern forces were driven back from Chattanooga in humiliating rout and preparations commenced for the concerted advance of Grant's and Sherman's mighty war machines in the spring of 1864, confidence again reached floodtide.

In this setting Vallandigham's candidacy for the governorship of Ohio appeared less frightening. Vallandigham himself, safe in Canada but with orders on file for his arrest and imprisonment in Fort Warren if he should be found within the boundaries of the United States,[6] tried to shift position in response to the changed outlook. In an address sent across the border to the people of Ohio on July 15, and in subsequent open letters to Democratic rallies, he stressed the argument that after the overthrow of the Confederacy the Democratic party would be best qualified for the task of bringing about the spiritual reconciliation of the sections without which no mere physical reunion could be lasting.[7] Many of his followers, however, seemed to perceive that in the minds of the electorate his candidacy was inextricably identified with the advocacy of immediate peace. They consequently continued their previous line of argument. The *Crisis* pictured an immense reserve strength in the Confederacy, minimized the significance of the recent victories, and pronounced the effort of the federal government to fill up losses in the army by conscription a "perfect failure." It insisted, too, that military possession of the Mississippi River would bring no economic relief to the Midwest, since Eastern interests dominating the administration would see to it that prohibitive regulations on river trade would prevent any competition with railroad and canal routes leading to the north Atlantic coastal cities.[8] In the Democratic campaign every effort was made to use the old reliable issues of civil rights and the danger of a freedman inundation of the Northwest. The exiled nominee symbolized the first of these themes, and at campaign rallies a popular feature was a procession of young women bearing placards inscribed, "Fathers, Save Us from Negro Equality." [9]

But the Republicans of Ohio had the advantage, and they exploited it to the full. Sobered by the reverses suffered in the 1862 elections and shocked at the amount of anti-war sentiment revealed by the military setbacks of the previous year, they were now firmly united. The recent victories in the field provided just the right amount of confidence to nerve them for a vigorous campaign.

Seeing that the Democrats had stranded themselves upon commitments to an extremist leadership they set out to exploit the opportunity by doing everything possible to invite conservative Democrats to cross the party line. In the terminology of the organization "Republican" was discreetly set aside for "Union"; the state nominating convention adopted the keynote sentiment that "in the present exigencies of the Republic we lay aside personal preferences and prejudices, and henceforth, till the war is ended, will draw no party line but the great line between those who sustain the government and those who rejoice in the triumph of the enemy," and chose as candidate for governor a former Democrat, John Brough, whose fifteen-year retirement from active politics had freed him from connection with controversial issues; attention was directed to Generals John A. Logan of Illinois and John A. Dix of New York as examples of prominent Democrats whose patriotism was causing them to lead the way to membership in the consolidated war party; and, if partisan traditions still proved too strong for some, an alternative road was provided by the device of having independent "Democratic" local conventions indorse the Unionist slate of candidates. (A meeting of this type held in September in the neighboring state of Wisconsin was presided over by the former lieutenant-governor, Judge Arthur MacArthur, grandfather of General Douglas MacArthur.) [10] The Democratic strategy of 1862 was copied in the subordinating of debatable issues to a broad appeal for a patriotic and united support of the war. Emancipation and arbitrary acts of government were kept in the background. President Lincoln himself lent a hand by squelching General Burnside when that obtuse functionary ordered the suppression of the Chicago *Times*.[11] Shortly thereafter the chastened general ordered the freeing of all political prisoners in his department who could be released with safety and advised his subordinates to use all possible restraint in the making of further arrests.[12]

On election day the success of the Union party was overwhelming. Out of a total vote of more than 476,000 in Ohio, Brough received a majority of 62,000 of the home and 39,000 of the soldier ballots, and his supporters won 29 out of 34 seats in the state senate and 73 of 97 in the house.[13] The *Crisis* and other bitter partisans charged the result to fraud, based upon the fact that 100,000 more

ELECTIONS OF 1863. Black counties—50% or more for Democratic candidates
for highest state office in six states.

votes had been recorded than in the previous year,[14] but the New
York *World,* viewing the election with more detachment, was nearer
to the truth in its conclusion that Vallandigham's nomination, raising to first place in the campaign the issue of peace rather than that
of arbitrary government, had been a mistake.[15] Certainly, it was un-
timely in a period when the war was going well. But had such an
election been held during the previous period of despair or had
military success been some weeks or months delayed, the outcome
might have been quite different. In spite of the many handicaps
which it had to face, Vallandigham's candidacy had succeeded in
getting the votes of 36,000 more people than had supported the
Democratic nominee of 1861 and of 3000 more than the party had

polled in its victories in the state in the previous year. An amazing strength, all considered, had been demonstrated by the peace men; only the complete co-operation of every faction in the Union party and tremendous exertions in getting out the vote had insured the defeat of the advocate of open surrender. If the mood of discouragement and recrimination that had prevailed earlier had continued, this might not have been possible. But in the timing of events good fortune had once more befallen the Union cause. And there could be no denying that it had been greatly advanced. Comparable victories were scored in other parts of the Midwest. In Iowa, Wisconsin, and Minnesota Union-Republican governors and legislatures were returned by wide margins, and local elections in Michigan, Indiana, and Illinois showed that the tide was running in the same direction in those states.[16]

Thus the danger of political obstruction of the war by Democratically controlled state governments had been dispelled—for the time being. But there was still work to be done in keeping the armies in the field recruited to the strength that would enable them to complete their task. Here there were continuing dangers from public apathy and outright resistance. An executive call of March 3, 1863, for 300,000 militia provided for a draft on September 8 to fill quota deficiencies. The preliminary enrollment of men subject to call had been completed in most localities by the end of June. In spite of some new evidences of opposition, believed to have been spurred by the New York draft riot in July in which hundreds of lives were lost before the police and detachments from the Army of the Potomac restored order, the work was finished up everywhere within the next few weeks.[17]

There were signs that actual drafting might encounter much more serious opposition. Arms were still being brought in and distributed in a manner that implied an intent to offer resistance; in the larger cities the Irish were especially restive; [18] and from many rural areas came continuing reports of military drill by members of the secret orders and other opponents of conscription.[19] Outbreaks of violence here and there pointed to an underlying stratum of passion that might break out in bloody revolt. On July 17 an enrolling officer in Sullivan County, Indiana, was shot and killed from ambush,[20] and at Danville, Illinois, on August 24 the attempt of a

mob to overpower a provost marshal resulted in the death of
five persons.[21] Fortunately, because of volunteering and surpluses
credited on previous calls, drafting was found unnecessary in Ohio,
Indiana, and Illinois, states where the portents had been most
ominous. This gave time for the people to adjust themselves to the
prospect of future conscription. After having relieved their feelings
by much bold talk and having found clandestine drilling more irk-
some and less romantic than they had anticipated, most of them
would later decide either to hire substitutes or to submit to conscription when the necessity should come. In Michigan and Wisconsin the authorities were alert and prepared for trouble, and
consequently encountered none. In Detroit, the focal point of any
expected difficulty in the former state, a force of eight companies of
sharpshooters (six of them having been returned to the state for
the ostensible purpose of completing the organization of a regiment), a company of the Invalid Corps serving as provost guards,
and some forty or fifty cavalry were all ready for service. They were
sufficient to make it clear that opposition would be useless, and the
spirit of resistance faded.[22]

The provost marshal service now found its hands freer for its
other major responsibility, the apprehension of deserters. In the
past eighteen months this practice had become so widespread that
it threatened to dominate whole communities. It was most prevalent where disaffection with the war policy was strongest, but there
was hardly a township in which there were not some who would
offer a hiding place, if necessary, and employment, if possible, to
deserters. In the most favorable areas they were organized and
armed against efforts to arrest them and were credited with deeds
of increasing violence and provocativeness.[23] In Union County,
Illinois, four men in the provost marshal service were killed in the
latter half of 1863 in endeavoring to make arrests.[24] A deserter
murdered a deputy provost marshal in De Kalb County, Indiana,
the *Crisis* making its attitude abundantly clear by headlining the
story "Murderer at Heart Himself Murdered." [25]

The officials of the service were determined to use the forces at
their command in a concerted effort to put down such challenges.
Whenever found, the armed bands were dispersed and their mem-

bers hunted down. A cavalry force of 250 assigned to the provost marshal of the southernmost district of Illinois for emergency duty found about 130 deserters and their supporters entrenched in a crude fort on the Muddy River in Williamson County. The rebels suddenly lost their taste for fighting on sight of the troops and fled without offering battle. Thereafter some 400 deserters were arrested in the locality, and a period of relative peace ensued.[26] A sanguinary engagement took place in notorious Isabel Township, Fulton County, Illinois, in which a cavalry detachment led by the provost marshal surprised a camp of about 400 deserters and their Copperhead friends, killing several, capturing about a dozen, and putting the rest to flight.[27] In Fayette and Effingham counties in Illinois and Coshocton County, Ohio, troops and posses were attacked by bands of deserters, but in each case the deserters got the worst of the encounter.[28] These affairs had the effect of discouraging others who might have entertained thoughts of resistance. In Illinois alone, 2000 deserters were arrested between June and October 1863,[29] and by the end of that year 800 were reported to have been taken in the four counties of Perry, Saline, Jackson, and Williamson, in the southern portion of the state.[30]

Arrests were also made of those who had given encouragement or assistance to desertion. An examination by the author of records in the office of the Clerk of the United States District Court of the Southern District of Illinois at Springfield has revealed some thirty indictments of civilians on such charges by the federal grand jury during January and February 1864. There were several convictions and a number of sudden departures from the community or state, some of those indicted setting out for the Far West.[31] By the spring of 1864 there was reason for believing that the problem of desertion had been brought under some measure of control, although it had by no means ceased to be a problem.[32]

This respite from the necessity of raising additional recruits was short-lived. On October 17 the Washington authorities, with the purpose of placing armies in the field in the spring of 1864 that would be able to complete the suppression of the rebellion, issued a call for 300,000 volunteers. Drafting to fill deficiencies was to take place on January 5. The call was twice amended until, as finally issued on March 15, 1864, a total of 700,000 enlistments was required, with conscription to begin on April 15 or as soon thereafter as might be feasible.[33]

Even with the promising outlook in the field and aid from re-enlistments of the veteran three-year volunteers of 1861, the task of raising this huge force revealed that both the holiday enthusiasm of 1861 and the determination of the summer of 1862 had almost everywhere disappeared. A prime example of this flagging spirit was to be found in Illinois, the state that eighteen months before had led all others in the Union in its outpouring of manpower. Abetting the general indifference was the attitude of the Democratic press, which disclaimed any responsibility for further support of the war. The *State Register* of December 4 grumpily observed that

. . . at the late election, the patriotic loyal leaguers were as busy as bees bringing men up to the polls to vote against the democracy. . . . It now remains for these superlatively loyal men to prove their loyalty by something more than words. Their votes do not contribute to put down the rebellion. . . .

We should be pleased to do all in our power . . . to induce the democrats to enlist, but the democrats are disheartened by the mischievous policies the administration has seen fit to adopt. They can only anticipate permanent and hopeless ruin for the country unless those policies are abandoned. . . .

With the loyal leaguers it is different. These policies are precisely what they approve, and what they have been clamoring for.

And the Joliet *Signal* of December 22 expressed a comparable attitude:

On the fifth of January, therefore, the lottery of life and death is to be drawn. It is truly hard for men who do not believe in the war or approve of the policy upon which it has been conducted, to be dragged from their homes in the dead of winter, but the fate seems inevitable. The strong arm of military power will encircle them, from which there is little chance to escape. Democrats and lovers of the constitution, who abhor the policy of the war and believe that it can only result in ruin to the country, it is said will be the principal victims of the draft—and we fear it will be so.

Such papers were also busy with charges that the troop calls were unfairly constructed. The provision in the draft act by which service could be avoided by the payment of $300 or by the hiring of a substitute was especially vulnerable to attack, and was seized on as one more evidence of the administration's disposition to grant favors to the wealthy at the expense of the poor. Some of the more extreme oppositionists expressed the fear that the real purpose of the call for 700,000 was to make possible the military subjugation of the North, this being adduced from the assumption that such a large body of men could not possibly be required for the battlefield alone.[34] Only a trickle of new volunteers came in.[35] For a time it appeared that the state would be unable to fill its quota by volunteering[36]—in spite of surpluses in earlier calls, credits obtained for Illinois men who had enlisted in the regiments of other states,[37] the enlistments of Negroes,[38] and the increase of bounties to totals ranging as high as $400 or $500 plus local appropriations and private donations for soldiers' families.[39] The mortification felt by the state officials was apparently the chief cause of another unseemly squabble that broke out between the state and federal authorities over the functioning of the recruiting service. This quarrel, or rather series of quarrels and misunderstandings, eventually involved to some extent the Secretary of War, Chief of Staff Halleck, Provost Marshal General Fry, and General Samuel Peter Heintzelman, a "Pennsylvania Dutchman," veteran of the Eastern campaigns and Burnside's successor as commander of the Department of the Ohio, on the one hand, and Governor Yates and Adjutant-General Fuller of Illinois of the other.[40]

Eventually Illinois was able to meet her quota and thus again escape conscription, but it was largely by virtue of heavy veteran re-enlistments. The men who had volunteered in 1861 for a three-year period, with little material inducement, were now eager to get the attractive bounties offered to veterans. They were appealed to, also, by the promise of furloughs home for all who re-enlisted before the end of their original terms of service. Having developed an *esprit* of their own distinct from that of the civilian population, they had been less subject to defeatist influences, although they shared in the current feeling that the offensive planned for 1864 would complete the triumph of the Union.[41]

Another suggestion of the decline of the spirit that had animated the Middle West earlier in the conflict was offered by the fate of the last attempt made at pure volunteering. On April 21, 1864, the President announced the acceptance of an offer of 85,000 "hundred-day" volunteers (curiously misconstrued by the War Department as 100,000) made by the governors of Ohio, Indiana, Illinois, Wisconsin, and Iowa. These troops, to be mustered within twenty days and not to receive bounties or to be credited on the draft, were expected to administer the *coup de grâce* to the Confederacy. In spite of energetic efforts on the part of all concerned to elicit enthusiasm for the project it fell far short of its intent except in Ohio. Illinois, though granted an extension of the original time limit, hardly more than half filled her quota.[42] After a conference with Governor Morton the head of the recruiting service in Indiana reported to Washington:

The Governor says that if more men are required they must be drafted; that it will be impossible to procure volunteers, and that it would be injurious to make the effort and fail in it.

I think the difficulty of procuring volunteers, even for 100-days' service, shows that he is right in this opinion.[43]

While evidences accumulated of the difficulty of providing the manpower required by the ambitious military undertakings planned for 1864, organized sentiment for the abandonment of the war was still manifesting itself on the political level. The defeat of their most prominent leader in the Ohio gubernatorial contest had disappointed the peace Democrats of the Middle West, but it had not caused them to abandon or to modify their position. They seemed, rather, to throw off such restraints as the campaign had imposed upon them and prepared to define their attitude more clearly than ever before. More heartened by the size of Vallandigham's vote than discouraged by his failure to be elected, and refusing to admit that recent victories for the Union actually presaged a final triumph,[44] they openly set their goal at committing the national Democratic organization to an unconditional peace platform and peace candidate in the approaching presidential contest. Here and there were evidences that the movement was getting under way. In Chicago on December 3, 1863, a somewhat shadowy "consulting convention of the Democracy of the Northwestern states" was held at which resolutions were adopted declaring:

. . . that whatever be the theory of constitutional power, war as a means of restoration of the Union, is a delusion, involving the waste of human life, national bankruptcy, and the downfall of the republic.
. . . That we are in favor of *Peace*—an unconditional *Peace*.
. . . That we are in favor of the call of a convention to adjust existing differences among the states, believing that it is the only way contemplated and provided by the constitution for the settlement of such controversies.[45]

At a Jackson Day Banquet held at Columbus, Ohio, on January 8, 1864, William M. Corry, a spokesman of the extreme anti-war wing, declared that the party must give only incidental attention to the secondary issues of personal liberty and the conduct of the war and take its stand unequivocally on the essential issue of peace.[46]

But it was in Congress that the most striking avowals were made. On February 19, 1864, Representative Chilton A. White of Ohio told his colleagues, then sitting in Committee of the Whole on the naval appropriation bill:

I maintain that the war in which we are at present engaged is wrong in itself; that the policy adopted by the party in power for its prosecution is wrong; that the Union cannot be restored, or, if restored, maintained by the exercise of the coercive power of the Government, by war; that the war is opposed to the restoration of the Union, destructive of the rights of the States and the liberties of the people. It ought therefore, to be brought to a speedy and immediate close.

. . . .

The Union cannot be restored either in semblance or form by war. If we should succeed in overrunning the South with our arms, and reducing them to a state of subjection by force, we would be far, very far, from a restoration of the Union. That would be a Union founded in force, and not consent, the very opposite of that established by the wisdom of our fathers. It would be the union of England with Ireland, of Poland with Russia, of Hungary with Austria, a Union to be execrated and despised by every true American who breathes that spirit of patriotic piety that animated the bosoms of our fathers. It would be a Union of Hate pinned together by bayonets, a Union which it would cost us our liberties to maintain, which could only be preserved by the unholy trinity of perpetual war, perpetual taxation, and perpetual conscription. It may in the estimation of some be disloyal of me to say it but I think it, and will therefore say it. I have no heart for such a Union as that; I reject it, and should regard its establishment as the greatest calamity that ever befell my country except the war which produced it. It has already cost twenty million people at the North their liberties in the effort to establish it, and if it should be established they will never regain them while it endures.[47]

White believed, or affected to believe, that a peaceable compromise reunion was possible, but no such pretense was offered by another Ohio congressman, Alexander Long, who on April 8 demanded disunion as the price of peace. He declared:

If the time ever was when the Union could have been restored by war (which I do not believe) it has long since been dispelled by emancipation, confiscation, amnesty, and like proclamations. . . .

. . . .

. . . Much better would it have been for us in the beginning, much better would it be for us now, to consent to a division of our magnificent empire and cultivate amicable relations with our estranged brethren, than to seek to hold them to us by the power of the sword.

. . . Here let me say on the experience of my individual belief, that if it had been understood in the North as in the South that by the terms of the Federal compact a State had the right to secede from the Union, this disruption would never have occurred. . . .

. . . . It is said that no confederacy can exist by a recognition of this principle, but such was not the view of the fathers of the Government. It was not the view of Jefferson and Madison in their immortal resolutions of 1798 and 1799.

. . . .

. . . As will be judged, perhaps, by the tenor of these remarks, I am reluctantly and despondingly forced to the conclusion that the Union is lost never to be restored. I regard all dreams of the restoration of the Union . . . as worse than idle. . . .

. . . .

I do not share in the belief entertained by many of my political friends on this floor and elsewhere, that any peace is attainable upon the basis of union and reconstruction. If the Democratic party were in power to-day I have no idea, and honesty compels me to declare it, that they could restore the Union of thirty-four States. My mind has undergone an entire change upon that subject; and I now believe that there are but two alternatives, and they are either an acknowledgement of the independence of the South as an independent nation, or their complete subjugation and extermination as a people; and of these alternatives, I prefer the former.

. . . I do not believe there can be any prosecution of the war against a sovereign State under the Constitution, and I do not believe that a war so carried on can be prosecuted so as to render it proper, justifiable or expedient. *An unconstitutional war can only be carried on in an unconstitutional manner,* and to prosecute it further . . . as a war waged against the confederates as an independent nation, for the purpose of conquest and subjugation . . . I am equally opposed.

I say further, Mr. Chairman, that if this war is to be still further prosecuted, I, for one, prefer that it shall be done under the auspices of those who now conduct its management, as I do not want the party with which I am connected to be in any degree responsible for its result, which cannot be otherwise than disastrous and suicidal; let the responsibility remain where it is, until we can have a change of policy instead of men, if such a thing is possible. Nothing could be more fatal to the Democratic party than to seek to come into power pledged to a continuance of the war policy. Such a policy would be a libel upon its creed in the past and the ideas that lay at the basis of all free government, and would lead to its complete demoralization and ruin. I believe the masses of the Democratic party are for peace, that they would be placed in a false position if they should nominate a war candidate for the Presidency and seek to make the issue upon the narrow basis of how the war should be prosecuted.

For my own part, as I have already indicated, I fear that our old Government cannot be preserved, even under the best auspices and with any policy that may be now adopted, yet I desire to see the Democratic party, with which I have always been connected, preserve its consistency and republican character unshaken.[48]

Long's pronouncement, than which it would be hard to imagine anything less ambiguous, brought a storm in the House. Speaker Colfax left the chair to move the expulsion of the outspoken Ohioan. Republicans gave their support to the resolution, arguing that the avowal of sentiments in favor of disunion, when not absolutely forced by complete military defeat, was a violation of the congressman's oath of office; Democrats upheld the right of a member of the House to express whatever views he might hold provided that he did not violate the decorum of that body.[49] In the end Democratic strength made impossible the two-thirds vote required for expulsion, although resolutions of censure were voted in which a majority of the Democrats concurred.[50]

In the country at large Long received some support,[51] but the Democratic press and party leaders were in general not willing to commit themselves to so forthright a position. Political expediency had more appeal than rigid principle, no matter what views might be entertained in private, and they were aware that more votes could be drawn from those tired of the war if the lure of negotiated reunion were kept on view. Such an attitude prevailed in the Ohio state Democratic convention held in Columbus on March 23, 1864, and resulted in a partial setback for the peace-at-any-price group. The slate of the latter faction for delegates-at-large for the national nominating convention consisting of Vallandigham, Medary (editor of the *Crisis*), Edson B. Olds (martyr of arbitrary imprisonment), and Chilton A. White, was rejected for one giving representation to varying shades of opinion, consisting of George H. Pendleton, William Allen, Allen Thurman, and Rufus P. Ranney. In keeping with this policy a series of resolutions was adopted that was a masterpiece of ambiguity susceptible of interpretation to satisfy all views. The key resolution asserted that

. . . we are opposed to the prosecution of the war for the subjugation of States, or for the purpose of depriving them of their sovereignty, or impairing their constitutional rights, and being satisfied that its continued prosecution for such objects will in the end prove the utter destruction of civil liberty, we, therefore, demand the immediate inauguration of peaceable means to attain an honorable settlement and the restoration of the Union under the Constitution.[52]

By no means discouraged in their project to commit the party nationally to their views, though disgusted by the equivocation displayed in this convention, the out-and-out peace men of the section determined to carry the fight to the congressional districts. Here, where the true popular sentiment would be most apparent and where the occupational timidity of the professional politician would be less felt, it was hoped that delegates fully committed to peace would be chosen. And circumstances would soon operate to give this hope foundation.

Meanwhile another movement for bringing the war to an end was in progress. During the first two years of the war the secret anti-war societies of the Midwest had been essentially local bodies, designed to protect their members against mob violence or arbitrary arrest, to oppose conscription, and in an extremist fashion to foster the interests of the Democratic party. The lodges of the Knights of the Golden Circle had had a somewhat uniform ritual and a community of purpose, but there had been no effective central governing authority. In the summer of 1863, however, a movement got under way for bringing these autonomous chapters together into a new, centralized organization. In the process a distinctly revolutionary cast began for the first time to appear. A certain Phineas C. Wright, a native of New Orleans, had in 1862 been permitted to move to St. Louis. There he became associated with a Missouri organization bearing the exotic title of the Corps de Belgique. This society was similar to the Knights of the Golden Circle but, because of conditions in Missouri, was more truly pro-Confederate in its views. Under Wright's direction the Corps was sometime in the spring of 1863 transformed into the Order of American Knights, with Wright as Supreme Grand Commander. A grandiloquent ritual was adopted, in certain aspects distinctly treasonable. In the second degree of the order an initiate took an oath, "At all times, if needs be, to take up arms in the cause of the oppressed—in my country first of all—against any monarch, prince, potentate, power, or government usurped, which may be found in arms and waging war against a people or peoples who are endeavoring to establish or have inaugurated a government for themselves of their own free choice in accordance with and founded upon the eternal principles of Truth." [53]

Soon the new organization spread into adjoining states. On June 17, 1863, Wright authorized the setting up of a hierarchy for Illinois. S. Corning Judd, a Democratic politician of little more than local influence residing in Lewistown, was elected Grand Commander for the state. Toward the latter part of August a similar organization for Indiana was established in a meeting at Terre Haute, with Harrison H. Dodd as Grand Commander. Thereupon the Order of American Knights apparently absorbed most of the former membership of the Knights of the Golden Circle in the Midwest and even spread to New York and other Eastern states.[54]

It can hardly be doubted that a large part of the membership did not regard the new fraternity as differing essentially in its purpose from the old, and many probably joined it merely as a party club. Others were aware of a changed direction and some dropped out in consequence, but a great many seemed to welcome the new militancy. Elements disposed toward some sort of revolutionary orientation had been steadily increasing in the areas where the society's strength was greatest. Certain of the peace Democrats had been convinced by Vallandigham's defeat that they must resort to revolution if they were to succeed in realizing their aims; deserters, draft evaders, and other desperate men constituted a nucleus for revolt; and a series of incidents involving returned soldiers tended to inflame the public mind. After the uproar over the Vallandigham case the administration had attempted to avoid military arrests of citizens for crimes of opinion,[55] but the actions of soldiers home on furlough served to arouse the tempers of peace men to a fighting pitch. Many of these soldiers had been planning chastisement of opponents of the war for some time,[56] and on their homecoming they turned to Democratic newspaper offices and leaders as objects of their resentment. In the spring of 1863 the *Crisis* and the Marietta (Ohio) *Republican* (a Democratic paper) had suffered at the hands of soldier mobs, the former sustaining damages estimated at between $600 and $800.[57] The next year a number of other newspapers in the Midwest, including, in Ohio, the Mahoning *Sentinel,* Lancaster *Ohio Eagle,* Dayton *Empire,* and Fremont *Messenger,* and the Chester (Illinois) *Picket Guard* and the Keokuk (Iowa) *Constitution-Democrat* suffered similar visitations.[58] In Greenville, Ohio, in April a company of returned soldiers staged a general riot, assaulting Democratic citizens and breaking up the law office of former Congressman (and later Governor) William Allen.[59]

Violent clashes between soldiers and Copperheads were, under the circumstances, all but inevitable. Near South English, Keokuk County, Iowa, in August 1863 an encounter (remembered as the "Skunk River War") took place in which several men were killed, including a preacher named Cyphert Tally, a principal leader of the peace faction of the region. To prevent a local civil war the governor was forced to call out eleven companies of home guards.[60] Other clashes occurred at Canton, Ohio, in March [61] and at Lewistown, Illinois, in May 1864, neither with serious consequences. In the latter affair the Copperheads, after having come into town with the boasted purpose of "cleaning out" a number of soldiers home on furlough, fled when someone fired a gun.[62] A more sanguinary encounter took place at Paris, in Edgar County, Illinois. On March 2 John M. Eden, Democratic congressman from the district, was scheduled to speak, but a group of furloughed soldiers, who had already engaged in a number of bouts of drunken rowdyism, apparently determined to prevent this. Eden canceled the engagement when he became aware of the danger in the situation, but some of his followers nevertheless got into a fracas with the soldiers in which three men were wounded. The first reports that got out had matters more serious still, and the military commander of the Department of the Ohio, General Heintzelman, was ordered by the Secretary of War to take command of the situation—until investigation on the spot proved such a step unnecessary.[63] A few days later a similar situation at Charleston, Illinois, led to a virtual pitched battle. Here a group of Democrats, led by Sheriff John O'Hair, had come to a rally with guns concealed in their farm wagons in anticipation of trouble. When a fist fight started, the guns were suddenly produced and turned on the soldiers with fatal effect.[64] A major and five other men of the 54th Regiment and three citizens were killed and four soldiers and eight civilians wounded.[65] Another fatal encounter was reported at Hardin in Calhoun County, Illinois, as sequel to the alleged shooting by a returned soldier of a man who had cheered for Jeff Davis.[66]

All such affairs, in which a large share of the initial blame was ascribable to the soldiers, served to stimulate the growth and stiffen the attitude of the secret orders. Republican papers were aware of a quickening of the activities of the organization,[67] although Democratic papers, with what can hardly be regarded as other than a brazen disregard for truth, were still denying the existence of any such association.[68] On February 17, 1864, a military division of the Order of American Knights was instituted for Indiana, a step of such import that a number of fairly prominent politicians in the state, who had been previously affiliated with the society in anticipation of assistance to their own undertakings, severed their connections. By this withdrawal the order tended to come under the control of its more extreme leaders, few of them men of more than local influence, such as county office holders or members of the legislature.

On February 22, 1864, an important change took place in the affairs of the O.A.K. On that day a so-called national meeting of its moving spirits took place in New York in which the name was changed to the Sons of Liberty, thus claiming spiritual kinship with the patriotic society of the Revolutionary period. The ritual was reformed to delete any oaths of a treasonable nature, although a promise of strict obedience to the officers still left the way open for committing the membership to dangerous projects. On the way to the gathering two of the delegates went through Canada and secretly inducted Vallandigham into membership, at the same time securing his consent for his name to be proposed for the office of Supreme Commander. The proposal was submitted and adopted, and a leader of national importance for the first time was in direction of affairs.[69] Vallandigham's motives in the transaction can, necessarily, be only surmised. Possibly the military outlook was such that he was beginning to feel that, unless a diversion were made in the North, the Confederacy would soon be overwhelmed, a result which he sincerely believed would also destroy the foundations of the government of the United States. Then, too, seeing in actions by the Democratic party in Ohio indications that he was being relegated to a minor position in that organization, he may have seized upon the pledge of unquestioning support of the membership of this body as a means of rehabilitating his political influence. Except in Missouri, the members of the Order of American Knights in the West accepted the new name, ritual, and leadership and prepared to follow the latter toward whatever goal might be decided upon.

The revolutionary schemes of the Sons of Liberty were now to be given assistance and direction from a new source. With Grant and Sherman beginning to encircle the Confederacy in a crushing embrace while the blockade served to sap its energies for the critical encounter, the South was finally impelled to give direct attention

Captain THOMAS H. HINES at 23

to her last resource—the promotion of disaffection in the Midwest. On March 16, 1864, the Confederate Secretary of War placed the chief responsibility for such an undertaking in the hands of Captain Thomas H. Hines, formerly of Morgan's cavalry, a man who would in later years achieve the staid eminence of the chief justice-ship of Kentucky but whose wartime exploits would merit the pen of an E. Phillips Oppenheim. Credited with having been the master mind in the escape of his commander and himself from the Ohio State Penitentiary after the fiasco of the Morgan raid through Indiana and Ohio in the previous year, he had prevented the recapture of Morgan on the flight back to the Confederate lines by permitting himself to fall into the hands of a federal scouting troop and then had again made his escape. For months during 1864 he traveled at will through enemy territory, his life every moment in danger, but seemingly able to elude apprehension with almost fictional ease. He was a slender young man with a sleepy-eyed appearance that belied his quick mind, favored a sweeping mustache, and had just a suggestion of the lurking panther in his carriage. He was eminently qualified to undertake the task assigned to him, although he would be strangely omitted from the usual listings of the great secret service operatives of the war. Hines was to go to Canada to arrange for the return to the South of the considerable number of sorely needed Confederate soldiers who had managed to make their way there after escape from Northern prison camps. In addition, he was to undertake any larger schemes for assistance to the Confederacy that might appear feasible from information obtained in the Middle West and Canada.

About a month later President Davis appointed a commission consisting of Jacob Thompson, Secretary of the Interior under Buchanan, Clement C. Clay, member of the United States Senate and then the Confederate Senate from Alabama, and J. P. Holcomb, with directions to proceed through the blockade to Canada on a similar undertaking. After futile efforts to subsidize Northern newspapers for propaganda purposes and unproductive conferences at Niagara Falls with Horace Greeley and former Attorney General Jeremiah Black, the commission broke up. Holcomb proceeded to Europe, Clay elected to remain in eastern Canada to promote schemes of his own, and Thompson, from the safety of the Canadian side of the international boundary, turned his attention to the Midwest. On May 27 Captain Hines was directed to place himself under Thompson's direction, although he remained the real driving force in the schemes that followed. The possibility of utilizing the Sons of Liberty in measures favorable to the Confederacy was readily apparent. A meeting between Thompson and Vallandigham on June 11 was followed by other conferences. The Supreme Commander did Thompson the honor of initiating him into the Sons of Liberty and, although insisting upon his warm desire for the restoration of the Union on its original basis, was willing to discuss the practicability of creating a "Western Confederacy" through a revolutionary uprising. Other leaders of the order were even less circumspect in their discussions with the Confederate representatives. Gradually there evolved a scheme for the seizing of the governments of Illinois, Indiana, Ohio, Kentucky, and Missouri and the institution of provisional control by the officers of the Sons of Liberty. The armed forces that were to effect the overturn would consist of three contingents—Confederate refugees in Canada (chiefly soldiers escaped from Northern prison camps), the military section of the Sons of Liberty, and the prisoners still held in large numbers in camps of the Northwest. For the arming of the Sons of Liberty and their transportation to crucial points at the proper time money was lavishly provided by the Confederate commissioners, nearly $500,000 all told. Vallandigham, with that meticulous, legalistic desire to keep the record straight that was so characteristic of him, refused personally to accept the funds. But since he not only gave tacit approval of their purpose but recommended the adjutant-general of the order, James A. Barrett, as a proper person to distribute them, his later claims of perfect innocence in the matter became subject to something more than doubt. Hines and his coadjutors seem to have been tongue-in-cheek about the more grandiose expectations of the plot, but they nevertheless thought that it had possibilities of usefulness to the Confederacy that made it worth the investment involved. Aware of the uncertain character of their allies, and that they had a far greater propensity for big talk than for decisive action, the Confederate agents nevertheless hoped to maneuver them into some overt action from which they would be unable to retreat. In such circumstances their very instability might cause them to fight in desperation. At least enough might be set on foot to effect the release and arming of the inmates of the prison camps. These men, veterans of many battles and presumably at such a pitch of exasperation from long confinement that they would be ripe for any desperate undertaking, were of an entirely different caliber. For some months they had given evidences of restlessness that suggested a readiness to support such an undertaking to the utmost.[70] Having once overpowered the feeble garrisons confining the prisoners, the Confederate agents expected to arm the prisoners from federal arsenals which were in several cases close at hand and thus collect an effective fighting force in the heart of the North. The Sons of Liberty would serve as auxiliaries. They did not put much stock in the Copperhead talk of overthrowing the state governments of the Midwest, but they did feel that there was a chance that, once set in motion, this activity might create a diversion that would force a partial withdrawal of federal troops from the South to crush it. In view of the military situation, and considering, too, the general deterioration of morale in the section (a fact they had discerned through numerous individuals with whom they had come in contact), the whole aspect of the conflict might possibly be reversed.[71]

Vallandigham proposed to return to Ohio, where his anticipated arrest by the federal authorities would give the signal for revolt. It remained to be seen whether such an uprising could be called forth and, if so, whether it could materially affect the outcome of the war.

CHAPTER VIII

The Period of Weariness

(June 3–September 2, 1864)

THE project of an armed uprising against the war was now to be jeopardized from an unexpected, even paradoxical, quarter. Early in the summer of 1864 the military situation took a sharp turn for the worse, with the result that prospects for overthrowing the administration at the polls and replacing it with a President and Congress pledged to peace suddenly became so bright that the use of force to achieve this end seemed unnecessary. As the veteran, powerful, and splendidly equipped armies of Grant and Sherman had begun their concerted offensive in May, few in the North had doubted that the war was entering the final phase. It had seemed impossible that the Confederacy would be able for long to offer an effective defense against the sheer crushing weight of such forces. But an early blight fell upon their movements. Grant's flanking action from the Wilderness to the James River, marked by unprecedented casualties culminating on June 3 in the slaughter at Cold Harbor, came on June 19 to a standstill in front of Petersburg. Here, in almost the position held by McClellan when the Peninsular campaign had been abandoned two years before, the Army of the Potomac lay powerless, unable to pierce the elaborate system of forts and entrenchments which Lee had constructed in the months of respite since Gettysburg. Likewise, Sherman's thrusts against the flawless parries of Joe Johnston were blocked at Kenesaw Mountain on June 27. Ahead lay the fortifications about Atlanta, comparable in strength to those of Richmond and Petersburg. The war had become a stalemate. The two great military leaders of the Confederacy were evolving a new type of warfare based on large-scale semi-permanent field entrenchments, prophetic of the Western Front of the First World War.

Lee, always keenly aware of the psychological aspects of war, seized on this moment to give the North a dramatic reminder that the Confederacy was still very much alive. In 1862 he had relieved the pressure on Richmond by sending Stonewall Jackson to threaten Washington. Now to play a similar role he chose General Jubal Early, bald, bent, piercing-eyed, whose shrill treble was reputed to be capable of the most lurid profanity in the Confederate army. In spite of his almost legendary eccentricity Early, who opposed secession in 1861 but afterward became such an "unreconstructed rebel" that he would go to his grave without having taken an oath of submission, was a first-rate fighting man. With such troops as Lee could spare he dashed down the Shenandoah Valley, swept through Hagerstown and Frederick, and in the second week of July entered the District of Columbia, which had been stripped of its defenders to reinforce Grant. The Northern capital, it appeared, was more in danger than the Southern. Although repelled by the last-minute arrival of troops sent back from Grant's army, the Confederate force succeeded in making a leisurely and unimpeded return to the Shenandoah Valley, laden with prisoners and booty. The whole episode seemed a final demonstration of the clumsiness and ineptitude of the leadership of the Northern forces. Hopes had been equally bright in the spring of 1862, and incompetence had dissipated them. Was the story to be repeated? Millions in the North began to wonder.

On June 7, before the full reaction to military reverses was felt, the Union Republican convention, meeting at Baltimore, had renominated Lincoln. The popular conviction still persisting at that time that the war could best be carried on under the existing experienced leadership had made the nomination possible, for without it the fabulously clever wire-pulling of Lincoln and his political henchmen could hardly have been successful. It had been accomplished, however, in the face of powerful opposition, and certain of the sharp expedients that had been employed to bring it about had left many of the other party leaders nursing rancorous and rebellious feelings. Beneath the apparent unity of the convention there were emotions that needed only some marked setback to the administration to effect their release.[1] Before the convention one of Senator Trumbull's constituents had attempted to analyze the state of opinion as he observed it:

. . . The fact is the people are not satisfied with the loose way in which the war is carried on. Yet they dare not say much and they hardly dare change, yet it would take but little to throw them into confusion and loose [*sic*] us the election. If the democrats nominate McClellan and we nominate Mr. Lincoln and some of the dissatisfied start out on Butler or Fremont we should be whipped. . . .[2]

The change in the military situation now constituted an ideal precipitant for discontent within the Republican fold. Democratic prospects brightened.

Not only were the chances of Democratic success increased; the peace faction within that party was strengthened. The change in sentiment was illustrated by developments in Ohio. When the state convention had met at Columbus on March 23 to choose delegates-at-large, the general expectation of Union victory lent cautiousness to the stand taken on the question of peace. A noncommittal platform had been adopted and the general state delegation selected was dominated by moderates.[3] But, when the time came for the picking of delegates from each congressional district, the military outlook was becoming daily more gloomy, and the result was that these more popularly chosen representatives were men generally identified with the peace faction.[4] Many of the district conventions adopted at the same time positive declarations against the war. The resolutions of the Ninth (Sandusky) District called for immediate peace; [5] the convention of the Eleventh, meeting at Portsmouth, specifically instructed its delegates to support none but peace candidates and peace measures in the national convention; [6] that of the Fourteenth at Ashland voted that "the delegates to the National Democratic Convention from this Congressional District are hereby instructed to use all honorable means as delegates to the Chicago Convention, to secure the nomination only of peace candidates upon a peace platform, for the Presidency and Vice Presidency of the United States"; [7] and the Fourth District meeting at Piqua adopted a statement of belief that there existed in the federal government no constitutional power to use force against a sovereign state.[8] Vallandigham and former Governor Thomas H. Seymour of Connecticut were understood to be looked upon with most favor as possible candidates by the peace element of Ohio.[9] The *Crisis,* unequivocating advocate of peace at any cost,

was sent into raptures. Under the heading "OHIO FOR PEACE—
THE PEOPLE HAVE SPOKEN AND THE VICTORY IS WON!" the editor
wrote, "Let the Democrats of Ohio rejoice—let the friends of Peace
everywhere rejoice, that Ohio will stand in the Chicago Convention almost unanimous for PEACE—a peace candidate and a peace
platform." [10] From an examination of the list of the delegates selected it appeared to the editor that no more than eight would support Representative S. S. Cox's plan of nominating General Mc-
Clellan and adopting a platform condemning the abandonment of
the war but favoring the calling of a peace convention while the
fighting continued. The remaining thirty-six, possibly more, were
believed to be committed to the peace view, and included such
men as Vallandigham, Chilton A. White, Medary himself, Edson
B. Olds, Archibald McGregor, and Alexander Long.[11] The editorial concluded, "Ohio may, therefore, be set down as triumphantly for the peace policy, and as goes Ohio, so will go the
Union." [12]

To add volume to the expression of their wishes the peace men
called local meetings throughout the Midwest to declare their opposition to any equivocation on the question of continuing the war.
The Democratic Club of Galena, Jo Daviess County, Illinois, unanimously voted approval of the position taken by Alexander Long
and announced "that it is to such men we look for leadership!" [13]
Legislator James W. Singleton of Illinois told a meeting of the
Young Men's Democratic Union Association of New York that his
state would insist upon a peace platform for the party,[14] and a convention of the Hendricks County, Indiana, Democrats heard Harrison H. Dodd, commander of the Sons of Liberty in that state, advance the proposal of a Northwest Confederacy as a temporary
expedient looking to a reunion with the South. Dodd threatened
civil war if the administration should attempt military interference
with this or any other action which the Democratic party should
attempt to achieve through the regular channels of politics.[15] Many
gatherings of this type were reported in Ohio. The Democrats of
Jackson Township, Jackson County, adopted resolutions warning
that they would support none but peace candidates; [16] a joint gathering from Franklin, Licking, and Delaware counties, held at Columbus on July 23, heard speakers urge the people not to submit

to further conscription and to resort to insurrection if arbitrary arrests were resumed, and listened to promises that regardless of whether a peace or war man were elected president "we will never consent to the prosecution of this war"; [17] and a great peace meeting at Bucyrus, Crawford County, resolved its opposition to further conscription and insisted that the war should be no longer continued.[18] Actions of the same nature were reported by meetings in Union, Delaware, Athens, Stark, and Ashland counties.[19]

The anti-war press also swung into action in the old familiar way —reveling in reports of checks, disasters, and slaughter visited upon the Union armies, describing each with loving detail, exaggerating reverses and casualties, giving credence to rumors of disasters about to overtake Grant and Sherman, and insinuating that the troops were ripe for mutiny. It slyly suggested, in contrast to this dismal prospect, that the South would be willing to listen to a reasonable proposal for reunion.[20] An editorial in the *Crisis* observed, "If nothing else would impress upon the people the absolute necessity of stopping this war, its utter failure to accomplish any results to encourage the most enthusiastic advocate of subjugating the South, [the war news of the week] would be sufficient," [21] and prominence was given to still more extreme expressions from contributors.[22] The Chicago *Times* of August 1 concluded that a Northwest Confederacy might well be the result of almost inevitable defeat:

The continuance of this war on present terms is as certain to result in the independence of the seceded States as night and day are to follow each other. It is just as certain that the different sections of the Republic, after one extended division, will ally themselves with such portions as can and will most practically assist in the advancement of their respective interests.

Another factor complicated the reigning uncertainty. On July 19, 1864, the President issued a call for 500,000 additional volunteers, deficiencies on assigned quotas to be drafted on September 5.[23] All the obstacles to recruiting that had been increasing during the previous two years were by now fully developed. Democrats sought to discredit the call by charging it with discrimination against the Midwestern states. The La Crosse *Democrat* snarled,

"If the people of Wisconsin were not natural born cowards . . . if they were not as great slaves as the blacks this war is now being conducted to benefit, they would stand shoulder to shoulder and swear by the living God that not a man nor a dollar should be sent to war from the West until the East had filled her quotas." [24] Another paper bitterly charged:

Before making this last call, Mass. was advised that it would be made, and the provisions were arranged to suit her case exactly. She had time to hunt up negro substitutes for her quota, as if they were deemed good enough to stand side by side with the brave sons of Indiana and Illinois! Her patriotic (!) Gov. Andrew the most clamorous for the war, the most blatant for equality of negroes with white men, has bent every energy and beat every bush, to find negro substitutes for the *brave* boys of the Old Bay State.

. . . Illinois can afford to enroll her chivalrous and stalwart sons alongside of southern niggers, and who have been picked up wherever they could be had for the money, by Gov. Andrew, who cannot spare any Mass. men from the field of labor in which they are engaged, when calico brings fifty-cents a yard, and brown muslins that formerly brought four or five cents range from twenty-five to thirty cents! . . .[25]

Although high bounties were offered and contributions were being received for the relief of the families of those enlisting, such inducements were counterbalanced by the attraction of greatly increased civilian wages, even farm hands being paid from $2 to $5 a day in the harvest field.[26] The public was apathetic and volunteering was meager—a fact not only apparent from the statistics but implicit in charges going back and forth that recruiting agents were attempting to lure men from other states,[27] in the efforts being made to get quotas decreased, and in authorization for the enlistment of rebel prisoners.[28] Governor Brough of Ohio begged the Secretary of War, "For the first time in my varied and extensive official correspondence with you I ask a reduction of the military forces you demand from Ohio." [29]

It was readily apparent that the greater part of the call would have to be filled by drafting, and state and federal officials were agreed that this task would have to be performed in the face of possible widespread resistance.[30] Governor Brough feared that from

10,000 to 15,000 soldiers might be required to enforce conscription in Ohio; [31] Lieutenant-Colonel Charles S. Lovell, acting assistant provost marshal general for Wisconsin, forwarded to his superior in Washington reports from all over that state of incipient trouble, coupled with the recommendation that at least a company of troops be assigned to each congressional district; [32] and General Heintzelman, commanding the Department of Ohio and not by habit an alarmist, thought that not less than 25,000 troops might be needed in Ohio, Indiana, and Illinois. [33] Yet so great was the need for these troops at the front that General Rosecrans, in command at St. Louis, informed Governor Yates that he could not spare 150 soldiers requested by the latter to assist in the enforcement of writs in Montgomery and Fayette counties. [34] The best that the federal authorities could do was to offer arms, subsistence, pay, and transportation for such forces as the states might be able to muster for this special need. [35] The problem had aspects other than the danger of armed resistance. Republicans feared and Democrats hoped that the unpopularity of a draft carried out at the height of a political campaign would insure Lincoln's defeat. [36] And, finally, there was the question whether men so opposed to entering the army as to require such a force to compel them to serve would have any worth as soldiers.

Again, as in the campaign of 1862, the Republicans, faced by widespread discontent among the people and an aggressive Democratic attack, seemed more intent on quarreling among themselves than on preserving a united front against the common enemy. The congressional radicals had tried hard to prevent Lincoln's renomination. In January 1864, members of the National Executive Committee, headed by Senator Samuel C. Pomeroy, of Kansas, had distributed a pamphlet savagely attacking Lincoln and endeavoring to promote the candidacy of Chase. Alleged precedents for a one-term principle were advanced and it was asserted that

there is still another and more forcible objection to the nomination of Mr. Lincoln.

The people have lost all confidence in his ability to suppress the rebellion and restore the Union. It is impossible to put out of view the fact that there is a general feeling of disappointment in the loyal North, that after such a wasting of its precious blood, and such a vast expenditure of treasure, the rebellion continues unsubdued; and all the promises of the Administration time and again for its speedy overthrow have been falsified.

. . . .

. . . The responsibility rests *alone* upon him. He has been weak and vascillating [sic] throughout, seemingly incapable of settling upon any definite line of policy in regard to the rebellion.

. . . .

Should Mr. Lincoln be forced upon the country in defiance of the better judgement of the Republican party, and the Democratic party be judicious in planting a candidate for the prosecution of the war. . . . Mr. Lincoln will be most unquestionably defeated, unless he should be tempted in an evil hour, to use the military power in his hands by suppressing the freedom of elections in the loyal States. . . .[37]

Combining denunciation of Lincoln with the assertion, astounding from a Republican source, that the President could have secured the peaceable return of the Southern states to the Union had he been willing to guarantee the integrity of slavery, the publication was disposed not only to inflame intra-party resentments but to provide the Democrats with weapons of which they were not slow to take advantage.[38] Shortly afterward, from the same general source had come the "Pomeroy Circular" of similar import, followed on March 10 by an explanatory speech before Congress by Senator Pomeroy.[39] Lincoln's hold on the imagination of the Republican masses and his clever, and not infrequently ruthless, manipulation of party machinery succeeded in bringing about his renomination by the national convention with the open opposition of only one state delegation, that of Missouri,[40] but the radicals, foreseeing an approaching struggle over reconstruction as well as nursing resentments for past disagreements,[41] could muster little enthusiasm for the ticket.

As the summer wore on and the unpromising military outlook was re-emphasized by each day's news, even the popularity that Lincoln had built up among the common people began to fade, not so much taking the shape of specific criticisms of the administration as manifesting itself in a general dejection that seemed ready to admit the hopelessness of the war policy that it was attempting to pursue. One observer reported:

Within the last few weeks Mr. Lincoln's popularity as a candidate for reelection has had such an abatement that it may be said not to have any existence at all in this section of the State. At the rate this thing is going on now there will soon be no hope of his reelection. . . . If the election were to come off now not a few who at the last election voted for Lincoln would if McClellan were a candidate vote for him some would vote for Fremont and more would not vote at all. I hope this state of things will not continue long but that the confidence of the people in their cause and its final success as well as in themselves may be restored.[42]

Another wrote, "I am stating my honest conviction when I tell you he is daily losing strength here, and there is (sic) in more than one mouth murmurs of dissatisfaction where there was lately nothing but praise." [43] Military victories would be likely to dissipate much of this feeling, but further defeats would greatly augment its strength.

A potentially dangerous factor in the situation was the Fremont ticket. At the time of the nomination of the Republican candidate of 1856 by a haphazard convention of malcontents at Cleveland on May 31, 1864 this ticket had been something of a joke. But in the developments of the next three months it came increasingly to be feared that disgruntled elements, particularly the Germans, marshaled by the St. Louis *Missouri Democrat* and their own language press, might support him in such numbers as to effect not his election but the defeat of Lincoln by the Democratic candidate.[44]

The issuance of the Wade-Davis Manifesto on August 5, 1864, savagely denouncing Lincoln for his conciliatory reconstruction policy, added to the dissension, and nine days later a further division seemed about to take place. On the 14th day of August a meeting of New York journalists and others, including David Dudley Field, Congressman Henry Winter Davis, and Professor Francis Lieber, took stock of the situation. Agreeing that Lincoln's chances were hopeless, they decided to issue a private call for a new national convention to be held in Cincinnati on September 28, at which Lincoln would be replaced by a more promising candidate.[45] Salmon P. Chase, who had petulantly resigned from the cabinet after Lincoln's renomination, was being urged by many of his supporters to bolt the Union ticket [46] and had returned answers that led some to believe that he might be prevailed upon to accept an independent nomination for the presidency.[47] With discouragement general, with Horace Greeley badgering him through the widely read *Tribune* to attempt a negotiated peace, and his own party apparently disintegrating into mutually repellent factions, Lincoln had little reason to be in any way hopeful for the future. On August 23 he secretly recorded the conviction that his reelection and the victorious conclusion of the war were unlikely if not impossible.[48]

On the other hand the revolutionary designs of the Sons of Liberty and their secret allies had been suffering repeated setbacks. First, Vallandigham's return to Ohio in the middle of June failed to provide the expected occasion for rising because the Washington authorities decided, after some hesitation, not to order his arrest.[49] The next occasion chosen was the meeting of the Democratic national convention, scheduled for July 4 in Chicago, and that was spoiled by the postponement of the convention. July 16 was then selected, it being expected that opponents of the war would be stirred up by a new call for troops. But the Copperhead leaders were showing definite signs of loss of nerve and their lack of preparation and co-ordination was becoming increasingly apparent. The arrest of some of the principal "S.O.L.'s" in Kentucky, after their return from conferences in Canada with the Confederate representatives, was definitely disturbing and created a fear that spies and informers were learning their secrets. Accordingly the leaders of the Sons of Liberty were forced to report to their Confederate friends that further devices for arousing the public mind would have to be provided before an uprising could be brought about. On June 22, at a conference between the Copperheads and the Southern agents at St. Catharines, Ontario, their plans were redrafted and preparations were made to stage a series of huge demonstrations for peace at Peoria, Springfield, and Chicago, successively. The meeting at Chicago on August 16 was to be the occasion for the revolt, simultaneous gatherings being arranged for other cities on the same date. Jacob Thompson paid over large sums to be used to defray the transportation costs involved. The attendance at the Peoria meeting was gratifying, and the people applauded the sentiments of the principal speaker, Amos Green of Edgar County, who was in charge of the military preparations of the Sons of Liberty in Illinois:

There is no longer a question before us as to whether we can subjugate the South.—The great question with us is, whether we will be able to save from the wreck our own liberties. . . .

. . . .

In September next a heartless and relentless call for five hundred thousand more men—a heartless and relentless conscription—is to be enforced throughout the State. One of Lincoln's Provost Marshals will cross your threshold, drag you from your home, tear you from your loved ones to die under the torrid Sun of the South or be stricken down in battle. . . . Let us no longer crouch at the feet of power with our petitions. Let us stand up and *demand* that the rights and liberties bequeathed us by our fathers be respected, and proclaim if they are not respected, we will maintain them as our fathers achieved them.[50]

On August 15 a smaller gathering at Hamilton, Ohio, adopted resolutions declaring that

the States have the right to withdraw their consent to the Union, and resume their independence, by repealing their ordinance of accession, and passing ordinances of secession.

. . . That a State having been withdrawn from the Federation . . . cannot be invaded with a purpose to compel its return.

. . . .

. . . We but perform a natural and social duty in declaring "to all whom it may concern," that *no citizen of Ohio, resident of Butler county,* shall be compelled to join the Federal army to consummate the avowed designs of the enemies of State rights, even should it prove necessary to give effect to this decision *by force and with arms.*

Resolved that the citizens of this country, who are opposed to a further prosecution of the war, *should prepare for such a contingency.*

And on August 13 a meeting at Fort Wayne, Indiana, resolved "that the honor, dignity, and safety of *the people demand that against ruin and enslavement, they must afford to themselves the protection which usurpation and tyranny denies them."* [51] One at Iowa City adopted comparable resolutions.[52] But at Peoria and elsewhere it was apparent that in demanding peace and the abandonment of

JACOB THOMPSON

conscription most of the audience looked to political rather than revolutionary activity to achieve these ends.

The rallies at Springfield and Chicago brought out comparatively small crowds and were otherwise discouraging to the revolutionaries. Members of the State Central Committee of the Democratic party in Indiana, some of whom were or had been members of the Sons of Liberty, acted to head off the attempt of Grand Commander Harrison H. Dodd to have a party mass meeting at Indianapolis on the 16th. They wanted nothing to interfere with a political outlook that was growing daily more promising. On August 13 they issued a public announcement urging people of the state not to resist conscription but to seek redress in political action.[53] In the face of opposition from such sources, the arrests made in Kentucky, and the parallel publication of their rituals and the revelation of some of their activities it was decided that the prospects for a successful *coup d'état* were inauspicious. August 16 came and passed without disturbance.[54]

The Confederate agents, however, were determined not to abandon the project, and another conference was held at London, Canada. The Sons of Liberty still professed to be willing to undertake a revolt if a suitable occasion could be found, and it was agreed that the Democratic national convention at Chicago, finally scheduled for August 29, would offer the most favorable opportunity. This time the Confederates determined to see that the chance should not be wasted and made arrangements to be on hand themselves. About 70 former soldiers of the Confederate armies, under the command of Captains Hines and Castleman, made their way to the convention city. The Copperhead "generals" promised to have 50,000 of their followers present, and Charles Walsh of Chicago had been supplied with funds to equip two regiments of revolutionaries which he claimed to have ready for action in that city. Additional sums were advanced for the purchase of arms and the transportation of the various units of the order, in particular to Amos Green in Illinois, Harrison H. Dodd and John C. Walker in Indiana, and T. C. Massie of Ohio. At Camp Douglas in Chicago there were nearly 5000 Confederate prisoners. It was hoped that their guard of 1000 men, largely made up of invalids of the Veteran Reserve Corps, could be overpowered and the liberated men armed from the federal arsenal to strike a blow at the vitals of the North. At the signal Southern sympathizers throughout the North were to rise, sever all telegraphic and railway communications, free the prisoners in the other camps of the area, and, if possible, seize control of the governments of the Northwest.[55]

There is no justification for assuming that all these expectations were mere daydreams of overexcited Copperheads. If there were no concerted revolt there might well be local resistance to conscription at many points which could develop into something definitely serious. Both civil and military authorities in the Middle West received reports of heavy shipments of arms into many parts of the region. Early in August, Governor Brough inquired of Stanton if there were anything that could be done to stop the selling of Henry rifles in the state to persons who seemed likely to use them against the government. One agent selling on commission for the New Haven Arms Company of Connecticut, the governor reported, had sold fifty rifles in Columbus in two days and was taking orders to supply the surrounding region. Other agents were operating in other sections of Ohio, the manufacturers refusing to recognize any responsibility for the ultimate use of the guns.[56] In southern Illinois the guerrilla outfits, such as the John Carlin and Clingman gangs, were spreading terror,[57] and although some of them were broken up during the course of the summer by vigorous action on the part of the authorities, the problem was so widespread and the resources available for checking it so limited that Governor Yates urged the sending of a considerable body of soldiers to the district and the appointment of a federal military commander for the state.[58] Governor Morton reported a similar state of affairs in southern Indiana,[59] and General Heintzelman admitted that he dared not make military arrests for fear of provoking an uprising which he would not have sufficient force to put down. He also voiced fears for the security of the Confederate prisoners and, with the commander of the Department of the Northwest, General Pope, at Milwaukee, predicted that drafting would provoke resistance beyond the power of the forces stationed in the Midwest to control. Counting up all the demands made upon him for troops for the preservation of order in the Middle West, General Halleck, in one of his few evidences of humor in official correspondence, remarked to Grant, "Add these requisitions to those from New York, Pennsylvania, New Jersey, and Delaware, and I think we can dispose of a few hundred thousand men, if you can spare them from the James River." But he continued, "Seriously, I think much importance should be attached to the representations of General Heintzelman in regard to the condition of affairs in the West." [60] In June, in a message recommending that because of the disturbed conditions in the Middle West the Confederate prisoners be sent to the East, Governor Brough had predicted, "External raids and internal trouble in Indiana and Illinois promise a warm summer's work." [61] As disguised Confederates, armed Sons of Liberty, and Democratic delegates converged on Chicago in the last week of August these threats were apparently approaching fulfillment and the Union seemed menaced by a twofold danger—political and insurrectionary.

The Democratic leaders, eager to be in a position to take the fullest possible advantage of Republican embarrassments, had postponed the meeting of their national convention to the latest practicable date. The deliberations of the convention itself, beginning on August 29, bore witness to the same intent. The military situation still remained such that its final outcome appeared unpredictable, and it would be politic, therefore, to spread a net as broad as possible. Compromise and evasion ruled. A large proportion of the Midwestern delegates, led by the Ohio contingent, had come to the meeting favoring a peace program and nominee, but Governor Horatio Seymour of New York and most of the Eastern men, on the other hand, were certain that such a course would alienate the moderates everywhere and prove fatal to the party in the Northeast. To this group the most desirable and promising move would be the nomination of General George B. McClellan as the party standard bearer on a platform calling for the prosecution of the war on its original basis (i.e., abandonment of emancipation), meanwhile endeavoring to secure reunion by negotiation. Such an appeal, it was thought, would take the fullest advantage of all shades of dissatisfaction with the incumbent administration. But there remained the danger that the insistent peace elements of the Midwest, if overridden entirely, might carry out threats to bolt the party. Accordingly Vallandigham was approached—so at least was the general understanding about the convention hall—and a bargain arranged. McClellan was nominated for the presidency, although a small block of Ohio and Indiana delegates led by Alexander Long joined with border states delegates in opposing him to the end,[62] peace advocate George H. Pendleton of Ohio was unopposed for the vice-presidency, and the platform was drafted to meet the demands of the peace faction. The crucial second plank of the platform read:

Resolved, That this Convention does explicitly declare as the sense of the American people, that after four years of failure to restore the Union by the experiment of war, during which, under the pretense of a military necessity, or war power higher than the Constitution, the Constitution itself has been disregarded in every part, and public liberty and private rights alike trodden down, and the material prosperity of the country essentially impaired justice, humanity, liberty and the public welfare demand that immediate efforts be made for a cessation of hostilities with a view to an ultimate convention of all the States, or other peaceable means to the end that at the earliest practicable moment peace may be restored on the basis of the Federal Union of the States.

With this statement, which might mean much or nothing, the peace faction had to be content. They were determined that it should mean a great deal. Outside the convention hall they set the tone of the meeting. On street corners semi-impromptu gatherings heard speakers such as Fernando Wood of New York, Vallandigham, Henry Clay Dean of Iowa, and other eccentrics of the stripe of that crank of cranks, George Francis Train, demand immediate and unconditional peace, urge forcible resistance to conscription and arbitrary arrest, and depict the attractiveness of a union in which the Midwest and South would be rejoined but New England excluded.[63] It was evident that the peace men were conscious of their strength and determined that their views should not be ignored in a final settlement after political victory. The rumor circulated among them that McClellan's supporters had agreed to move for peace on any terms as soon as their candidate was safely elected, if only the issue were not pressed during the campaign.[64]

But while the peace Democrats who sought to gain their objectives by political means were winning at least a partial victory, those who looked to revolutionary action had seen the complete failure of their plans. A meeting of the conspirators at the Richmond House in Chicago on August 28 revealed the hopeless outlook for a successful rising. For a number of reasons the commanders of the Sons of Liberty had lost enthusiasm for the project. Their backwoods forces, scattered throughout the town and bewildered by unfamiliar big city surroundings, were neither organized nor nerved for an outbreak. The arrest of their fellow-conspirators in Missouri and Kentucky and a raid in Indiana, instigated by Governor Morton, that had uncovered records, correspondence, and arms of the Sons of Liberty in the office of state Grand Commander Dodd in Indianapolis had resulted in successive depressions of their confidence and courage. Finally the promise of Democratic victory seemed to make such a hazardous venture unnecessary and ill-advised. Their Supreme Commander, Vallandigham, had been taken back into the councils of the party and now appeared to find his exalted position in the order an embarrassment and liability of which he would be happy to rid himself. Other party leaders in contact with the society brought pressure to prevent any untoward action that might furnish political capital for their opponents. When delegate Edson B. Olds of Ohio sought a hearing in the convention for a communication from the Sons of Liberty he was howled down and induced to abandon his motion.[65] To cap all, the federal authorities, getting wind of the conspiracy, had fortified the garrison at Camp Douglas to a point where a prison break could hardly succeed under the most favorable conditions.[66] Reviewing these circumstances at their conference Confederates and Copperheads agreed that the plot would have to be abandoned. As the convention broke up, the Sons of Liberty returned quietly to their homes, and the Confederate adventurers, knowing that strangers would be conspicuous in the city with the departure of delegates and spectators of the convention, either returned to Canada or else went into hiding with sympathizers in the Middle West.[67]

Although the revolutionary movement had fizzled, the political threat against continuation of the war loomed formidably enough. The Democrats seemed united. In McClellan they had nominated a candidate who would appeal to the war Democrats, both those who had been co-operating for the past three years with the Republicans and those who had remained undeviatingly faithful to the party. He might through his personal popularity and appeal also win considerable numbers of votes from independent sources and perhaps even from discontented Republicans. The peace Democrats, it was expected, would be held in line by the platform and the nominee for the vice-presidency. Declining confidence in the war's outcome, suggested by the fall in value of paper currency to one-third of the price of gold, and other indications of widespread spiritual fatigue seemed to forecast Democratic victory. The Republicans were divided, wrangling and exchanging blame among themselves, and thoroughly discouraged.[68] In a district that in normal circumstances was stanchly Republican one party worker admitted:

I think the *Democratic party will be a unit on McClellan, and that unless "Old Abe" is withdrawn from the Canvass, and another man put in his place who can unite the Republican strength, McClellan will be elected!* Since I came home, I learn of a number who have been, *and are,* Republicans, who have been supposed to be all right for Lincoln, who declare, since the Chicago Nomination, that as between Lincoln and McClellan, *they are for McClellan.* . . . The Democracy are going *unanimously* for McClellan—Lincoln's course has not only dissatisfied but *embittered* many thousands of Republicans, particularly Germans, against him; the Fremont party, and the Chase and Wade-Davis movement, and the anti-slavery dissatisfaction in New England, weakens him greatly; there is no enthusiasm for him, and cannot be, while every saloon, and concert hall will ring and re-echo with songs for McClellan.[69]

And if McClellan were elected, what then? Although classified as a supporter of the war, his susceptibility to the pressure of those about him left room for fears that his personal predilections would be no guarantee that the war would be energetically pursued until the Union should be restored.[70] He would be dependent upon a Congress and state authorities whose support of such a policy seemed at best doubtful. Democratic victories in the state elections of Indiana and Illinois were anticipated, victories essentially for the peace Democrats. A Republican political worker confided:

. . . I think Indiana is lost for both Lincoln & Morton. I was told at Indianapolis last week by some of Morton's best friends that it was extremely doubtful whether he could carry the State. There is a dreadful apathy prevailing in all this region of Ohio & nearly all of Indiana. . . .[71]

The Democratic candidate for governor of Illinois, Congressman James C. Robinson, was closely identified with the extreme peace partisans, and during the campaign accepted $40,000 from Jacob Thompson, giving in return assurances which satisfied Thompson that the Confederate interests would be advanced to that extent by his election. One-half of this sum was used to repay an advance to the Illinois Democratic State Central Committee from C. H. McCormick, who may well not have known the source of these funds. A notation in Thompson's official journal for October 24, 1864, recorded:

When Mr. J. A. Barrett of Illinois and B. P. Churchill of Cincinnati visited Mr. Thompson, bringing a letter from Honorable Alex Long, and assurances from Messrs. Vallandigham, Develin of Indiana, Green and Robinson of Illinois, and others, that it was of the last importance to secure the election of Mr. Robinson as governor of Illinois, and asking that money should be advanced for that purpose, stating that Robinson had pledged himself to them, that if elected he would place the control of the militia and the 60,000 stand of arms of that state in the hands of the order of the Sons of Liberty. Mr. Thompson agreed that whenever proper committees were formed of responsible persons to use the money effectually and in good faith to secure that end, that he would furnish the money.

Robinson promptly gave written assurances concerning his objectives as would-be governor in a letter addressed to "Messrs. Green, O'Melveny and others" but apparently intended for Thompson, to whom it was forwarded. It read:

Gentlemen: Your letter of enquiry came duly to hand and its contents noted.

In reply I would state that if elected governor of the state I will see that its sovereignty is maintained, the laws faithfully enforced and its citizens protected from arbitrary arrest, and if necessary for these purposes will, after exhausting the civil, employ the entire military force

of the state. I will also be happy to avail myself of the counsel and aid
of the executive committee of the Peace Democracy in the conduct
and organization of the militia of the state, recognizing the fact that
a well organized militia is necessary for the maintenance of state rights
as well as the liberties of the people. Hoping that the Democracy may
be successful in the great contest and that Constitutional liberty may
again be reinstated in the full plenitude of her power, I remain

Yours truly,

James C. Robinson [72]

Even if the national contest were not won, the Southern emissaries
could see promising possibilities in having officials in control of
one of two important states who would withdraw those states from
support of the war. If that should occur, who could say that the
war was yet lost to the South? On one thing political watchmen
of all varieties seemed to be in agreement, that on the military
events of the next few weeks depended the outcome of the elections,
state and national.[73] Even as the Democrats were choosing their
nominee and writing their platform and the revolutionary conspirators were attempting to decide upon a course of action, the
issue was approaching a decision on the field of battle. At Atlanta,
the economic capital of the Confederacy, a red-haired, outspoken
military genius, General Tecumseh Sherman, was throwing his en-
veloping lines around the city. His success or failure would be the
heaviest ballot cast in the election campaign.

Rome Nov 7th 1864

Gentlemen
    Your letter of enquiry came duly to hand & its contents noted.
In reply I would state that if elected Governor of the State I will see that its sovereignty is maintained the laws faithfully enforced and its citizens protected from Arbitrary arrest & if necessary for these purposes will after exhausting the civil, employ the entire Military force of the State. I will also be happy to avail myself of the Counsel & aid of the Executive Committee of the Peace Democracy in the Conduct & organization of the Militia of the said Recognizing the fact that a well organized Militia is necessary for the Maintenance of State rights as well as the liberties of the people. Hoping that the Democracy may be successfull in the great contest of tomorrow & that Constitutional liberty may again be Reinstated in the full plenitude of her power I Remain
    Yours truly
Messrs Green Quinby & others
    James C. Robinson

FACSIMILE OF LETTER OF JAMES C. ROBINSON

Received Toronto Canada Nov 15th 1864 of Jacob Thompson Twenty Thousand Dollars to pay a note executed by the central committee for Expense incurred in election   James A Barret

Recd of James A Barret Twenty Thousand Dollars to pay note to C. H. McCormick signed by him & others Chicago Nov 17. 1864
    W. C. Gowdy
    of Central Com.

FACSIMILE OF RECEIPTS OF W. C. GOWDY

CHAPTER IX

The Period of Victory

(September 2, 1864–April 9, 1865)

FATE dealt unkindly with the Democratic party in 1864. In the hope of being able to take advantage of last-minute developments, the national convention had been postponed as long as possible—to no avail. The military situation at the time of the meeting had been such that some sort of appeal to the widespread desire for peace appeared to be good political strategy, but hardly had the last of the delegates left Chicago before a pent-up flood of Union victories broke all restraints. On September 2 Atlanta fell into the hands of Sherman. General Phil Sheridan during September and October decisively defeated Early and laid waste the Shenandoah Valley, ending the possibility of another Confederate raid against Washington. These triumphs, together with Farragut's capture of Mobile, convinced the volatile public that the stalemate was broken. Relief found expression in celebrations that generally turned into rallies for the Union party, and Republican politicians who had observed McClellan's nomination with anxiety now expressed returning confidence in Lincoln's chances.[1] The St. Paul *Press* headlined the news:

VICTORY!!

GLORY!

Lincoln's Last Joke.

Atlanta is Ours!

Old Abe's Reply to the Chicago Convention.

Is the War a Failure?

* * * * * * * * * * * * * * * * *

Consternation and Despair Among the Copperheads.

The Southern Confederacy and Democratic Party Tumbling in a Common Ruin.[2]

"Good feeling prevailed over the Glorious News from Atlanta. I find more enthusiasm & more faith of ultimate success among our *rural* people generally than among our Politicians. Political skies are brightening every day," was a typical report.[3] Sulking radicals, including Chase and Greeley, came out of their tents and hastened to board the band wagon as it began to gather speed, although some, such as Alphonso Taft of Cincinnati, grandfather of the present Ohio senator, were sour in their private expressions about Lincoln.[4] Fremont's withdrawal from the canvass on September 22 removed the last danger of a split in the Republican vote.

Thus the chief issue of the campaign of 1864, that of whether the conduct of the war had resulted in failure or success, was settled by victories for the Union arms. But the Republican campaign was not yet out of the woods. Another problem still remained to disturb the politicians. In response to the President's call of July 19 for 500,000 men, conscription had been ordered to begin on September 5. As the time for the filling of the quotas approached, it was found that, in spite of unprecedentedly high bounties and other inducements, such as appropriations by local governing bodies and contributions by private citizens for the assistance of the families of those who enlisted,[5] a much more extensive conscription would be necessary than on any previous call. For the first time every state of the Middle West would be to some extent subject to the draft. Coming at the time it did, the prospects of conscription bore a double hazard. On the one hand, failure to raise a sizable body of troops promptly and efficiently would endanger the recent promise of the military situation; on the other, such an undertaking, disagreeable at best, might stir up public sentiment in a way to endanger the anticipated political triumph of the Republicans.

Democrats gave volunteering little support and were, of course, disposed to make as much political capital as possible out of any unpopular aspects of the situation. Their press frequently expressed the idea that those who expected to vote for Lincoln were the ones who ought to feel obligated to meet the government's call for more troops. After victories for the state tickets of the Republicans in Pennsylvania, Ohio, and Iowa, the Chicago *Times* jeered:

We wish to encourage enlistments. The President has called for three hundred thousand volunteers, very properly taking it for granted that, if five or six hundred thousand men had endorsed all his war policies, and voted for a vigorous prosecution of the war, in only three States, he ought to have no difficulty in securing three hundred thousand soldiers in the entire North. Now, Curtin men, Brough men, Stone men, where are you? You have said to the administration, "Go on with this war, just as you have been prosecuting it during the last year. Never stop fighting until you have freed the last slave in the South. Confiscate their property; subjugate them; offer them no terms but unconditional submission." How is the administration to follow your dictation unless you come to its support? . . .[6]

And readers were warned that

. . . if Mr. Lincoln should be re-elected, the necessity for like exertions would again arise within a few months . . . to re-elect Mr. Lincoln is to perpetuate the present political policies, and to perpetuate these policies is to inaugurate the draft as a regular arrangement to be repeated three or four times a year.

It is in this light that the prevailing heroic efforts of the workingmen of Chicago to rid themselves of the impending draft seem melancholy. Success in these efforts is only to put the evil day off, unless the workingmen can, at the proper time, also rid themselves and the country of Mr. Lincoln and his war policies.[7]

Even such a conservative Democratic paper as the Columbus *Ohio Statesman* on the eve of the election emphasized as its leading argument the assertion that a vote for Lincoln was a vote for a draft.[8]

Certain aspects of the problem held particular liabilities from the political point of view. Democratic newspapers fostered rumors that frauds were being perpetrated in the drawings of names of those liable to service so as to make the draft bear heaviest upon Democrats and the foreign-born. The Germans were told that they were to be singled out in revenge for their growing estrangement from the national administration over the past three years.[9] A more tangible cause for dissatisfaction was a new ruling of the War Department by which each sub-district, many of them illogically constructed, must make good all deficiencies on this and previous calls, regardless of whether or not the state as a whole might have filled its quota. In Illinois, where the state possessed a considerable excess of credits on previous calls, the ruling produced acute dissatisfaction [10] which the Democratic press sought with all its energy to exploit.[11] A committee of officers and members of the Union League of Illinois made a hurried trip to Washington to urge an adjustment of the matter, warning that the current situation contained possibilities for the defeat of the Republican ticket in the state.[12] Governor Yates sought to underwrite this admonition with a stern communication to the President, Secretary of War, and provost marshal general:

The total deficiency against this state for all calls was 13,440 on the 1st of this month, and yet the assistant provost-marshal-general here informs me that he is instructed to draft by sub-districts for the total deficiency of such sub-districts. Such deficiency was 28,058 on the 1st of this month, or more than double the balance against us as a State. . . . I had . . . urged that if a draft was insisted upon it should only be made for the deficiency against [us] as a State. No attention has been paid to these matters. If a draft is now insisted upon for 28,058, I will not be responsible for consequences. In my opinion it will not only endanger the peace of the State, but will hopelessly defeat us in the coming election. Our Republican papers will universally denounce it, and our Union men in the State will be left without the means of defending the fatal policy.[13]

Another irritant was the requirement that each district must make up the deficiencies caused by the failure of those drafted to report for duty, many holding that the apprehension of these deserters should be the responsibility of the federal officials and not of the people of the draft districts.[14]

All in all, discontent with conscription, or with some of its special features, seemed to offer the last hope for Democratic success in the Middle West. A communication to the Chicago *Times* from Livingston County, Illinois, reported:

The draft is helping the democratic ticket throughout this whole region. In the first place, the Germans are becoming very much excited, in Milwaukee there was scarcely any but Germans drafted. In St. Clair county, in this state, 700 Germans were drafted out of 900. In Woodford county about 100 Germans were drafted; about half the number drafted in Quincy. The Germans bear the brunt. The publication of the names in Chicago papers of drafted men in that city shows that almost every other man is a German. Why is this? It seems strange that, in a fair draft, nobody but Germans are called upon to do military duty. Is it because so many of them are turning democrats and going for McClellan that they are drafted? . . . Very few of the Germans in Woodford County are responding. They have sold out their farms, their homes, the products of all their labor since immigrating to this country, including money brought by them from the old country. Thus they have realized a thousand dollars and purchased a substitute and are now homeless. These things are telling strongly against the Lincoln party. . . .[15]

Republican politicians showed evidences of fright and some of the leading figures of the party urged the administration to postpone the draft until after the election.[16] Many of them also sought to delay the forwarding of recruits to the front until after they had been able to cast their ballots. Speaker of the House Schuyler Colfax of Indiana went farther and asked General Sherman to furlough home certain regiments from his district whose support he needed in the election, receiving for his pains a sharp lecture on both the impropriety and the selfishness of the request, at a time when the troops were pressingly needed in the nation's service.[17] When Senator John Sherman tried to intervene in the controversy on behalf of Colfax he received an even more sulphurous dressing down from his politician-detesting brother, at grips with Hood at Atlanta. So great was the pressure of this sort that Stanton finally called upon General Grant for moral support, saying:

. . . I would be glad if you would send me a telegram for publication urging the necessity of immediately filling up the Army by draft. The worst difficulty is likely to be in Ohio, Indiana, and Illinois, from the desire of candidates to retain their men until after the election. We have not got a single regiment from Indiana. Morton came here especially to have the draft postponed, but was peremptorily refused. But the personal interest to retain men until after the election requires every effort to procure troops in that State, even by draft.

Illinois is much the same way. Not a regiment or even company there has been organized. A special call from you would aid the Department in overcoming the local inertia and personal interests that favor delay.[18]

Grant immediately acquiesced in a statement from City Point, Virginia, on September 13:

We ought to have the whole number of men called for by the President in the shortest possible time. A draft is soon over, and ceases to hurt after it is made. The agony of suspense is worse upon the public than the measure itself. Prompt action in filling our armies will have more effect upon the enemy than a victory over them. They profess to believe, and make their men believe, there is such a party North in favor of recognizing Southern independence that the draft cannot be enforced. Let them be undeceived.

Deserters come into our lines daily who tell us that the men are nearly universally tired of war, and that desertions would be much more frequent, but they believe peace will be negotiated after the fall elections. The enforcement of the draft and prompt filling up of our armies will save the shedding of blood to an immense degree.[19]

Lurking in the shadows of this subject was still the possibility of armed resistance and perhaps widespread uprisings. In southern Illinois guerrilla bands were active, having apparently taken up bank-robbing and counterfeiting as sidelines. It was believed that they were in touch with similar bands in Missouri.[20] Near Girard, Illinois, Provost Marshal Cherry and Deputy Enrolling Officer Wolf were set upon and seriously injured on October 3 by a gang reported to number between thirty and forty. In the long-troublesome area on the west side of the Illinois River in Fulton and Rush counties a number of men in the provost marshal service were attacked. Deputy Provost Marshal Randolph was killed in an effort to arrest a draft dodger, Assistant Provost Marshal Charles Phelps was shot from ambush, and two other deputy provost marshals were fired upon, one being slightly injured.[21] Colonel James G. Jones, acting assistant provost marshal general for Indiana, sent in alarming statements of prospects in that state. The Sons of Liberty and other bands, he reported, were getting ready to oppose enforcement of the draft and plotting in some localities to seize control of the polling places in order to prevent Republicans from voting. Owen, Orange, Sullivan, Clay, and Crawford counties were designated as particular centers of disaffection. Colonel Jones believed that no less than 4000 soldiers would be required to maintain order in the state; otherwise he feared that more men would fail to report than would present themselves under the draft.[22] "We are," he warned, "upon the very verge of Civil War in Indiana." [23] Even after discounting possible exaggeration in such reports Secretary of War Stanton was apprehensive of some difficulty in these two states.[24]

The War Department nevertheless determined to go resolutely ahead with conscription. The only delay permitted was one of four days to allow the last-minute completion of certain details.[25] Communications from Grant and Sherman, including the warning that any wavering on conscription would cost the Republicans the soldier vote,[26] were used to get action from state officials. Illinois's protests over her quota were met by an arrangement for the reduction by fifty per cent of the number of recruits required from the state and by permission to rearrange the draft districts according to local wishes.[27] Instructions were issued to generals commanding the departments to be prepared to render prompt military aid in case of resistance to the levy.[28] Special attention was given to Indiana: a regiment of the Veteran Reserve Corps was sent from Albany, New York, for guard duty in the various draft districts; General Hovey, military commander of the state, was sent $5,000 from the secret service fund for emergency use; arrangements were made for arming the loyal civilian population if necessary; and the newly appointed commander of the Department of the Ohio, Joseph Hooker, himself went to Indianapolis to be prepared to take charge in case of an uprising.[29] The report of a special agent sent to Indiana having represented Colonel Jones as timid, overimaginative, and lacking in efficiency, Provost Marshal General Fry on October 9 removed Jones and replaced him with Brigadier-General Thomas G. Pitcher, who had proved his capacity in a similar post in Vermont.[30]

Faced with the inevitability of conscription, opposition of all types collapsed. Republican politicians decided that if the draft were going to be made it would be well to hurry, get it over, and then be able to forget about it while devoting all energies to an aggressive campaign for Lincoln's re-election on a platform of wholehearted confidence in approaching military triumph.[31] Troops were in readiness to meet any trouble that might arise, and by the device of conscripting various districts at different dates it was possible to use a small number of soldiers with a maximum of effectiveness. Under these circumstances virtually no resistance was encountered. By the early part of October drafting was about completed amid reports that draftees were accepting their calls with good-natured acquiescence.[32] It was remarked, however, that no small factor in this spirit of acceptance was the growing conviction that the war was making rapid progress toward a successful termination. The Chicago *Tribune* observed that "the dread of the conscription is really much diminished by the shining promise that after the war the Union will not be long in reaching its glorious conclusion; that the conscripts of this draft will be in at the death of the rebellion." [33]

Military victories and the successful conclusion of the draft had the effect of safeguarding the Republican ticket from the two issues capable of being of greatest trouble to it. By October 1864 it was fairly apparent that the party would be victorious not only in the national election but in the state contests of the Middle West as well. But there was still need for a line of attack that would drive home the victory. After all, the refutation of the charge that the war was a failure and the successful carrying out of conscription were, from the party point of view, essentially defensive measures. What was wanted was an aggressive issue with which the Democratic party might be attacked in their own camp, and given the state of public feeling, the most effective approach would be to fix upon them the stigma of treason. In March 1864 Colonel J. P. Sanderson had been appointed provost marshal general of the military Department of Missouri and had at once begun an investigation of the secret anti-war societies in that state. In this he secured the co-operation of members who for reasons of their own were willing to betray their associates, and he was also able to insinuate spies into the organizations. As time went on he even extended his researches into the neighboring states of Illinois, Indiana, and Kentucky. On June 12 he reported his findings to Major-General W. S. Rosecrans, commander of the Department, in a lengthy document which in spite of numerous errors and misconceptions did give an approximate picture of the ritual, organization, and purposes of the Order of American Knights.[34] Numerous arrests were made, including those of Charles L. Hunt, Charles E. Dunn, and Green B. Smith, Grand Commander, Deputy Grand Commander, and Grand Secretary, respectively, of the order in Missouri. This resulted in further revealing confessions.[35] A month later the War Department ordered Judge-Advocate-General Joseph Holt to investigate the situation in regard to treasonable societies in Ohio,

Indiana, Illinois, Kentucky, and Missouri. Holt consulted Colonel Sanderson, General Rosecrans, and various others. With information drawn largely from Sanderson's investigations and from a report made by Brigadier-General Henry B. Carrington to Governor Morton he advised the Secretary of War on August 5 of his findings. Holt represented the movement as extensive, armed, and bent on a revolutionary uprising.[36]

In all these revelations, however, only indirect connections with the Democratic party were proved. A more definite tie-up was required for political use, and it was shortly furnished in Indiana, where Governor Morton was virtually the autocrat of the state. In the second week of September a number of the officers and members of the Sons of Liberty of Indiana, including state Grand Commander Harrison H. Dodd, were arrested and, without loss of time, were on September 22 placed on trial before a military commission at Indianapolis. Conspiracy and treason were the charges. The testimony of federal detectives, some of whom claimed to have penetrated into the inner councils of the order, was buttressed by the usual confessions. In the process a sufficient number of members of some consequence in the Democratic party in the state were involved to forge an effective link, in the public mind, between the party and the secret order. Horace Heffren, Democratic leader in the state House of Representatives, was identified as one of the state officers of the Sons of Liberty. J. J. Bingham, chairman of the Democratic state committee and editor of the *State Sentinel,* leading party organ of the state, admitted membership in the order and, with Heffren, made a damaging confession concerning the plans of the Sons of Liberty for an uprising, although the former insisted, probably quite correctly, that he had done all in his power to block such action. Another prominent Democrat, Colonel William A. Bowles, commander of a regiment at the Battle of Buena Vista and owner of a large hotel at French Lick, was proved to be one of the state leaders of the society. Finally the evidence that the national commander was Vallandigham, regarded as the principal author of the Democratic national platform, completed the linking of party and secret society. The testimony eventually revealed also that S. Corning Judd, Democratic nominee for lieutenant-governor of Illinois, had been Grand Commander of the Order of American

Knights in that state and that other candidates there and elsewhere had held membership.[37] This trial plus arrests and confessions by less important men in other states gave the Republican journals campaign ammunition with which they mercilessly bombarded their opponents.[38] To help the cause along, the Republican Congressional Committee published a brief edition of Judge-Advocate-General Holt's report [39] and made ample use of the other materials of this type in numerous pamphlets with which it flooded the country. Against this attack the Democrats had virtually no defense, and merely revealed their intense chagrin by the billingsgate denunciation which they poured upon the heads of Sanderson, Carrington, Holt, and others for their part in the disclosures. Some attempt was made to assert that the Sons of Liberty had been secretly organized by the federal government to trap ignorant folk, and this alternated with the claim that it was an entirely peaceable political organization whose military character was being created by perjured testimony to provide an excuse for the Union League to suppress the Democratic party by force.[40] But it was a dismal undertaking. Even less defensible, under the circumstances, was the position of the Chicago *Times* that neither

. . . Lincoln, nor Heintzelmann, nor Carrington, has any right to inquire what citizens in States obedient to law are going to do with arms. It is none of their business. If the weapons are unlawfully used the parties may be punished, but their arms cannot be seized under a plea that they may be used unlawfully.[41]

The events that brightened the outlook for the Republicans threw their opponents' plan of campaign into confusion. As a rule the peace faction acted on the assumption that the Democratic party had too far committed itself against the war policy to make a successful change of front. Many of their newspapers attempted a curious course of denying that victories had been won or, where this could not be maintained, insisting that they had come about through no contributions of the administration. The surly Chicago *Times* observed that, if the disasters of the summer had continued, Lincoln would have been the most unpopular man in the country and warned that Stanton might use his control of the telegraph to manufacture mythical victories for electioneering purposes.[42] Un-

PRINCIPALS AT THE TRIAL FOR TREASON, 1864

der the heading "Abolition Lies—Lincoln's Stock in Trade" another paper played up rumors that Sherman's capture of Atlanta
had only served to place his army in an untenable position and took
comfort in the belief that Hood had not yet finished *his* campaign.
It concluded:

Lincoln is to be hurrahed through the campaign. The war fervor is
to be raised to fever heat and the people to be again fooled into voting
for Lincoln, and more war, and more ruin. Victories are to be shouted
over that never were gained, and the *tellie*graph to be used for the purpose of aiding Abolition by magnificent achievements.

All this is the shoddy contractor's plan of engineering. The plunder-
ers, quartermasters, contractors, &c., wish to keep the people's attention
directed away from themselves and their evil deeds.[43]

The *Crisis* insisted that Sherman's army was half starved, deci-
mated, and about to be forced out of Atlanta by Hood's masterly
strategy. The whole Union campaign in the West, it held, had been
a failure and the Confederates would soon be able to carry the
war back into Tennessee and Kentucky, beginning over again the
whole fruitless action of the first two years; Grant's movement was
a complete, costly, bloody fiasco; Sterling Price was threatening Jefferson City and St. Louis. As to Sheridan's rout of Early at Cedar
Creek, there were flat denials by the *Crisis* that it had occurred, it
being stated that no fighting had taken place after two o'clock in
the afternoon (up to which time the Confederates had had the advantage) and that the administration had used Early's voluntary
retirement with great stores of booty and numbers of prisoners as
the basis for claiming a spurious victory. On the eve of election
the paper printed last-minute rumors of catastrophe, picturing
Sherman's army threatened with being cut off and captured and
Grant in full retreat, harried by Lee's cavalry.[44]

Other Democrats tended toward a virtual abandonment of the
peace issue. McClellan, the nominee—urged by his friends of the
conservative Eastern wing of the party,[45] and no doubt moved by
changes in the military situation [46]—adopted this point of view. In
his acceptance speech on September 8 he virtually repudiated the
second plank of the Democratic platform. Conservative Democrats
were gratified and relieved, holding that his decisive action had
retrieved the errors of the Chicago convention.[47] Some of the peace

faction likewise gave their endorsement, perhaps regarding the pronouncement as having become a practical necessity,[48] and Pendleton, the vice-presidential candidate, began to explain in his speeches that peace would be acceptable only on the basis of reunion.[49] But in the minds of many others, both inside and outside the Democratic party, the intentions of the party remained embodied in the platform. Supporters of the war could not forget that at Chicago Vallandigham had moved to make the nomination unanimous, and throughout the campaign Democratic local rallies in the Middle West continued to emphasize the demand for peace at any price, obtainable only under Democratic auspices.[50]

All the same, much resentment was created among the peace faction by McClellan's repudiation, for his nomination had been none too palatable in the beginning and was acceptable only as the maximum price that would be paid for party unity and a peace platform.[51] Vallandigham, apparently getting wind of what McClellan was about, had begged him not to betray this group, writing on September 4:

Pardon the liberty I take, but for Heaven's sake, hear the words of one who has now nothing so much at heart as your success. Do not listen to any of your Eastern friends who in an evil hour, may advise you to *insinuate* even, a little war into your letter of acceptance. We have difficulty in preventing trouble now, tho. all will come right; but if any thing implying war is presented, two hundred thousand men in the West will withhold their support, and may go further still. Accept the word, on this subject of one who knows, & whose heart's desire is that nothing may be done to take away his power to aid you with his whole might in this campaign.[52]

This element had now the alternatives of bolting the party or of unenthusiastically staying with it in the hope of being able to shape its policy after the election. A few extremists attempted the former course. On September 14 about fifty representatives of the faction held a meeting at the St. Nicholas Hotel in New York to discuss the feasibility of putting up a separate candidate. Benjamin Wood of the New York *News* and James McMaster of the *Freeman's Journal* were apparently the moving spirits of the gathering.[53] And a month later, on October 18 and 19, a convention of Midwestern peace men was held in Cincinnati over which William

M. Corry of Ohio presided. Others of some prominence in attendance included James W. Singleton of Illinois, Lafe Develin of Indiana, and Congressman Alexander Long of Ohio. Resolutions were adopted declaring that the first Kentucky Resolution of 1798 was the cornerstone of the Democratic party, demanding a rigid adherence to the doctrines of state rights, and announcing:

. . . We . . . declare THE WAR WHOLLY UNCONSTITU-TIONAL, and on that ground we hold it should be stopped. If a majority of the copartnership States can retain a member by force, they may expel one by force, which has not yet been pretended by any body. The Federal Agency, at Washington, backed up by a majority of the States in Congress, without right, in the vain attempt to subjugate the minority of the States, is destroying their liberty, and crushing the federal system to atoms by thus attacking the Constitution. The Administration, and that majority, are the real enemies of the Union, which cannot, and ought not to exist after its conditions are destroyed. The Chicago Platform, and General McClellan and his war-record letter, which he has laid over it, must all be repudiated by Democrats for the same reason. If we admit that the war is constitutional, we must not murmur at the monstrous abuses which attend it, for they all naturally grow out of the original atrocity.

The administration was further charged with attempting to favor the industrial interests of the East at the expense of the agriculturists of the Midwest; slavery was held to be the only possible system of life for the American Negro; McClellan's nomination was challenged as a violation of party principles, and a new presidential candidate was demanded. When, however, Alexander Long declined the honor of such a nomination the convention had to abandon that project, as it was deemed too late to find another suitable standard bearer.[54] The extremists would have to yield support to the Chicago ticket with mental reservations or register a silent protest by refraining from voting. Considerable numbers probably followed the latter course. The *Crisis* refused to carry McClellan's name at its masthead and bitterly denounced the nomination as a sell-out to Wall Street and the Rothschild interests, as represented in the Chicago convention in the person of August Belmont.[55]

The Democratic campaign, which began with high hopes in the

spring and summer, wilted in that autumn. After the mind of the electorate was made up on the great issue—whether or not the administration in office could be depended upon to conclude the war and restore the Union within a reasonable time—there was little that the Democrats could do. It was vain to thresh old straw. Arguments that the Republicans were responsible for the war, that they had ridden down the civil rights of individuals, violated all manner of precepts inherited from the fathers of the republic, had never tried to stop the war by compromise when the South might possibly have been willing to discuss such a thing, that they would upset the social order by the freeing of the Negroes, that monetary inflation had raised the cost of living to the disadvantage of the poor, that the contracting of a huge war debt would burden the nation for generations to come, that peculation had run riot in high places, that the Republicans were planning to carry the election by force and fraud [56]—these arguments were all disbelieved or disregarded. What did they matter if only the nation could be reconstituted in such a manner that no future attempt at its disruption would ever be made?

As the election campaign went into its final period, the Republicans were in full strength engaged in a terrific onslaught against the Democratic ranks. They pounded them without mercy and without respite with charges of treasonable activities and association, using the votes of Democratic congressmen against war measures, quoting four years of pronouncements by Democratic newspapers and speakers, and utilizing the revelations of the Sons of Liberty as ammunition.[57] Republican stump speakers found their audiences little interested in any arguments except emotional denunciations of the Democrats as traitors and Copperheads,[58] this with other indications evidencing the growth of a grim and vindictive spirit in the people of the North as the end of the war came into view.[59] Against these attacks the Democrats had no effective defense. Instead, they quarreled among themselves, the conservatives blaming their predicament upon the fatal second plank of the Chicago platform,[60] and the peace Democrats sulking over McClellan's repudiation of their policy.[61]

Remorselessly the Republicans drove home the argument that an experienced administration which had succeeded in maintaining an ever-tightening blockade of the ports of the Confederacy, which had cut the South into three parts and reoccupied three-fourths of its total area, and which was now about to deliver the *coup de grâce* to rebellion ought not to be replaced by an uncertain quantity like McClellan, in whose election it was alleged many Southerners professed to see their last hope of independence.[62] The mass of voters were primarily concerned with the question of how the war might best be brought to an end and the Union restored. The victories of Sherman, Farragut, and Sheridan had convincingly demonstrated that the existing regime was qualified to execute that task; charges of treason against the Democratic party supplied the emotional overtone needed to arouse interest and enthusiasm in the campaign. Declarations that the war for reunion was a success and that the Democrats were Copperheads constituted a double-barreled weapon of Republican campaigners.

No group of voters was overlooked in the appeal for Lincoln's re-election. In order to get as many Democrats as possible to break away from their habitual affiliations a great show was made of support given the ticket by war Democrats. Statements from Democratic generals or other public figures urging such action were given wide circulation.[63] On November 1 a gathering of leading war Democrats of the East at Cooper Institute helped to signalize the trend.[64] Special attention was given to winning the German vote and a number of the Republican campaign pamphlets were translated into German. The Democratic party, the Germans were told, was the vehicle of state sovereignty, pro-slavery, and nativism, and only the Republican organization could offer the strong government that would insure economic opportunity and social equality for the immigrant.[65] Care was taken also to win the soldier's vote.[66] No one was overlooked. Even old campaigners such as the former Whig cabinet member Thomas Ewing were brought out of retirement to contribute their bit to insuring a Union victory. Ewing made a speech at Circleville, Ohio, seated in a chair on the platform, centering his arguments on casting doubts upon McClellan's loyalty and questioning his desire to defeat the Confederacy.

In the election not only was Lincoln triumphantly returned to the presidency, with a greatly enlarged majority in Congress, but in the Middle West the Democratic party was virtually pulverized. Only one of the fourteen United States senators from the section —Hendricks of Indiana, a holdover from the election of 1862— and less than one-seventh of the members of the federal House of Representatives were Democrats. Every governor was a Republican. And, except for Indiana, in which the two parties had an equal number of votes in the state senate, both houses of every legislature in the Midwest had Republican majorities. When the ballots were counted, it was plain that the last hope of the Confederacy had faded forever. And as the ballots were being cast and almost as though to symbolize the failure of the peace faction upon which Southern expectations had been built, there came the news that Samuel Medary was dead. The owner and editor of the *Crisis,* the most determined journalistic spokesman of the Midwestern peace group, had died with his movement.[67]

Had McClellan been elected he might have allowed his genius for inactivity to palsy the military drives that were striking at the vitals of the Confederacy. The South, suffering more, perhaps, from discouragement than from any other factor, might have been encouraged to carry on the war with new vigor. Had such men as James Robinson in Illinois been elected governors of the states in the Midwest they might have found ways of crippling the further successful prosecution of the war. But all such possibilities had faded. The people had spoken. One of Lincoln's supporters analyzed his own attitude:

I have felt tried, like yourself, by many things in Mr. Lincoln's course. I have felt and do feel that he lacks much of the firmness, decision and sternness with which God so usefully blessed Andrew Jackson. But I made up my mind, months ago, that we could not risk a change—a change of President might be a change of every thing—Generals, Cabinet &c., and I determined to work with all my might, "in season and out of season," for Mr. Lincoln's re-nomination and re-election, and I have done so, faithfully and earnestly.[68]

And a soldier stationed in Florida expressed a sentiment that would also have fitted the civilian population of the North:

. . . It is election day, but there is no more stir than usual, the boys having made up their minds that Old Abe had better remain at the

ELECTION OF 1864. Black counties—50% or more for McClellan.

White House four years more and see the thing through. There were but two votes for McClellan in our Company! Don't you believe that nonsence [*sic*] that our folks have been preaching to you—the war will end just as quick if Lincoln is re-elected, if not quicker. If he is elected it will do more to discourage the rebels than to lose a doszen [*sic*] battles—they will see that we are in earnest and mean to put the thing through. . . . Gen Grant is doing pretty well and if he keep [*sic*] on with his successes I think the rebs will have to cave in this winter.[69]

But what if the military victories that had so changed opinion had been delayed? If the stalemate had been prolonged at Atlanta as well as at Richmond, what then?

The time of the election also witnessed the crushing of the last gesture toward a revolutionary uprising against the war policy. In spite of the failure of their plans for an outbreak in Chicago at the time of the Democratic National Convention, the wily Confederate Captain Hines and his associates had not entirely given up hope of being able to strike a telling blow in the Midwest. About seventy Confederates had been in Chicago at the end of August. When the convention broke up about one-third returned to Canada, another third set out to make their way to the Southern lines, and the daring remainder elected to remain in the section in hope of finding new opportunities for action. Under the leadership of Hines and Captain Castleman this group went into hiding, mostly in the vicinity of Mattoon and Marshall, Illinois, taking part in a number of acts of incendiarism against government stores and steamboats while waiting for a chance to undertake a more significant action. Their contacts with the Copperhead chieftains at Chicago had convinced them that although the high officials of the secret societies were impractical visionaries many of the subordinates were prepared for real violence. Accordingly, plans were revived for freeing the prisoners at Camp Douglas, now numbering some eight or nine thousand men. After the failure of the August plot the garrison had been again weakened and consisted of about eight hundred men. A considerable number of these were unfit for duty, so that only about two hundred and fifty were on guard at any time. Only these guards and a twelve-foot board fence stood between the prisoners and liberty. Castleman was captured at Sullivan, Indiana, where he had gone to confer with local Copperheads, probably betrayed by someone in the order. Hines and his remaining men, plus a number of Confederates who had again come from Canada, certain Sons of Liberty from Fayette and Christian counties, Illinois, and Chicago Copperheads under Charles Walsh gathered at the designated time and place. Agents had been placed in other districts to cut the telegraph lines and destroy railroad connections. Under cover of election night, November 8, the plot was to be carried out. A few days before, however, word of what was planned reached the ears of federal detectives. Acting on this information Colonel Sweet, commanding at Camp Douglas, secured reinforcements for his garrison. Sweet also made a deal with one of the Confederate prisoners in Camp Douglas by which the prisoner was permitted to "escape" and join the conspirators. The information thus betrayed enabled Colonel Sweet to ferret out and arrest more than a hundred of the plotters and add them to the inmates of Camp Douglas. But Captain Hines, like the spies of fiction that he so closely approximated, managed to escape and eventually made his way to Richmond. In surrounding the house of Dr. Edward W. Edwards at 70 Adams Street, where Hines was staying, a detachment of soldiers made enough noise to warn those within. Hines hid himself within the box springs of a bed on which Mrs. Edwards pretended to be very ill. Later, escorting a woman who had come to call on the pretended sick woman, he simply walked past the guard that had been left at the house, went to Cincinnati, where he put up with another family of Southern sympathizers, and stayed there until he was convinced that any further effort was hopeless. But otherwise the circumvention of the plot was complete.[70]

Affairs in the Midwest after the election ceased to have any important bearing on the outcome of the war. A few Democratic politicians and newspapers continued obstinately to insist that victory was as far removed as ever, only serving to emphasize the failure of the peace cause. In Wisconsin the La Crosse *Democrat* answered Lincoln's re-election with the threat that the next effort at conscription would precipitate a revolution in the North, running frightening captions at the head of its leading editorial:

> The Union of States is gone forever.
> The South never will be subjugated.
> A revolution, already rife in the North, will burst with bloody
> fury at no distant day.
> A Central and Northwestern Confederacy will surely be established.
> The Northwestern Confederacy will join hands with the South,
> regardless of politics, for commercial interests.[71]

In mid-March the Galena (Illinois) *Weekly Democrat* was still insisting that the war would be likely to go on for years, after having long since destroyed the old union of "consent." [72] The *Crisis,* now edited by Medary's son, continuing to belittle every victory for the Union arms, talked of the likelihood of French and British intervention, and would not admit until Lee's surrender the certainty of Northern triumph.[73] In Congress, Representative Chilton A. White insisted that slavery could not be abolished even by constitutional amendment,[74] and Alexander Long was still maintaining that the Union could not be re-established by force.[75] Even an occasional Republican, such as unstable Joseph Medill of the Chicago *Tribune,* might be momentarily overtaken by misgivings in which he would wonder whether Sherman's raid was not merely spectacular rather than meaningful, whether the armies could be kept supplied with sufficient replacements for the completion of their tasks, whether the currency situation might not presage immediate ruin, and whether the blockade had really deprived the Southerners of anything essential.[76] But events moved on inexorably.

Cyrus H. McCormick, more practical as a reaper-manufacturer than as a statesman, still had hopes of a peace conference with the Southern leaders, which he broached through open letters to the Chicago *Times* and the New York *World.*[77] He offered, if necessary, to go to Richmond, either as Lincoln's representative or on his own responsibility.[78] Nothing came of it. Wilbur F. Storey, publisher of the Chicago *Times,* advised him that the time had gone by when such a project was conceivable.[79] In January resolutions were introduced in the Ohio legislature by Senator Connell from Fairfield County, calling for a thirty-day armistice and a peace conclave between the sections to consider terms of peace on the basis of reunion and a gradual abolition of slavery,[80] and a similar proposal was advanced in the same body in March by Senator Lang of Seneca County,[81] but both were received with an indifference that evidenced the complete apathy of even Democrats toward the topic. The peace movement of the Midwest was dead. Toward the end of the struggle the former peace advocates were gravitating to a position of support of President Lincoln, believing that he represented the best hope for effecting a true reconciliation of the people of the two sections, a tendency that might have been of the first importance had it not been for the great President's tragic death.[82]

There yet remained one task to be performed by the civilian population in the work of completing the overthrow of the Confederacy. On December 21, 1864, the President issued his final call for troops. Three hundred thousand were asked for, with deficiencies to be met by conscription on February 15.[83] The response suggested that enthusiasm for the war, even in the face of approaching victory, was almost as dormant in the Middle West as the peace movement. Democrats indicated that it was up to the supporters of Lincoln's re-election to enlist. Republican officials seemed more concerned to find means of reducing their quotas than to provide the largest possible number of men for the completion of the great work. The Illinois administration entered into another prolonged controversy with the War Department, thoroughly profitless and accompanied by display of bad temper on both sides; Secretary Stanton had one of his typical outbursts of impatience and arrogance, and the Illinois officials delivered long homilies upon the honor and dignity of the commonwealth which they represented.[84]

Nor did men subject to military duty show enthusiasm for being in at the final triumph. Fraudulent certificates of service or of physical incapacity enjoyed a considerable vogue.[85] Many joined draft protective associations which, under arrangements with the provost marshals, were permitted to furnish substitutes in proportion to their numbers.[86] Local districts seemed interested only in compliance with the letter of the law, regardless of the probable usefulness to the government of their contingents, and made efforts to enlist runaway Southern Negroes, Confederate prisoners, and even convicts.[87] Large numbers of those induced to enlist by the generous bounties offered proved to be chronic "bounty jumpers" who deserted at the first opportunity.[88] The governors of Illinois and Indiana and the legislatures of Indiana and Wisconsin entered pleas for the postponement of the draft.[89] Despite the filling of quotas with human odds and ends and a two-month postponement of conscription, the number of deficient districts was greater than ever before. Drafting had begun, when Lee's capitulation caused the discontinuance of recruiting to be ordered on April 13, 1865. Even such districts as were later able to boast of never having been subject to drafting were in many cases able to do so only because conscripting officials had not reached them. A profound spirit of apathy, of exhaustion of morale rather than resources, seemed to indicate that at the end of the great struggle the will to fight had departed from the Middle West almost as much as it had from the expiring Confederacy.

CHAPTER X

The Heritage
of the Defeatist Movement

With Lee's surrender and the collapse of the Confederacy the movement for peace without victory came to an end, joining the innumerable lost causes and "might-have-beens" that line the road of history. Its failure had perhaps been due more to chance than to inherent weaknesses, but it had reflected little credit upon either the patriotism or the intelligence of its participants. Some had taken part in it because they were opposed to the aims and purposes of the war, either from the beginning or after the abolition of slavery had been introduced as an added objective in the midst of the conflict. There were men of Southern birth or descent who found the idea of a war upon their kinsmen abhorrent, and many of the Irish joined them in fearing that emancipation would result in the Negroes' becoming their economic competitors and social equals. Some could not see beyond the bitter party warfare that in some respects was to the middle decades of the nineteenth century what religious controversy had been to the seventeenth century and economic issues would be to the twentieth. Poor people resented having to support a war whose burdens often fell unequally upon them, and business men felt the pinch of high transportation rates, the loss of Southern trade, and the disturbance of the currency. Added to such positive advocates of peace were their unwitting supporters, those who wanted victory but who were too easily discouraged and too prone to find fault with those who were directing the war.

To see the Midwestern Copperhead movement with a wider perspective it should be remembered that there had been kindred or parallel developments in the other sections of the loyal states, although nowhere else did defeatism so seriously endanger the Union cause. The movement in each such section was conditioned by its own set of circumstances and motives. In the Northeast opposition to the war effort came from manufacturers and merchants who had built up a flourishing trade with Southern planters, from recently arrived immigrant groups, particularly the Irish, from narrow Democratic partisans, and from those whose understanding was circumscribed by social conservatism and psychological inertia. In 1860 the cotton mills of Massachusetts and Rhode Island were dependent on the plantations of the South for their raw material, while manufacturers of all sorts had built up some of their most important markets there. The shoemakers of the Bay State shod Southern feet, both white and black, the harnessmakers and carriage-manufacturers of Connecticut enabled the planters to ride abroad, and the stovemakers of New Jersey warmed them from the chill of the winter months. The sixty carriage factories of New Haven, employing more than fifteen hundred men, sold three-fourths of their product in the South. It was estimated that all New England exported goods to the value of $60,000,000 per year to the Southern states and received about $50,000,000 worth in return. From New York, Philadelphia, and other seaboard cities wholesale merchants had developed profitable trade in a great variety of commodities, while their banking interests had helped to finance railroad and other enterprises for which they had taken bonds and notes and even, through inevitable foreclosures, had sometimes acquired ownership of Negro slaves put up as collateral. Faced with the dismaying fact of secession most of them would have preferred acquiescence to war, firmly convinced that they could still do business with an independent Confederacy. Profiteering war contracts and the succulent Republican tariff and financial legislation that came later only gradually and partially reconciled them to a course of action which interrupted that business. The numerous foreign-born proletariat, led by the Irish and with the Germans in second place, like their brethren in the Middle West feared potential competition and association with liberated Negroes and generally looked upon the Republican party as the chief heir of the Know Nothing movement which had been so active in this section in the previous decade. Unlike the Middle West, where loyalty to Douglas and enthusiasm for popular sovereignty had reduced administration Democrats to a mere office-hungry clique after the party split over the Lecompton Constitution, an influential part of the Northeastern Democrats had favored the Buchanan-Breckinridge faction. Consequently the virus of state sovereignty had spread widely among them, with a resultant disposition to reject coercion by the national government. The innate conservatives were primarily of two types, consisting on the one hand of people of established wealth and on the other of slow-minded rustics—the hill farmers of Massachusetts and Connecticut, the stubborn "Bergen County Dutch" of New Jersey, and the stolid colonial Germans of Pennsylvania. They agreed in wanting no disturbance of their settled lives and habits. Like all such people they wished to close their ears to any higher call upon themselves and to hate the voice that sought to rouse them. In the chill precincts of the Friday and Somerset clubs in Boston patriotism was at so low an ebb that in 1863 a group of which Oliver Wendell Holmes was a member organized the rival Union Club. Loyalists in New York left the conservative Union Club of that city to form the Union League Club. An indignant member of the venerable Philadelphia Club once declared "this place reeks of Copperheads."

The most outspoken peace Democrats in the East were to be found in New York City and the adjacent portion of New Jersey. They were led by a gentlemanly blackguard, Fernando Wood, Philadelphia-born, by turns wine and cigar merchant, grocer, ship chandler, auctioneer, Know Nothing and Democrat, once elected to Congress and three times chosen mayor of New York. He had finally become too much even for Tammany Hall and withdrew with his riff-raff following and with some support of the remnants of the up-state Hunkers, to form Mozart Hall, a center of sedition throughout the war. James Brooks, a Constitutional Unionist in 1860, who would later be singled out for formal censure by the national House of Representatives for his role in the Credit Mobilier scandal, became his chief New York lieutenant. Wood, who in January 1861, toward the end of his last term as mayor, had broached to the city council the proposal that New York become a free city able to trade on equal terms with both the United States and the Confederacy, kept in close touch with the peace Democrats of New Jersey. They were led by another well-born rascal with impeccable manners, James W. Wall of Burlington, assisted by former Governor Rodman M. Price, State Senator Daniel Holsman, and Assemblyman Dr. Thomas Dunn English, best remembered as the author of "Ben Bolt." The central leadership of the Democratic party in Connecticut, dominated by men of Breckinridge antecedents, was less blatant in its expression but of much the same mind. Former Governor Thomas H. Seymour, whom it tried repeatedly to return to the gubernatorial chair, announced his opposition to the war at the outset and never retracted that statement. William Eaton of Hartford, the behind-the-scenes manager of the party in the state throughout the period, never lost an opportunity to denounce the idea of coercion, and James Gallagher, New Haven leader, called for resistance to the federal government if necessary. A snarling pack of newspapers also disseminated the views of these men. In New York City this included brother Benjamin Wood's *Daily News,* the *Express,* the *Metropolitan Record,* and James McMaster's Roman Catholic *Freeman's Journal.* In New Jersey it was represented by the Newark *Journal,* owned by William Wright, and by the *Bergen County Democrat,* which until May 1862 had as its editor C. Chauncey Burr, a specialist in extremism whose career had ranged from being an Abolitionist newspaperman in Ohio to having served as press-agent for the American tour of the notorious Lola Montez. The Pottsville (Pennsylvania) *Democratic Standard* was of the same stripe. The somewhat more sedate and influential New Haven *Register,* Hartford *Times,* and Philadelphia *Pennsylvanian* and *Age* shared the same basic attitudes.

The peace Democrats in these states offered their supreme challenge in the first six months of 1863. On January 13 Daniel Holsman of Bergen County introduced a series of resolutions into the New Jersey senate calling for an armistice of six months and advocating the strengthening of the state militia in order to defend the state's sovereignty against the national authority by force if necessary. James W. Wall, who had been jailed for sedition in September 1861 by the United States marshal, was elected to fill out an unexpired term in the United States Senate and William Wright was chosen for a full term. The Democratic state convention of Connecticut met at Hartford on February 18 and nominated Thomas Seymour for the governorship on a peace platform. In Pennsylvania, which fortunately for the Unionists held its principal elections in odd-numbered years, George W. Woodward was selected as the party's candidate for governor. He was an outspoken apologist for secession in 1861 and in November 1863 would, as a member of the state supreme court, vote against recognizing the constitutionality of the federal Conscription Act. Spurred on by a visit from Vallandigham to New York, the General Committee of Mozart Hall in March unanimously called upon the governor to prevent the enforcement of the act in that state. They also sponsored a series of mass meetings in the city on April 7, May 18, and June 3 which took progressively stronger positions in opposition to the war.

The Eastern peace Democrats, however, never succeeded in capturing the party machinery as they did in the Middle West. In New York the ultra-cautious New York Central Railroad group led by Dean Richmond, Erastus Corning, Horatio Seymour, and Samuel J. Tilden—heirs to the senescent stewardship of the "Albany Regency"—was able with the intermittent support of Tammany Hall to checkmate the designs of Vallandigham's friends. Elected governor in the political revulsion of 1862, Seymour refused to set the machinery of the state in direct opposition to the federal government. That was true too of Democrat Joel Parker, who assumed the governorship of New Jersey at the same time and by using tactics of yielding defense was able to tone down the anti-war resolutions before their final passage by the legislature. These men contented themselves with a less clear-cut type of obstructionism. They bitterly denounced arbitrary arrests and the suppression of disloyal newspapers without being willing to admit the circumstances that provoked them or attempting to co-operate with the federal authorities to work out a more discriminating system; they attacked the emancipation policy as though it had become the primary goal of the administration rather than recognizing the truth that it had been adopted as an essential weapon for preserving the Union; and they indirectly fostered resistance to conscription by constantly endeavoring to cast doubts upon its legality. They did not oppose the war, they merely indulged themselves in a fussy constitutionalism and in irresponsible criticism, with the determined purpose of making party capital. That such actions might contribute to the dissolution of the Union was to them apparently a regrettable but unavoidable hazard. This observation could also be made of such "respectable" newspapers as the New York *World,* Albany *Argus,* and the Trenton *True Democrat.* It was a much shrewder course from a partisan point of view, for in those states where the party was more openly defeatist it lost out. Even in that spring of despair of 1863, Thomas Seymour fell 2633 votes short of persuading the people of Connecticut to give up their annual custom of re-electing Republican Governor William A. Buckingham. And after Gettysburg, Governor Curtin would triumph over Woodward in Pennsylvania.

During the course of the war the East experienced a certain number of violent incidents. Massachusetts, Connecticut, New York, New Jersey, and Pennsylvania were all reputed to have chapters of the Knights of the Golden Circle, and the Sons of Liberty apparently made a somewhat more modest showing. A sore spot of opposition to the draft was Cass Township in Schuylkill County, Pennsylvania. In October 1862, more than 500 coal miners, mostly Irish-born members of the Molly Maguire organization, forcibly prevented a trainload of draftees from leaving Tremont and Pottsville. That area, plus certain parts of Philadelphia, Pittsburg, and Berks and Cambria counties, remained troublesome throughout the war, and many draft evaders took refuge in the sparsely settled northwestern portion of the state. On July 13, 1863 the great New York draft riot began, provoking reverberations in Troy and other cities of that state, uneasiness in New Haven and Hartford, and a brief flare-up in the North End of Boston which the prompt and vigorous action of Governor Andrew, contrasting with the temporizing course of New York's Seymour, quickly put down. Confederate agents also gave the section some attention. On October 19, 1864, ununiformed Confederates under Lieutenant Bennett H. Young slipped over the border to St. Albans, Vermont, looted three banks of more than $200,000, killed one citizen, and then rushed back to Canada, where the courts found reasons to avoid acting against them. Somewhat later the Confederate guerrilla John Yates Beall, who had been unsuccessful in an attempt to surprise the American revenue cutter *Michigan* on Lake Erie in order to use it as a means of setting free the Confederate prisoners at Johnson's Island, was apprehended in a train-wrecking venture near Niagara Falls and executed. And on November 25 a bizarre effort was made to set on fire a number of hotels in New York City, including the Astor, St. Nicholas, Metropolitan, and Fifth Avenue, plus, of all things, Barnum's Museum. One participant, Robert Kennedy, was captured and hanged after confessing his part in the scheme.[1]

The border slave states were less comparable with the Middle West. Unique conditions operated there in the widespread desire for adherence to the Confederacy, in the actual ownership of slaves in great numbers, and in the presence during the conflict of powerful Union military forces. It was touch and go in most of these states as to whether they would cast their lot with the North or the South after Sumter, and about as many soldiers wore the Confederate gray as served in the ranks of the Federals, most of them being formed into regiments that bore the names of their states. After the issuance of the Emancipation Proclamation there were strong demands in Kentucky for mustering their regiments out of the Union army, and at a sign from their legislature the overwhelming majority of Kentuckians might have attempted to withdraw from the war. But none of these states was a free agent by the autumn of 1861. After the bloody effort of a Baltimore mob to prevent the passage of Northern troops through the city on April 19, General John A. Dix arrested members of the Maryland legislature who were suspected of favoring secession. Military intervention in Kentucky helped to prevent the election to the governorship of the peace Democrat Charles A. Wickliffe in 1863. And in the fall of 1862, Federal troops who were sent into Delaware to "supervise" the election did their work so well that the Union candidate, William Cannon, squeezed through to the governor's chair by 111 votes. This caused all but fifteen Democrats in the entire state to boycott the election held a year later under the same type of supervision. Kent and Sussex counties were the heart of pro-Southern feeling in this state, and from them large numbers of young men made their way across Chesapeake Bay to the Confederate lines. On June 27, 1861, more than 1500 people gathered on Dover Green to express their preference for division of the Union to war, and at the end of January 1863 the two houses of the legislature by joint resolution announced that they would no longer support a war of emancipation and arbitrary arrests but would demand the arrangement of an armistice. Expressions of this sort, however, were of little practi-

cal effect, and such protesting representatives in Congress as Henry
May and Benjamin G. Harris of Maryland and Senators Garrett
Davis and Lazarus W. Powell of Kentucky, or the lamentations of
such a paper as the Louisville *Democrat* were unheeded voices in
the wilderness. Secret societies operated in all the border states, and
in the summer of 1864 the chief justice of Kentucky, Joshua F.
Bullitt, was taken into custody as a high official of the Sons of
Liberty.[2]

Affairs in the new states west of the Missouri River had comparatively little effect on the outcome of the war. Here recent emigrants
from older sections had had little time for their views to take on
much of the color of their new environment. Many returned to
their former homes to enlist. The oldest of these commonwealths
was California. Perhaps a third of the population was of Southern
origin and formed the principal support for a scheme of United
States Senators William M. Gwin and Milton S. Latham and Oregon's Senator Joseph Lane (Breckinridge's running mate in 1860) to
set up an independent Pacific Confederacy, which although too remote to be an integral part of the Southern Confederacy could assist
it with a supply of precious metals that would have supported its
financial system. When this plot fell of its own weight the Southern
element, particularly in California, remained unregenerate. Such
papers as the Los Angeles *Star, Tribune,* and *Expositor,* Visalia
Equal Rights Expositor and *Post,* San Jose *Tribune,* Stockton *Argus*
and *Democrat,* Tulare *Post,* Marysville *Express,* and Mariposa *Free
Press* were most outspoken. The Reverend Dr. W. A. Scott, pastor
of the Calvary Presbyterian Church of San Francisco, provoked an
uproar by offering prayers for Jefferson Davis, and in such towns as
Visalia, Sonoma, and indeed many places in the San Joaquin and
Santa Clara valleys, the southerners were dominant and flaunted the
Confederate flag. Castles (as the local chapters were called) of the
Knights of the Golden Circle were reputed at one time to have
1600 members, including former Governor Bigler. The majority of
Californians, however, gave such assistance as they could to the
Union cause. Led by men of the type of Thomas Starr King, they
formed a Home Guard to watch the Confederate partisans, con-
tributed $1,000,000 to the Sanitary Commission, and sent 15,000
men into the army. A California column in 1862 crossed the Sierras

to drive the Confederate General Henry Hunter Sibley back into Texas, after a force from Colorado under Colonel John B. Slough by a brilliant maneuver destroyed Sibley's supply train at La Glorieta and thus prevented his reaching the gold fields. The story of dissent in Kansas during the war was a fitting interlude between the civil war of 1856 and the Jesse James depredations of the post-war period. Kansas "Red-Legs," so called from their habit of affecting red morocco leggings, made thieving forays into Missouri, and pro-slavery settlers who had retreated into Missouri retaliated in kind. The climax came in the plundering of Lawrence on August 21, 1863, and the slaughter in cold blood of more than 150 citizens by a band of Missouri Confederate guerrillas led by a former resident of the city, the stupidly brutal William Clarke Quantrill.[3]

It was in the Middle West, however, that the Copperhead movement had its principal seat, where it was generated and flourished. So far as the records indicate, there was no formal dissolution of the secret anti-war societies. In the spring of 1865 they simply faded out like the Cheshire cat, although the smile was no doubt lacking.

But the Copperhead leaders lived on, for the most part in careers that seemed strangely unaffected by their wartime activities. Vallandigham's later years were anti-climactic. Returning to the practice of law, he was refused the nomination for United States senator which he craved in 1867, but was selected as a delegate to the Democratic National Convention of 1868, and was nominated for Congress in 1868 but defeated in the election by the Republican incumbent. His death, however, was characteristically spectacular. It came from a pistol shot accidentally self-discharged as he attempted to demonstrate a point in a murder case in which he was counsel. Alexander Long was soured on politics after 1864 and until 1876 refused to vote for any presidential candidate. But in Cincinnati he maintained a position of respect and served as a member of the Board of Education and of the Trustees of the Public Library. Chilton A. White returned to the practice of law in his old home and birthplace, Georgetown, Ohio, served in the state constitutional convention of 1873, and was defeated in the race for secretary of state in 1896. Some others were more successful. George Hunt Pendleton, "Gentleman George," defeated for Congress in 1866, became a leading sponsor of the "Ohio idea" of repaying the

federal war bonds in greenback currency and was a leading con-
tender for the presidential nomination in 1868. In 1869 he was the
unsuccessful opponent of Rutherford B. Hayes for the governorship but then became president of the Kentucky Central Railroad.
From 1879 to 1885 he was a member of the United States Senate
and carried through the first great Civil Service Reform Act, and
thereafter until his death was our minister to Germany. That quasi-
Copperhead, cultured and witty Samuel Sullivan Cox, marked for
life by the name "Sunset" for a newspaper sketch that he had once
written, cannily moved from Ohio to New York in search of a more
dependably Democratic district. He was thus able to return to Congress in 1868, and in 1885 he became minister to Turkey. Another
cautious defeatist, Daniel Wolsey Voorhees of Indiana, who had
managed to sidestep most of the unpleasantness when the secret
societies had been broken up in his state, remained in Congress until February 1866, returned to it from 1869 to 1873, and served in
the Senate from 1877 to 1897. Famed for his full-steam oratory, the
"Tall Sycamore of the Wabash" as Chairman of the Finance Committee led Cleveland's fight for the repeal of the Sherman Silver
Purchase Act in 1893 and was influential in the erection of the present Library of Congress building.

Among the Illinois peace Democrats, James C. Robinson, safe
during his lifetime from revelation by his Southern co-conspirators
of his part in the Copperhead plot to seize the Northwest in 1864,
was re-elected to Congress in 1870 and 1872. William Joshua Allen,
once a victim of arbitrary imprisonment, became in 1877 Judge of
the United States District Court for the Southern District of Illinois. James W. Singleton became president of the Quincy and
Toledo and the Alton and St. Louis railroads, and in 1878 and 1880
was elected to Congress. S. Corning Judd, forsaking Copperhead
Lewistown for Chicago, served as postmaster of the latter city from
1885 to 1889. Iowa became too strongly Republican for such men
to flourish there politically. George Wallace Jones in time became
an indulged and venerated "old settler," Henry Clay Dean would be
remembered by Mark Twain in *Life on the Mississippi* as an anti-
quated freak, and Dennis Mahoney seems to have dropped into
obscurity.

Among the bellwethers of the Copperhead press in the Midwest the *Crisis* declined after the death of Samuel Medary and the failure of the cause which he advocated, but his descendants continued to occupy a position of respect and influence in the community. In brawny, cosmopolitan Chicago, Wilbur F. Storey's *Times* went on to achieve a great financial success. But in the attitude of even its own readers and in the cynical sensationalism of its tone there was a note suggesting the consciousness that somewhere in its career the paper had sold its birthright. Storey would later tell one of his employees that, regardless of the circumstances, it would never again oppose any war in which the United States might become involved. After the owner's death the paper eventually lost its identity in that series of mergers which would in the end convert Chicago into a journalistic Dead Sea. Only the Cincinnati *Enquirer*, under a change of ownership and politics, would continue to occupy a position of importance down to our own day.

All the conspirators connected with the Northwest Conspiracy managed to escape any very severe punishment. Four of those tried at Indianapolis were in December 1864 sentenced to death: Harrison H. Dodd, William A. Bowles, Stephen Horsey, and Lambdin P. Milligan. Dodd escaped from prison during the trial and fled to Canada. Three days before the execution of the others was to take place on May 19, 1865, President Johnson commuted Horsey's sentence to life imprisonment and postponed the hanging of the other two. Eventually the issue of whether or not a military commission had had the right to try civilians on such charges came before the Supreme Court of the United States, with J. E. McDonald, Jeremiah S. Black, James A. Garfield, and David Dudley Field representing the case for the prisoners. On April 3, 1866, the court, in the case of Milligan, decided that the entire procedure had been illegal, and the prisoners were discharged. All were then indicted in the civil courts but the cases never came to trial. When, however, Milligan attempted to sue the members of the military commission for damages he was awarded a paltry $5. The Camp Douglas conspirators were tried before another military commission at Chicago from January 9 to April 19, 1865. One Confederate, Colonel Benjamin M. Anderson, committed suicide in prison. Two others, Charles T. Daniels and Colonel George St. Leger Grenfell, an Englishman who had once been General John Morgan's chief-of-staff, were sentenced to death; Charles Walsh of Chicago and Confederate R. T. Semmes were sent to prison but shortly freed; and Judge Buckner C. Morris of Chicago and Colonel Vincent Marmaduke were acquitted. Daniels escaped during the trial and Grenfell, whose sentence was commuted to life imprisonment, escaped from Fort Jefferson, Florida, in 1868, possibly drowning in the attempt. John B. Castleman was held in custody until after the war. Fearing that he might be executed as a spy, a pro-Union uncle, Samuel Breckinridge, rushed to Washington from Kentucky to get a secret order from the President reprieving the young man. Years later the uncle became tired of Castleman's slurs on Lincoln and presented him with the original of the order. In the Civil War the government and people showed a characteristic reluctance to punish either espionage or disloyalty with the rope and firing squad. Thereby they undeniably fostered the American tradition of tolerance, individual liberty, and civil rights. Perhaps, however, they also tended thereby to give a measure of encouragement to enemies of the nation, foreign and at home, in times to come.

Although few of those who gave aid and comfort to the Confederacy either through political maneuvering or revolutionary plotting were ever directly punished for their activities, the Democratic party suffered severely for the extent to which it permitted itself to be used as an instrument of the Copperheads. Disloyalty during the War of 1812 had given the death blow to the Federalist party, and opposition to the Mexican War played a part in the demise of the Whigs. Had it not been for its strength in the South, where from the Southern point of view it had been the "loyal" party during the war and Reconstruction, the Democratic party might have disintegrated as a result of the Civil War. As it was, it lay under a cloud in the North for decades after the war. A strong opposition party was needed after 1865 to check the rapacious Eastern industrial interests that, following Lincoln's death, seized control of the Republican party. But these interests were little hindered as they plundered the natural resources of the continent and bound farmer and laborer with tariff exactions, deflationary financial policies, and unregulated business monopolies. The weak efforts of third parties to stand against them availed little. It was the Democratic party that should have been the most suitable implement for opposing

CAPTAIN JOHN B. CASTLEMAN AT 22

the advance of the industrial oligarchy, and under its banner the agriculturalists and common people of the South and West might have united for their mutual benefit. But Midwesterners found it hard to bring themselves to join that combination, however strong might be the practical incentives. Psychological and emotional obstacles stood in the way, products of the bitter memories of the war. Reconciliation was not impossible with opponents such as the soldiers of the South had been, but it was against nature to join hands with men in one's own section who had seemed intent upon a betrayal of their country in its time of need. Republican campaigners were keenly aware of the weapon that they held and used it for half a century. It was an important part of the technique of "waving the bloody shirt" that could be counted upon to rally Midwesterners to the Grand Old Party in crucial elections. Anti-war speeches or activities during the course of the conflict were disinterred years afterward to besmirch the reputations of Democratic candidates for office,[4] and the Democratic party as a whole was smeared with the indelible stigma of Copperheadism. In the campaign of 1868 one Republican paper reminded veterans of the war:

The Peoria Transcript, in speaking of the Soldiers and Sailors who have united their fortunes with the Democratic party, gives them some sensible advice. It says that during the late war, the Democracy could find no curse too deep, no epithet too foul to be used against them. "Hireling" and "Dog" were the mildest terms that this party . . . hurled in their faces then.

. . . .

We beg our conservative soldiers and sailors to pause a moment, . . . and think of these things.[5]

During the Hayes-Tilden contest of 1876 the Chicago *Tribune* advised its readers:

We print this morning an interesting and significant leaf from the War record of the Democratic party in Illinois, copied out of the journal of the House of Representatives. [The story of the peace resolutions of 1863.] . . . This was the Democracy in 1863, not alone in Illinois, but in New York and Indiana, where *Samuel J. Tilden* and *Thomas A. Hendricks* were no less busily engaged in the attempt to cripple the Union army and hinder and hamper the Federal Government in the prosecu-

tion of the War. They were all alike then, and they are all alike now—
enemies to the highest good and truest prosperity of the nation.[6]

All things considered, it is hard to find much good in the leaders
of the peace movement. In their opinionated views many of them
were willing to sacrifice the Union rather than permit the carrying
out of a policy that had been adopted against their wishes, and they
seemed incapable of looking beyond party victory or defeat. Some
were willing to connive with the agents of the Confederacy; and
Vallandigham, ablest and most determined of these men but an
epitome of arrogant political egoism, was a type that is dangerous
in a democracy.

The assessment of these men is not simply an effort to pass moral
judgment on individuals long dead and almost forgotten. They
were a type that has appeared repeatedly in our history and which
we may expect to encounter in times to come. Narrow, clinging to
prejudice as though it were principle, capable of plausible but
twisted logic, they necessitate a constant vigilance in any period that
they may be identified and combated. It is a mark by which they
may be known that they appeal always to the basest and most selfish
instincts, and call pandering to such motives wisdom.

But in the peace movement there was reassurance as well as warnings for democracy. The great majority of the people, often misled
and given to alternate excesses of optimism and despair, were in
the end willing to carry the war through to its close. When they
could believe that the Union would be restored, they were willing
to pay the costs. Often foolish, they were never base. In their conduct and reactions were to be seen the dangers that must be guarded
against in time of crisis among a free people; but also there were the
convincing evidences of their soundness and their strength.

Appendix

THE COPPERHEAD OATH
(Knights of the Golden Circle)

I,———, in the presence of God! and many witnesses, do solemnly declare, that I do herein, freely, and in the light of a good conscience, renew the solemn vows which I plighted in the V[estibule]. I do further promise that I will never reveal, nor make known, to any man, woman or child, any thing which my eyes may behold, or any word which my ears may hear, within this sacred T[emple], nor in any other T., nor in any other place where the brotherhood may be assembled. That I will never speak of, nor intimate any purpose or purposes of this order, whether contemplated or determined, to any one except to a brother of this order, whom I know to be such. That I will never exhibit any or either of the emblems or insignia of the order, except by express authority granted to that end, and that I will never explain their use or signification to any one not a brother of this order, whom I know to be such, under any pretense whatsoever, neither by persuasion nor by coercion. That I well never reveal nor make known, to any man, woman or child, any or either of the signs, hails, passwords, watchwords, initials nor initial letters belonging to this order, neither by voice, nor by gesture, attitude or motion of the body, nor any member of the body; nor by intimation through the instrumentality of any thing animate or inanimate, or object in the heavens, or on the earth, or above the earth, except to prove a man if he be a brother, or to communicate with a brother whom I shall have first duly proved or know to be such. That I will never pronounce the name of this order in the hearing of any man, woman or child, except to a brother of this order, whom I know to be such. That I will ever have in my most holy keeping each and every secret of this order, which may be confided to me by a brother, either within or without the T., and rather than reveal which, I will consent to any sacrifice, even unto *death by torture.* . . . I do further promise that I will, at all times, if needs be, take up arms in the cause of the oppressed—*in my country first of all*—against any Monarch, Prince, Potentate, Power or Government usurped, which may be found in arms, and waging war against a people or peoples, who are endeavoring to establish, or have inaugurated, a Government for themselves of their own free choice, in accordance with, and founded upon, *the eternal principles of Truth!* which I have sworn in the V., and now in this presence do swear, to maintain inviolate, and defend with my life. *This* I do promise, without reservation or evasion of mind; without regard to the name, station, condition or destination of the invading or coercion power, whether it shall arise within or come from without! . . . . All this I do solemnly promise and swear sacredly to observe, perform and keep, with a full knowledge and understanding, and with my full assent, that the penalty which will follow a violation of any or either of these, my solemn vows, *will be a shameful death!* while my name shall be consigned to infamy, while this sublime order shall survive the wrecks of time, and even until the last faithful brother shall have passed from earth to his service in the Temple not made with hands! Divine Essence! and ye men of Earth! witness the sincerity of my soul touching these, my vows!

Amen!

(Sons of Liberty)

. . . .

6th. The Government designated the United States of America has no sovereignty, because that is an attribute belonging to the people in their respective State organization, and with which they have not endowed that government as their common agent. It was by the terms of this compact, constituted by the States, through the express will of the people thereof severally, such common agent to use and exercise certain specified and limited powers. It was authorized so far as regards its status and relations, as a common agent in the exercise of the powers carefully and jealously delegated to it, to call itself "supreme," but not "sovereign." Supremacy, as plainly intended by the tenor and spirit of article VI of the Constitution, was created, defined and limited by the sovereignties themselves.

7th. In accordance with these principles, the Federal Government can exercise only delegated power; hence, if those who shall have been chosen to administer that Government, shall assume to exercise power not delegated, they should be regarded and dealt with as usurpers.

8th. The claim of "inherent power," or "war power," as also "State necessity," or "military necessity," on part of the functionaries of a constitutional government, for sanction of any arbitrary exercise of power, we utterly reject and repudiate.

9th. All power resides in the people, and is delegated always to be exercised for the advancement of the common weal.

10th. Whenever the officials, to whom the people have intrusted the powers of the government, shall refuse to administer it in strict accordance with its constitution, and shall assume and exercise power or authority not delegated, it is the inherent right, and imperative duty of the people, to resist such officials, and, if need be, expel them by force of arms. Such resistance is not revolution, but is solely the assertion of right.

11th. It is incompatible with the history and nature of our system of government, that federal authority should coerce by arms a sovereign State; and all intimations of such power or right, were expressly withheld in the Constitution, which conferred upon the Federal Government all its authority.

12th. Upon the preservation of the sovereignty of the States, depends the preservation of civil and personal liberty.

13th. In a convention of delegates, elected by the people of a State, is recognized the impersonation of the sovereignty of that State. The declaration of such convention upon the subject matter for which it was assembled, is the ultimate expression of that sovereignty. Such convention may refer its action back to its constituents, or the people may reverse the action of one convention by the voice of another. Thus sovereignty resides in the people of each State, and speaks alone through their conventions. . . .

References

CHAPTER I

1 Edward L. Pierce, *Memoir and Letters of Charles Sumner* (Boston: Roberts Bros., 1877–93), IV, 114

2 Speech by Thomas Corwin, quoted in Lloyd Lewis, *Sherman, Fighting Prophet* (New York: Harcourt, Brace & Co., c. 1932), p. 74

3 Speech by Senator Benjamin H. Hill, "Address Delivered before the Southern Historical Society, at Atlanta, Georgia, February 18, 1874," in Benjamin Harvey Hill, Jr., *Senator Benjamin H. Hill of Georgia: His Life, Speeches, and Writings* (Atlanta: T. H. P. Bloodworth, 1893), p. 410

4 Frank Lawrence Owsley, *State Rights in the Confederacy* (Chicago: University of Chicago Press, c. 1925) and "Defeatism in the Confederacy," *North Carolina Historical Review*, III (July 1926), 446–56; Albert Burton Moore, *Conscription and Conflict in the Confederacy* (New York: Macmillan Co., 1929); Georgia Lee Tatum, *Disloyalty in the Confederacy* (Chapel Hill: University of North Carolina Press, 1934)

5 See Frederick Jackson Turner, *The United States, 1830–1850: the Nation and Its Sections* (New York: Henry Holt & Co., c. 1935), pp. 253–351; see Isaiah Bowman, *Forest Physiography: Physiography of the United States and Principles of Soils in Relation to Forestry* (New York: J. Wiley & Sons, 1911), pp. 460–97; also Ernst Antevs, "Maps of the Pleistocene Glaciations," *Bulletin of the Geological Society of America*, XL (December 1929), 631–720; Joseph Schafer, *Four Wisconsin Counties, Prairie and Forest*. Wisconsin Domesday Book, General Studies, II (Madison: State Historical Society of Wisconsin, 1927), pp. 1–14

6 Frederic L. Paxson, "The Railroads of the Old Northwest before the Civil War," *Transactions of the Wisconsin Academy of Sciences, Arts and Letters*, XVII (Madison 1912), 247–67; Charles Henry Ambler, *A History of Transportation in the Ohio Valley, with Special Reference to Its Waterways, Trade, and Commerce from the Earliest Period to the Present Time* (Glendale, Cal.: Arthur H. Clark Co., 1932), pp. 185–264

7 Royal B. Way, "The Commerce of the Lower Mississippi in the Period 1830–1860," *Proceedings of the Mississippi Valley Historical Association*, X (July 1920), 57–68; A. H. Kohlmier, "Commerce and Union Settlement in the Old Northwest in 1860," *Transactions of the Illinois State Historical Society for the Year 1923*, pp. 154–61; Ambler, *op. cit.*, pp. 17–132

8 Way, *op. cit.*, pp. 57–68; Ambler, *op. cit.*, pp. 133–84; James William Putnam, *The Illinois and Lake Michigan Canal: A Study in Economic History*. Chicago Historical Society Collections, Vol. X (Chicago: University of Chicago Press, 1918), pp. 99–111

9 *De Bow's Review of the Southern and Western States*, XII (May 1852), 502

[10] United States, Department of the Interior, *Population of the United States in 1860, Compiled from the Original Returns of the Eighth Census under the Secretary of the Interior by Joseph C. G. Kennedy, Superintendent of Census* (Washington: Government Printing Office, 1864), pp. iv, xxxi–ii, 104, 130, 156, 248, 262, 398, 544; Robert Emmett Chaddock, *Ohio before 1850: A Study of the Early Influence of Pennsylvania and Southern Populations in Ohio*. Studies in History, Economics, and Public Law Edited by the Faculty of Political Science of Columbia University, Vol. XXXI, No. 2 (New York: Columbia University Press, 1908), pp. 13–46; Arthur Clinton Boggess, *The Settlement of Illinois, 1778–1830.* Chicago Historical Society Collections, Vol. V (Chicago: Chicago Historical Society, 1908), *passim;* William Vipond Pooley, *The Settlement of Illinois from 1830 to 1850.* Bulletin of the University of Wisconsin, No. 220, History Series, Vol. I, No. 4 (Madison, 1908), pp. 307–74; Evarts Boutell Greene, "Sectional Forces in the History of Illinois," *Transactions of the Illinois State Historical Society for the Year 1903,* pp. 75–8; Carl Russell Fish, "The Decision of the Ohio Valley," *Annual Report of the American Historical Association for 1910,* pp. 155–6; Avery Odell Craven, *Soil Exhaustion as a Factor in the Agricultural History of Virginia and Maryland, 1606–1860.* University of Illinois Studies in the Social Sciences, Vol. XIII, No. 1 (Urbana: University of Illinois, 1925), pp. 62–4, 72–82, 115–50, 122–5; Cyrenus Cole, *A History of the People of Iowa* (Cedar Rapids: Torch Press, 1921), pp. 127–31, 236–41; William O. Lynch, "The Flow of Colonists to and from Indiana before the Civil War," *Indiana Magazine of History,* XI (March 1915), 1–8

[11] Judson Fiske Lee, "Transportation, a Factor in the Development of Northern Illinois Previous to 1860," *Journal of the Illinois State Historical Society,* X (April 1917), 57, 67–8; Chaddock, *op. cit.,* pp. 13–29; Edward Conrad Smith, *The Borderland in the Civil War* (New York: Macmillan Co., 1927), pp. 10–14

[12] Lois Kimball Mathews, *The Expansion of New England: the Spread of New England Settlement and Institutions to the Mississippi River 1620–1865* (Boston: & New York: Houghton Mifflin Co., 1909), pp. 4–10, 138–250; Pooley, *op. cit.,* pp. 307–74, 482, 559–74; Greene, *op. cit.,* pp. 78–83; Solon J. Buck, "The New England Element in Illinois Politics before 1833," *Proceedings of the Mississippi Valley Historical Association, 1912–1913,* pp. 49–61; Paul Wallace Gates, *The Illinois Central Railroad and Its Colonization Work.* Harvard Economic Studies, Vol. XLII (Cambridge: Harvard University Press, 1934), 225–43

[13] Albert Bernhardt Faust, *The German Element in the United States, with Special Reference to Its Political, Moral, Social, and Educational Influence* (New York: Steuben Society of America, 1927), I, 432–90; Pooley, *op. cit.,* pp. 493–5; Carl Wittke, *We Who Built America: The Saga of the Immigrant* (New York: Prentice-Hall, 1939), pp. 187–261; U.S., *Population of the United States in 1860,* p. xxix

[14] Pooley, *op. cit.,* p. 499; Wittke, *op. cit.,* pp. 129–86; William Forbes Adams, *Ireland and the Irish Emigration to the New World from 1815 to the Famine* (New Haven: Yale University Press, 1932), *passim;* U.S., *Population of the United States in 1860,* p. xxix

[15] George Henry Porter, *Ohio Politics during the Civil War Period.* Studies

in History, Economics, and Public Law Edited by the Faculty of Political Science of Columbia University, Vol. XL, No. 2 (New York: Columbia University Press, 1911), pp. 16–18, 42, 49; James Albert Woodburn, "Party Politics in Indiana during the Civil War," *Annual Report of the American Historical Association for 1902*, I, 226; Arthur Charles Cole, *The Era of the Civil War, 1848–1870*, Vol. III of *The Centennial History of Illinois*. Edited by Clarence Walford Alvord (Chicago: A. C. McClurg & Co., 1922), pp. 53–74, 101–201; Floyd Benjamin Streeter, *Political Parties in Michigan from the Admission of the State to the Civil War*. Michigan Historical Publications, University Series, Vol. IV (Lansing: Michigan Historical Commission, 1918), pp. 4–192; Cyrenus Cole, *op. cit.*, pp. 205–9; William E. Dodd, "The Fight for the Northwest, 1860," *American Historical Review*, XVI (July 1911), 774–88, should be compared with Joseph Schafer, "Who Elected Lincoln," *Ibid.*, XLVII (October 1941), 51–63; Buck, *op. cit.*, pp. 49–61; Library of Congress, Lyman Trumbull MSS., Ebenezer Peck, Chicago, July 10, 1856, to Trumbull; Robert Fergus, Comp., *Chicago River-and-Harbor Convention; an Account of Its Origin and Proceedings. . . .* Fergus Historical Series, No. 18 (Chicago: Fergus Printing Co., 1882), *passim*

CHAPTER II

[1] *The* (Painesville, Ohio) *Press and Advertiser*, Nov. 21, 1860

[2] *Chicago Press and Tribune*, Oct. 11, 1860; also (Springfield) *Illinois State Journal*, July 16, 1860; also *The Beloit* (Wisconsin) *Journal and Courier*, Oct. 18, 1860

[3] *The Chicago Daily Times and Herald*, Oct. 10, 12, 30, 1860; *The Daily* (Columbus) *Ohio Statesman*, Oct. 9, 1860

[4] (Davenport, Iowa) *Weekly Democrat and News*, Nov. 15, 1860

[5] *The* (Cleveland, Ohio) *National Democrat*, Sept., Oct., 1860

[6] *The Connersville* (Indiana) *Telegraph*, July 20, Sept. 8, 1860

[7] *The* (Chicago) *Daily Times and Herald*, Oct. 11, 1860; *The Detroit Free Press*, Oct. 26 to Nov. 4, 1860; *The Daily Ohio Statesman*, Oct. 28, 31, Nov. 3, 4, 6, 1860; *The Cincinnati Daily Enquirer*, Oct. 23, 1860; *The Indianapolis Daily Sentinel*, Oct. 26, 27, 29, Nov. 2, 1860

[8] *The Chicago Daily Tribune*, Nov. 7, 8, 1860; (Springfield) *Illinois State Journal*, Nov. 12, 13, 15, 1860; (Champaign) *Central Illinois Gazette*, Nov. 14, 1860; *Cincinnati Daily Commercial*, Nov. 10, 12, 24, 1860; *Detroit Daily Advertiser*, Nov. 12, 17, 1860; Library of Congress, Benjamin F. Wade MSS., Senator Lyman Trumbull, Springfield, Ill., Nov. 9, 1860, to Wade

[9] Library of Congress, John Jordan Crittenden MSS., *passim;* University of Chicago Library, Stephen Arnold Douglas MSS., *passim;* Illinois State Historical Library, Richard Yates MSS., John Wilson, Washington, D.C., Jan. 1, 1861, to Yates; *Ibid.*, E. Ethridge, Washington, Jan. 14, 1861, to Yates

[10] *Daily Fort Wayne* (Indiana) *Sentinel*, Dec. 17, 1860; (Indianapolis) *Daily State Sentinel*, Jan. 22, 1861; *The Detroit Free Press*, Jan. 29, 1861; *The Cincinnati Daily Enquirer*, Dec. 20, 1860; Indiana State Historical Library, William H. English MSS., James A. Cravens (former state senator), Hardinsburg, Ind., Jan. 20, 1861, to English

[11] McCormick Historical Association Library, Cyrus H. McCormick MSS., William S. McCormick, Chicago, Feb. 6, 1861 to Jno. Churchman; Indiana State Library, Allen Hamilton MSS., I. D. G. Nelson, Fort Wayne, Ind., Feb. 4, 1861, to Hamilton

[12] *New York Weekly Tribune,* Nov. 10, 1860, *et seq.* See Ralph Ray Fahrney, *Horace Greeley and the Tribune, in the Civil War* (Cedar Rapids, Iowa: Torch Press, 1936), pp. 1–3, 43–64

[13] *New York Weekly Tribune,* Nov. 17, 1860

[14] *The Congressional Globe,* 36th Cong., 2nd sess., p. 698, appdx., pp. 129–37, speech of Representative James Wilson of Iowa; Library of Congress, John McLean MSS., E. M. Huntington (federal district judge), Indianapolis, Nov. 27, 1860, to McLean; Library of Congress, Lyman Trumbull MSS., George T. Allen, Alton, Ill., Dec. 27, 1860, to Trumbull; *Ibid.,* Th. Gregg, "Representative Office," Hamilton, Ill., Dec. 29, 1860, to Trumbull; *Ibid.,* Johnson H. Jordan, M.D., Cincinnati, Feb. 26, 1861, to Trumbull; (Jefferson, Ohio) *Ashtabula Sentinel,* Feb. 13, 1861

[15] George W. Bassett, *A Northern Plea for the Right of Secession* (Ottawa, Ill.: Office of the *Free Trader*), *passim; The Indianapolis Daily Journal,* Nov. 28, Dec. 10, 11, 1860

[16] Dec. 15, 1860. Also Dec. 8, 1860

[17] *Fort Wayne* (Indiana) *Times,* quoted in *The Cincinnati Daily Enquirer,* Jan. 6, 1861

[18] See George H. Porter, *Ohio Politics during the Civil War Period.* Studies in History, Economics, and Public Law edited by the Faculty of Political Science of Columbia University, Vol. XL, No. 2 (New York: Columbia University Press, 1911), pp. 50–2; *Daily* (Columbus) *Ohio State Journal,* Nov. 13, 1860; *Cincinnati Daily Commercial,* Nov. 14, 1860

[19] Dec. 1, 1860

[20] Ohio State Archaeological and Historical Society Library, Joshua R. Giddings MSS., John A. Bingham, Washington, Jan. 14, 1861, to Giddings; *The Congressional Globe,* 36th Cong., 2nd sess., p. 499, appdx., pp. 75–6

[21] John McLean MSS., Judge H. H. Leavitt, Cincinnati, Dec. 20, 1860, to McLean; *Ibid.,* John Reeves, Cincinnati, Jan. 10, 1861, to McLean; Library of Congress, Schuyler Colfax MSS., John H. Harper, South Bend, Ind., Feb. 25, 1861, to Colfax; *Belleville* (Illinois) *Weekly Advocate,* Jan. 11, 1861; *The* (Madison) *Wisconsin Daily Patriot,* Jan. 15, 1861; *The Indianapolis Daily Journal,* Dec. 7, 1860

[22] Chicago Historical Society Library, Richard Yates MSS., Colfax, Washington, Jan. 12, 1861, to Yates; Illinois State Historical Library, Oliver H. Browning MSS., Colfax, Jan. 18, 1861, to Browning

[23] *The Congressional Globe,* 36th Cong., 2nd sess., pp. 691, 820, appdx., pp. 192–6; Illinois State Historical Library, William Jayne MSS., Lyman Trumbull, Washington, Feb. 17, 1861, to Jayne

[24] William Dudley Foulke, *Life of Oliver P. Morton* (Indianapolis & Kansas City: Bowen Merrill Co., 1899), I, 89–96; *The Indianapolis Daily Journal,* Nov. 27, 1860

[25] Fessenden MSS., D. D. Stewart, St. Albans, Mich., March 30, 1861, to Fessenden; *Baraboo* (Wisconsin) *Republic,* Dec. 6, 1860; *Conneaut* (Ohio) *Reporter,* Jan. 31, 1861; *Painesville* (Ohio) *Telegraph,* Jan. 3, 1861

[26] Ohio State Archaeological and Historical Society Library, Columbus, Joshua Reed Giddings MSS., from Columbus, Ohio, Jan. 31, 1861

[27] This letter became public and, printed in Democratic papers, served as a basis of contention by the latter that party interests had guided the Republican policy of this period. Library of Congress, Zachariah Chandler MSS., Governor Austin Blair, Lansing, Mich., Feb. 27, 1861, to Chandler; *The Cincinnati Daily Enquirer*, Aug. 30, 1861; *The Congressional Globe*, 36th Cong., 2nd sess., pp. 1246–7. Chandler (1813–79), born in New Hampshire, acquired great wealth in Detroit, was senator from 1857 to 1875 and in 1879, member of the Joint Committee on the Conduct of the War, secretary of the Interior under Grant, during most of his career undisputed Republican boss of Michigan.

[28] Giddings MSS., New York, Feb. 5, 1861. Giddings (1795–1864) was born in Pennsylvania of New England parents, was the Abolitionist representative of the Ashtabula district of Ohio's Western Reserve from 1839 to 1859, consul-general to Canada from 1861 to his death, by turns Whig, Free Soiler, and Republican.

[29] George W. Julian, *Political Reminiscences, 1840 to 1872*, pp. 193–4. Julian (1817–99) was a native of Indiana, Abolitionist and one-time Free Soiler, member of Congress 1849 to 1851 and 1861 to 1871, radical Republican leader during Reconstruction, in 1876 supporting Tilden, and thereafter remaining a Democrat.

[30] Chase MSS., E. B. Taylor, Greenville, Ohio, Dec. 14, 1860, to Chase; *Ibid.*, Milton Sutcliff, Warren, Ohio, Feb. 14, 1861, to Chase; Trumbull MSS., James I. Ferrie, Waukegan, Ill., Dec. 24, 1861, to Trumbull; *Ibid.*, Ebenezer Peck, Chicago, Jan. 1, 1861, to Trumbull; *Ibid.*, A. B. Barrett, Mount Vernon, Ill., Jan. 5, 1861, to Trumbull

[31] Library of Congress, Joshua R. Giddings–George W. Julian MSS., William Brisbane, Madison, Wis., Jan. 31, 1861, to Julian

[32] Trumbull MSS., Johnson H. Jordan, Cincinnati, Feb. 26, 1861

[33] Letters to William Kellogg, Elihu B. Washburne, J. T. Hale, Thurlow Weed, and William H. Seward, Dec. 11, 1860, to Feb. 1, 1861, in John G. Nicolay and John Hay, *Abraham Lincoln, Complete Works* (New York: Century Co., c. 1894), I, 657–60, 664, 668–9

[34] Dec. 17, 1860

[35] Nov. 10, Dec. 7, 20, 1860. Illinois State Historical Library, John A. McClernand MSS., Charles H. Lanphier (editor of the *State Register*), Dec. 19, 1860, to McClernand. Some of the editorials were, indeed, of Lincoln's own composition.

[36] Trumbull MSS., James I. Ferrie, Waukegan, Ill., Dec. 24, 1860, to Trumbull; *Ibid.*, A. B. Barrett, Mount Vernon, Ill., Jan. 5, 1861, to Trumbull; Library of Congress, William Pitt Fessenden MSS., Milton Sutcliff, Columbus, Ohio, Feb. 15, 1861, to Fessenden; Wade MSS., Salmon P. Chase, Cincinnati, Nov. 21, 1860, to Wade; *Ibid.*, R. M. Corwine, Cincinnati, Dec. 20, 1860, to Wade; *Ibid.*, J. D. Cox, Warren, Ohio, Dec. 21, 1860, to Wade; *Ibid.*, C. Delano, Mount Vernon, Ohio, Dec. 21, 1860, to Wade; Yates MSS. (I), John Young Scammon, Chicago, Dec. 27, 1860, to Yates; *Ibid.*, Trumbull, Washington, Dec. 19, 1860, to Yates

[37] *The Chicago Daily Tribune*, Dec. 5, 1860; *The Cincinnati Commercial*, Jan. 7, 1861

38 Library of Congress, Salmon P. Chase MSS., copy of letter from Chase, Columbus, Ohio, Jan. 1861, to William H. Seward; Library of Congress, Elihu Washburne MSS., Joseph Medill, Chicago, March 21, 1864, to Washburne; Joshua R. Giddings MSS., John A. Bingham, Washington, Jan. 28, 1861, to Giddings. For the stated reasons for Republican opposition to compromise see *The Congressional Globe*, 36th Cong., 2nd sess., speeches of Senators Wade, pp. 99–104, and Sherman, pp. 450–6, of Ohio, and Harlan, of Iowa, p. 332, appdx., pp. 42–8, and Congressmen Ashley, p. 438, appdx. pp. 61–70, Blake, p. 1043, appdx., pp. 223–5, Bingham, p. 512, appdx., pp. 80–84, Edgerton, p. 680, appdx., pp. 127–9, Gurley, pp. 416–21, Hutchins, appdx., pp. 199–203, Trimble, p. 762, appdx., pp. 160–4, and Edward Wade, p. 1043, appdx., pp. 228–31, of Ohio, Case, p. 820, appdx., pp. 185–9, and Pettit, p. 1040, appdx., pp. 280–7, of Indiana, Farnsworth, p. 677, appdx., pp. 118–21, Lovejoy, appdx., pp. 84–7, and Morris, p. 421, appdx., pp. 48–57, of Illinois, and Kellogg, p. 1157, appdx., pp. 269–72, of Michigan. Most of these and other speeches were printed and circulated in pamphlet form.

39 Trumbull MSS., W. Jayne, Springfield, Jan. 28, 1861, to Trumbull. Trumbull (1813–96), born in Connecticut, was chief justice of Illinois from 1848 to 1854, senator from 1855 to 1873, a Democrat to 1855 and after 1876, Republican and Liberal Republican in the interim, recognized as one of the ablest statesmen of his generation.

40 Foulke, *op. cit.*, I, 104–6

41 United States, *The War of the Rebellion: a Compilation of the Official Records of the Union and Confederate Armies* (hereinafter referred to as *O.R.*), Ser. III, Vol. I, 55–7, Samuel J. Kirkwood, to Joseph Holt; Fessenden MSS., C. N. Bodfish, Clinton, Iowa, Jan. 29, 1861, to Fessenden; Wisconsin State Historical Society Library, Wisconsin Civil War Governors' Letters, letters to Alexander W. Randall from Major-General James Sutherland, Janesville, Jan. 5, from Captain George E. Bryant, Madison, Jan. 9, from forty persons of Ripon, Jan. 14, Colonel S. L. Lefferts, Fond du Lac, Jan. 16, from Sergeant John Rohr, Fort Atkinson, Feb. 2, from Captain Gustavus Hammer, Maysville, Feb. 25, 1861; Yates MSS., Lyman Trumbull, Washington, Jan. 2, 1861, to Yates; *Chicago Daily Tribune*, Jan. 3, 1861; *The Beloit* (Wisconsin) *Journal and Courier*, Jan. 3, 1861

42 *The Cincinnati Daily Enquirer*, Jan. 13, 1861; *Chicago Daily Tribune*, March 20, 1861

43 Chicago Historical Society Library, Douglas MSS., Theo. Williams, North California, Ohio, Apr. 1, 1861, to Douglas; Indiana State Library, Allen Hamilton MSS., Congressman William S. Holman, Washington, D.C., Dec. 13, 28, 1860, to Hamilton; *Ibid.*, Aurora, Ind., Apr. 13, 1861; *The Congressional Globe*, 36th Cong., 2nd sess., pp. 367–73, 418–21, 803, appdx., pp. 167–70

44 Dec. 7, 22, 1860, Jan. 2, 1861

45 Jan. 5, 18, 1861

46 Dec. 29, 30, 1860

47 Nov. 8, 1860. English MSS., Senator Jesse D. Bright, Dec. 1860, to English

48 Quoted in *Belleville Weekly Advocate*, Nov. 16, 1860

49 *Cairo* (Illinois) *City Gazette*, Dec. 6, 1860; *Ottawa* (Illinois) *Free Trader*, Dec. 29, 1860; *The* (Columbus, Ohio) *Crisis*, Jan. 31, 1861

50 Quoted in *The* (Columbus, Ohio) *Crisis*, Apr. 11, 1861

51 Jan. 11, 1861

52 See speeches of Senators Stephen A. Douglas of Illinois and George E. Pugh of Ohio, and Congressmen Samuel S. Cox, Clement L. Vallandigham, and George H. Pendleton of Ohio, and John A. Logan of Illinois, as well as those of Holman, McClernand, and Allen already cited in note 43. *The Congressional Globe,* 36th Cong., 2nd sess., pp. 157, 243, 450, 759, 803, 836–9, 1067, appdx., pp. 29–42, 70–5, 167–70, 178–81, 235–42

53 *The Cincinnati Daily Enquirer,* Jan. 13, 24, March 12, 1861; *The Detroit Free Press,* Jan. 1861, *passim*

54 *The* (Columbus, Ohio) *Crisis,* Jan. 31, 1861; Foulke, *op. cit.,* I, 110–2; (Indianapolis) *Daily State Sentinel,* Jan. 31, 1861; (Springfield) *Illinois State Register,* Jan. 15, 16, 1861

55 Ottawa (Illinois) *Free Trader,* Feb. 9, 16, 1861; *The Cincinnati Daily Enquirer,* Jan. 6, 13, 24, Feb. 19, March 5, 6, 7, 12, 1861. The basis of this policy, in so far as it arose from sincere motives rather than from partisan maneuvering, was a firm belief in a powerful Union sentiment in the South which needed only reassurance of Northern respect for Southern rights to arise and check secession in mid-course. Such was its vitality that it would persist as a cardinal article of faith with the peace Democrats throughout the conflict.

56 Patton, Charles and William, Collection, Springfield, Ill., Charles H. Lanphier MSS., Washington, Feb. 4, 1861, to Lanphier; also letter of Dec. 3, 1860. Lanphier was editor of the *Illinois State Register.* McClernand (1812–1900) was born in Kentucky, served in Congress from Illinois from 1843 to 1851 and 1859 to 1861, was made brigadier-general in 1861 and major-general in 1862. Removed by Grant for insubordination in the Vicksburg campaign, he was restored to command in 1864. Throughout the war he was unfailing in his support of the administration and its war policy.

57 Allen Johnson, *Stephen A. Douglas; a Study in American Politics* (New York: Macmillan Co., 1908), pp. 447–8. Original in Lanphier MSS., Washington, Dec. 25, 1860, to Lanphier; *The Congressional Globe,* 36th Cong., 2nd sess., p. 243, appdx., pp. 35–42. This was also issued and distributed in pamphlet form.

58 Chase MSS., James M. Ashley, Washington, Dec. 18, 1860, to Chase; *Ibid.,* H. G. Blake, Washington, Dec. 18, 1860, to Chase. See speech of Pugh, *The Congressional Globe,* 36th Cong., 2nd sess., p. 157, appdx. pp. 29–35. Pugh (1822–76) was captain in the Mexican War, strong supporter of Douglas and spokesman for his faction in the Democratic convention in 1860, and senator from 1855 to 1861. *The Daily* (Columbus) *Ohio Statesman,* Dec. 27, 1860

59 *Ibid.,* pp. 1067, 450, appdx., pp. 235–42, 70, 72. Pendleton (1825–89) was a descendant of Virginia aristocracy, married to a daughter of Francis Scott Key and niece of Roger B. Taney, and known in Ohio politics by the sobriquet of "Gentleman George." Law partner of Pugh, he was congressman from 1857 to 1865 and Democratic nominee for vice-president in 1864.

60 *The* (Columbus, Ohio) *Crisis,* Feb. 7, 1861. Thurman (1813–95), born in Virginia, was member of Congress from Ohio from 1845 to 1847, chief justice of Ohio from 1854 to 1856, senator from 1867 to 1881, and Democratic nominee for vice-president in 1888.

61 *The Chicago Tribune,* Jan. 16, 1861

62 (Chicago) *Daily Times and Herald,* Sept. 12, 1860. See also *The Cincinnati*

Daily Enquirer, Dec. 21, 1860; English MSS., J. A. Cravens, Hardinsburg, Ind., Apr. 9, 1861, to English

63 *The* (Columbus, Ohio) *Crisis*, Jan. 31, 1861. See also *The Daily Chicago Times*, Dec. 6, 1860; (Davenport, Iowa) *Weekly Democrat and News*, Nov. 15, 1860; *The Cincinnati Daily Press*, Jan. 28, 1861 (pamphlet reprint); *The Jonesboro* (Illinois) *Weekly Gazette*, Apr. 6, 1861; Crittenden MSS., N. P. Tallmadge, former U. S. Senator, Fond du Lac, Wis., Dec. 17, 1860, to Crittenden

64 *The Cincinnati Daily Enquirer*, Jan. 17, 1861; *Ottawa* (Illinois) *Free Trader*, March 16, 1861; Hamilton MSS., Congressman W. S. Holman, Aurora, Ind., Nov. 18, 1860, to Hamilton

65 *The* (Columbus, Ohio) *Crisis*, Jan. 31, 1861

66 Library of Congress, Crittenden MSS., James F. Noble, Cincinnati, Dec. 3, 1860, to Crittenden; Douglas MSS., S. S. Hayes, Chicago, Dec. 18, 1860, to Douglas; *The* (Columbus, Ohio) *Crisis*, Feb. 7, 1861; *The Appleton* (Wisconsin) *Crescent*, Dec. 22, 1860; *The Cincinnati Daily Enquirer*, Jan. 13, 1861. Logan (1826–86) was lieutenant in the Mexican War, in Congress from 1859 to 1861 and 1867 to 1871, became colonel in 1861, brigadier-general in 1862, major-general in 1863, was an organizer of the Grand Army of the Republic, senator from 1871 to 1877 and from 1879 to his death, was a Democrat to 1864 and Republican thereafter, nominee of the latter party for vice-president in 1884.

67 (Indianapolis) *Daily State Sentinel*, Jan. 8, 1861

68 Trumbull MSS., S. E. Flannigan, Benton, Ill., Apr. 9, 1861, to Trumbull

69 (Indianapolis) *Daily State Sentinel*, Jan. 14, 1861; *Canton* (Illinois) *Weekly Register*, Jan. 29, Apr. 9, 1861; *Joliet* (Illinois) *Signal*, Dec. 25, 1860

70 *The Cincinnati Daily Enquirer*, Jan. 18, Feb. 3, 1861; *The* (Columbus, Ohio) *Crisis*, Jan. 31, Feb. 21, March 28, Apr. 4, 1861; *Joliet* (Illinois) *Signal*, Feb. 25, 1861

71 (Springfield) *Illinois Daily State Journal*, Jan. 14, 1861

72 Jan. 29, 1861

73 Jan. 23, 1861. See also Douglas MSS., John A. Trimble, Hillsboro, Ohio, Dec. 29, 1860, to Douglas

74 Feb. 19, 1861

75 William Watts Folwell, *A History of Minnesota*, (St. Paul: Minnesota Historical Society, 1921), II, 70–1

76 Jan. 3, 1861

77 *The Detroit Free Press*, Feb. 2, 3, 1861

78 Jan. 26, 1861

79 Jan. 29, 1861

80 *The Cincinnati Daily Enquirer*, Jan. 25, 1861; *The* (Columbus, Ohio) *Crisis*, Jan. 31, 1861

81 (Indianapolis) *Daily State Sentinel*, Jan. 9, 1861

82 (Springfield) *Illinois State Register*, Jan. 17, 1861

83 *The* (Columbus, Ohio) *Crisis*, April 4, 1861; *Joliet* (Illinois) *Signal*, Apr. 22, 1861

84 Douglas MSS., Charles H. Fox, Jacksonville, Ill., March 13, 1861

85 Library of Congress, Thomas Ewing MSS., copy of letter from Thomas Ewing, Jr., Vincennes, Ind., Apr. 15, 1861, to Hugh Ewing. See also Chase MSS., A. Harris, Eaton, Ohio, Dec. 25, 1860, to Chase; Trumbull MSS., Horace White,

of the *Chicago Tribune*, Chicago, Dec. 30, 1860, to Trumbull; Gustave Koerner, *Memoirs of Gustave Koerner*, II, 119. Thomas Ewing, Jr. (1829–96), was law partner with his brother Hugh and his brother-in-law W. T. Sherman in Kansas, chief justice of Kansas from 1861 to 1862, entered the war in 1862, became a brigadier-general in 1863 and checked Sterling Price's invasion of Missouri in 1864, for which feat he was breveted a major-general in 1865. After the war he became a leader of the Greenback wing of the Democratic party in Ohio, serving in Congress from 1877 to 1881 and running unsuccessfully as his party's candidate for governor in 1879. Hugh Boyle Ewing (1826–1905) enlisted at the outset of the war, became a colonel in 1861, a brigadier-general in 1862, and was breveted a major-general in 1865, having served with particular distinction in the Antietam and Vicksburg campaigns.

[86] Apr. 3, 1861. Also Yates MSS. (I), S. R. Hay, Newton, Ill., April 14, 1861, to Yates

[87] *The Cincinnati Daily Enquirer,* Jan. 8, 1861

[88] Edward Channing, *A History of the United States,* VI (New York: Macmillan Co., 1927), 314–5

CHAPTER III

[1] *The* (Columbus, Ohio) *Crisis,* Apr. 18, 1861; also (Indianapolis) *Daily State Sentinel,* Apr. 15, 1861; (Springfield) *Illinois State Register,* Apr. 16, 20, 1861; (Springfield, Illinois) *Weekly State Journal,* Apr. 17, 20, 24, 1861; *The Cincinnati Daily Enquirer,* Apr. 17, 18, 19, 20, May 7, 1861; *Aurora* (Illinois) *Beacon,* Apr. 18, May 2, 1861; *Ottawa* (Illinois) *Weekly Republican,* Apr. 20, 1861; *Ottawa* (Illinois) *Free Trader,* Apr. 20, 27, 1861; (Rockford, Illinois) *Rock River Democrat,* Apr. 23, 1861; *Rockford* (Illinois) *Register,* May 4, 1861; (Champaign) *Central Illinois Gazette,* May 8, 1861; Library of Congress, John Jordan Crittenden MSS., N. M. Ross, Indianapolis, Apr. 23, 1861, to Crittenden; Library of Congress, Salmon Portland Chase MSS., Joshua Hanna, Pittsburg, Apr. 24, 1861, just after trip through Midwest, to Chase; *Ibid.,* Henry Converse, Wyocena, Wis., May 6, 1861, to Chase; *O.R.,* Ser. III, Vol. I, 121–2, W. H. Osborn, President of the Illinois Central R.R., New York, Apr. 26, 1861, to Secretary of War Cameron; *Ibid.,* pp. 181, 219, Governor Yates, Springfield, May 9, 1861, to Lincoln, Cameron, May 21, 1861, to Yates; Jane Martin Johns, *Personal Recollections of Early Decatur, Abraham Lincoln, Richard J. Oglesby, and the Civil War* (Decatur, Ill.; Decatur Chapter of the Daughters of the American Revolution), pp. 142–6; Theodore Calvin Pease and James Garfield Randall, eds., *The Diary of Orville Hickman Browning,* I (Springfield: Illinois State Historical Library, 1925), 463

[2] Wisconsin State Historical Society Library, James Corydon Howard MSS., Jonathan Dean Howard, Portage City, Wis., Apr. 28, 1861, to J. C. Howard

[3] Library of Congress, Edwin M. Stanton MSS., Bancroft, New York, Jan. 27, 1862, to Stanton

[4] *O.R.,* Ser. III, Vol. I, 70, Oliver Perry Morton, Indianapolis, Apr. 15, 1861, to Abraham Lincoln; *Ibid.,* p. 72, Alexander W. Randall, Madison, Apr. 15, 1861, to Simon Cameron; *Ibid.,* p. 73, William Dennison, Columbus, Apr. 15, 1861, to Lincoln; *Ibid.,* pp. 80–1, Richard Yates, and others, Springfield, Apr. 17, 1861, to Lincoln; *Ibid.,* p. 85, Samuel J. Kirkwood, Davenport, Apr. 18,

1861, to Cameron; *Ibid.*, p. 91, Randall, Madison, Apr. 19, 1861, to Cameron; *Ibid.*, p. 88, Austin Blair, Lansing, Apr. 19, 1861, to Cameron; *Ibid.*, p. 103, Ignatius Donnelly, St. Paul, Apr. 23, 1861.

5 Wisconsin Governors' Letters during the Civil War MSS., letters from Charles H. Larrabee (Democratic member of Congress and former justice of the Wisconsin Supreme Court), Horicon, Apr. 14, 1861; Lysander Cutler (later major-general), Milwaukee, Apr. 15; S. T. Harshaw, Horicon, Apr. 16; William Blake, Fox Lake, Apr. 16; N. S. Murphy, Whitewater, Apr. 16; George Strong, Hudson, Apr. 16; Lucas M. Miller, Oshkosh, Apr. 17; E. F. Herzberg, Milwaukee, Apr. 18; Wilson Colwell, La Crosse, Apr. 18, to Randall; *O.R.*, Ser. III, Vol. I, 74–5, Governor Kirkwood, Davenport, Apr. 16, 1861, to Cameron; *Ibid.*, p. 75, Governor Morton, Indianapolis, Apr. 16, 1861, to Cameron; *Ibid.*, p. 116, Governor Yates, Springfield, Apr. 26, 1861, to Cameron; *Ibid.*, pp. 125–6, Morton, Indianapolis, Apr. 28, 1861, to Cameron; *The Cincinnati Daily Enquirer*, Apr. 17, 18, 1861; *The Chicago Daily Tribune*, Apr. 19, 1861, Ottawa (Illinois) *Free Trader*, Apr. 27, June 11, 1861; Ohio Archaeological and Historical Society Library, Ohio Executive Records, Correspondence, Joseph Ankeny, Millersburg, Ohio, Apr. 28, 1861, to Governor Dennison

6 *O.R.*, Ser. III, Vol. I, 84–5, Governor Dennison, Columbus, Apr. 18, 1861, to Cameron; (Springfield, Illinois) *Weekly State Journal*, Apr. 24, May 29, 1861; (Springfield) *Illinois State Register*, July 15, 1861; State of Illinois, *Report of the Adjutant General of the State of Illinois*, I (Springfield: Phillips Bros., State Printers, 1900), 7–8; Augustus Harris Burley, *The Cairo Expedition: Illinois' First Response in the Civil War; the Expedition from Chicago to Cairo* (Chicago: Fergus Printing Co., 1892), *passim;* Library of Congress, Lyman Trumbull MSS., Joseph Medill, Chicago, Apr. 16, 1861

7 *O.R.*, Ser. III, Vol. I, 80, Governor Morton, Indianapolis, Apr. 17, 1861, to Secretary of War Cameron, Cameron to Morton; *Ibid.*, p. 97, Senator Zachariah Chandler, Detroit, Apr. 21, 1861, to Cameron; *Ibid.*, pp. 101–2, Governor Dennison, Columbus, Apr. 22, 1861, to Cameron; *Ibid.*, p. 113, Governor Yates, Springfield, Apr. 25, 1861, to Cameron; *Ibid.*, p. 127–8, Governor Kirkwood, Davenport, Apr. 29, 1861, to Cameron; *Ibid.*, p. 145, Dennison, Columbus, May 2, 1861, to Cameron; *Ibid.*, p. 214, Yates, Springfield, May 18, 1861, to Congressman John A. McClernand; *Ibid.*, p. 162, Kirkwood, Davenport, May 6, 1861, to Cameron; *Ibid.*, p. 189, Governor Randall, Madison, May 11, 1861, to Cameron; *Ibid.*, p. 217, Dennison, Columbus, May 19, 1861, to Cameron; *Ibid.*, p. 273, Yates, Springfield, June 16, 1863, to Lincoln; (Springfield) *Illinois State Register*, May 2, 1861; (Springfield, Illinois) *Weekly State Journal*, May 29, June 5, 1861; *The Chicago Daily Tribune*, May 31, 1861; Ottawa (Illinois) *Weekly Republican*, June 8, 1861; Illinois, *Report of the Adjutant General*, I, 11

8 (Springfield) *Illinois State Register*, Apr. 16, 20, 1861; *Weekly Racine* (Wisconsin) *Advocate*, Apr. 24, 1861; *The Detroit Free Press*, Apr. 16, 17, 26, 1861; Chase MSS., Philip V. Herzing, St. Marys, Ohio, Apr. 16, 1861, to Chase; *Ibid.*, Edward D. Mansfield, Cincinnati, Apr. 18, 1861, to Chase; *O.R.*, Ser. III, Vol. I, 78, Senator Zachariah Chandler, Detroit, Apr. 17, 1861, to Secretary of War Cameron

9 *The Racine* (Wisconsin) *Democrat*, Apr. 21, 1861; also *The Detroit Free Press*, Apr. 19, 1861; *The* (Madison) *Wisconsin Daily Patriot*, Apr. 17, 1861;

The Manitowoc (Wisconsin) *Pilot,* Apr. 19, 1861; *Beaver Dam* (Wisconsin) *Argus,* Apr. 26, 1861; *The Appleton* (Wisconsin) *Argus,* Apr. 27, 1861

10 *The Cincinnati Daily Enquirer,* Apr. 17, 21, 1861

11 *Ottawa* (Illinois) *Free Trader,* Apr. 27, 1861

12 (Springfield) *Illinois Weekly State Journal,* Apr. 24, July 17, 1861; *Prairie Farmer,* July 25, 1861. An additional stimulus to enlistment was the fact that the prices for farm products were currently low and that in many districts army worms, locusts, and chinch bugs were making serious inroads on the crops. *Ibid.,* June 20, July 10, 25, 1861

13 *The Cincinnati Daily Enquirer,* Apr. 21, 1861

14 Chase MSS., F. W. Fee, Cincinnati, Apr. 14, 1861, to Chase

15 *Ibid.,* J. H. Jordan, Cincinnati, May 8, 1861, to Chase

16 (Springfield) *Illinois Weekly State Journal,* Apr. 17, 1861. Also *The Detroit Free Press,* Apr. 16, 1861; *O.R.,* Ser. II, Vol. II, 1321–39, intercepted letter from William M. Hill, Magnolia, La., May 14, 1861, to the editor of the *Union* (Virginia) *Democrat*

17 (Indianapolis) *Daily State Sentinel,* Apr. 13, 15, 18, 19, 29, 1861; *The Detroit Free Press,* Apr. 16, 1861; *The Cincinnati Daily Enquirer,* Apr. 17, 18, 19, 21, 24, May 21, 1861; (Canton, Ohio) *Stark County Democrat,* Apr. 17, May 1, 1861; *The* (Columbus, Ohio) *Crisis,* Apr. 18, 1861; *The Circleville* (Ohio) *Watchman,* Apr. 19, May 24, 1861; *The Kenosha* (Wisconsin) *Democrat,* Apr. 19, 1861

18 Wisconsin Governors' Letters, Horn, Cedarburg, Wis., Apr. 18, 1861, to Governor Randall

19 McCormick MSS., suppressed pro-war editorial written by Dr. Willis Lord for the *Presbyterian Expositor; Ibid.,* William S. McCormick, Chicago, May 6, 1861, to Alexander Steele, New Orleans; *Ibid.,* May 21, 1861, to James Henry, Steele's Tavern, Virginia. For a detailed presentation and analysis of McCormick's views throughout the war period see William T. Hutchinson, *Cyrus Hall McCormick: Harvest, 1856–1884* (New York & London: D. Appleton-Century Co., 1935), pp. 37–63

20 *The Cincinnati Daily Enquirer,* June 27, 1861; Pease, *op. cit.,* I, 464

21 *The Cincinnati Daily Enquirer,* Apr. 20, 1861

22 Quoted in *The Chicago Daily Tribune,* Apr. 30, 1861. *The Jonesboro* (Illinois) *Weekly Gazette,* Apr. 27, May 25, 1861

23 *The Chicago Daily Tribune,* Apr. 23, 1861, from the *Marion* (Illinois) *Intelligencer; Ibid.,* Apr. 30, 1861, from the Carbondale, Illinois, *Times,* Apr. 27, 1861. Other evidence of such an attitude is to be found in Illinois State Historical Library, Richard Yates MSS., letters to Yates from Parker Earle and Charles Colby, Colden, Union County, Ill., Apr. 21, 1861; "A Unionist," Nashville, Washington County, Ill., Apr. 22, 1861; T. M. Seawell, Nashville, Ill., Apr. 23, 1861; Jas. L. Gage, St. Louis, Mo., Apr. 23, 1861

24 (Springfield, Illinois) *Weekly State Journal,* May 8, 1861; (Springfield) *Illinois State Journal,* July 30, 1862; *The Cincinnati Daily Enquirer,* May 30, 1861; *The Chicago Times,* Aug. 3, 1861, from the *Mt. Vernon* (Illinois) *Guardian,* July 31, 1861; (Rockford, Illinois) *Rock River Democrat,* Feb. 18, 1863

25 *The Chicago Times,* Oct. 31, 1876, letter of recollections from C. H. Lanphier, editor of the (Springfield) *Illinois State Register* during the war and confidant of Senator Douglas; Koerner, *op. cit.,* II, 124

26 *The Cincinnati Daily Enquirer,* Apr. 23, 24, 28, 1861; *The Daily* (Columbus, Ohio) *Statesman,* Apr. 23, 25, 1861; *The* (Columbus, Ohio) *Crisis,* Apr. 25, 1861; *The Chicago Daily Tribune,* May 2, 1861; *Weekly* (Springfield, Illinois) *State Journal,* May 8, 1861; *Ottawa* (Illinois) *Free Trader,* May 11, 1861; Lanphier MSS., Douglas, Bellaire, Ohio, Apr. 22, 1861, telegram to C. H. Lanphier; Pease, *op. cit.,* I, 465–6; Stephen A. Douglas, *Speech of Senator Douglas before the Legislature of Illinois, April 25, 1861, in Compliance with a Joint Resolution of the Two Houses* (7 pages; no publishing data given); Yates MSS. (I), A. C. Clayton, *Jerseyville* (Illinois) *Prairie State,* Apr. 10, 1861, to Yates

27 *The Cincinnati Daily Enquirer,* Apr. 27, 28, May 22, 23, June 10, 1861; (Indianapolis) *Daily State Sentinel,* Apr. 30, 1861; *The Joliet* (Illinois) *Signal,* Apr. 30, 1861

28 McCormick MSS., undated clipping from *Chicago Times; Ibid.,* William S. McCormick, Chicago, May 3, 1861, to J. B. McCormick, St. Louis; *Ibid.,* May 6, 1861, to Alex. Steele, New Orleans; May 9 and May 21, 1861, to Jas. Henry, Steele's Tavern, Va. On June 1, 1861, C. H. McCormick sold the *Times* to Wilbur F. Storey, owner of the *Detroit Free Press,* which was now sold to another party. Storey took charge on June 8. *The Daily Chicago Times,* June 8, 1861; *The Cincinnati Daily Enquirer,* June 8, 1861. On Richardson, see *Joliet Signal,* May 14, 1861, from the Quincy *Herald.*

29 *The Cincinnati Daily Enquirer,* Apr. 21, 1861; (Springfield, Illinois) *Weekly State Journal,* May 22, 1861; Buford Wilson, "Southern Illinois during the Civil War," *Transactions of the Illinois State Historical Society for the Year 1911,* pp. 99–103; Yates MSS. (I), A. H. Warford, Equality, Gallatin County, May 16, 1861, to Yates

30 Sept. 1, 1861; see also *Ibid.,* May 5, 8, 15, 19, 21, 27, June 7, 21, 28, Aug. 15, Sept. 3, 5, 6, 7, Nov. 5, 1861; *The Daily Chicago Times,* June 8, 12, 14, 16, 18, 19, 25, 27, 28, July 26, Aug. 14, Sept. 3, Oct. 15, 1861, Jan. 5, 8, 1862

31 Apr. 25, 1861

32 Library of Congress, John Alexander Logan MSS.; also *Ibid.,* Washington, July 16; *Ibid.,* Washington, July 16, 1861, to Capt. ? , referred to as his closest friend. Logan went out to the Battle of Bull Run as a spectator but reported that he got hold of a musket and fought for the last four hours of the engagement, also helping carry off the wounded. *Ibid.,* Washington, July 20, 1861, to Mrs. Logan. On July 25 he wrote to her that he had decided to enlist as soon as he returned home.

33 Clement L. Vallandigham, *Speeches, Arguments, Addresses, and Letters of Clement L. Vallandigham* (New York: J. Walter & Co., 1864), pp. 324–5

34 Chase MSS., F. A. Waldo, Cincinnati, July 29, 1861, to Chase; also *The Chicago Times,* July 20, 23, 26, 1862; *Milwaukee Morning Sentinel,* July 23, 24, 25, 1861; (Alma, Wisconsin) *Buffalo County Journal,* July 25, 1861; *The Cincinnati Daily Enquirer,* July 23, 1861; Library of Congress, Lyman Trumbull MSS., Grant Goodrich, Chicago, July 29, 1861, to Trumbull

35 Aug. 17, 1861. *The Prairie Farmer,* July 25, 1861; (Springfield, Illinois) *Weekly State Journal,* Apr. 24, 1861. See also *O.R.,* Ser. III, Vol. I, 343, Governor Yates, Springfield, Ill., July 23, 1861, to Secretary Cameron; *Ibid.,* p. 350, Cameron, Washington, July 25, 1861, to Yates; *Ibid.,* p. 432, Governor Randall, Madison, Wis., Oct. 19, 1861, to Cameron; *Ibid.,* p. 450, Yates, Aug. 24, 1861, to Cameron; *Ibid.,* p. 466, Governor Morton, Indianapolis, Aug. 30, 1861, to

Assistant Secretary of War Thomas A. Scott; *Ibid.,* Scott, Washington, Aug. 31, 1861, to Morton; *Ibid.,* pp. 489–90, Morton, Sept. 7, 1861, to Scott; *Ibid.,* p. 544, Governor Blair, Jackson, Mich., Sept. 27, 1861, to Cameron; *Ibid.,* p. 548, Assistant Adjutant-General John L. Loomis, Springfield, Sept. 30, 1861, to Cameron; (Springfield, Illinois) *Weekly State Journal,* July 17, Aug. 7, 1861; *Belleville* (Illinois) *Democrat,* Aug. 3, 1861; *Ottawa* (Illinois) *Free Trader,* Aug. 17, Nov. 23, 1861; *Canton* (Illinois) *Weekly Register,* Aug. 13, Sept. 3, 1861, Jan. 21, 1862; *Rockford* (Illinois) *Republican,* Oct. 10, 1861

³⁶ *O.R.,* Ser. III, Vol. I, 698–708

³⁷ Trumbull MSS., C. H. Kettler, Waterloo, Ill., Dec. 22, 1861

³⁸ *The Cincinnati Daily Enquirer,* Sept. 26, 1861, resolutions of the Dearborn County Democratic meeting, Lawrenceville, Ind., Sept. 21, 1861

³⁹ *Ibid.,* July 19, Aug. 20, Sept. 6, 13, Oct. 6, 22, Nov. 1, 5, Dec. 5, 1861; *St. Charles City* (Iowa) *Republican Intelligencer,* Aug. 1, Sept. 12, 19, 26, 1861; *The* (Columbus, Ohio) *Crisis,* Aug. 29, 1861; *Burlington* (Iowa) *Daily Hawk-Eye,* Sept. 2, 3, 4, 13, 16, 21, 25, 28, 1861; (Madison) *Wisconsin Patriot,* Oct. 5, 26, 1861; (Indianapolis) *Daily State Sentinel,* Jan. 3, 1861

⁴⁰ *The Cincinnati Daily Enquirer,* June 4, 1861; also *Ibid.,* July 9, Aug. 28, 1861; *The Daily Chicago Times,* June 14, 27, July 18, 1861; *The* (Columbus, Ohio) *Crisis,* Aug. 8, Oct. 24, 1861, Jan. 2, Feb. 5, 1862. It is interesting to note that only some two or three of the eighty or ninety Democratic papers in Ohio would join the Union party movement in that state in 1861. *The Cincinnati Daily Enquirer,* Aug. 17, 1861

⁴¹ *The Cincinnati Daily Enquirer,* Aug. 9, 11, 13, Sept. 21, 26, Dec. 1, 29, 1861; *The Chicago Times,* Jan. 5, 31, 1862; (Rockford, Illinois) *Rock River Democrat,* Jan. 21, 1862; Chase MSS., Peter Linn, House of Representatives, Columbus, Ohio, Jan. 9, 1862, to Chase

⁴² *The Cincinnati Daily Enquirer,* June 22, 1861

⁴³ *Ibid.,* May 5, 17, June 6, 7, 21, July 10, Oct. 9, 1861; *The Chicago Times,* July 6, 1861; (Indianapolis) *Daily State Sentinel,* Aug. 10, 12, 1861; *The Daily* (Columbus) *Ohio Statesmen,* June 30, 1861

⁴⁴ *The Cincinnati Daily Enquirer,* Aug. 15, 1861

⁴⁵ *Ibid.,* May 21, Sept. 5, 7, 1861; (Indianapolis) *Daily State Sentinel,* July 17, 1861; *Coshocton* (Ohio) *Democrat,* Sept. 18, 1861; *The Chicago Times,* Aug. 2, 1861, Jan. 8, 1862; *The* (Columbus, Ohio) *Crisis,* Aug. 22, 1861; Trumbull MSS., Hiram Sears, Elsah, Ill., July 18, 1861, to Trumbull

⁴⁶ Library of Congress, Carl Schurz MSS., E. L. Buthick, Milwaukee, Sept. 15, 1861, to Schurz; *Milwaukee Wisconsin,* Sept. 9, 1861, quoted in *The Chicago Times,* Sept. 10, 1861

⁴⁷ *The Chicago Times,* July 10, 1861; (Springfield) *Illinois State Register,* Aug. 20, 1861; *Joliet* (Illinois) *Signal,* Dec. 17, 1871; *The Cincinnati Daily Enquirer,* Dec. 8, 1861

⁴⁸ *The Cincinnati Daily Enquirer,* Aug. 1, 1861; also *Ibid.,* Dec. 28, 1861

⁴⁹ *Ibid.,* July 9, 1861; also May 8, 10, June 20, 26, July 2, 14, Aug. 8, 1861

⁵⁰ *The Cincinnati Daily Enquirer,* July 9, 12, Sept. 7, 1861; (Indianapolis) *Daily State Sentinel,* Aug. 9, 15, 1861; (Springfield) *Weekly Illinois State Journal,* Feb. 5, 1862

⁵¹ *O.R.,* Ser. II, Vol. II, 56, Samuel Hill (postmaster), Deer Creek, Ohio, Sept. 7, 1861, to Simon Cameron, enclosing clipping

52 *The Cincinnati Daily Enquirer*, Apr. 17, 19, 20, May 19, June 20, July 7, 9, 12, 17, 1861; (Canton, Ohio) *Stark County Democrat*, Apr. 24, 1861; *The* (Columbus, Ohio) *Crisis*, May 30, June 20, July 4, 1861; McCormick MSS., William S. McCormick, Chicago, May 7, 1861, to J. B. McCormick, St. Louis

53 *The Cincinnati Daily Enquirer*, June 20, 1861; *Rockford* (Illinois) *Republican*, June 26, 1861

54 *The Cincinnati Daily Enquirer*, Aug. 17, 1861

55 (Indianapolis) *Daily State Sentinel*, July 30, 1861; *The Cincinnati Daily Enquirer*, Sept. 6, 1861; *The* (Columbus, Ohio) *Crisis*, Sept. 5, 1861

56 *Ibid.*, Aug. 29, Sept. 12, 1861; *The Cincinnati Daily Enquirer*, Sept. 1, 7, Oct. 22, 1861

57 Aug. 23, 1861

58 *The* (Columbus, Ohio) *Crisis*, Aug. 29, 1861; also *The Chicago Times*, July 11, 1861; *The Cincinnati Daily Enquirer*, Aug. 4, 1861

59 *Ibid.*, Apr. 19, 1861, from the (Indianapolis) *Daily State Sentinel*

60 *O.R.*, Ser. II, Vol. II, 1295–1302; *Burlington Daily Hawk-Eye*, July 3, 1862. Born in Vincennes, Indiana, son of a commissary of George Rogers Clark, Jones (1804–96) had been successively territorial delegate first from Michigan and then from Wisconsin, one of Iowa's first two senators (1849–59), and under Buchanan minister to Colombia. On his release from prison he withdrew from politics. John Carl Parish, *George Wallace Jones* (Iowa City: State Historical Society of Iowa, 1912), pp. 3–71

61 Jesse David Bright (1812–75), born in New York state, was state senator in Indiana from 1841 to 1843, lieutenant-governor from 1843 to 1845, and United States senator from 1845 to 1862.

62 *The Chicago Times*, July 11, 1861, Jan. 31, 1862; *The Congressional Globe*, 37th Cong., 2nd sess. (Washington: Congressional Globe Office, 1862), pp. 40–5, speech of Representative George H. Pendleton, of Ohio, Dec. 10, 1861; also circulated in pamphlet form.

63 *The Cincinnati Daily Enquirer*, July 7, 12, 17, Aug. 4, 1861

64 Ollinger Crenshaw, "The Knights of the Golden Circle," *The American Historical Review*, XLVII (Oct. 1941), 23–50, deals with the society before the war; Mayo Fesler, "Secret Political Societies in the North during the Civil War," *Indiana Magazine of History*, XIV (Sept. 1918), 185–224; J. W. Pomfrey, *A True Disclosure and Exposition of the Knights of the Golden Circle, Including the Secret Signs, Grips, and Charges of the Three Degrees, as Practiced by the Order* (Cincinnati: printed for the author, c. 1861); *K.G.C.: a Full Exposure of the Southern Traitors, the Knights of the Golden Circle; Their Startling Schemes Frustrated; from Original Documents Never Before Published* (Boston: E. H. Bullard & Co., *The Five Cent Monthly*, 1860–61?); *Cairo* (Illinois) *City Gazette*, Apr. 5, 1860; *Canton* (Illinois) *Weekly Register*, May 21, 1861; *The Cincinnati Daily Enquirer*, June 4, 1861; *The* (Frankfort, Kentucky) *Commonwealth*, July 31, 1861, referred to in Curtis Hugh Morrow, "Politico-Military Secret Societies of the Northwest," *Social Science*, IV (Nov. 1928–Aug. 1929), 9–31, 222–42, 348–61, 463–76, V (Nov., 1929), 73–84

65 Yates MSS., (I), Griffin Gariand, Attila, Williamson County, Ill., Apr. 23, 1861, to Yates; *Salem* (Illinois) *Advocate*, Aug. 8, 1861, quoted in *Chicago Daily Tribune*, Aug. 12, 1861; *Charles City* (Iowa) *Republican Intelligencer*, Sept. 12, 1861; *Jonesboro* (Illinois) *Gazette*, Oct. 5, 1861; *Chicago Daily Tribune*, Oct. 10,

1861, from *Du Quoin* (Illinois) *Mining Journal;* (Springfield, Illinois) *Weekly State Journal,* Dec. 11, 1861, Jan. 1, 1862; (Jerseyville, Illinois) *Prairie State,* quoted in *Weekly State Journal,* Jan. 1, 1862; Salmon P. Chase MSS., Enoch T. Carson, Cincinnati, July 15, 1861, to Chase; Richard Yates MSS. (C), Brig.-Gen. U. S. Grant and Brig.-Gen. John A. McClernand, Camp Cairo, Ill., Nov. 5, 1861, to Yates; *O.R.,* Ser. II, Vol. II, 54, William H. Seward, Washington, D.C., Sept. 3, 1861, to Flamen Ball, U.S. District Attorney, Cincinnati, Ohio, *The Cincinnati Daily Enquirer,* Oct. 17, 19, 31, Nov. 1, 1861; *The* (Columbus, Ohio) *Crisis,* Oct. 17, 24, Nov. 28, 1861; (Indianapolis) *Daily State Sentinel,* Jan. 3, 1862; Library of Congress, Zachariah Chandler MSS., W. S. Wood, Detroit, Jan. 3, 1862, to Chandler

⁶⁶ (Canton, Ohio) *Stark County Democrat,* May 1, 1861; *The Cincinnati Daily Enquirer,* July 18, 1861; *St. Charles City* (Iowa) *Republican Intelligencer,* Sept. 5, 1861; *Jonesboro* (Illinois) *Gazette,* Oct. 5, 1861; *The* (Columbus, Ohio) *Crisis,* Nov. 7, 1861; *O.R.,* Ser. II, Vol. II, 113–4, Secretary of State Seward, Washington, Oct. 21, 1861, to U.S. Marshal H. M. Hoxie, Des Moines, Iowa; *Ibid.,* Ser. III, Vol. I, 473, Governor Morton, Indianapolis, Aug. 31, 1861, to Assistant Secretary of War Thomas A. Scott; Chicago Historical Society Library, Richard Yates MSS., Brigadier-General U. S. Grant and Brigadier-General John A. McClernand, Camp Cairo, Ill., to Governor Yates

⁶⁷ *O.R.,* Ser. II, Vol. III, 297, Adjutant-General A. C. Fuller, Springfield, Ill., Feb. 21, 1862, to Major-General Halleck; Frederick F. Cook, *Bygone Days in Chicago: Recollections of the "Garden City" of the Sixties* (Chicago: A. C. McClurg & Co., 1910), 129–30

⁶⁸ *Ibid.,* July 23, 1861, also July 3, 1861

⁶⁹ *The Cincinnati Daily Enquirer,* June 22, July 20, Aug. 9, 10, 1861; *The* (Columbus, Ohio) *Crisis,* June 27, July 18, Aug. 22, 29, 1861; (Indianapolis) *Daily State Sentinel,* Aug. 10, 14, 1861; *The* (Canton, Ohio) *Stark County Democrat,* Aug. 7, 1861. The greater boldness of the Eastern papers raises an interesting speculation as to the cause. Perhaps a more marked tendency in men of the Middle West to use violence in stifling such sentiments may partially provide the answer.

⁷⁰ *The Congressional Globe,* 37th Cong., 2nd sess., pp. 40–5, 331, also circulated in pamphlet form; *The Cincinnati Daily Enquirer,* Aug. 1, 1861; *The Chicago Times,* Aug. 2, 1861

⁷¹ *The Cincinnati Daily Enquirer,* Aug. 8, 13, 17, 29, Sept. 27; *The* (Columbus, Ohio) *Crisis,* Aug. 9, 1861. See Osman Castle Hooper, *The Crisis and the Man: an Episode in Civil War Journalism.* Contributions in Journalism, No. 5. Columbus: Ohio State University Press, 1929, pamphlet

⁷² *The Cincinnati Daily Enquirer,* Aug. 6, 1861; also *Ibid.,* Aug. 1, 2, 1861; *The* (Columbus, Ohio) *Crisis,* June 20, July 2, 25, Aug. 8, 1861; (Indianapolis) *Daily State Sentinel,* July 9, Aug. 12, 14, 16, 26, 27, Sept. 26, 1861; (Canton, Ohio) *Stark County Democrat,* Aug. 7, 1861; *The Chicago Tribune,* Sept. 21, 1861

⁷³ *Burlington* (Iowa) *Daily Hawk-Eye,* Sept. 18, 1861

⁷⁴ Trumbull MSS., W. A. Baldwin, Chicago, Dec. 16, 1861; see also Chase MSS., Congressman J. M. Ashley, Toledo, May 5, 1861, to Chase.

⁷⁵ Chase MSS., Eli Nichols, Wolpen Springs, [Ohio?], Apr. 18, 1861

⁷⁶ Trumbull MSS., J. M. Palmer, camp near Tipton, Mo., Oct. 13, 1861, to

Trumbull; Chicago Historical Society Library, George Schneider MSS., J. L. Scripps, Chicago, Nov. 27, 1861, to Schneider; Detroit Public Library, Burton Historical Collection, Austin Blair MSS., J. P. Christiancy, Monroe, Mich., Sept. 14, 1861, to Blair; Zachariah Chandler MSS., Christiancy, Monroe, Sept. 14, to Chandler; *Ibid.*, Senator Benjamin F. Wade, Jefferson, Ohio, Sept. 23, 1861, to Chandler

77 Trumbull MSS., Yates, Springfield, Feb. 14, 1862, to Trumbull; *Ibid.*, Senator James W. Grimes, Burlington, Iowa, Oct. 24, 1861, to Trumbull; Library of Congress, Elihu B. Washburne MSS., William Bross, Chicago, Dec. 30, 1861, to Simon Cameron; Richard Yates, *Speech of Governor Yates at the Great War Meeting in Chicago, August 1, 1861,* pamphlet, no date, taken from *Chicago Tribune*

78 Chase MSS., J. H. Jordan, Cincinnati, Apr. 26, 1861; *Ibid.*, Wm. Mills, Yellow Springs, Ohio, Aug. 6, 1861, to Chase; Trumbull MSS., Gustave Koerner, Belleville, Ill., July 29, 1861, to Trumbull; *Ibid.*, Dec. 6, 1861; *Ibid.*, C. H. Ray, editor of the *Chicago Tribune,* Chicago, Dec. 12, 1861, to Trumbull; *Burlington* (Iowa) *Daily Hawk-Eye,* Oct. 30, 1861; *The Cincinnati Daily Enquirer,* May 2, 11, 21, June 13, 1861; *The Daily Chicago Times,* June 11, 1861; *The Daily* (Columbus) *Ohio Statesman,* June 23, 1861; Zachariah Chandler MSS., Benjamin F. Wade, Jefferson, Ohio, Oct. 8, 1861, to Chandler; *Ibid.*, Chandler, St. Louis, Oct. 12, 1861, to Mrs. Chandler; *Ibid.*, Oct. 27, 1861

79 *The Cincinnati Daily Enquirer,* Sept. 26, 1861

80 Trumbull MSS., Gustave Koerner, Belleville, Ill., Jan. 2, 1862, to Trumbull; *Ibid.*, J. M. Palmer, Camp Lamine, Mo., Feb. 3, 1862; Logan MSS., John A. Logan, New York, Jan. 3, 1862, to Mrs. Logan; *Cincinnati Daily Times,* Jan. 18, 1862; Zachariah Chandler MSS., I. J. Bagley, Detroit, Dec. 6, 1861, to Chandler; *Ibid.*, Thurlow Weed, London, Dec. 7, 1861, to Chandler; Yates MSS. (I), S. M. Wilson, Chicago, Jan. 31, 1861 (sic. 1862), to Yates

81 *O.R.,* Ser. III, Vol. I, 416, Governor Dennison, Columbus, Aug. 15, 1861, to Secretary of War Cameron; *Ibid.*, p. 500, Governor Yates, Springfield, Sept. 12, 1861, to Cameron; *Ibid.*, pp. 520–1, C. C. Nourse, Attorney General of Iowa, Des Moines, Sept. 16, 1861, to Cameron; *Ibid.*, p. 539, Cameron, Washington, Sept. 25, 1861, to Governor Kirkwood, Des Moines; *Aurora* (Illinois) *Beacon,* July 4, 11, 1861

82 *The Cincinnati Daily Enquirer,* May 2, 5, 7, 31, July 9, 1861; (Springfield, Illinois) *Weekly State Journal,* May 15, 1861; *Belleville* (Illinois) *Weekly Advocate,* June 14, 1861; (Champaign) *Central Illinois Gazette,* May 8, 1861; *Jonesboro* (Illinois) *Gazette,* Nov. 2, 1861; (Urbana) *Champaign County Democrat,* Jan. 30, 1862; *O.R.,* Ser. III, Vol. I, 519–20, Congressman Jno. A. Gurley, Cincinnati, Sept. 16, 1861, to Lincoln

83 *O.R.,* Ser. II, Vol. II, 34–5, Brigadier-General B. M. Prentiss, Cairo, Ill., July 26, 1861, to Secretary of War Cameron; *Ibid.*, p. 46, Secretary of State Seward, Washington, Aug. 24, 1861, to Senator Chandler, Detroit; *Ibid.*, p. 52, Seward, Sept. 2, 1861, to William H. Barse, Detroit, and John C. Miller, Chicago; *Ibid.*, Sept. 14, 1861, to U.S. District Attorney Flamen Ball, Cincinnati; *Ibid.*, p. 73, Sept. 20, 1861, to Miller, Chicago, Barse, Detroit, and Hollis White, Niagara Falls; *Ibid.*, p. 82, Seward, Sept. 28, 1861, to Postmaster General Montgomery Blair; *Ibid.*, p. 83, Sept. 30, 1861, to Albert G. Davis, Washington, D.C.; *Ibid.*, p. 98, Barse, Detroit, Oct. 11, 1861, to Assistant Secretary of State

F. W. Seward; *Ibid.,* p. 114, F. W. Seward, Washington, Oct. 21, 1861, to Samuel Hill, Deer Creek, Ohio; *Ibid.,* pp. 127–9, U.S. Marshal A. C. Sands, Cincinnati, Nov. 5, 1861, to W. H. Seward, with enclosures; *Ibid.,* p. 133, Miller, Chicago, Nov. 9, 1861, to Seward; *Ibid.,* p. 137, Seward, Nov. 13, 1861, to Barse; *Ibid.,* p. 170, Seward, Dec. 4, 1861, to Alexander H. Stowell, Detroit; *Ibid.,* p. 170, Seward, Dec. 5, 1861, to U.S. Marshal D. L. Phillips, Springfield, Ill.; *Ibid.,* p. 176, Seward, Dec. 12, 1861, to Barse, Detroit; *Ibid.,* p. 179, Seward, Dec. 20, 1861, to Phillips, Cairo, Ill.: *Ibid.,* p. 185, Phillips, Springfield, Jan. 2, 1862, to Seward; *Ibid.,* p. 246, Seward, Feb. 25, 1862, to the chiefs of police of the United States; *Ibid.,* p. 323, memorandum of case of S. R. Burnett of Pulaski County, Ill.; *Ibid.,* p. 331, case of J. R. Hawley of Cincinnati; *Ibid.,* pp. 343–4, cases of Robert W. Buckles, Thomas Mathews, Thomas O'Leary, and John Rigal of Olney, Illinois; *Ibid.,* p. 344, case of Mrs. William Smith; *Ibid.,* pp. 711–21, record of case of John C. Brain of Michigan City, Ind.; *Ibid.,* pp. 982–1008, case of John G. Shaver, of Detroit; *Ibid.,* pp. 1041–76, case of Matthew F. Maury, of New Orleans, arrested at Cleveland; *Ibid.,* pp. 1244–67, cases of Dr. Guy S. Hopkins, Isaac Butler, and David C. Wattles of North Branch, Lapeer County, Michigan; *The Cincinnati Daily Enquirer,* Apr. 18, May 2, July 14, 1861; *Cairo* (Illinois) *City Gazette,* Nov. 14, 1861

[84] *The Congressional Globe,* 37th Cong., 2nd sess., pp. 552–4, also published in pamphlet form

[85] Trumbull MSS., State Treasurer William Butler, Springfield, Ill., Feb. 4, 1862; also Yates MSS., circular sent out by the Committee on Military Affairs of the Convention, date Jan. 23, 1862; Illinois State Historical Library, Orville Hickman Browning MSS., Butler and Secretary of State Jesse I. Dubois, Springfield, Feb. 8, 1862, to Senator Browning

CHAPTER IV

[1] Chicago Historical Society, Richard Yates MSS., James G. Blaine, speaker of the House, and John H. Goodenow, president of the Senate, March 19, 1862, to Yates

[2] State Historical Society of Wisconsin Library, Madison, Lucius Fairchild MSS., Fairchild (later governor of Wisconsin), Camp Tillinghast, Va., Feb. 17, 1862, to his sister; Ohio Archaeological and Historical Society Library, J. S. Robinson MSS., Robinson, Headquarters, 82nd Regiment, Grafton, Va., Feb. 17, 1862, to L. T. Hunt

[3] Charles C. Coffin, *My Days and Nights on the Battlefield* (2nd ed., Boston: Ticknor & Fields, 1864), pp. 119–20. An extensive search, in spite of the appreciated assistance of *The New York Times* and of Dr. Paul M. Angle of the Illinois State Historical Library, has failed to disclose the authorship or original place of appearance of this poem. Coffin was mistaken in crediting it to the *Atlantic Monthly.*

[4] Library of Congress, Lyman Trumbull MSS., Mark Skinner, Chicago, March 20, 1862, to Trumbull

[5] Yates MSS. (C), Feb. 6, 1862

[6] Library of Congress, Giddings-Julian MSS., Baxter Harrison, Feb. 15, 1862, to Julian. See also *Ibid.* W. G. Snethen, Baltimore, Jan. 20, 1862, to Julian, and *Ibid.,* from Josephus S. Gentry, Butter Creek, Ind., Feb. 27, 1862

[7] Trumbull MSS., B. Godfrey, Alton, Ill., Apr. 11, 1862, to Trumbull

[8] *Ibid.* (signature missing, stationery of Illinois Mutual Fire Insurance Company), Du Quoin, Ill., Apr. 11, 1862, to Trumbull

[9] *The Chicago Weekly Times,* Feb. 18, 1862

[10] *The* (Columbus, Ohio) *Crisis,* Feb. 19, Mar. 5, Apr. 9, May 7, 1862; (Indianapolis) *Daily State Sentinel,* Apr. 14, 1862

[11] *The Chicago Times,* March 18, Apr. 15, 1862

[12] Feb. 26, 1862, weekly edition

[13] Trumbull MSS., E. Peck, Chicago, Feb. 15, 1862, to Trumbull; *Ibid.,* M. C. Flagg, Madison County, Ill., May 30, 1862, to Trumbull; *The Chicago Times,* weekly, Feb. 18, 1862

[14] Yates MSS. (C), William Cam, Lieutenant-Colonel, 14th Illinois Infantry, Jefferson City, Mo., Feb. 12, 1862, to Singleton; *Ibid.,* E. A. Carr, Colonel, 3rd Illinois Cavalry, Camp Halleck, Ark., Feb. 27, 1862, to Singleton; *Ibid.,* John A. Logan, Colonel, 32nd Illinois Infantry, Fort Henry, Tenn., March 1, 1862, to Singleton; *Ibid.,* U. S. Grant, Major-General, Savannah, Tenn., March 24, 1862, to Singleton; *Weekly* (Springfield, Illinois) *State Journal,* Jan. 29, 1862

[15] *Ibid.,* Frank W. Partridge, 13th Illinois Infantry, Rolla, Mo., Feb. 15, 1862, to Singleton

[16] Yates MSS. (C), Quincy McNeil, Major, 2nd Illinois Cavalry, Paducah, Ky., Feb. 16, 1862, to Singleton; also in (Springfield) *Weekly Illinois State Journal,* Feb. 26, 1862

[17] Library of Congress, Edwin M. Stanton MSS., Joseph Medill, Chicago, Jan. 21, 1862, to Stanton; *Ibid.,* Joseph Cable, Van Wert, Ohio, Feb. 5, 1862; Yates MSS. (C), Lyman Trumbull, Washington, Feb. 6, 1862, to Yates; *Cincinnati Daily Times,* Jan. 23, 1862; *The Chicago Times,* Jan. 25, 1862

[18] *O.R.,* Ser. II, Vol. II, 263–4, W. Hoffman, Commandant General of Prisoners, Chicago, March 15, 1862, to M. C. Meigs, Quartermaster-General

[19] Trumbull MSS., Gustave Koerner, Belleville, Ill., May 20, 1862, to Trumbull

[20] *O.R.,* Ser. III, Vol. II, 2–3

[21] See Fred Albert Shannon, *The Organization and Administration of the Union Army* (Cleveland: Arthur H. Clark Co., 1928), I, 266–7

[22] *O.R.,* Ser. III, Vol. II, pp. 44, 61, 70, 75, dispatches of Adjutant-General Thomas and Stanton, May 19, 21, 24, 25, 26

[23] *Ibid.,* p. 44, Adjutant-General Allen C. Fuller, Springfield, Ill., May 19, 1862, to Thomas; *Ibid.,* p. 63, Governor Tod, Columbus, May 21, 1862, to Thomas; *Ibid.,* pp. 110–43, Edward Salomon, Madison, June 6, 10, 1862, to Stanton; *Ibid.,* pp. 142–3, Governor Blair, Jackson, Mich., June 10, 1862, to Stanton; *Ibid.,* pp. 212–3, Morton and other officials, Indianapolis, July 9, 1862, to Lincoln

[24] *Ibid.,* pp. 44, 61, 69, 70, 75, 87, 92, 97–9, 100–1, 106, 108, 109–10, 175–6, 179; (Springfield) *Illinois State Journal,* June 10, 1862; *Canton* (Illinois) *Weekly Register,* June 10, 1862

[25] *O.R.,* Ser. III, Vol. II, p. 109

[26] *Ibid.,* pp. 181, 183, 187–8, 291–2

[27] *O.R.,* Ser. III, Vol. II, p. 104. Also Trumbull MSS., Gustave Koerner, Belleville, Ill., May 20, 1862, to Trumbull; (Springfield, Illinois) *State Register,* Aug. 7, 1862; McCormick Historical Association Library, Chicago, McCormick

MSS., Wm. S. McCormick, Chicago, Sept. 27, 1862, to Cyrus H. McCormick, in Europe; *The* (Columbus, Ohio) *Crisis,* Aug. 27, 1862

28 *O.R.,* Ser. III, Vol. II, 201, July 3, 1862

29 *O.R.,* Ser. II, Vol. IV, 343, Oliver P. Morton, Indianapolis, Aug. 5, 1862, to General Henry Halleck

30 Library of Congress, William Allen MSS., Jo. H. Riley, Columbus, Aug. 18, 1862

31 *O.R.,* Ser. III, Vol. II, 468, Governor Tod, Columbus, Aug. 26, 1862, to Stanton; *Ibid.,* Stanton to Tod

32 *The* (Columbus, Ohio) *Crisis,* Sept. 24, 1862, speech at Dayton

33 *Rockford* (Illinois) *Register,* Apr. 19, 1862; *Rockford Republican,* May 10, July 31, 1862; (Rockford) *Rock River Democrat,* July 29, Aug. 5, 19, 1862; *Aurora* (Illinois) *Beacon,* Aug. 14, 1862; *Ottawa* (Illinois) *Weekly Republican,* Aug. 16, 1862; *O.R.,* Ser. III, Vol. II, 187, Stanton, July 1, 1862, to Seward

34 *O.R.,* Ser. III, Vol. II, 253, Congressman Isaac N. Arnold, Chicago, July 26, 1862, to Stanton; *Aurora* (Illinois) *Beacon,* Aug. 14, 1862

35 *O.R.,* Ser. III, Vol. II, 357, Edward Salomon, Madison, Aug. 11, 1862, to Stanton

36 *Canton* (Illinois) *Weekly Register,* Aug. 5, 1862

37 (Rockford, Illinois) *Rock River Democrat,* Aug. 15, 1862

38 Aug. 23, 1862

39 (Springfield) *Weekly Illinois State Journal,* July 23, Aug. 13, 1862; *Ottawa* (Illinois) *Weekly Republican,* Aug. 16, 1862

40 *O.R.,* Ser. III, Vol. II, 213, C. P. Wolcott, Asst. Sec. of War, July 10, 1862, to governors of Indiana, Ohio, Wisconsin, and Michigan, and the president of the Military Board of Kentucky

41 *O.R.,* Ser. II, Vol. IV, 361; *Ibid.,* Ser. III, Vol. III, 234, 251, 269, 270, 361; Library of Congress, William Tecumseh Sherman MSS., John Sherman, Mansfield, Ohio, Aug. 8, 1862, to W. T. Sherman

42 *O.R.,* Ser. III, Vol. IV, 1264–70

43 *Ibid.,* Ser. III, Vol. V, 647–8

44 *Prairie Farmer,* July 12, 26, Aug. 9, 23, Sept. 13, 1862; *Ottawa* (Illinois) *Free Trader,* July 26, 1862

45 *O.R.,* Ser. III, Vol. II, 208, 264, 289, 316, 317–8, 323, 324, 337, 338, 360, 374–5, 382, 399, 408, 415, 429, 440, 455, 463, 417; *Canton* (Illinois) *Weekly Register,* July 1, 1862; *Ottawa* (Illinois) *Weekly Republican,* Aug. 2, 1862; (Springfield) *Illinois State Register,* Aug. 5, 13, 1862; *Cairo* (Illinois) *City Gazette,* Aug. 7, 1862; (Rockford, Illinois) *Rock River Democrat,* Aug. 12, 1862; (Springfield) *Weekly Illinois State Journal,* Aug. 13, 1862; *Belleville* (Illinois) *Democrat,* Aug. 30, 1862

46 *Rockford Republican,* Aug. 14, 1862

47 (Springfield) *Illinois State Journal,* Aug. 2, 16, 1862

48 *O.R.,* Ser. III, Vol. II, 429

49 *Joliet Signal,* Aug. 26, 1862; also *Belleville Democrat,* Aug. 16, 1862

50 *O.R.,* Ser. II, Vol. II, 221–3, 249

51 *Ibid.,* pp. 240–4, 249, 273. They were Dr. John M. Clemerson, James D. Pully, A. P. Corder, C. C. Carpenter, and Dr. Duff Green

52 *Ibid., O.R.,* Ser. III, Vol. II, 321–2; (Springfield) *Weekly Illinois State Journal,* Aug. 13, 1862

53 (Springfield) *Weekly Illinois State Journal*, Aug. 13, 1862; *Belleville* (Illinois) *Democrat*, Aug. 16, 1862; *Chicago Daily Tribune*, Aug. 26, 1862; Chicago Historical Society Library, Madison Y. Johnson MSS., *passim*. Allen (1829–1901), born in Tennessee, entered Democratic politics of Illinois under the tutelage of his father, a member of Congress from Illinois from 1851 to 1855. The son, after serving in the legislature, entered Congress in June 1862 and was re-elected that autumn. From 1887 to his death he was United States district judge for the Southern District of Illinois.

54 Dennis A. Mahoney, *The Prisoner of State* (New York: Carleton, publ., 1863), *passim*

55 *Ibid.; The* (Columbus, Ohio) *Crisis*, Aug. 20, 1862; John A. Marshall, *American Bastille: a History of the Illegal Arrests and Imprisonment of American Citizens during the Late Civil War* (Philadelphia: Thomas W. Hartley, 1869), *passim*

56 Henry Clay Dean, *Crimes of the Civil War and Curse of the Funding System* (Baltimore: William T. Smithson, 1868), pp. 11–24; see also Samuel Langhorne Clemens, *Life on the Mississippi* (New York: Grosset & Dunlap, c. 1874, etc.), pp. 463–6 for a character sketch of Dean.

57 *The* (Columbus, Ohio) *Crisis*, Apr. 9, 1862, quoted from the *Watchman*. Also *The* (Columbus, Ohio) *Crisis*, July 9, 23, 1862

58 *Rockford* (Illinois) *Republican*, July 10, 1862; *The* (Columbus, Ohio) *Crisis*, Aug. 20, 1862; (Springfield) *Illinois State Journal*, Aug. 22, 1862, from the (Bloomington, Illinois) *Pantagraph*

59 Library of Congress, Franklin Pierce MSS., Robert McClelland, Detroit, Jan. 15, 1862, to Pierce; *The* (Columbus, Ohio) *Crisis*, May 7, Sept. 10, 1862, correspondence

60 *Aurora* (Illinois) *Beacon*, Aug. 7, 1862; *Cairo* (Illinois) *City Gazette*, Aug. 8, 1862; *O.R.*, Ser. II, Vol. IV, 358–9, Ser. III, Vol. II, 316

61 *The Chicago Daily Tribune*, Aug. 11, 22, 1862; (Rockford, Illinois) *Rock River Democrat*, Aug. 12, 1862; *Ottawa* (Illinois) *Weekly Republican*, Aug. 23, 1862

62 (Springfield) *Illinois State Journal*, July 28, Aug. 22, 1862; *Ottawa* (Illinois) *Weekly Republican*, Aug. 9, 1862; *The* (Columbus, Ohio) *Crisis*, Aug. 20, 1862

63 *O.R.*, Ser. III, Vol. II, 471, 477, Governor Salomon to Stanton, and reply

64 See, for example, Trumbull MSS., U.S. Marshal D. L. Phillips, Springfield, Ill., March 22, 1862, to Trumbull

65 McCormick MSS., letter of introduction of McCormick from Horace Greeley to William L. Dayton, United States minister at Paris, July 14, 1862; *Ibid.*, William S. McCormick, Chicago, July 20, Aug. 3, 1862, to Cyrus H. McCormick

66 *O.R.*, Ser. II, Vol. III, 277, Yates and others, Springfield, Feb. 18, 1862, to General Halleck; also *Ibid.*, Ser. II, Vol. II, 272, 274

67 *Ibid.*, Vol. IV, 37–8, 42, 87–8, 89

68 *The Congressional Globe*, 37th Cong., 2nd sess., p. 2537, appdx., pp. 242–9; *The* (Columbus, Ohio) *Crisis*, June 18, 1862. The pamphlet reprint of this speech and subsequent references to it, including Cox's own *Three Decades of Federal Legislation*, erroneously give June 6 as the date.

69 *The Chicago Times,* March 25, 1862; *The* (Columbus, Ohio) *Crisis,* March 26, May 28, 1862; *Burlington* (Iowa) *Daily Hawk-Eye,* July 1, 1862

70 *The* (Columbus, Ohio) *Crisis,* Apr. 23, 1862; Norman Dwight Harris, *The History of Negro Servitude in Illinois and of the Slavery Agitation in That State* (Chicago: A. C. McClurg, 1904), pp. 238–9

71 Library of Congress, Horace Greeley MSS., Greeley, New York, Aug. 27, 1862, to George W. Wright, Washington; *The Chicago Times,* Mar. 25, Apr. 15, 1862; (Springfield, Illinois) *State Register,* July 15, 1862; *Jonesboro* (Illinois) *Gazette,* Aug. 9, 1862

72 *The* (Columbus, Ohio) *Crisis,* Apr. 30, May 21, 28, 1862; *The Chicago Times,* May 11, 26, 1862; speech of Daniel W. Voorhees in the House of Representatives, May 21, 1862, *The Congressional Globe,* 37th Cong., 2nd sess., pp. 2265–71, also distributed in pamphlet form

73 *Carlinville* (Illinois) *Free Democrat,* quoted in (Springfield) *Weekly Illinois State Journal,* June 11, 1862; *Illinois State Journal* (daily), June 23, Aug. 22, 1862; *The Chicago Tribune,* Aug. 3, 1862

74 *O.R.,* Ser. II, Vol. II, 275–6, H. B. Barnes, editor of the *Tribune,* Detroit, March 28, 1862, to Seward; *Detroit Advertiser and Tribune,* Aug. 26, 1862

75 *O.R.,* Ser. III, Vol. II, 105, Columbus, June 2, 1862

76 *Ibid.,* 176–7, Indianapolis, June 25, 1862; copy in Indiana State Library, Indianapolis, Oliver P. Morton MSS., Letter Press Books, I, 9–18

77 *The* (Columbus, Ohio) *Crisis,* Oct. 8, 1862

78 *The Chicago Times,* Mar. 18, 25, 1863

79 *The* (Columbus, Ohio) *Crisis,* Apr. 9, 16, 1862; *The Chicago Times,* Apr. 15, 1862; Pierce MSS., A. P. Stinson, St. Joseph, Mich., March 24, 1862, to Pierce

80 *The Chicago Times,* March 18, 25, Apr. 15, May 11, 26, 1862; *Weekly Illinois State Journal,* June 11, 1862

81 March 26, Apr. 30, May 7, 21, 28, 1862

82 *Address of Democratic Members of Congress to the Democracy of the United States* (Washington: L. Towers & Co., printers, 1862), *passim; Speeches, Arguments, Addresses, and Letters of Clement L. Vallandigham* (New York: J. Walter & Co., 1864), pp. 362–9; *The* (Columbus, Ohio) *Crisis,* May 14, 1862

83 *The Congressional Globe,* 37th Cong., 2nd sess., pp. 2206–8, 2265–71, 2537, appdx., pp. 242–9, delivered May 19, May 21, and June 3, respectively; *The Chicago Times,* May 26, 1862; *The* (Columbus, Ohio) *Crisis,* June 4, 1862

84 May 16, 1862, quoted in the (Springfield) *Weekly Illinois State Journal;* also see latter, June 11, 1862; Indiana State Historical Library, William H. English MSS., James A. Cravens, Hardinsburg, Ind., June 25, 1862; *The Detroit Free Press,* May 11, 19, 1862

85 *The* (Columbus, Ohio) *Crisis,* May 21, June 18, July 2, 1862

86 *Burlington* (Iowa) *Daily Hawk-Eye,* July 22, 1862

87 *Ibid.,* Aug. 26, 1862

88 *Ibid.,* June 11, 1862

CHAPTER V

1 *O.R.,* Ser. III, Vol. II, 508, Governor Tod, Columbus, Ohio, Sept. 2, 1861, to Secretary of War Stanton; Library of Congress, Salmon P. Chase MSS.,

Simeon Nash, Racine, Wis., Sept. 5, 1862, to Chase; *Ibid.,* S. G. Arnold, *"North American* Office," Newark, Ohio, Sept. 12, 1862, to Chase; *Ibid.,* O. Follett, Sandusky, Ohio, Sept. 16, 1862, to Chase; *Ibid.,* Rev. R. P. A. (?), Cincinnati, Sept. 17, 1862, to Chase; *Ibid.,* N. H. Swayne, Columbus, Ohio, Sept. 17, 1862, to Chase; Library of Congress, James Rood Doolittle MSS., M. Romero, Washington, Sept. 9, 1862, to Doolittle, Racine, Wis.; *Burlington* (Iowa) *Daily Hawk-Eye,* Sept. 8, 1862

² *The Chicago Times,* Oct. 15, 1862

³ *O.R.,* Ser. III, Vol. II, 525–6

⁴ *O.R.,* Ser. II, Vol. IV, 503–4, W. Hoffman, Commissary General of Prisoners, Detroit, Sept. 10, 1862, to Stanton, in *re* arrest of Dr. L. D. Boone; *Ibid.,* pp. 567–8, Judge Advocate L. C. Turner, Washington, Sept. 27, 1862, to U.S. District Marshal H. M. Hoxie, Des Moines; *The* (Columbus, Ohio) *Crisis,* Sept. 24, 1862; *Ibid.,* Nov. 5, 1862, in *re* arrest of Dr. T. Horton of Bluffton, Ind., taken from Fort Wayne *Times; Ibid.,* Nov. 19, 1862, in *re* arrest of Warren Stanton of Kingsville, Ohio; *Ibid.,* Oct. 22, 1862, in *re* arrest of Peter N. Reitzell and of A. McGregor at Massillon, Ohio; (Springfield, Illinois) *State Register,* Sept. 22, 1862, quoted in *The* (Columbus, Ohio) *Crisis,* Oct. 8, 1862; Chicago Historical Society, Madison Y. Johnson MSS., Johnson, Ft. Lafayette, N.Y., Sept. 16, 1862, to Louis Shissler, Richard Kingsland, and others; *Ibid.,* Fort Delaware, Dec. 8, 1862, to President Lincoln; *Ibid.,* Dec. 8, 1862, to George O. Collins; *Ibid.,* Oct. 28, 1862, to Senator O. H. Browning. Some of these are copies or first drafts of letters sent. One, at least, is an original which the prison authorities refused to dispatch. Johnson's manuscript diary is also in these papers.

⁵ *The Chicago Times,* Oct. 8, 1862

⁶ *The* (Columbus, Ohio) *Crisis,* Dec. 10, 1862

⁷ *Ibid.,* Nov. 5, 1862

⁸ Sept. 23, 1862; also Oct. 4, 5, 7, 19, 1862; see also *Milwaukee Daily Sentinel,* Sept. 24, 25, 26, 1862

⁹ Sept. 24, 1862

¹⁰ *O.R.,* Ser. III, Vol. II, 569, 663; *The Toledo Blade,* July 8, 9, 10, 1862; *The* (Columbus, Ohio) *Crisis,* July 2, 16, 1862; *The Chicago Times,* Sept. 23, Oct. 5, 10, 1862

¹¹ *Quincy Herald,* Oct. 24, 1862, quoted by *The Chicago Times,* Oct. 26, 1862

¹² *O.R.,* Ser. III, Vol. II, 586–7, Lieutenant-Governor Francis A. Hoffman, Springfield, Sept. 24, 1862, to Lincoln

¹³ *The* (Columbus, Ohio) *Crisis,* Sept. 24, 1862

¹⁴ *Ibid.,* July 2, 23, Sept. 24, Oct. 1, 1862; *The Chicago Times,* July 20, Sept. 23, 24, Oct. 1, Nov. 14, 1862

¹⁵ Indiana State Library, George Washington Julian MSS., J. W. Gordan, an Indianapolis man in command of Fort Independence, Boston harbor, July 27, 1862, to Julian

¹⁶ Indiana State Library, Oliver Perry Morton Letter Press Books, W. R. Holloway, private secretary to Governor Morton, Indianapolis, Oct. 24, 1862, to John G. Nicolay, private secretary to President Lincoln; Library of Congress, Schuyler Colfax MSS., Gil. Pierce, Paducah, Oct. 30, 1862, to Colfax

¹⁷ Library of Congress, Lyman Trumbull MSS., Chicago, July 4, 1862

¹⁸ *Ibid.,* Gerritt Nichols, Milton Station, Ill., July 15, 1862, to Trumbull

[19] Library of Congress, Joshua Rood Giddings-George Washington Julian MSS., Ashtabula, Ohio, Sept. 29, 1862

[20] Library of Congress, Edwin M. Stanton MSS., Detroit, to Assistant Secretary of War P. W. Watson

[21] Trumbull MSS.

[22] *O.R.,* Ser. III, Vol. II, 441, 454, 463, 472, 681–2, Lincoln, Washington, Aug. 23, 1862, to Yates; Yates, Springfield, Aug. 23, to Lincoln, endorsement by William Butler and Jesse K. DuBois; Lincoln, Aug. 25, to Yates; Assistant Secretary of War Buckingham, Washington, Aug. 26, to Illinois Adjutant-General Fuller; Yates, Springfield, Aug. 27, to Buckingham; Mustering Officer Ketchum, Springfield, Oct. 24, 1862, to Stanton

[23] *The Chicago Times,* Sept. 18, 1862

[24] *O.R.,* Ser. III, Vol. II, 508–9, Madison, Sept. 2, 1862

[25] *Ibid.,* p. 518, Stanton, Washington, Sept. 5, 1862, to Salomon; *Ibid.,* pp. 522–3, Salomon, Madison, Sept. 5, to Stanton

[26] Chase MSS., M. D. Potter, of the *Cincinnati Commercial,* Cincinnati, Sept. 12, 1862, to Chase

[27] *The* (Columbus, Ohio) *Crisis,* July 16, 1862; also Clement Laird Vallandigham, *Speeches, Arguments, Addresses, and Letters of Clement L. Vallandigham* (New York: J. Walter & Co., 1864), pp. 384–96

[28] Oct. 10, 1862

[29] *The Chicago Times,* Sept. 30, 1862; *Greenville* (Ohio) *Democrat,* Sept. 10, 1862, quoted in *The Crisis,* Sept. 24, 1862; *The Daily* (Columbus) *Ohio Statesman,* Sept. 16, 1862

[30] Vallandigham, *op. cit.,* pp. 415–7

[31] *Ibid.,* pp. 397–415, Aug. 2, 1862

[32] *The Chicago Times,* Oct. 11, 1862

[33] *Proceedings of Democratic State Convention Held at Columbus, Ohio, Friday, July 4, 1862,* pp. 11–12

[34] (Indianapolis) *Daily State Sentinel,* July 31, 1861. The convention met in Indianapolis on July 30. The Democrats of Minnesota convened at St. Paul on July 2, followed a similar line of approach. *The* (St. Paul) *Pioneer and Democrat,* July 3, 1862; also *The* (Columbus, Ohio) *Crisis,* Sept. 10, 1862; *The Chicago Times,* Nov. 2, 1862

[35] *The Chicago Times,* Oct. 15, 1862

[36] *Ibid.,* Aug. 10, 1862; also *Joliet* (Illinois) *Signal,* Aug. 12, 1862

[37] Sept. 24, 1862; see also July 9, Sept. 10, 1862

[38] *The Tribune Almanac for 1863,* pp. 18–19, 55–62

[39] Chase MSS., H. S. Bundy, defeated candidate for Congress, Reeds Mills, Ohio, Oct. 18, 1862, to Chase; *Ibid.,* S. G. Arnold, Newark, Ohio, Oct. 20, 1862; *Ibid.,* R. S. Newton, Cincinnati, Oct. 20, 1862; *Ibid.,* R. C. Parsons, Cleveland, Oct. 21, 1862; *Ibid.,* C. Kingsley, editor of the *Western Christian Advocate,* Cincinnati, Oct. 22, 1862; *Ibid.,* M. Welker, defeated candidate for Congress, Columbus, Ohio, Oct. 24, 1862; *Ibid.,* Edw. D. Mansfield, Morrow, Ohio, Oct. 25, 1862; Library of Congress, Carl Schurz MSS., A. Lincoln, Washington, Nov. 10, 1862, marked "Private and Confidential," to Schurz; *Ibid.,* Schurz, Centreville, Va., Nov. 20, 1862, to Lincoln (second draft); *Ibid.,* Lincoln, Washington, Nov. 24, 1862, to Schurz; Chicago Historical Society, Richard Yates MSS., Governor Morton, Indianapolis, Nov. 13, 1862, to Yates; Library of Congress,

William Tecumseh Sherman MSS., John Sherman, Mansfield, Ohio, Nov. 16, 1862, to W. T. Sherman; Library of Congress, John Jordan Crittenden MSS., Thos. Dowling, Terre Haute, Ind., Dec. 1, 1862, to Crittenden; *Daily* (Indianapolis) *State Sentinel,* Nov. 8, 1862; *Burlington* (Iowa) *Daily Hawk-Eye,* Nov. 6, 1862

[40] *O.R.,* Ser. II, Vol. IV, 746–7, General Orders, No. 193; *The* (Columbus, Ohio) *Crisis,* Nov. 12, 19, Dec. 17, 1862

[41] Chase MSS., David Chambers, Zanesville, Ohio, Oct. 25, 1862, to Chase; Library of Congress, Zachariah Chandler MSS., Senator Lyman Trumbull, Springfield, Ill., Nov. 9, 1862, to Chandler

[42] *O.R.,* Ser. III, Vol. II, 583–4

[43] *O.R.,* Ser. III, Vol. II, 512, 650, 669, 693, 867, 881

[44] *The* (Columbus, Ohio) *Crisis,* Oct. 8, 1862

[45] Indiana, Adjutant General's Office, *Report of the Adjutant General of Indiana,* I (Indianapolis, 1869), 44

[46] *O.R.,* Ser. III, Vol. II, 265–6, Congressman James F. Wilson, Fairfield, Iowa, 28, 1862, to Stanton

[47] *Milwaukee Daily Sentinel,* Nov. 10, 12, 13, 17, 19, 21, 1862, with reprint from the *Ozaukee Advertiser and Democrat; O.R.,* Ser. III, Vol. II, 765, Governor Salomon, Madison, Nov. 12, 1862, to Stanton

[48] Wisconsin State Historical Society Library, Wisconsin Governors' Telegrams MSS., Draft Commissioner William A. Prentis, Milwaukee, Nov. 8, 1862, to Governor Salomon; *Milwaukee Daily Sentinel,* Nov. 11, 1862

[49] *Ibid.,* Nov. 11, 19, 1862; *O.R.,* Ser. II, Vol. IV, 718, 786, V, 24, Ser. III, Vol. II, 786, Salomon, to Stanton. On January 13, 1863, the Wisconsin Supreme Court held the arrest of these men under the suspension of the habeas corpus by the President (General Orders, No. 141, Sept. 25, 1862) invalid. In order to avoid a conflict with the state authorities, Stanton on January 19, 1863, authorized the release on parole of the prisoners. *O.R.,* Ser. II, Vol. V, 174, 179, 190; *Ibid.,* Ser. III, Vol. III, 15. In view of the existing membership of the United States Supreme Court, Attorney General Bates advised Stanton not to permit the case to come before that body. Stanton MSS., Jan. 31, 1863

[50] Quoted in *The* (Columbus, Ohio) *Crisis,* Oct. 15, 1862

[51] *Weekly* (Springfield), *Illinois State Journal,* Sept. 18, Oct. 15, 29, 1862

[52] *Belleville* (Illinois) *Weekly Advocate,* Oct. 31, 1862

[53] *O.R.,* Ser. II, Vol. IV, 278–9, Col. Joseph H. Tucker, Commandant of Camp Douglas, Chicago, July 23, 1862, to Colonel William Hoffman, Commissary-General of Prisoners; *Ibid.,* pp. 323–4, Hoffman, Detroit, Aug. 1, 1862, to Stanton; *Ibid.,* p. 379, Major John G. Fonda, Commandant of Camp Butler, Springfield, Ill., Aug. 12, 1862, to Hoffman

[54] *O.R.,* Ser. I, Vol. XIII, 525–6, John Wood, Quartermaster-General of Illinois, Frank P. Blair, Jr., and J. Samuel Holmes, St. Louis, Aug. 1, 1862, to Major-General Halleck

[55] *O.R.,* Ser. III, Vol. II, 351, Springfield, Aug. 11, 1862

[56] *Jacksonville* (Illinois) *Journal,* Sept. 25, 1862

[57] *O.R.,* Ser. II, Vol. IV, 499, Stanton, Washington Sept. 9, 1862, to Governor Tod of Ohio; *Ibid.,* p. 562, Stanton, Sept. 26, 1862, to Governor Morton of Indiana

[58] *Ibid.,* p. 546, Wallace, Columbus, Sept. 22, 1862, to Adjutant-General

Thomas; *Ibid.,* p. 563, Wallace, Sept. 26, 1862, to Stanton; *Ibid.,* pp. 600, 644–5, Tyler, Chicago Oct. 5, 23, 1862, to Thomas

59 *O.R.,* Ser. II, Vol. V, 33, Capt. J. M. Rice, Cincinnati, Dec. 6, 1862, to Col. William Hoffman

60 *O.R.,* Ser. II, Vol. IV, 949–50, Lieut.-Col. Robert P. Blount, Provost Marshal, First Corps, Army of Northern Virginia, Richmond, Nov. 20, 1862, to President Davis. Endorsed by Davis "Valuable information."

61 *The Crisis,* Nov. 29, 1862

62 Nov. 10, 1862

63 *The Chicago Times,* weekly, Dec. 16, 1862

64 Dec. 17, 1862

65 *The Congressional Globe,* 37th Cong., 3rd sess., p. 15; *The* (Columbus, Ohio) *Crisis,* Dec. 10, 24, 1862

66 McCormick Historical Association Library, Chicago, Cyrus Hall McCormick MSS., Chicago, Dec. 11, 1862; also letters of Sept. 28, Oct. 5, 19, 1862

67 Library of Congress, Stanton MSS., Springfield, Nov. 10, 1862, "true copy"

68 *Ibid.,* Indianapolis, Oct. 27, 1862, to Lincoln

CHAPTER VI

1 *The Congressional Globe,* 37th Cong., 3rd sess., p. 314, appdx., pp. 52–60; Clement Laird Vallandigham, *Speeches, Arguments, Addresses, and Letters of Clement L. Vallandigham* (New York: J. Walter & Co., 1864), pp. 418–53; *The* (Columbus, Ohio) *Crisis,* Jan. 28, 1863. Also *The Congressional Globe,* 37th Cong., 3rd sess., p. 130; *Weekly* (Springfield) *Illinois State Journal,* Dec. 24, 1862; *Belleville* (Illinois) *Weekly Advocate,* Jan. 30, 1863; *The Crisis,* March 11, 1863

2 *The Congressional Globe,* 37th Cong., 3rd sess., p. 1226, appdx., pp. 172–7; Vallandigham, *op. cit.,* pp. 454–78

3 *The New York World,* Feb. 16, 1863. This is not included in the volume of Vallandigham's published speeches except in fragmentary form.

4 Vallandigham, *op. cit.,* pp. 479–502; *The* (Columbus, Ohio) *Crisis,* March 25, 1863

5 *The Congressional Globe,* 37th Cong., 3rd sess., pp. 783–6. Also circulated in pamphlet form as Paper No. 2 of the Society for the Diffusion of Political Knowledge. Delivered on February 7th.

6 *The* (Columbus, Ohio) *Crisis,* Jan. 21, 1863. Also published in pamphlet form. Delivered on Jan. 13, 1863.

7 Jan. 16, 1863. Also *The Crisis,* Dec. 17, 24, 1862, Jan. 28, 1863; *The Chicago Times,* Dec. 30, 1862; *The Detroit Free Press,* Jan. 1, 13, 1863; (Indianapolis) *Daily State Sentinel,* Jan. 3, 1863; *Jonesboro* (Illinois) *Gazette,* Jan. 10, 17, Feb. 28, Apr. 4, 1863; *The Joliet* (Illinois) *Signal,* Jan. 27, Apr. 14, 1863; (Davenport) *Democrat and News,* Jan. 30, 1863, quoted in *Davenport Daily Gazette,* Jan. 31, 1863; *Davenport Daily Gazette,* Feb. 3, 7, 1863. Only in Minnesota did the journals of the party fail to come up to the new position of the Democratic party in the Middle West. There the party was weak, connections with the war remote and overshadowed to a considerable extent by frontier conditions. Consequently the Democratic press in that state apparently

contented itself with criticism of the efficiency rather than the objectives of the federal administration. *The Saint Paul Union,* a strongly Republican organ, played up Copperhead activities in such states as New York, Indiana, and Illinois, but it apparently found no cases of such overt opposition or even of clear statements of attitude against the war in Minnesota. See issues from Jan. 21 to Feb. 28, 1863, also *The Saint Paul Pioneer,* Jan. 3, 23, 1863 and *Mankato Independent,* Feb. 27, 1863.

The *Dubuque Herald* bluntly announced, "Permit us to say as a matter of record, that we consider separation and the acknowledgement of the Southern Confederacy as a fixed thing. Gov. Seymour says that a war for the restoration of the Union would be right. In that we disagree with him. Mr. Vallandigham says that separation is impossible. In that we disagree with him. The South will gain its independence—we have always believed so and said so." Quoted in *Davenport Daily Gazette,* March 7, 1863.

⁸ *The* (Columbus, Ohio) *Crisis,* Dec. 24, 1862, Jan. 14, Feb. 25, June 3, 1863; also March 25, 1863, from the *Wayne County* (Ohio) *Democrat; Davenport* (Iowa) *Daily Gazette,* Jan. 13, 1863, quotation from *Dubuque Herald*

⁹ Dec. 24, 1862, Jan. 14, 1863. The effect on the readers of such papers is suggested by a letter of William S. McCormick to his brother, Cyrus H., saying, "The atrocities of the Federal Army in Va. have been inhuman, devilish, beastly, brutal, barbarous—I suppose no language could express it." McCormick Historical Association Library, McCormick MSS., Chicago, Feb. 15, 1863; also *Ibid.,* Mrs. William S. McCormick, Chicago, Feb. 17, 1863, to Mrs. C. H. McCormick

¹⁰ *The Detroit Free Press,* Feb. 16, 1863

¹¹ *Davenport* (Iowa) *Daily Gazette,* Jan. 31, Feb. 4, 1863, quotations from (Davenport) *Democrat and News* and *Dubuque Herald,* respectively

¹² Quoted in *Davenport* (Iowa) *Daily Gazette,* Jan. 10, 1863

¹³ *The* (Columbus, Ohio) *Crisis,* Apr. 22, 1863

¹⁴ (Springfield, Illinois) *State Register,* March 12, 1863

¹⁵ (Indianapolis) *Daily State Sentinel,* Jan. 8, 1863   ·

¹⁶ *The Detroit Free Press,* Feb. 11, 1863

¹⁷ (Springfield, Illinois) *State Register,* Feb. 27, 1863

¹⁸ *Davenport* (Iowa) *Daily Gazette,* Apr. 8, 1863

¹⁹ *Ibid.*

²⁰ *The Detroit Free Press,* Feb. 12, 1863. For reports of other meetings in the various Midwestern states see (Indianapolis) *Daily State Sentinel,* Jan. 8, 9, 1863; *Jonesboro* (Illinois) *Gazette,* Feb. 7, 14, 28, 1863; *The Detroit Free Press,* Feb. 11, 12, 1863; (Springfield) *Illinois State Journal,* Feb. 18, 1863; *The* (Columbus, Ohio) *Crisis,* Feb. 18, 25, March 18, 25, Apr. 1, 22, 29, May 13, 1863; (Springfield, Illinois) *State Register,* Feb. 11, March 2, 3, 13, Apr. 6, 1863; *The Chicago Times,* March 6, 1863; *Davenport* (Iowa) *Daily Gazette,* Apr. 8, 16, 1863; *Canton* (Ohio) *Stark County Democrat,* June 3, 8, 1863

²¹ *Chicago Tribune,* Feb. 18, 1863; John Sherman MSS., A. H. Dunlevy, Lebanon, Ohio, Jan. 13, 1863, to Sherman

²² *Chicago Times,* Dec. 27, 1862; *Jonesboro* (Illinois) *Gazette,* Jan. 3, 1863; *Appleton* (Wisconsin) *Crescent,* Jan. 3, 1863

²³ (Springfield) *Illinois State Journal,* Mar. 10, 1863

²⁴ (Indianapolis) *Daily State Sentinel,* Jan. 9, 1863

²⁵ Jan. 21, 1863

26 Library of Congress, John Sherman MSS., Daniel Hamilton, Milan, Ohio, Dec. 25, 1862, to Sherman; also *Ibid.*, David Wyrick, Newark, Ohio, Dec. 31, 1862, to Sherman; Library of Congress, William Tecumseh Sherman MSS., John Sherman, Washington, Jan. 2, 1863, to W. T. Sherman; Library of Congress, Lyman Trumbull MSS., H. Barber, Richview, Ill., Feb. 2, 1863, to Trumbull; *Ibid.*, J. G. Bowman, Vincennes, Ind., Jan. 22, 1863, to Trumbull; Library of Congress, Benjamin F. Wade MSS., Isaac Welsh, Ohio State Senate, Columbus, Jan. 31, 1863, to Wade

27 Library of Congress, Elihu Washburne MSS., J. F. Ankeny, Freeport, Ill., Feb. 3, 1863, to Washburne

28 Trumbull MSS., William Butler, state treasurer, Springfield, Ill., Jan. 29, 1863 to Trumbull; also Yates MSS. (I), letters to Yates from R. I. McCartney, Loami, Ill., March 1, 1863; C. H. Kettler, Waterloo, Ill., March 29, 1863; Richard Aten, Astoria, Fulton County, Ill., June 12, 1863

29 *O.R.*, Ser. III, Vol. III, 23, Lincoln, Washington, Feb. 1, 1863, to Morton

30 Trumbull MSS., John M. Palmer, Nashville, Tenn., Dec. 19, 1862, to Trumbull; *Ibid.*, Grant Goodrich, Chicago, Jan. 26, 1863, to Trumbull; *Ibid.*, Bernard G. Farrar, Office of the General Supervisor of Confiscated and Contraband Property of the Department of Missouri, St. Louis, Jan. 30, 1863, to Trumbull; Washburne MSS., Geo. E. Haskell, Lee Center, Ill., Jan. 6, 1863, to Washburne; *Ibid.*, G. S. Hamilton, Galena, Ill., Jan. 18, 1863

31 Library of Congress, Salmon P. Chase MSS., M. D. Potter of the *Cincinnati Commercial*, Dec. 18, 1862, to Chase; John Sherman MSS., J. W. Wigton, Lucas, Ohio, Dec. 31, 1862, to Sherman; Washburne MSS., Joseph Medill, Chicago, Feb. 18, 1863, to Washburne

32 Library of Congress, Charles Butler MSS., E. B. McCagg, Chicago, Jan. 20, 1863, to Butler

33 John Sherman MSS., A. L. Brewer, New Lisbon, Ohio, Jan. 14, 1863, to Sherman

34 *Ibid.*, J. Purdy, Mansfield, Ohio, Jan. 10, 1863, to Sherman; Chase MSS., George S. Denison, Collector's Office, New Orleans, Jan. 8, 1863, to Chase; Trumbull MSS., Colonel Elias S. Dennis, Memphis, Jan. 17, 1863, to Trumbull; *Ibid.*, D. L. Phillips, U.S. Marshal for the Southern District of Illinois, Jan. 30, 1863, to Trumbull; *Ibid.*, Grant Goodrich, Chicago, Jan. 31, 1863, to Trumbull; Washburne MSS., J. F. Ankeny, Freeport, Ill., Feb. 3, 1863, to Washburne

35 Chase MSS., Galena, Ill., Apr. 4, 1863

36 Washburne MSS., Chicago, Jan. 14, 1863; Ralph Ray Fahrney, *Horace Greeley and the Tribune in the Civil War Period* (Cedar Rapids: Torch Press, 1936), pp. 140–84

37 *The Cincinnati Gazette,* Dec. 19, 1862, quoted in *The* (Columbus, Ohio) *Crisis,* Dec. 24, 1862; John Sherman MSS., R. M. Corwine, Cincinnati, Dec. 26, 1862, to Sherman; Library of Congress, Zachariah Chandler MSS., Chandler, Washington, Dec. 18, 1862, to Mrs. Chandler; Illinois State Historical Library, Miscellaneous MSS., Lyman Trumbull, Washington, Jan. 21, 1863, to Norman G. Flagg

38 Washburne MSS., B. H. McClellan, Galena, Ill., Jan. 13, 1863, to Washburne; (Columbus) *Daily Ohio State Journal,* Jan. 14, 1863; Library of Congress, Thomas Ewing MSS., Senator Orville Hickman Browning, Quincy, Ill., June 15, 1863, to Ewing

[39] Library of Congress, Benjamin R. Curtis MSS., Curtis, Washington, Jan. 1, 1863, to Greenough

[40] *O.R.*, Ser. III, Vol. III, 106–7

[41] *Ibid.*, p. 4, Morton, Indianapolis, Jan. 3, 1863, to Stanton; Library of Congress, Edwin M. Stanton MSS., Governor Yates, with endorsements by O. M. Hatch and Jesse K. Du Bois, Springfield, Ill., Feb. 2, 1863, to Chase; *Ibid.*, Governor Morton, Indianapolis, Feb. 9, 1863, to Stanton. This last communication, seven pages in length, was taken to Washington by Robert Dale Owen. Also *Weekly* (Springfield) *Illinois State Journal*, Jan. 7, 1863; (Springfield, Illinois) *State Register,* Jan. 9, 1863; Washburne, MSS., Daniel Richards, state senator from Whiteside County, Illinois, Springfield, Apr. 14, 1864; Illinois State Historical Library, Richard Yates MSS., Yates, Springfield, Ill., Jan. 19, 1863, to Governor Morton ("copy"); *Ibid.,* Yates, State Treasurer William Butler, Secretary of State O. M. Hatch, and Auditor Jesse K. Du Bois, Springfield, March 1, 1863, to Lincoln

[42] (Indianapolis) *Daily State Sentinel,* Jan. 15, 1863; *Indianapolis Daily Journal,* Jan. 30, 1863

[43] *Daily* (Springfield) *Illinois State Journal,* Feb. 5, 13, 1863; *The* (Columbus, Ohio) *Crisis,* Jan. 14, 21, Feb. 18, 1863

[44] *Chicago Tribune,* March 18, 1863

[45] W. T. Sherman MSS., W. T. Sherman, Memphis, Dec. 20, 1862, to John Sherman

[46] *O.R.*, Ser. II, Vol. V, 216

[47] Washburne MSS., copy of the proclamation, dated Feb. 12, 1863, from Memphis

[48] *O.R.*, Ser. II, Vol. V, 83, Department of the Ohio, General Orders, No. 31, Cincinnati, Dec. 14, 1862; *Ibid.,* pp. 214–5, W. Hoffman, Commissary-General of Prisoners, Washington, Jan. 26, 1863, to Quartermaster-General M. C. Meigs

[49] Wisconsin State Historical Society Library, Lucius Fairchild MSS., Fairchild, Belle Plain, Va., Jan. 30, 1863, to "Sarah"

[50] *Jonesboro* (Illinois) *Gazette,* Feb. 28, 1863

[51] *Mt. Vernon* (Ohio) *Banner,* quoted with approving comments in *The* (Columbus, Ohio) *Crisis,* Dec. 24, 1863; (Springfield) *Illinois State Journal,* Feb. 18, 1863; Ewing MSS., Brigadier-General Hugh Ewing, before Vicksburg, Apr. 28, 1863, to Thomas Ewing

[52] *Missouri Democrat,* quoted in (Springfield) *Illinois State Journal,* Jan. 30, 1863

[53] *Canton* (Illinois) *Weekly Register,* Apr. 20, 1863, letter of Ed. Mosher, Cuba, Fulton County, Ill., March 1, 1863, to Richard Speake, Co. A, 16th Illinois Volunteers. Also see (Springfield) *Illinois State Journal,* Feb. 25, Apr. 14, 1863; *Missouri Democrat,* quoted by the *Illinois State Journal,* Jan. 28, 30, 1863; *Michigan History Magazine,* I (Oct. 1917), pp. 4–5; Yates MSS. (I), T. Wildman, Unity, Ill., Feb. 4, 1863, to Yates

[54] (Springfield) *Illinois State Journal,* March 31, July 20, 1863

[55] Indiana State Library, Oliver P. Morton MSS., Morton, Indianapolis, Jan. 2, 1863, to Stanton; Stanton MSS., Morton, Indianapolis, Feb. 9, 1863, to Stanton, Robert Dale Owen, bearer; *O.R.*, Ser. II, Vol. V, 227–8, H. W. Freedley, Capt., 3rd Infantry, Indianapolis, Jan. 30, 1863, to Col. W. Hoffman, Commissary-General of Prisoners; *Ibid.,* Ser. III, Vol. III, 62, Governor Kirk-

wood, Iowa City, March 10, 1863, to Stanton; *Ibid.,* Ser. II, Vol. VI, 3, Brigadier-General O. B. Willcox, Commander of the District of Indiana and Michigan, Indianapolis, June 11, 1863, to Hoffman; *Ibid.,* pp. 19–20, June 15, 1863; Yates MSS. (I), John W. Beems, Mason, Ill., Feb. 9, 1863, to Yates; *Ibid.,* Andrew Miller, Litchfield, Ill., Jan. 21, 1863, to Yates; *Ibid.,* Clark E. Carr, Galesburg, Ill., Feb. 15, 1863, to Yates

⁵⁶ *O.R.,* Ser. III, Vol. III, 79–81, Wright, Cincinnati, to Adjutant-General Lorenzo Thomas; *Ibid.,* p. 116, Governor Yates, Springfield, Ill., Apr. 3, 1863, to Stanton; *Jacksonville* (Illinois) *Journal,* March 19, 1863

⁵⁷ *O.R.,* Ser. II, Vol. V, 108, Carrington, Indianapolis, Dec. 22, 1862, to Stanton; *Ibid.,* Ser. III, Vol. III, 19–20, Carrington, Indianapolis, Jan. 24, 1863, to Adjutant-General Thomas; *Ibid.,* Ser. II, Vol. V, 363–7, Carrington, Indianapolis, March 19, 1863, to "the President and the honorable Secretary of War"; *Ibid.,* Ser. III, Vol. III, 68–9, Hoxie, Des Moines, Feb. 21, 1863, to Major L. C. Turner, Judge Advocate, Washington, with enclosures. Hoxie reported Polk, Warren, Lucas, and the neighboring counties as the chief seats of unrest. See also *Ibid.,* pp. 62–3, 66–72, 82–4, Governor Kirkwood, Iowa City, Mar. 11, 13, 23, 1863, to Stanton; *Ibid.,* pp. 124–5, U.S. Senator James Grimes, Burlington, Iowa, Apr. 20, 1863, to Stanton; Yates MSS. (I), Uri Manly, Marshall, Ill., March 7, 1863, to Yates

⁵⁸ *Ibid.,* Ser. III. Vol. III, 75–6, Colonel Carrington, Indianapolis, March 19, 1863, to Adjutant-General Thomas; *Ibid.,* Ser. II, Vol. V, 221, Lieut. Simpkins, 66th Illinois Volunteers, Paris, Illinois, Jan. 28, 1863, to Secretary Stanton, forwarded by Governor Yates; *Ibid.,* Ser. III, Vol. III, 71, Colonel George A. Henry, Winterset, Iowa, Feb. 24, 1863, to Governor Kirkwood; *Ibid.,* pp. 66–72, Kirkwood, Iowa City, March 13, 1863, to Stanton, with enclosures; *Ibid.,* Ser. II, Vol. V, 363–7, Carrington, Indianapolis, March 19, 1863, to Lincoln, etc.; Stanton MSS., Jas. A. Gager, Carbondale, Ill., Jan. 13, 1863, to Secretary Chase; Chase MSS., Carrington, Indianapolis, Apr. 13, 1863, to Chase; *Belleville* (Illinois) *Democrat,* March 21, 1863; *Ottawa* (Illinois) *Weekly Republican,* March 28, 1863; (Rockford, Illinois) *Rock River Democrat,* Apr. 22, 1863; *Chicago Tribune,* May 5, 1863; (Springfield) *Illinois State Journal,* Jan. 21, 28, May 7, June 10, July 20, 1863; *Cairo* (Illinois) *City Gazette,* June 18, 1863; Morton MSS., Letter Books, W. R. Holloway, secretary to Morton, Indianapolis, Apr. 18, 1863, to Morton, Cincinnati; *Ibid.,* Telegram Books, Capt. Jas. Thompson, Bloomington, Ind., Apr. 20, 1863, to Morton; *Ibid.,* James B. Mulkey, *et al.,* Bloomington, Apr. 22, 1863, to Morton; *Ibid.,* Morton, Indianapolis, Apr. 25, 1863, to J. I. Brown, New York; *Ibid.,* N. Jones, *et al.,* Centreville, Ind., May 2, 1863, to Morton; *Ibid.,* Morton to Jones, *et al.;* W. H. H. Terrell, Adjutant-General of Indiana, May 4, 1863, to Morton, Cincinnati; *Ibid.,* Morton, Indianapolis, June 5, 1863, to Colonel R. W. Thompson, Terre Haute; *Ibid.,* Lieutenant Wm. Cockran, White Licks, Ind., June 11, 1863, to Morton; *Saint Paul* (Minnesota) *Daily Union,* Feb. 28, 1863

⁵⁹ *Evansville* (Indiana) *Daily Journal,* May 6, 1863

⁶⁰ *O.R.,* Ser. II, Vol. V, 506, S. R. Curtis, St. Louis, Apr. 22, 1863, to General-in-Chief H. W. Halleck

⁶¹ Stanton MSS., Jas. L. Gager, Carbondale, Ill., Jan. 13, 1863, to Secretary Chase; (Springfield, Illinois) *State Register,* March 9, 1863; *O.R.,* Ser. II, Vol. V, 516, Brigadier-General Asboth, Columbus, Ky., Apr. 24, 1863, to Major-General

Hurlbut, Memphis; *Ibid.*, pp. 521–2, Brigadier-General N. B. Buford, Cairo, Ill., Apr. 25, 1863, to Stanton; *Ibid.*, p. 585, Buford, May 10, 1863, to Major-General Burnside

⁶² *The Detroit Free Press,* Mar. 6, 7, 8, 11, 1863; *Detroit Advertiser and Tribune,* March 7, 8, 9, 10, 11, 12, 13, 14, 16, 17, 1863; *The* (Columbus, Ohio) *Crisis,* March 18, 1863

⁶³ *The Joliet* (Illinois) *Signal,* Jan. 27, June 23, 1863; *Jonesboro* (Illinois) *Gazette,* Apr. 4, 1863; *Belleville* (Illinois) *Democrat,* Apr. 11, 1863

⁶⁴ *O.R.,* Ser. III, Vol. III, 35–6, Tod, Columbus, Feb. 1, 1863, to Secretary Stanton

⁶⁵ *Ibid.*, Vol. V, 627, summary report of Provost Marshal General Fry to Stanton. See also *Ibid.*, Vol. III, 410–1, General A. E. Burnside, Cincinnati, June 22, 1863, to Provost Marshal General Fry, Washington

⁶⁶ *The* (Columbus, Ohio) *Crisis,* Feb. 25, March 4, Apr. 1, 15, 1863; (Springfield, Illinois) *State Register,* Feb. 28, 1863; *The Congressional Globe,* 37th Cong., 3rd sess., pp. 1224–6, 1230–4, 1367–70, appdx., pp. 91–4, 172–7, speeches of Senator Turpie and Representative Voorhees of Indiana and Congressmen Vallandigham, Pendelton, and Chilton A. White, of Ohio. Forty-nine members of the House voted against the bill.

⁶⁷ *O.R.,* Ser. III, Vol. III, 88–93

⁶⁸ *Ibid.*, p. 74. General Order No. 67, signed by Adjutant-General Lorenzo Thomas. Simeon Draper had originally been appointed to the office. On Sept. 24, 1862, his work, chiefly the apprehension of deserters, had been defined in General Order No. 140. To aid him a number of special provost marshals were appointed and stationed in such cities as Cleveland, Columbus, Cincinnati, Indianapolis, Detroit, and Quincy, Illinois. Under Draper more than 6,000 deserters were arrested by emissaries of the Bureau and some 200 persons were taken into custody on charges of resistance to the authorities, aiding deserters, rioting, destruction of government property, and spying. See *O.R.,* Ser. III, Vol. II, 65; *Ibid.*, 936–41. The latter is Draper's report of operations, dated Dec. 6, 1862.

⁶⁹ *Ibid.*, Vol. III, pp. 125–46, 167–72, 320, 322–3. Original appointees for the Midwest were Colonel Edwin A. Parrott, Ohio; Colonel Conrad Baker, Indiana; Lieutenant Colonel James Oakes, Illinois; Major Thomas Duncan, Iowa; Major Bennett H. Hill, Michigan; Lieutenant-Colonel Charles S. Lovell, Wisconsin; and Captain Anderson D. Nelson, Minnesota

⁷⁰ *Ibid.*, pp. 323–4

⁷¹ *Ibid.*, p. 349, Governor Tod, Columbus, June 12, 1863, to Stanton; *Ibid.*, pp. 349–50, Acting Assistant Provost Marshal General E. A. Parrott, Columbus, June 12, 1863, to Provost Marshal General Fry; *Ibid.*, pp. 403–4, D. P. Leadbetter, Millersburg, Ohio, June 22, 1863, to Governor Tod

⁷² *Ibid.*, pp. 338–40, Acting Assistant Provost Marshal Conrad Baker, Indianapolis, June 11, 1863, to Fry; *Ibid.*, p. 347, June 12, 1863; *Ibid.*, p. 354, Fry, June 13, 1863, to Baker; *Ibid.*, pp. 354–6, Baker, June 13, 1863, to Fry, enclosing copy of report of Provost Marshal McQuiston to General Willcox; *Ibid.*, pp. 396–7, Baker, June 22, 1863, to Fry; *Ibid.*, pp. 413–4, John C. McQuiston, Greensburg, Ind., June 24, 1863, to Baker

⁷³ *Ibid.*, pp. 391–4, including report of Provost Marshal R. W. Thompson,

Terre Haute, June 18, 1863, to Baker; *Ibid.,* pp. 391–4, General Willcox, Indianapolis, June 20, 1863, to General Burnside; *Ibid.,* Burnside to Willcox, Willcox to Burnside, Baker, Indianapolis, to Fry; *Ibid.,* pp. 396–7, Baker, June 22, 1863, to Fry

74 *Ibid.,* pp. 354–6, Baker, Indianapolis, June 13, 1863, to Fry; *Ibid.,* p. 375, June 17; *Ibid.,* pp. 393–4, Provost Marshal R. W. Thompson, Terre Haute, June 18, 1863, to Baker; *Ibid.,* pp. 392–4, Baker, June 20, 1863, to Fry; *Ibid.,* pp. 464–5, Baker, July 2, 1863, to Fry; Morton MSS., Telegram Copy Books, J. A. Watson, Greencastle, Ind., June 15, 1863, to Morton (?); Trumbull MSS., Caleb B. Smith, June 19, 1863, to Trumbull

75 *The Chicago Tribune,* June 26, 27, 1863. Also see *Ibid.,* June 23, 1863; (Springfield) *Illinois State Journal,* March 23, Apr. 2, 1863

76 *O.R.,* Ser. III, Vol. III, 503–4, Luke Elliott, Summum, Ill., June 22, 1863, to Captain B. F. Westlake, endorsed by Justice of the Peace Joel Onion; *Ibid.,* Wm. McComb, Lewistown, Ill., June 23, 1863, to Provost Marshal B. F. Westlake; *Ibid.,* p. 504, Acting Assistant Provost Marshal General James Oakes, Springfield, Ill., July 1, 1863, to Westlake; *Ibid.,* p. 505, R. R. Randall, Rushville, Ill., July 9, 1863, to Westlake; *Canton* (Illinois) *Weekly Register,* June 29, 1863

77 *Ibid.,* p. 103, T. O. Howe, Madison, Wisconsin, Mar. 25, 1863, to Stanton; *Ibid.,* pp. 248–9, Provost Marshal J. M. Tillapaugh, Racine, Wis., June 2, 1863, to Fry; *Ibid.,* pp. 247–8, Acting Assistant Provost Marshal General Charles S. Lovell, Madison, June 2, 1863, to Fry; *Ibid.,* p. 368, Fry, Washington, June 15, 1863, to Lovell; *Ibid.,* pp. 395–6, Pope, Milwaukee, June 20, 1863, to Fry

78 *Ibid.,* p. 367, Acting Assistant Provost Marshal B. H. Hill, Detroit, June, 15, 1863, to Fry

79 *Ibid.,* pp. 421–2, Fry, Washington, June 28, 1863, to Baker

80 *Lewistown* (Illinois) *Democrat,* quoted in *Canton* (Illinois) *Weekly Register,* June 29, 1863

81 Vallandigham, *op. cit.,* pp. 502–4; also pp. 42–3

82 *O.R.,* Ser. III, Vol. III, 467

83 *Indianapolis Daily Journal,* Jan. 15, 1863

84 *Weekly* (Springfield) *Illinois State Journal,* Jan. 28, 1863; Isaac Jenkinson, *The Peace Party and Its Policy: Speech of Isaac Jenkinson at Fort Wayne, Indiana, March 16, 1863* (Fort Wayne, 1863), pamphlet

85 *Quincy* (Illinois) *Daily Whig and Republican,* Feb. 27, 1863; *Davenport* (Iowa) *Daily Gazette,* Feb. 27, March 14, 18, 1863; *The Echo from the Army: What Our Soldiers Say about the Copperheads* (Loyal Reprints, No. 1. New York, 1863), pamphlet; Yates MSS. (I), Lieutenant-Colonel Edward S. Salomon, 82nd Illinois Regiment, Stafford Court House, Va., Feb. 14, 1863, to Yates; *Ibid.,* Brigadier-General M. Brayman, Bolivar, Tenn., Feb. 16, 1863, to Yates

86 Library of Congress, Samuel Henry Eells MSS., Eells, Assistant Surgeon, 12th Michigan Infantry, Middlebury, Tenn., Feb. 12, 1863, to his aunt (name not given)

87 *Davenport* (Iowa) *Daily Gazette,* Feb. 23, 24, 1863

88 *Saint Paul* (Minnesota) *Daily Union,* Feb. 24, 1863

89 Washburne MSS., S. [or L.] Noble, Dixon, Ill., Feb. 6, 1863, to Washburne

90 *The* (Columbus, Ohio) *Crisis,* Apr. 1, 1863

⁹¹ *Joliet* (Illinois) *Signal*, Feb. 10, 1863; *The* (Columbus, Ohio) *Crisis*, June 24, 1863; Yates MSS. (I), Yates, Springfield, June 10, 1863, to Adjutant-General A. C. Fuller, Chicago

⁹² William Dudley Foulke, *Life of Oliver P. Morton* (Indianapolis: Bowen-Merrill Co., 1899), I, 236–9; Indiana State Historical Society Library, William H. English MSS., Frederick W. Matthis, Corydon, Ind., March 6, 1863, to English; Indiana State Library, Richard W. Thompson MSS., W. R. Holloway, secretary to Governor Morton, March 12, 1863, to Thompson

⁹³ Trumbull MSS., Jesse K. Du Bois, Auditor, Springfield, Ill., Feb. 2, 1863, to Trumbull; Washburne MSS., C. Lansing, Marengo, Ill., Feb. 21, 1863; Ewing MSS., Senator Edgar Cowan, Greensburg, Pa., March 17, 29, 1863, to Ewing; *The* (Columbus, Ohio) *Crisis*, Apr. 8, 1863; Chicago Historical Society Library, William B. Ogden MSS., W. H. Green, Metropolis, Ill., May 2, 1863, to Ogden; Library of Congress, John Dean Caton MSS., J. W. Sheahan, *The Chicago Morning Post*, Chicago, March 19, May 9, 1863, to Caton; *Ibid.*, Caton, Ottawa, Ill., March 24, 1863, to John W. Merritt, Silas L. Bryan (father of William Jennings Bryan), and H. K. S. O'Melveny, Salem, Ill., copy; *Ibid.*, Amos Kendall, Washington, D.C., March 26, 1863, to Caton; J. S. Buckles, Geneseo, Ill., March 26, 1863, to Caton; *Ibid.*, M. McConnel, Jacksonville, Ill., Apr. 15, 1863, to Caton; *Ibid.*, S. S. Marshall, McLeansboro, Ill., May 2, 1863, to Caton

⁹⁴ *Indianapolis Daily Journal*, Jan. 9, 1863; *Canton* (Illinois) *Weekly Register*, June 22, 1863; Washburne MSS., [?] Russ, Chicago, Feb. 20, 1863, to Washburne

⁹⁵ Morton MSS., Telegram Books, W. R. Holloway, secretary to the Governor, Indianapolis, May 16, 1863, to W. H. H. Terrell, Adjutant-General of Indiana; E. Bently Hamilton, "The Union League: Its Origin and Achievement in the Civil War," *Transactions of the Illinois State Historical Society*, 1921, pp. 110–5. Mark Bangs of Marshall County and George H. Harlow of Tazewell County were the first state president and secretary, respectively. Joseph Medill was a member of the executive committee.

⁹⁶ Trumbull MSS., H. G. McPike, Alton, Ill., Feb. 23, 1863, to Trumbull; also see Washburne MSS., Charles C. Royce, Ogle Station, Ill., Feb. 23, 1863, to Washburne; Yates MSS. (I), letters to Yates from John D. Bartlett, *et al.*, Rio, Ill., Feb. 17, 1863; William A. Woods and Havillah G. Smith, Ingraham P.O., Clay County, Ill., March 1, 1863; F. J. Riggs, Bloomington *Pantagraph* Office, March 2, 1863; Mayor A. J. Merriman, Bloomington, June 10, 1863; W. T. Sylvester, Arcola, Coles County, Ill., June 22, 1863; John T. Wilson, Commander-in-Chief of "The Strong Band," Chicago, July 1, 1863; Geo. H. Harlow, secretary of the Illinois state council, Union League of America, Springfield, July 6, 1863; John S. Wolfe, Champaign, Ill., July 12, 1863

⁹⁷ Washburne MSS., S. W. McMaster, Galena, Ill., Feb. 26, 1863, to Washburne

⁹⁸ *O.R.*, Ser. II, Vol. V, 555, Captain D. R. Larned, Burnside's assistant adjutant-general, Cincinnati, May 4, 1863, to Charles G. Hutton; *Ibid.*, p. 567, Burnside, Cincinnati, May 7, 1863, to General-in-Chief H. W. Halleck; *Ibid.*, pp. 633–46, Burnside, Cincinnati, May 18, 1863, to Halleck; *Ibid.*, pp. 573–84, record of hearing before Judge Leavitt, of the U.S. Circuit Court for the

Southern District of Ohio, May 9, 11, 1863; *Ibid.*, p. 608, Burnside, Cincinnati, May 14, 1863, to Stanton

99 *The Daily* (Columbus) *Ohio Statesman*, May 7, 1863; *Davenport* (Iowa) *Daily Gazette*, May 16, 1863, quoting the *Dubuque Herald; The* (Columbus, Ohio) *Crisis*, May 13, 27, 1863; *O.R.*, Ser. II, Vol. V, 654–6, Erastus Corning *et al.*, Albany, May 19, 1863, to Lincoln; *Ibid.*, Vol. VI, 4–10, Lincoln, June 12, 1863, to Corning *et al.; Ibid.*, Vol. V, 566, Capt. G. Hutton, Dayton, May 6, 1863, to Burnside; *Ibid.*, to Major-General John Parke, Cincinnati. The officer in command of the detail of troops sent to Dayton reported the discovery in the office of *The Empire* of two hundred muskets and a small cannon, probably a provision against mob attack, although possibly having more sinister implications.

100 *O.R.*, Ser. II, Vol. V, 657–8, Stanton, May 19, 1863, to Burnside, Burnside to Stanton, Stanton to Burnside, Stanton to Rosecrans; *Ibid.*, Brigadier-General E. R. S. Canby to Major-General Rosecrans; *Ibid.*, pp. 665–6, Burnside, Cincinnati, May 20, 1863, to Stanton, Canby, Washington, to Burnside; *Ibid.*, p. 717, Burnside, May 29, 1863, to Lincoln, Lincoln to Burnside; *Ibid.*, pp. 664–5, General-in-Chief Halleck, Washington, May 20, 1863, to Burnside

101 *The* (Columbus, Ohio) *Crisis*, June 17, 1863; *O.R.*, Ser. II, Vol. VI, pp. 48–53, 56–9, 64–8

102 *Ibid.*, Vol. V, pp. 705–6, Major Wm. Wiles, provost marshal, Murfreesboro, Tenn., May 25, 1863, to Brigadier-General Garfield; *Ibid.*, p. 958, General Braxton Bragg, Shelbyville, Tenn., May 26, 1863, to Vallandigham; *Ibid.*, pp. 959–60, Bragg, Shelbyville, May 27, 1863, to Adjutant and Inspector-General S. Cooper, Richmond; *Ibid.*, p. 963, Secretary of War James A. Seddon, Richmond, May 30, 1863, to Bragg; *Ibid.*, 963–4, Vallandigham, Shelbyville, May 31, 1863, to Bragg; *Ibid.*, p. 965, Bragg, Shelbyville, June 1, 1863, to Cooper; *Ibid.*, Jefferson Davis, Richmond, June 2, 1863, to Bragg; *Ibid.*, p. 966, Charles Martin, Hampden Sydney College, Va., June 2, 1863, to Seddon; *Ibid.*, p. 968, Seddon, Richmond, June 5, 1863, to Robert Ould, Commissioner for the Exchange of Prisoners; *Ibid.*, p. 969, Davis, Richmond, June 8, 1863, to Bragg

103 *Daily* (Springfield) *Illinois State Journal*, June 18, 1863; *Ottawa* (Illinois) *Weekly Republican*, June 20, 1863. See also Morton MSS., Telegram Books, W. R. Holloway, Indianapolis, May 20, 1863, to Morton; *O.R.*, Ser. I, Vol. XXVII, pt. 3, pp. 140, 241, Richard Yates, Springfield, June 15, 20, 1863, to Stanton; *Jacksonville* (Illinois) *Journal*, June 4, 1863; *Belleville* (Illinois) *Weekly Advocate*, July 24, 1863

104 *Davenport* (Iowa) *Daily Gazette*, July 11, 1863

105 *The* (Columbus, Ohio) *Crisis*, Apr. 8, 15, 1863, Indiana State Library, Morton Telegram Copy Books, no. 10, p. 247, J. Jenkinson, Fort Wayne, Ind., n.d.

106 Alexander Harris, *A Review of the Political Conflict in America* (New York: Y. H. Pollock, 1876), pp. 331–2

107 *Proceedings of the Great Peace Convention, Held in the City of New York, June 3d, 1863; Speeches, Addresses, Resolutions, and Letters from Leading Men Abridged from the Elaborate Report Published in the New York "Daily News," June 4th, 1863; The* (Columbus, Ohio) *Crisis*, June 17, 1863

108 *Davenport* (Iowa) *Daily Gazette*, Jan. 13, 1863, quoting speech of Jeffer-

son Davis at Jackson, Mississippi, in which he stated that he "confidently looked to the North-West for the first gleam of peace." *Belleville* (Illinois) *Democrat,* Feb. 7, 1863, quoting Atlanta, Georgia, *Intelligencer; Belleville* (Illinois) *Weekly Advocate,* Feb. 13, 1863, quoting *Chattanooga Rebel; Illinois State Journal,* March 10, 1863, from *Richmond Enquirer,* Feb. 12, 1863; *The* (Columbus, Ohio) *Crisis,* Mar. 25, 1863, from the *Richmond Dispatch,* March 12, 1863, telling of the introduction of resolutions in the Confederate Congress to recognize the peace sentiment in the North; *O.R.,* Ser. IV, Vol. II, 487–95, Gov. John Milton of Florida, Apr. 15, 1863, enclosing pamphlet, to Davis

109 Library of Congress, Trumbull MSS., Gustave Koerner, minister to Spain, Madrid, March 22, 1863, to Trumbull

110 *O.R.,* Ser. I, Vol. XXVII, pt. 2, pp. 302, 305; *Ibid.,* pt. 3, p. 382; Library of Congress, E. B. Washburne MSS., [?] Russ, Office of the U.S. Marshal for the Northern District of Illinois, Chicago, July 4, 1863, to Washburne; Mc-Cormick MSS., Mrs. William S. McCormick, Chicago, June 29, 1863, to Mrs. C. H. McCormick in Europe. The Dubuque *Herald* called Governor Seymour a "fool" for forwarding troops from New York to aid in repelling Lee, saying that he should have seized the opportunity to inform Lincoln that "he paused to see what kind of government it was for which we were asked to pour out our blood and treasure." Quoted in *Davenport* (Iowa) *Daily Gazette,* June 30, 1863; *O.R.,* Ser. III, Vol. III, 196, O. P. Morton, Indianapolis, May 7, 1863, to Stanton.

CHAPTER VII

1 *O.R.,* Ser. III, Vol. III, 731–4, Lincoln, Washington, Aug. 26, 1863, to James Conkling, Springfield, Ill. Also Library of Congress, Elihu B. Washburne MSS., John Lorrain, Galena, Ill., July 8, 1863, to Washburne; *Daily* (Springfield) *Illinois State Journal,* July 9, 10, 1863

2 Library of Congress, Lyman Trumbull MSS., N. B. Judd, U.S. Minister to Germany, Berlin, Sept. 8, 1863, to Trumbull; *Dodgeville* (Wisconsin) *Chronicle,* May 26, 1864

3 McCormick Historical Association Library, Cyrus H. McCormick MSS., July 12, 1863; Library of Congress, Franklin Pierce MSS., Samuel S. Cox, Washington, March 17, 1864, to Pierce; *Ibid.,* Robert McClelland, Detroit, Apr. 13, 1864, to Pierce, *Ibid.,* Daniel W. Voorhees, Washington, Apr. 18, 1864, to Pierce

4 Trumbull MSS., Jesse M. Fell, Cincinnati, Aug. 11, 1863, to Trumbull. Also *Ibid.,* John M. Palmer, Chattanooga, Tenn., Dec. 18, 1863, Jan. 24, 1864, to Trumbull; *Ibid.,* John Gordon, Lynnville, Ill., Jan. 11, 1864, to Governor Yates; *Ibid.,* W. H. Hanna, Bloomington, Ill., Feb. 5, 1864, to Trumbull; Library of Congress, Thaddeus Stevens MSS., L. G. Wells, Cincinnati, Dec. 19, 1863, to Stevens; Library of Congress, Julian-Giddings MSS., Mary J. Lewis, Washington, Sept. 4, 1863, to [?]; George W. Julian, *Political Recollections* (Chicago: Jansen, McClurg & Co., 1884), pp. 237–8; *The Saint Paul Press,* Apr. 6, 1864; *Green Bay* (Wisconsin) *Advocate,* Apr. 18, 1864

5 *Cairo* (Illinois) *Morning News,* Oct. 15, 1863; *The* (Richmond, Indiana) *Quaker City Telegram,* Aug. 15, 1863; Trumbull MSS., Col. F. Hecker, Lookout Valley, Tenn., Feb. 8, 1864, to Trumbull; Library of Congress, Thomas Ewing

MSS., Brigadier-General Hugh Ewing, Camp Sherman, Miss., Aug. 8, 1863, to Thomas Ewing; *Ibid.*, Scottsboro, Ala., Jan. 22, 1864

⁶ *O.R.*, Ser. II, Vol. VI, 231–2, 276

⁷ Clement Laird Vallandigham, *Speeches, Arguments, Addresses, and Letters of Clement L. Vallandigham* (New York: J. Walter & Co., 1864), pp. 507–20; *The* (Columbus, Ohio) *Crisis*, July 22, Aug. 12, 1863

⁸ *Ibid.*, July 22, Aug. 19, Sept. 16, 23, 30, Oct. 7, 1863. See George Henry Porter, *Ohio Politics during the Civil War Period*. Studies in History, Economics, and Public Law Edited by the Faculty of Political Science of Columbia University, Vol. XL. No. 2 (New York: Columbia University Press, 1911), pp. 167–89, also *Coshocton* (Ohio) *Democrat*, Sept. 2, 1863

⁹ *The* (Columbus Ohio) *Crisis*, Sept. 2, 16, 23, 1863; *The Cincinnati Daily Enquirer*, Sept. 19, 25, 26, Oct. 3, 10, 12, 13, 1863

¹⁰ Library of Congress, John Sherman MSS., Edward Kinsman, Ohio House of Representatives, Columbus, Jan. 8, 1863, to Hon. Geo. B. Sentis [?]; Library of Congress, Salmon P. Chase MSS., Jos. H. Geiger, Columbus, July 13, 1863, to Chase; Richard A. Harrison, *Oration of the Honorable Richard A. Harrison, Delivered at Pleasant Valley, Madison County, Ohio, on the Fourth of July, A.D. 1863* (London, Ohio: *Madison County Union*, printers, 1863); John Sherman, *Valandigham's* [sic] *Record Reviewed; A Political Traitor Unmasked: Speech by Hon. John Sherman, U.S. Senator from Ohio, Delivered at Delaware, Ohio, July 28th, 1863* (Dayton: *Daily Journal*, printer, 1863; John Alexander Logan, *Speech of Major-General John A. Logan on Return to Illinois after Capture of Vicksburg. Reported by "Mack" of the Cincinnati Commercial.* Loyal Publications of the National Union Association of Ohio, No. 4 (Cincinnati: Caleb Clark printer, 1863); John Adams Dix, *Letter from John A. Dix to the War Democracy of Wisconsin* (New York, 1863), Arthur McArthur, *Address by the Loyal Democracy of Wisconsin to the People of the State. Reported by Arthur McArthur and Adopted in Convention in Janesville, September 17, 1863* (Milwaukee: *Daily Wisconsin* Steam Press Establishment, 1863); *Davenport* (Iowa) *Daily Gazette*, June 23, 1863; *The* (Findlay, Ohio) *Hancock Jeffersonian*, June 26, July 3, Aug. 14, Oct. 9, 1863. *The* (Richmond, Indiana) *Quaker City Telegram*, Aug. 15, 1863; see also Porter, *op. cit.*, pp. 167–89. On October 1 a state convention of the Illinois war Democrats was held at Decatur. (Springfield) *Illinois State Register*, Oct. 5, 1863; *Jacksonville* (Illinois) *Journal*, Oct. 15, 1863. A gathering of war Democrats from all the Northern states met in Chicago on November 25, 1863. *The Chicago Times*, Nov. 26, 1863.

¹¹ *O.R.*, Ser. II, Vol. V, 723–6, Stanton, Washington, June 1, 1863, to Burnside. This letter was accompanied by newspaper clippings of an undignified squabble carried on with the newspapers by Brigadier-General Hascall, commanding the Military District of Indiana. Burnside was advised to remove Hascall. See also *O.R.*, Ser. III, Vol. III, 252, Assistant Adjutant-General E. D. Townshend, Washington, June 4, 1863, to Burnside; *Ibid.*, Ser. II, Vol. V, 741, General Order No. 91, Department of the Ohio, June 4, 1863; Burnside had also forbidden the circulation of the *New York World* in his district.

¹² *O.R.*, Ser. II, Vol. V, 739–40, General Order No. 90

¹³ *The Tribune Almanac for 1864*, pp. 60–1

¹⁴ Oct. 21, 1863

¹⁵ Quoted in *The Crisis*, Oct. 28, 1863

16 *The Tribune Almanac for 1864,* pp. 60–7; *Davenport* (Iowa) *Daily Gazette,* July 11, 14, 28, 29, Aug. 10, 1863

17 *O.R.,* Ser. III, Vol. III, 35–6, 503–11, 626–7; *Joliet* (Illinois) *Signal,* July 21, 1863; *Canton* (Illinois) *Weekly Register,* July 27, 1863; (Springfield) *Illinois State Journal,* Aug. 19, 1863; *Canton* (Illinois) *Weekly Republican,* Aug. 24, 1863

18 *O.R.,* Ser. III, Vol. III, 488–9, Provost Marshal Jno. S. Newberry, Detroit, July 14, 1863, to Major B. H. Hill, Acting Assistant Provost Marshal General for Michigan; *Ibid.,* pp. 533–5, Provost Marshal J. M. Tillapaugh, Milwaukee, July 14, 1863, to Lieutenant-Colonel Charles S. Lovell, Acting Assistant Provost Marshal-General for Wisconsin; *Ibid.,* p. 567, Colonel Edward A. Parrott, Acting Assistant Provost Marshal General for Ohio, Columbus, July 24, 1863, to Provost Marshal General Fry

19 *Ibid.,* p. 508, Captain B. M. Veach, Tennessee, Ill., July 10, 1863, to Provost Marshal W. H. Randolph; *Ibid.,* p. 507, Randolph, Macomb, Ill., July 11, 1863, to Provost Marshal B. F. Westlake; *Ibid.,* 663, Provost Marshal R. W. Thompson, Terre Haute, Ind., Aug. 10, 1863, to Acting Assistant Provost Marshal General Conrad Baker; *Ibid.,* p. 697, Baker, Indianapolis, Aug. 20, 1863, to Provost Marshal General James B. Fry

20 Indiana State Historical Library, Oliver P. Morton MSS., W. R. Holloway (Morton's secretary), Indianapolis, July 18, 1863, to Morton, Washington, D.C.

21 *O.R.,* Ser. III, Vol. III, 560–1, Acting Assistant Provost Marshal General James Oakes, Springfield, Ill., July 23, 1863, to Fry, with enclosures

22 *Ibid.,* 520–1, 544–5, 551–2, 577–8, 637, 639, 795, 798–9, 863, 924, 1027–9

23 *Ibid.,* 506, 508, 509–10; (Springfield) *Illinois State Journal,* Nov. 19, 1863

24 National Archives, War Department Archives, Office of Provost Marshal, Reports of Operations, Illinois, Provost Marshal Isaac N. Phillips, Cairo, Ill., to Oakes

25 Sept. 9, 1863

26 National Archives, War Department Archives, Office of Provost Marshal, Reports of Operations, Illinois, Provost Marshal Isaac N. Phillips, Cairo, Ill., to Oakes

27 (Springfield) *Illinois State Journal,* Aug. 17, 1863; *Jacksonville* (Illinois) *Journal,* Aug. 20, 1863

28 *The Chicago Times,* Sept. 9, 1863; *O.R.,* Ser. III, Vol. III, 724–5, Deputy Provost Marshal William A. Johnston, Crawford Township, Coshocton, Ohio, Aug. 26, 1863, to Provost Marshal John A. Sinnet

29 *The Chicago Daily Tribune,* Oct. 19, 1863

30 *Belleville* (Illinois) *Advocate,* Jan. 1, 1864

31 Files, 430–2, 434–6, 438, 440–7, 452–6, 459–65, 468, 482, 568–9, 571

32 *Cairo* (Illinois) *Daily Democrat,* March 9, 1864

33 *O.R.,* Ser. III, Vol. III, 892, Vol. IV, 38–9, 57–8, 59, 154, 181

34 *Galena* (Illinois) *Daily Democrat,* Feb. 8, 1864. Also *The Chicago Times,* Oct. 31, Nov. 25, Dec. 18, Jan. 13, 1863; *Joliet* (Illinois) *Signal,* Nov. 24, 1863, Jan. 5, 1864; (Springfield, Illinois) *State Register,* Dec. 29, 1863; *The Chicago Tribune,* Dec. 25, 1863; *Cairo* (Illinois) *Daily Democrat,* July 3, 1864

35 Washburne MSS., James Mitchell, Stephenson County Bank, Freeport, Ill., Nov. 16, 1863, to Washburne; Trumbull MSS., John E. Detrich, Alton, Ill., Jan. 8, 1864, to Trumbull; (Springfield, Illinois) *State Register,* Dec. 2, 1863;

O.R., Ser. III, Vol. IV, 18–21, Adjutant-General A. C. Fuller, Springfield, Ill., Jan. 10, 1864, to Provost Marshal General Fry

36 *Rockford* (Illinois) *Register*, Dec. 19, 1863; (Springfield) *Illinois State Journal*, Jan. 5, 1864; *Canton* (Illinois) *Weekly Register*, Feb. 15, 1864; *Belleville* (Illinois) *Advocate*, March 4, 1864; *Canton* (Illinois) *Weekly Republican*, March 23, 1864

37 *O.R.*, Ser. III, Vol. III, 1098, Assistant Adjutant-General Vincent, Washington, Nov. 27, 1863, to Governor Yates; *Ibid.*, p. 1116; *The Chicago Tribune*, Dec. 24, 1863; *The Chicago Times*, Jan. 6, 1864; *Ottawa* (Illinois) *Free Trader*, Jan. 9, 1864

38 *O.R.*, Ser. III, Vol. III, 584, 736, 864–5, 876; *Ibid.*, Vol. IV, 55; *The Chicago Times*, Sept. 14, Oct. 6, 1863; Jan. 7, Feb. 26, Apr. 29, 1864; *Belleville* (Illinois) *Democrat*, Nov. 7, 1863; *The Chicago Tribune*, Dec. 8, 1863, Jan. 6, 1864; *Cairo* (Illinois) *Daily Democrat*, June 30, 1864

39 *The Chicago Times*, Oct. 3, Dec. 15, 1863; (Rockford, Illinois) *Rock River Democrat*, Nov. 11, Dec. 9, 1863, May 4, 1864; *Cairo* (Illinois) *Daily Democrat*, Nov. 17, 1863; *Rockford* (Illinois) *Register*, Nov. 28, Dec. 5, 12, 1863, Apr. 16, 1864; *Ottawa* (Illinois) *Weekly Republican*, Dec. 5, 1863; *Belleville* (Illinois) *Democrat*, Dec. 5, 1863, May 4, 1864; *Aurora* (Illinois) *Beacon*, Dec. 24, 1863, May 5, 1864; (Springfield, Illinois) *State Register*, Jan. 12, 1864; *O.R.*, Ser. III, Vol. IV, 26, 150

40 *O.R.*, Ser. III, Vol. IV, 9, 17–21, 46, 54, 61, 426, 428

41 (Springfield, Illinois) *State Register*, Jan. 22, 1864; *Cairo* (Illinois) *Daily Democrat*, Feb. 23, 1864

42 *O.R.*, Ser. III, Vol. IV, 237–40, 262, 264, 280–1, 288, 382–3, 385, 406, 412–3, 417; *The Chicago Tribune*, May 10, 1864

43 *O.R.*, Ser. III, Vol. IV, 399, Acting Assistant Provost Marshal General Conrad Baker, Indianapolis, May 21, 1864, to Provost Marshal General James B. Fry

44 *The* (Columbus, Ohio) *Crisis*, Dec. 2, 16, 1863, Apr. 27, 1864; (Springfield, Illinois) *State Register*, Dec. 5, 1863, quoting the (Pittsfield, Illinois) *Pike County Democrat*

45 *The Chicago Times*, Dec. 12, 1863; *The Chicago Post*, Dec. 15, 1863

46 *The* (Columbus, Ohio) *Crisis*, Jan. 20, 1864

47 *The Congressional Globe*, 38th Cong., 1st sess., pp. 763–6; *The* (Columbus, Ohio) *Crisis*, March 9, 1864

48 *The Congressional Globe*, 38th Cong., 1st sess., pp. 1499–503; *The* (Columbus, Ohio) *Crisis*, Apr. 20, 1864

49 *The Congressional Globe*, 38th Cong., 1st sess., pp. 1505–18, 1533–57, 1577–607, 1618–35, most notably speeches of Schenk of Ohio, Orth of Indiana, and Davis of Maryland for the Republicans and Pendleton and Cox of Ohio for the Democrats, all these speeches being circulated in pamphlet form.

50 *The Congressional Globe*, 38th Cong., 1st sess., pp. 1626, 1634–5; *The* (Columbus, Ohio) *Crisis*, Apr. 20, May 11, 1864

51 *The Cincinnati Daily Enquirer*, Apr. 9, 12, 13, 14, 1864; *Holmes County* (Ohio) *Farmer* and *Wayne County* (Ohio) *Democrat*, quoted in *The Crisis*, June 8, 1864; also see *The Crisis*, June 1, 6, 22, 1864

52 *Ibid.*, March 30, Apr. 6, 1864; *The Cincinnati Daily Enquirer*, March 24, 1864

[53] Mayor Fesler, "Secret Political Societies in the North during the Civil War," *Indiana Magazine of History*, XIV (Sept. 1918), 226–7

[54] *Ibid.*, pp. 224–41; (Springfield, Illinois) *State Journal*, Aug. 20, 1863

[55] *O.R.*, Ser. II, Vol. VI, 23, Burnside, Cincinnati, June 18, 1863, to Stanton; *Ibid.*, Stanton, transmitting Lincoln's decision, to Burnside. In June 1864 Stanton was considering the arrest of Congressman S. S. Cox of Ohio and of the editors of the *Cincinnati Enquirer*, but was persuaded to forbear. *Ibid.*, pp. 367–8; *Ibid.*, Ser. III, Vol. IV, 426–7

[56] (Springfield) *Illinois State Journal*, Jan. 16, 23, Feb. 4, 6, 13, 20, 21, 24, 27, 28, March 11, 18, 30, 1863; Trumbull MSS., Lieut.-Col. Edw. G. Salomon, 82nd Illinois Volunteers, Stafford County, Va., Feb. 14, 1863, to Congressman Owen Lovejoy

[57] *The* (Columbus, Ohio) *Crisis*, March 11, 18, Apr. 1, 1863

[58] *Ibid.*, Feb. 3, March 9, Apr. 27, Aug. 17, 1864; Cyrenus Cole, *A History of the People of Iowa* (Cedar Rapids, Iowa: Torch Press, 1921), p. 362

[59] *The Crisis*, Apr. 27, 1864

[60] Cole, *op. cit.*, pp. 361–2

[61] *The* (Columbus, Ohio) *Crisis*, March 18, 1863

[62] *Canton* (Illinois) *Weekly Register*, May 16, 1864

[63] *O.R.*, Ser. III, Vol. IV, 148–9, Governor Yates, Springfield, Ill., March 2, 1864, to Stanton, Stanton to Yates, General-in-Chief Halleck, Washington, to Heintzelman, Columbus, Ohio; *Ibid.*, pp. 150–1, Yates, March 3, to Heintzelman; *Ibid.*, pp. 152–3, March 4; *Ibid.*, p. 155, Heintzelman, Paris, Ill., March 5, 1864, to Halleck; *Ibid.*, pp. 221–2, Columbus, Ohio, Apr. 8, 1864; *The* (Columbus, Ohio) *Crisis*, Apr. 6, 1864; Library of Congress, Samuel P. Heintzelman MSS., Heintzelman diary, entries of March 4, 5, 1864

[64] (Springfield) *Illinois State Journal*, Apr. 4, July 2, 6, 1864

[65] Charles H. Coleman and Paul H. Spence, "The Charleston Riot, March 28, 1864," The Illinois State Historical Society, *Journal*, XXXIII (March 1940), 7–56, describes the affair in great detail.

[66] *The Chicago Tribune*, March 9, 1864

[67] *Ibid.*, March 28, 1864

[68] *The* (Columbus, Ohio) *Crisis*, March 2, 1864

[69] Fesler, *op. cit.*, pp. 233–41

[70] See *O.R.*, Ser. II, Vol. VI, 371, 400–2, 415, 434–5, 448–50, 495, 500–1, 521, 584–5, 632, 637–8, 841, 855, 860–1, 893, 986, VII, 123–4, 184–5, 187–8, 193; Ser. III, Vol. III, 1008, 1012–3, 1018–9, 1024, 1031–3

[71] This story has been reconstructed largely from the accounts of the leading Confederate agents, Hines and his close friend and fellow-officer under Morgan, John Breckinridge Castleman, the latter a colonel in the Confederate army and later, in the Spanish-American War, to be a brigadier-general in the forces of the United States. These are virtually the only sources of any value on the matter. Fortunately, these men wrote of their experiences under conditions and at a time when they had no cause to distort what had occurred. Fortunately, too, they did not need to rely upon their memories but had access to the papers of Jacob Thompson, many of the more important documents from which are reproduced photographically in Castleman's work. Thomas H. Hines, "The Northwestern Conspiracy," *The Southern Bivouac: a Monthly Literary and Historical Magazine*, new series, II (1887), 437–45, 500–10; John B. Castleman,

Active Service (Louisville: Courier-Journal Job Printing Co., 1917), pp. 144–8; see also *O.R.*, Ser. I, Vol. XLIII, pt. 2, pp. 930–6, Jacob Thompson, Toronto, Dec. 3, 1864, to Judah P. Benjamin

CHAPTER VIII

1 Library of Congress, Salmon P. Chase MSS., Simeon Nash, Gallipolis, Ohio, Jan. 18, 1864, to Chase; *Ibid.*, U.S. District Attorney Flamen Ball, Cincinnati, Jan. 25, 1864, to Chase; Library of Congress, Elihu B. Washburne MSS., A. C. Jackson, Morrison, Ill., Feb. 10, 1864, to Washburne; *Ibid.*, Thomas J. Moore, Starfield, Ill., Apr. 14, 1864, to Washburne; *Ibid.*, Joseph Medill, Chicago, Apr. 29, 1864, to Washburne; *Ibid.*, May 30, 1864; *Ibid.*, James Miller, Chicago, May 26, 1864, to Washburne; *Ibid.*, Grant Goodrich, Chicago, Apr. 14, 1864, to Washburne; Library of Congress, Horace Greeley MSS., Greeley, New York, Apr. 9, 1864, to B. Brockway; Library of Congress, Lyman Trumbull MSS., F. R. Payne, Marshall, Ill., May 1, 1864, to Trumbull; Library of Congress, John Sherman MSS., I. R. Hubbell, Delaware, Ohio, July 27, 1864; *Ibid.*, J. F. Mayer, Cincinnati, July 30, 1864, to Sherman; *Ibid.*, Henry G. Curtis, Mount Vernon, Ohio, July 30, 1864, to Sherman; *Daily* (Columbus) *Ohio State Journal*, Feb. 27, 1864; *Evansville* (Indiana) *Daily Journal*, Feb. 11, 23, March 1, 1864; John Bigelow, ed., *Letters and Literary Memorials of Samuel J. Tilden* (New York & London: Harper & Bros., 1908) I, 232–3; Horace White, *The Life of Lyman Trumbull* (Boston & New York: Houghton Mifflin Co., 1913), pp. 217–8

2 Trumbull MSS., W. A. Baldwin, Chicago, Apr. 4, 1864, to Trumbull
3 See Chapter VII
4 *The* (Columbus, Ohio) *Crisis*, June 22, 1864
5 *Ibid.*, June 15, 1864
6 *Ibid.*
7 *Ibid.*
8 *Ibid.*, July 20, 1864
9 *Ibid.*, March 9, 1864
10 *Ibid.*, July 13, 1864
11 *Ibid.*
12 *Ibid.*, also July 29, 1864
13 *Rockford* (Illinois) *Register*, Apr. 30, 1864
14 *The* (Columbus, Ohio) *Crisis*, Aug. 3, 1864
15 *Ibid.*, July 6, 1864, from the Indianapolis *Sentinel*
16 *The* (Columbus, Ohio) *Crisis*, Aug. 10, 1864
17 *Ibid.*, July 27, 1864
18 *Ibid.*, Aug. 3, 1864; *Cincinnati Daily Gazette*, Aug. 1, 1864
19 *The Crisis*, Aug. 17, Sept. 7, 1864
20 *Ibid.*, July 6, 13, 20, 29, Aug. 17, 1864; *The* (Columbus) *Daily Ohio Statesman*, July 23, 1864
21 *Ibid.*, Aug. 24, 1864
22 *Ibid.*, July 13, Aug. 10, 1864
23 *O.R.*, Ser. III, Vol. IV, 515–6
24 Aug. 2, 1864. Also *Joliet* (Illinois) *Signal*, Aug. 23, 1864
25 *Cairo* (Illinois) *City Democrat*, July 23, 1864

²⁶ *The Prairie Farmer* (Chicago), July 16, 23, 30, Aug. 27, 1864. Also *Rockford* (Illinois) *Register,* Aug. 6, 1864; *Rockford Democrat,* Aug. 17, 24, 31, 1864

²⁷ *O.R.,* Ser. III, Vol. IV, 559–60, Adj.-Gen. L. Noble, Indianapolis, July 29, 1864, to Adj.-Gen. L. Thomas, Washington; *Ibid.,* p. 596, Gov. Yates, Springfield, Aug. 9, 1864, to Stanton

²⁸ *Ibid.,* Ser. III, Vol. IV, 494, Gov. Brough, Columbus, Ohio, July 14, 1864, to Stanton; *Ibid.,* p. 556, Yates, July 28, 1864, to Stanton; *Ibid.,* p. 633, Yates, Aug. 21, 1864, to Lincoln; *Ibid.,* p. 680; *Aurora* (Illinois) *Beacon,* Aug. 11, 1864

²⁹ *O.R.,* Ser. III, Vol. IV, 632–3, Youngstown, Ohio, Aug. 20, 1864

³⁰ *Canton* (Illinois) *Weekly Register,* Aug. 15, 1864; Archives of the United States, War Department, Provost Marshal, Reports of Operations, Illinois, report of Capt. B. F. Westlake, 9th District, Mt. Sterling, Ill., May 11, 1865; *Ibid.,* report of Capt. Wm. H. Collins, 12th District, Alton, Ill., May 23, 1865; *Ibid.,* report of Capt. A. B. Coon, 2nd District, Marengo, Ill., July 10, 1865; Library of Congress, Samuel P. Heintzelman MSS., Brigadier-General Henry B. Carrington, Indianapolis, Aug. 31, 1864, to Heintzelman; Illinois State Historical Library, Richard Yates MSS. letters to Yates from David Pierson, Carrollton, Ill., Aug. 13, 1864; Major-General E. A. Paine, Paducah, Ky., Aug. 3, 1864; A. H. Bodman, Chicago, Aug. 6, 1864; John D. Platt, Warren, Ill., Aug. 10, 1864; James McKee, Vermont, Fulton County, Ill., Aug. 11, 1864; Library of Congress, Benjamin F. Wade MSS., J. V. Binn, Adjutant-General for Provost Marshal Service for the State of Ohio, Columbus, Aug. 4, 1864, to Wade

³¹ *O.R.,* Ser. III, Vol. IV, 569, Columbus, Aug. 2, 1864, to Stanton; *Ibid.,* p. 599, Aug. 9, 1864

³² *Ibid.,* pp. 682–4, Madison, Wis., Sept. 1, 1864, to James B. Fry

³³ *Ibid.,* pp. 1286–7, S. P. Heintzelman, Columbus, Ohio, Aug. 9, 1864, to Chief of Staff H. W. Halleck

³⁴ *Ibid.,* Ser. I, Vol. XLI, pt. 2, 455, July 29, 1864

³⁵ *Ibid.,* Ser. III, Vol. IV, 620, Washington, Aug. 15, 1864, to Gov. Brough

³⁶ Ohio State Archaeological and Historical Society, Samuel Medary MSS., Charles Medary, son of Samuel, with the Army of the Potomac, July 20, 1864, to his father; John Sherman MSS., M. Welker, Wooster, Ohio, Aug. 31, 1864

³⁷ Pamphlet, unsigned, no place or date of publication, entitled, *The Next Presidential Election: Mr. Lincoln—The Presidency—Action of Legislatures—One Term Principle—Patronage—Prolonging the War—Inability and Vascillation [sic]—"Honest Old Abe"—Military Commander as a Candidate—The Candidate Wanted.* A copy of this pamphlet is in the Library of Congress, call number E458.4.P77. For the relation of this pamphlet to the Pomeroy Circular see Charles R. Wilson, "The Original Chase Organization Meeting and *The Next Presidential Election,*" *The Mississippi Valley Historical Review,* XXIII (June 1936), 61–79

³⁸ Democratic National Committee, Document No. 18, *Republican Opinions about Lincoln* (n.p., [1864])

³⁹ *The Congressional Globe,* 38th Cong., 1st sess. pp. 1025–8, also circulated in pamphlet form

⁴⁰ *Reasons Why the Radical Union Delegation from Missouri to the Baltimore Convention Should Be Admitted: Published on Behalf of the Delegation* (Washington: Gibson Bros., printers, 1864)

⁴¹ Speech of James M. Ashley in the House, March 30, 1864, *The Congres-*

sional Globe, 38th Cong., 1st sess., pp. 1354–9, also circulated in pamphlet form

42 Chase MSS., J. F. Morse, Painesville, Ohio, Aug. 2, 1864, to Chase

43 *Ibid.,* Dwight Bannister, Columbus, Ohio, Aug. 16, 1864, to Chase. See also *Ibid.,* Edward D. Mansfield, Morrow, Warren County, Ohio, Aug. 25, 1864, to Chase; John Sherman MSS., L. R. Hubbell, Delaware, Ohio, July 27, 1864, to Sherman

44 E. B. Washburne MSS., Joseph Medill, Chicago, Feb. 12, 1864, to Washburne; Trumbull MSS., U.S. District Marshal D. L. Phillips, Springfield, Ill., March 23, 1864, to Trumbull; *Ibid.,* John Fitch, Philadelphia, Apr. 12, 1864, to Trumbull

45 E. B. Washburne MSS., George Wilkes, New York, Aug. 31, 1864, to Washburne

46 Chase MSS., Congressman James M. Ashley, Toledo, Ohio, Aug. 5, 1864, to Chase; *Ibid.,* Lieutenant-Governor Charles S. May, Kalamazoo, Mich., Aug. 9, 1864, to Chase

47 *Ibid.,* Charles F. Schmidt, Office of the Auditor, Treasury Department, Washington, D.C., Aug. 28, 1864, to Chase

48 John G. Nicolay and John Hay, *Abraham Lincoln: a History* (New York: Century Co., 1890), IX, 218–9; John G. Nicolay and John Hay, eds., *Abraham Lincoln, Complete Works* (New York: Century Co., 1894), II, 568

49 *O.R.,* Ser. II, Vol. VII, 371–2, Gov. John Brough, Columbus, Ohio, June 16, 1864, to Stanton, Stanton to Brough. In President Lincoln's absence Stanton would probably have ordered the arrest had he not been dissuaded by Seward. Vallandigham's speech at Hamilton, Ohio, on June 15, is given in Vallandigham, *op. cit.,* pp. 527–31

50 *The* (Columbus, Ohio) *Crisis,* Aug. 17, 1864, from *The Chicago Times*

51 *Detroit Advertiser and Tribune,* Aug. 18, 1864

52 *The Saint Paul* (Minnesota) *Press,* August 30, 1864

53 *The Crisis,* Aug. 24, 1864

54 Thomas H. Hines, "The Northwestern Conspiracy," *The Southern Bivouac: a Monthly Literary and Historical Magazine,* new series, II (Jan. 1885) 506–10; John B. Castleman, *Active Service* (Louisville: Courier-Journal Job Printing Co., 1917), pp. 144–8

55 *Ibid.*

56 *O.R.,* Ser. III, Vol. IV, 606–7

57 (Springfield) *Illinois State Journal,* Aug. 2, 3, 4, 8, 1864; *Cairo* (Illinois) *Daily Democrat,* Aug. 19, 1864; Yates MSS. (I), letters to Yates from David Pierson, Carrollton, Ill., Aug. 13, 1864; William A. Grimshaw, Pittsfield, Ill., Aug. 17, 1864; W. K. Miner, Fidelity, Jersey County, Ill., Aug. 17, 1864

58 *O.R.,* Ser. III, Vol. IV, p. 558, Yates, Springfield, July 29, 1864, to Stanton; *Ibid.,* p. 575, Aug. 4, 1864; *Ibid.,* p. 581, Allen C. Fuller, Adjutant-General of Illinois, Washington, Aug. 6, 1864, to Provost Marshal General J. B. Fry. Also see Chicago Historical Society Library, Richard Yates MSS., Major-General W. S. Rosecrans, St. Louis, June 20, 1864, to Yates, reporting plans of O.A.K. for uprising on July 4; *Ibid.,* Yates, Springfield, Aug. 12, 1864, to I. Berdan *et al.;* and Heintzelman MSS., Rosecrans, May 25, June 26, 1864, to Heintzelman

59 *O.R.,* Ser. III, Vol. IV, 585, Indianapolis, Aug. 5, 1864, to Stanton

60 *Ibid.,* p. 613, Aug. 12, 1864

[61] *Ibid.,* p. 425, Columbus, June 9, 1864, to Stanton

[62] During the discussions of the floor preceding balloting Long, with Harris and Jones of Maryland, denounced McClellan as indistinguishable on the issue of continuing the war from Lincoln himself. On the final ballot 202½ votes went to McClellan and 23½ to former Governor (during the 1850's) Thomas H. Seymour of Connecticut, candidate of the irreconcilables. Delaware and Maryland cast all their votes, 3 and 7, respectively, for Seymour; Ohio 15 for McClellan and 6 for Seymour; Indiana 9½ for McClellan and 3½ for Seymour; and Missouri 7 for McClellan and 4 for Seymour.

[63] *The* (Columbus, Ohio) *Crisis,* Aug. 31, Sept. 7, 1864

[64] *Ibid.,* Sept. 7, 1864

[65] *Ibid.*

[66] There were a number of possible ways by which this information may have been obtained. Hines thought that some of the parties to the plot were given to talking too freely, particularly when under the influence of liquor; General Sweet, in command of Camp Douglas, was supposed to have intercepted communications between prisoners and plotters outside; federal detectives had for some time been infiltrating into the councils of the order; and one of the Confederates in Canada was supposed to have revealed the plans, for a consideration presumably, to Lietenant-Colonel B. H. Hill at Detroit, acting assistant provost marshal general for Michigan. Castleman, *op. cit.,* pp. 157–9; "The Chicago Conspiracy," *The Atlantic Monthly,* XVI (July 1865), pp. 108–20; William Bross, *Biographical Sketch of the Late Gen. B. J. Sweet; History of Camp Douglas* (Chicago: Jansen, McClurg & Co., 1878), pp. 17–20

[67] Hines, *op. cit.,* pp. 567–74; Castleman, *op. cit.,* pp. 157–9

[68] Library of Congress, W. T. Sherman MSS., John Sherman, Mansfield, Ohio, July 24, 1864, to W. T. Sherman; Library of Congress, Henry Broughton Bromwell MSS., Mrs. H. P. H. Bromwell, Corydon, Ind., July 1864, to her husband

[69] Trumbull MSS., Gershom Martin, Naperville, Ill., Sept. 2, 1864, to Trumbull; also W. T. Sherman MSS., John Sherman, Mansfield, Ohio, Sept. 4, 1864, to W. T. Sherman; John Sherman MSS., Joseph B. McCullough, Cincinnati, Sept. 6, 1864

[70] For evidence of McClellan's uncertain stand on the Democratic peace plank, see Charles R. Wilson, "McClellan's Changing Views on the Peace Plank of 1864," *The American Historical Review,* XXXVIII (April 1933), 498–505

[71] John Sherman MSS., A. Denny, Eaton, Ohio, Aug. 21, 1864, to Sherman

[72] Castleman, *op. cit.,* pp. 168–71

[73] *The Richmond* (Virginia) *Examiner,* Aug. 31, 1864, quoted in *The* (Columbus, Ohio) *Crisis,* Sept. 21, 1864; E. B. Washburne MSS., James Miller, Chicago, March 26, 1864, to Trumbull; Library of Congress, Ewing MSS., Thomas Ewing, Lancaster, Ohio, July 19, 1864, to Charles Ewing; W. T. Sherman MSS., John Sherman, Mansfield, Ohio, July, 24, 1864, to W. T. Sherman

CHAPTER IX

[1] Library of Congress, John Sherman MSS., R. M. Corwine, Cincinnati, Aug. 31, 1864, to Sherman; Library of Congress, W. T. Sherman MSS., John Pope, Milwaukee, Sept. 12, 1864, to Sherman; *Ibid.,* John Mason Loomis, Chicago,

Sept. 24, 1864, to Sherman; Library of Congress, Elihu B. Washburne, MSS., Lieutenant Evans Blake, 45th Illinois Infantry, Atlanta, Ga., Sept. 30, 1864, to Washburne; *The Bellefontaine* (Ohio) *Republican,* Sept. 23, 1861; Library of Congress, Gideon Welles MSS., Henry H. Elliott, New York, Aug. 31, Sept. 3, 1864

2 Sept. 4, 1864

3 John Sherman MSS., J. C. Devin, Mount Vernon, Ohio, Sept. 6, 1864, to Sherman

4 Library of Congress, Salmon P. Chase MSS., William B. Thomas, Gallipolis, Ohio, Sept. 18, 1864; Library of Congress, Zachariah Chandler MSS., letters from Chandler, Washington, Aug. 27, Sept. 2, New York, Sept. 6, 8, 1864, to Mrs. Chandler; Library of Congress, Benjamin F. Wade MSS., Alphonso Taft, Cincinnati, Sept. 8, 1864, to Wade

5 *Rockford* (Illinois) *Register,* Sept. 17, 1864; *Joliet* (Illinois) *Signal,* Sept. 20, 1864; *Cairo* (Illinois) *Daily Democrat,* Sept. 29, 1864; *Canton* (Illinois) *Weekly Register,* Oct. 3, 1864; *Belleville* (Illinois) *Advocate,* Oct. 14, 1861; *The Carthage* (Illinois) *Republican,* Oct. 20, 1864

6 Oct. 23, 1864

7 *Ibid.,* Oct. 1, 1864

8 Nov. 1, 1864

9 *The Chicago Times,* Oct. 7, 8, 9, 1864. That these charges may not always have been without foundation is hinted at from Republican sources in a special dispatch from Quincy, Illinois, to *The Chicago Tribune,* Sept. 24, 1864

10 *O.R.,* Ser. III, Vol. IV, 688, Gov. Richard Yates, Springfield, Sept. 3, 1864, to Sec. of War Stanton; *Ibid.,* p. 694, Provost Marshal General James B. Fry, Washington, Sept. 4, 1864, to Yates

11 *Cairo* (Illinois) *Daily Democrat,* Sept. 6, 10, 1864; (Springfield, Illinois) *State Register,* Sept. 6, 1864; *The Chicago Times,* Sept. 7, 1864; *Joliet* (Illinois) *Signal,* Oct. 11, 1864

12 *O.R.,* Ser. III, Vol. IV, 700–2

13 *Ibid.,* pp. 726–7

14 *Ibid.,* p. 744, Speaker of the House Schuyler Colfax, South Bend, Ind., Sept. 26, 1864, to President Lincoln; *Ibid.,* p. 754, Acting Assistant Provost Marshal General J. G. Jones, Indianapolis, Oct. 4, 1864, to Provost Marshal General Fry

15 *Chicago Times,* Oct. 4, 1864

16 *O.R.,* Ser. III, Vol. IV, 786, Congressman E. B. Washburne, Galena, Ill., Oct. 17, 1864, to Fry; *Ibid.,* 787, Fry, Oct. 18, 1864, to Washburne; *Ibid.,* Ser. III, Vol. IV, 786, Simon Cameron, Harrisburg, Pa., Oct. 18, 1864, to Secretary of War Stanton; *Ibid.,* 787, Senator Benjamin F. Wade, Cincinnati, Oct. 19, 1864, to Stanton; *Ibid.,* Fry to Wade

17 Library of Congress, William T. Sherman MSS., Sherman before Atlanta, Aug. 12, 1864, to Colfax

18 *O.R.,* Ser. III, Vol. IV, 709–10, Washington, Sept. 11, 1864

19 *Ibid.,* pp. 712–3, Grant to Stanton

20 *Cairo* (Illinois) *Daily Democrat,* Sept. 14, 1864; *O.R.,* Ser. I, Vol. XLV, pt. 1, p. 1055, Brigadier-General John Cook, Springfield, Ill., commanding District of Illinois, Nov. 25, 1864, to Major-General A. P. Hovey, commanding District of Indiana; *Ibid.,* Ser. I, Vol. XLI, pt. 3, p. 376, Major-General W. S.

Rosecrans, St. Louis, Sept. 26, 1864, to Governor Yates; (Springfield) *Illinois State Journal*, Oct. 4, 1864

[21] *Illinois State Journal*, Oct. 4, 1864; *Canton* (Illinois) *Weekly Register*, Oct. 10, 27, 31, 1864; *Rushville* (Illinois) *Times*, May 13, 20, 1869

[22] *O.R.*, Ser. III, Vol. IV, 711–2, 714, 748, 752, Jones, Indianapolis, Sept. 12, 13, 28, Oct. 2, 1864, to Provost Marshal General Fry

[23] *Ibid.*, p. 712, Sept. 12

[24] *Ibid.*, p. 713, Washington, Sept. 13, 1864, to Major-General W. T. Sherman

[25] *Ibid.*, pp. 724–5, Provost Marshal General Fry, Washington, Sept. 15, 1864, to all assistant provost marshals general; *Ibid.*, p. 726, to all governors

[26] *Ibid.*, p. 732, Stanton, Washington, Sept. 18, 1864, to Governor Morton

[27] *Ibid.*, p. 731, Provost Marshal General Fry, Washington, Sept. 17, 1864, to Governor Yates; *Ibid.*, pp. 749–50, Acting Assistant Provost-Marshal-General James Oakes, Springfield, Ill., Sept. 30, 1864, to Fry; *Ibid.*, p. 752, Fry, Washington, Oct. 1, 1864, to Oakes

[28] *Ibid.*, Stanton, Washington, Sept. 13, 1864, to Generals Dix, New York, Heintzelman, Columbus, Ohio, Couch, Chambersburg, Pa., Pope, Milwaukee, Rosecrans, St. Louis, and Wallace, Baltimore

[29] *Ibid.*, pp. 716–7, Assistant Adjutant-General E. D. Townshend, Washington, September 14, 1864, to Brevet Major-General A. P. Hovey; *Ibid.*, pp. 732–3, Provost Marshal General Fry, Washington, Sept. 18, 1864, to Acting Assistant Provost Marshal General Jones; *Ibid.*, 753, Fry, Washington, Oct. 3, 1864, to Major-General Hooker, *Ibid.*, p. 754, Townshend, Washington, Oct. 4, 1864, to Hooker

[30] *Ibid.*, pp. 757–60, United States Special Agent W. H. Riley, Washington, Oct. 8, 1864, to Fry; *Ibid.*, pp. 760–1, Fry, Washington, Oct. 9, 1864, to Governor Morton

[31] *Ibid.*, p. 742, Congressman James G. Blaine, Augusta, Me., Sept. 20, 1864, to Congressman E. B. Washburne, forwarded by Washburne to Stanton

[32] *The Chicago Tribune*, Oct. 27, 1864; (Springfield) *Illinois State Journal*, Oct. 3, 1864

[33] Sept. 27, 1864

[34] *O.R.*, Ser. III, Vol. IV, 228–58

[35] (Springfield) *Illinois State Journal*, Aug. 6, 1864, from the *St. Louis Democrat*

[36] *O.R.*, Ser. III, Vol. IV, 488, Assistant Adjutant-General E. D. Townshend, Washington, July 12, 1864, to Holt; *Ibid.* pp. 577–9, Holt, Washington, Aug. 5, 1864, to Stanton

[37] Benn Pitman, *The Trials for Treason at Indianapolis, Disclosing the Plans for Establishing a North-Western Confederacy* (Cincinnati: Moore, Wilstach & Baldwin, 1865), *passim;* (Indianapolis) *Daily State Sentinel*, Sept. 5, 7, 8, 20, 22, 23, 24, 26, 28, 29, Oct. 1, 3, 6, 7, 8, 1864

[38] *Cincinnati Daily Gazette,* July 30, 1864; (Springfield) *Illinois State Journal,* Aug. 6, 26, Oct. 15, Nov. 2, 8, 1864; *The Saint Paul* (Minnesota) *Press,* Aug. 9, 10, Nov. 3, 1864; *The Mankato* (Minnesota) *Weekly Union,* Aug. 19, 1864; *Detroit Advertiser and Tribune,* Aug. 24, 25, 30, Sept. 9, 1864; *The Bellefontaine* (Ohio) *Republican,* Sept. 23, 1864; *The Boscobel* (Wisconsin) *Broad-Axe,* Oct. 12, 1864; (Grand Rapids, Wisconsin) *Wood Country Reporter,* Oct. 13, 1864; (Champaign) *Central Illinois Gazette,* Oct. 21, 1864. *The Detroit*

Advertiser and Tribune ironically made an offer to the *Free Press* to pay half the cost of printing and circulating twenty thousand copies of the platform, resolutions, and speeches of the Democratic National Convention.

[39] *Report of the Judge Advocate General on "The Order of American Knights," Alias "The Sons of Liberty"; a Western Conspiracy in Aid of the Southern Rebellion* (Washington: Union Congressional Committee, 1864), 16 pp. Governor Morton wishes Holt to come to Indiana to aid in the political campaign. Library of Congress, Joseph Holt MSS., Morton, Indianapolis, Aug. 22, 1864, to Colonel W. M. Dunn, Louisville, Ky.

[40] *The Detroit Free Press*, Aug. 2, 1864; *The* (Columbus, Ohio) *Crisis*, Aug. 10, 1864; *The Daily* (Columbus) *Ohio Statesman*, Nov. 4, 1864

[41] Sept. 7, 1864

[42] Sept. 7, 22, 1864

[43] (Canton, Ohio) *Stark County Democrat*, Sept. 14, 1864

[44] Oct. 12, 26, Nov. 2, 1864; also *Daily Milwaukee News*, Sept. 4, 1864; *The Detroit Free Press*, Oct. 28, 1864

[45] Library of Congress, George B. McClellan MSS., Joel Parker (not the Governor of New Jersey), Cambridge, Mass., Aug. 27, 1864, to McClellan; *Ibid.*, George T. Curtis, New York, Sept. 1, 1864, to McClellan; *Ibid.*, William H. Aspinwall, "Rockwood," Sept. 4, 1864, to McClellan

[46] For a full charting of McClellan's hesitant approaches toward grasping the horns of his dilemma see C. R. Wilson, "McClellan's Changing Views on the Peace Plank of 1864," *The American Historical Review*, XXXVIII (Apr. 1933), 498–505

[47] McClellan MSS., Benjamin Rush, Philadelphia, Sept. 9, 1864, to McClellan; *Ibid.*, Amos Kendall, Washington, Sept. 10, 1864, to McClellan

[48] *The Chicago Times*, Sept. 10, 1861; McClellan MSS., Daniel W. Voorhees, Terre Haute, Ind., Sept. 15, 1864

[49] *The* (Columbus, Ohio) *Crisis*, Nov. 2, 1864

[50] (Canton, Ohio) *Stark County Democrat*, Sept. 14, 1864; *The Chicago Times*, Sept. 22, 1864, correspondence

[51] *The Circleville* (Ohio) *Watchman*, Sept. 2, 1864; (Canton, Ohio) *Stark County Democrat*, Sept. 7, 1864; *Coshocton* (Ohio) *Democrat*, Sept. 7, 1864; *The* (Columbus, Ohio) *Crisis*, Sept. 28, 1864

[52] McClellan MSS., from Dayton, Ohio. In a postscript Vallandigham informed McClellan that he would be in Trenton in about ten days.

[53] *New York Tribune*, Sept. 15, Oct. 10, 1864; Library of Congress, Jeremiah Sullivan Black MSS., Charles O'Connor, J. W. Singleton, J. A. McCarter (?), and A. Holloway, New York, Sept. 10, 1864, telegram to Black

[54] *The* (Columbus, Ohio) *Crisis*, Oct. 26, 1864; *Cincinnati Convention, October 18, 1864, for the Organization of a Peace Party upon State-Rights, Jeffersonian, Democratic Principles and for the Promotion of Peace and Independent Nominations for President and Vice-President of the United States*, 16-page pamphlet, no publication data

[55] On September 28, during Samuel Medary's absence, his son put the McClellan and Pendleton combination at the head of the editorial columns, but the former deleted it in subsequent issues—(Columbus) *Ohio State Journal*, Nov. 8, 1864, quoted in *The Crisis*, Nov. 23, 1864; also *The Crisis*, Sept. 9, 1864

[56] *Coshocton* (Ohio) *Democrat*, Nov. 16, 1864; *The Circleville* (Ohio) *Watch-*

man, Sept. 2, 1864; *An Address to the People of the United States and Particularly to the People of the States Which Adhere to the Federal Government* (Washington: 1864), 32 pp. by some forty Democratic members of Congress; Jeremiah S. Black, *The Doctrine of the Democratic and Abolition Parties Contrasted—Negro Equality—The Conflict between the "Higher Law" and the Law of the Land: Speech of Hon. Jeremiah S. Black, at the Hall of the Keystone Club, in Philadelphia, October 24, 1864* (Philadelphia: *Age* Office, n.d.), 8 pp.; *The Lincoln Catechism, Wherein the Eccentricities and Beauties of Despotism Are Fully Set Forth: a Guide to the Presidential Election of 1864* (New York: J. F. Feeks, n.d.), 46 pp., also published in German as *Der Lincoln Katechismus . . .* ; *Mr. Lincoln's Arbitrary Arrests: the Acts Which the Baltimore Platform Approves,* Document No. 13 (New York: Democratic National Committee, 1864), 24 pp.; *Corruptions and Frauds of Lincoln's Administration,* Document No. 14 (New York: Democratic National Committee, 1864), 8 pp.; McClellan MSS., Henry Clay Dean and nine others, Galena, Ill., Sept. 19, 1864, to McClellan; *Dayton Daily Empire,* Nov. 7, 1864

⁵⁷ *The Chicago Copperhead Convention; the Treasonable and Revolutionary Utterances of the Men Who Composed It: Extracts from All the Notable Speeches Delivered in and out of the National "Democratic" Convention—a Surrender to the Rebels Advocated—A Disgraceful and Pusilanimous Peace Demanded—The Federal Government Shamefully Vilified and Not a Word Said against the Crime of Treason and Rebellion* (Washington: Congressional Union Committee, 1864), 16 pp.; *George H. Pendleton, the Copperhead Candidate for Vice-President: His Hostility to the American Republic Illustrated by His Record as a Representative in Congress of the United States from the State of Ohio* (Washington: Union Congressional Committee, 1864), 8 pp.; *The Votes of the Copperheads in the Congress of the United States* (Washington, Union Congressional Committee, 1864), 8 pp.; Henry Conklin, *An Inside View of the Rebellion, and American Citizens' Text-Book* (Chicago: Tribune Book and Job Printing Establishment, 1864), 24 pp.; *Copperhead Conspiracy in the North-West: an Expose of the Treasonable Order of the "Sons of Liberty"—Vallandigham, Supreme Commander* (Union Congressional Committee, n.d.), William A. Cook, *Opinions and Practices of the Founders of the Republic in Relation to Arbitrary Arrests, Imprisonment of Tories, Writ of Habeas Corpus, Seizure of Arms and Private Papers, Domiciliary Visits, Confiscations of Real and Personal Estate, etc., etc., or the Administration of Abraham Lincoln Sustained by the Sages and Heroes of the Revolution* (Washington: William H. Moore, printer, 1864), 54 pp.; William Eaton Chandler, *The Soldier's Right to Vote: Who Opposes It? Who Favors It? or the Record of the MClellan Copperheads against Allowing the Soldier Who Fights the Right to Vote While Fighting.* Prepared for the Union Congressional Committee (Washington: Lemuel Towers, printer, 1864), 16 pp.; John D. Defrees, *Remarks Made before the Indiana Union Club of Washington, D.C., Monday Evening, August 1, 1864* (Washington: L. Towers, printer, 1864), 16 pp.

⁵⁸ Gustav Koerner, *Memoirs of Gustave Koerner, 1809–1896 . . .* (Cedar Rapids, Iowa: Torch Press, 1909), II, 434–6

⁵⁹ Thomas L. Wilson, *A Brief History of the Cruelties and Atrocities of the Rebellion Compiled from the Most Authentic Sources* (Washington: Union Congressional Committee, 1864), 8 pp.; W. T. Sherman MSS., H. W. Halleck,

Washington, Sept. 28, 1864, to Sherman; speech of Congressman George W. Julian in Cincinnati on Oct. 22, reported in the *Cincinnati Gazette*, Oct. 24, 1864, and quoted in *The* (Columbus, Ohio) *Crisis*, Nov. 2, 1864

60 McClellan MSS., R. McClelland, Detroit, Nov. 10, 1864, to William Wright

61 *The* (Columbus, Ohio) *Crisis*, Nov. 23, 1864, from (Columbus) *Ohio State Journal*, Nov. 8, 1864

62 William Swinton, *The Military and Naval Situation and the Glorious Achievements of Our Soldiers and Sailors* (Washington: Union Congressional Committee, 1864), 15 pp.; John Brough, *The Defenders of the Country and Its Enemies; the Chicago Platform Dissected: Speech of Governor Brough Delivered at Circleville, Ohio, Sept. 3*. From the *Cincinnati Gazette*, Sept. 5, 1864 (Cincinnati: Gazette Co., 1864), 16 pp.; Aaron Fyfe Perry, *Speech of Aaron F. Perry, Esq., Delivered before the National Union Association at Mozart Hall, Cincinnati, Sept. 20, 1864* (Cincinnati: National Union Association of Ohio, 1864), 15 pp.; *The Saint Paul* (Minnesota) *Press*, July 30, 1864; *Detroit Advertiser and Tribune*, Aug. 27, 1864; *The Bellefontaine* (Ohio) *Republican*, Sept. 16, 1864; *The Mankato* (Minnesota) *Weekly Union*, Oct. 28, Nov. 4, 1864

63 *What Genuine Democrats Think of the Rebellion* (New York: National Union Executive Committee, n.d.), 2 pp.; Democratic Loyal League of New York, *The Real Motives of the Rebellion: The Slaveholder's Conspiracy, Depicted by Southern Loyalists in Its Treason against Democratic Principles, as Well as against the National Union; Showing a Contest of Slavery and Nobility versus Free Government: Address of the Democratic League to the "Loyal Leagues" and Loyal Men throughout the Land* (New York, 1864), 16 pp.; *Stirring Appeals from Honored Veterans: Democratic Statesmen and Generals to the Loyal Sons of the Union—Views of Gens. Grant, Sherman, Dix, Wool, Butler, Edward Everett, John A. Griswold, and Others.* Union Campaign Documents, No. 8 (Albany: Weed, Parsons & Co., printers, 1864), pp. 83–96; Yates MSS. (C), Logan Uriah Reavis, editor of *Central Illinoisian*, Beardstown, Ill., Aug. 25, 1864, to Yates; *Ibid.*, Yates, Springfield, Sept. 9, 1864, to Reavis

64 *The* (Columbus, Ohio) *Crisis*, Nov. 2, 1864; David S. Coddington, *The Crisis and the Man: Address on the Presidential Crisis Delivered before the Union War Democracy at the Cooper Institute, New York, Nov. 1, 1864* (New York: Wm. Oland Bourne, 1865), pp. 2–16

65 Francis Lieber, *Lincoln or McClellan: Appeal to the Germans in America.* Translated from the German by T. C., No. 67 (New York: Loyal Publication Society, n.d.), 8 pp.

66 *O.R.*, Ser. III, Vol. IV, 751–2, Gen. Orders, No. 265, Washington, Oct. 1, 1864, signed by Assistant Adjutant-General E. D. Townshend; *Ibid.*, 871–2, Governor Yates, Springfield, Ill., Nov. 1, 1864, to Lincoln

67 *The* (Columbus, Ohio) *Crisis*, Nov. 16, 1864

68 Trumbull MSS., G. T. Allen, Cairo, Ill., Oct. 4, 1864, to Trumbull

69 McCormick Historical Association Library, G. W. Hannaford, St. Augustine, Fla., Oct. (?), 1864, to his wife

70 *The Chicago Times*, Nov. 17, 1864; *The Chicago Tribune*, Feb. 19, 1882, Sept. 2, 3, 1890; John B. Castleman, *Active Service* (Louisville: Courier-Journal Job Printing Co., 1917), pp. 155–9, 173–6, 189–95, 205; "The Chicago Conspiracy," *The Atlantic Monthly: a Magazine of Literature, Science, Art, and Politics*, XVI (July 1865), 108–20

[71] Nov. 21, 1864

[72] March 14, 1864; see also *Daily Milwaukee News,* Nov. 12, Dec. 30, 1864

[73] *The* (Columbus, Ohio) *Crisis,* Dec. 14, 1864, Jan. 4, 11, April 12, 1865

[74] *The Congressional Globe,* 38th Cong., 2nd sess., pp. 214–6; *The* (Columbus, Ohio) *Crisis,* Feb. 1, 1865

[75] *The Congressional Globe,* 38th Cong., 2nd sess., p. 654, appdx., pp. 55–61; *The* (Columbus, Ohio) *Crisis,* Feb. 22, 1865

[76] Washburne MSS., Chicago, Nov. 27, 1864, to Washburne

[77] *The Chicago Times,* Nov. 16, 1864; copies in the files of the McCormick Historical Association Library

[78] McCormick MSS., McCormick, Washington, Dec. 19, 1864, to Lincoln, copy

[79] *Ibid.,* Storey, Chicago, Dec. 17, 1864, to McCormick

[80] *The* (Columbus, Ohio) *Crisis,* Jan. 11, 1865

[81] *Ibid.,* March 15, 1865

[82] *Ibid.,* Apr. 19, 1865

[83] *O.R.,* Ser. IV, Vol. IV, pp. 1002, 1075; *Canton* (Illinois) *Weekly Register,* Dec. 26, 1864; *The Carthage* (Illinois) *Republican,* Dec. 29, 1864

[84] *O.R.,* Ser. III, Vol. IV, pp. 1070–1, Gov. Richard Oglesby, Springfield, Ill., Jan. 23, 1865, to Stanton; *Ibid.,* pp. 1090–1, Jan. 30, 1865, to Provost Marshal General Fry; *Ibid.,* 1190–1, Illinois Adjutant-General I. N. Haynie, Washington, Feb. 23, 1865, to Fry, notations by Fry and Stanton; *Ibid.,* Fry to Haynie; *Ibid.,* pp. 1191–2, Haynie, Feb. 24, 1865, to Fry; *Ibid.,* pp. 1194–7, Feb. 25, 1865; *Ibid.,* p. 1222, Haynie, Springfield, Mar. 4, 1865, to Fry; *Ibid.,* pp. 1258–9, Oglesby, Springfield, Apr. 6, 1865, to Stanton, Stanton, Washington, Apr. 7, to Oglesby; *The Carthage* (Illinois) *Republican,* Feb. 16, 1865; *Cairo* (Illinois) *Daily Democrat,* March 11, 1865

[85] *O.R.,* Ser. III, Vol. IV, 1149, Gov. Brough, Columbus, Ohio, Feb. 6, 1865, to Provost Marshal General Fry; *Ibid.,* pp. 1176–7, Fry, Washington, Feb. 16, 1865, to acting assistant provost marshals general

[86] *Rockford* (Illinois) *Register,* Jan. 28, 1865; *Ottawa* (Illinois) *Free Trader,* Feb. 4, 1865; *Cairo* (Illinois) *Daily Democrat,* Feb. 22, 1865; *Cairo Weekly Democrat,* Mar. 9, 1865; *Ottawa* (Illinois) *Weekly Republican,* Mar. 18, 1865

[87] *O.R.,* Ser. III, Vol. IV, p. 995, Adjutant-General Lorenzo Thomas to Stanton; *Ibid.,* p. 1185, Col. B. J. Sweet, Commanding, Chicago, Feb. 18, 1865, to Major-General Hooker, Cincinnati, forwarded by Hooker to Stanton, endorsed by Grant; *The Chicago Tribune,* Jan. 27, 1865

[88] *The Chicago Tribune,* Jan. 9, 1865

[89] *O.R.,* Ser. III, Vol. IV, p. 1169, Gov. Oglesby, Springfield, Feb. 13, 1865, to Stanton; *Ibid.,* pp. 1169–70, Gov. Morton, Indianapolis, Feb. 13, 1865, to Lincoln; *Ibid.,* p. 1179, Gov. James T. Lewis, Madison, Wis., Feb. 17, 1865, to Stanton; *Ibid.,* p. 1237, Oglesby, Springfield, Mar. 14, 1865, to Stanton

CHAPTER X

[1] An introduction to the story in this section can be found in Edith Ellen Ware, *Political Opinion in Massachusetts during the Civil War and Reconstruction.* Studies in History, Economics, and Public Law Edited by the Faculty of Political Science of Columbia University, Vol. LXXIV, No. 2 (New York:

Columbia University Press, 1916); J. Robert Lane, *A Political History of Connecticut during the Civil War* (Washington, D.C.: Catholic University of America, 1941); David Sidney Brummer, *Political History of New York State during the Period of the Civil War*. Studies in History, Economics, and Public Law Edited by the Faculty of Political Science of Columbia University, Vol. XXXIX, No. 2 (New York: Columbia University Press, 1911); Charles Merriam Knapp, *New Jersey Politics during the Period of the Civil War and Reconstruction* (Geneva, N.Y.: W. F. Humphrey, 1924); and Stanton Ling Davis, *Pennsylvania Politics, 1860–1863* (Cleveland: Bookstore, Western Reserve University, 1935). Robert Stewart Mitchell presents a sympathetic view of his subject in *Horatio Seymour of New York* (Cambridge, Mass.: Harvard University Press, 1938)

[2] Consult Charles Branch Clark, "Politics in Maryland during the Civil War," *Maryland Historical Magazine*, XXXVI (Sept., Dec. 1941), 239–62, 381–93; Sidney T. Matthews, "Control of the Baltimore Press during the Civil War," *Ibid.* (June 1941), 150–70; George L. P. Radcliffe, *Governor Thomas H. Hicks of Maryland and the Civil War*. Johns Hopkins University Studies in Historical and Political Science, Ser. XIX, No. 11 (Baltimore: Johns Hopkins Press, 1901); E. Merton Coulter, *The Civil War and Readjustment in Kentucky* (Chapel Hill: University of North Carolina Press, 1926); Sceva Bright Laughlin, *Missouri Politics during the Civil War* (Salem, Ore.: S. B. Laughlin, 1930); and Edward Conrad Smith, *The Borderland in the Civil War* (New York: Macmillan Co., 1927)

[3] See Joseph Ellison, *California and the Nation, 1850–1869: A Study of the Relations of a Frontier Community with the Federal Government* (Berkeley: University of California Press, 1927)

[4] *The Chicago Tribune*, Sept. 20, 1866, Mar. 18, 1867, Sept. 22, 1876, Oct. 21, 1878, Aug. 4, 1880

[5] *Joliet* (Illinois) *Republican,* June 27, 1868

[6] Sept. 21, 1876

Bibliography

A. PRIMARY SOURCES

1. Unpublished Materials

It is very regrettable that little of the correspondence of Midwestern Democratic leaders during the Civil War years has survived. This is particularly true for those identified with the peace faction. Much of this material was apparently destroyed deliberately, a fact that carries a significance of its own. It should be remarked also that some of the Republican collections show evidence of the removal of correspondence bearing on opposition to Lincoln.

Allen, William, MSS. Library of Congress

Bickley, George W. L., MSS. Chief Clerk's Office, Judge Advocate General, United States Army

Black, Jeremiah Sullivan, MSS. Library of Congress

Blair, Austin, MSS. Detroit Public Library

Bromwell, Henry Broughton, MSS. Library of Congress

Browning, Oliver Hickman, MSS. Illinois State Historical Library, Springfield

Buchanan, James, MSS. Library of Congress

Butler, Charles, MSS. Library of Congress

Caton, John Dean, MSS. Library of Congress

Chandler, William E., MSS. Library of Congress

Chandler, Zachariah, MSS. Library of Congress

Chase, Salmon Portland, MSS. Library of Congress

Colfax, Schuyler, MSS. Library of Congress

Colfax, Schuyler, MSS. Indiana State Library, Indianapolis

Confederate States of America. Department of State. Diplomatic Correspondence. Library of Congress

Creswell, John A. J., MSS. Library of Congress

Crittenden, John J., MSS. Library of Congress

Curtis, Benjamin R., MSS. Library of Congress

Cushing, Caleb, MSS. Library of Congress

Dana, Charles A., MSS. Library of Congress

Doolittle, James Rood, MSS. Library of Congress

Douglas, Stephen Arnold, MSS. University of Chicago Library

Eells, Samuel Henry, MSS. Library of Congress

English, William H., MSS. Indiana State Historical Library, Indianapolis

Ewing, Thomas, MSS. Library of Congress

Fairchild, Lucius, MSS. State Historical Society of Wisconsin Library, Madison

Fessenden, William Pitt, MSS. Library of Congress

Garfield, James A., MSS. Library of Congress

Giddings, Joshua R., MSS. Ohio State Archaeological and Historical Society, Columbus, Ohio
Giddings, Joshua R., and Julian, George W., MSS. Library of Congress
Grant, Ulysses S., MSS. Library of Congress
Greeley, Horace, MSS. Library of Congress
Hamilton, Allen, MSS. Indiana State Library, Indianapolis
Heintzelman, Samuel P., MSS. Library of Congress
Heintzelman, Samuel P., MS. Diary. Library of Congress
Holt, Joseph, MSS. Library of Congress
Howard, James Corydon, MSS. State Historical Society of Wisconsin Library, Madison
Jayne, William, MSS. Illinois State Historical Library, Springfield
Johnson, Andrew, MSS. Library of Congress
Johnson, Madison Y., MSS. Chicago Historical Society Library
Julian, George Washington, MSS. Indiana State Library, Indianapolis
Lanphier, Charles H., MSS. Charles and William Patton Collection, Springfield, Illinois
Logan, John Alexander, MSS. Library of Congress. Used by permission granted in 1930
Loomis, John S., MSS. Illinois State Historical Library, Springfield
McClellan, George B., MSS. Library of Congress
McClernand, John A., MSS. Illinois State Historical Library, Springfield
McCormick, Cyrus H., MSS. McCormick Historical Association Library, Chicago
McCulloch, Hugh, MSS. Library of Congress
McLean, John, MSS. Library of Congress
McPherson, Edward, MSS. Library of Congress
Medary, Samuel, MSS. Ohio Archaeological and Historical Society, Columbus
Morrill, Justin S., MSS. Library of Congress
Morton, Oliver Perry, MSS. Indiana State Library, Indianapolis
Ogden, William B., MSS. Chicago Historical Society Library
Ohio Executive Records. Correspondence. Ohio State Archaeological and Historical Society Library, Columbus
Pierce, Franklin, MSS. Library of Congress
Pratt, Daniel D., MSS. Indiana State Library, Indianapolis
Robinson, J. S., MSS. Ohio Archaeological and Historical Society Library, Columbus
Sanders, George N., MSS. Library of Congress
Schneider, George, MSS. Chicago Historical Society Library
Schurz, Carl, MSS. Library of Congress. Used by permission granted in 1935
Sherman, John, MSS. Library of Congress
Sherman, William Tecumseh, MSS. Library of Congress
Stanton, Edwin M., MSS. Library of Congress
Stevens, Thaddeus, MSS. Library of Congress
Thompson, Richard W., MSS. Indiana State Library, Indianapolis
Trumbull, Lyman, MSS. Library of Congress
United States. District Court. Southern District of Illinois. Office files of the Clerk, Springfield

United States. War Department. Provost Marshal General's Office. Historical Report of the Acting Assistant Provost Marshal General for Illinois from Organization to May 31, 1865. National Archives

United States. War Department. Provost Marshal General's Office. Records of Provost Marshals, Illinois. National Archives

Wade, Benjamin F., MSS. Library of Congress

Washburn, Israel, MSS. Library of Congress

Washburne, Elihu B., MSS. Library of Congress

Weed, Thurlow, MSS. Library of Congress

Welles, Gideon, MSS. Library of Congress

Wilson, Henry, MSS. Library of Congress

Wisconsin Adjutant-General's Letters during the Civil War. State Historical Society of Wisconsin Library, Madison. Typewritten copies made by Mr. Oliver, notes by Milo M. Quaife

Wisconsin Governors' Letters during the Civil War. State Historical Society of Wisconsin Library, Madison. Typed copies made under the direction of Milo M. Quaife

Wisconsin Governors' Telegrams. State Historical Society of Wisconsin Library, Madison

Yates, Richard, MSS. The Chicago Historical Society Library. Collected by Logan Uriah Reavis, one of Yates's closest friends, who planned, with Yates's co-operation, a biography of the latter. (This MSS. is referred to by letter C.)

Yates, Richard, MSS. Illinois State Historical Library. (Referred to by letter I.)

2. Official Documents

Illinois. *Blue Book of Illinois, 1913–14*. Compiled by Henry Woods, Secretary of State. Danville, Ill.: Illinois Printing Co., 1914

Illinois. *Report of the Adjutant General of the State of Illinois*. Vol. I. Revised by J. N. Reece, Adjutant General. Springfield: Phillips Bros., State Printers, 1900

Indiana, Adjutant-General's Office. *Report, 1861–66*. Indianapolis, 1865–67

United States Congress. House of Representatives. *Executive Document No. 50*. 39th Cong., 2nd sess. "Message from the President of the United States, in answer to a Resolution of the House of the 19th of December, Transmitting Papers Relative to the Case of George St. Leger Grenfell." Jan. 21, 1867

United States Congress. *The Congressional Globe*. . . .Washington: Printed at the Globe Office for the Editors, 1834–73

United States. Department of the Interior. *Population of the United States in 1860, Compiled from the Original Returns of the Eighth Census under the Secretary of the Interior by Joseph C. G. Kennedy, Superintendent of Census*. Washington: Government Printing Office, 1864

United States. Department of the Interior. *Statistics of the United States, (Including Mortality, Property, &c.,) in 1860*. . . . Washington: Government Printing Office, 1866

United States. War Department. *The War of the Rebellion: a Compilation of the Official Records of the Union and Confederate Armies*. 70 vols. Washington: Government Printing Office, 1880–1901

3. Newspapers and Periodicals
a. New York

New York Weekly Tribune   *The New York World*

*The Old Guard: a Monthly Journal Devoted to the Principles of 1776 and
    1787.* Vol. I begins Jan. 1863. New York: C. Chauncey Burr & Co.,
    117 Nassau St.

b. Ohio

Bellefontaine Republican
Bucyrus Weekly Journal
The (Canton) *Stark County Demo-
    crat*
Cincinnati Daily Commercial
Cincinnati Daily Courier
The Cincinnati Daily Enquirer
Cincinnati Daily Gazette
Cincinnati Weekly Gazette

(Cincinnati) *Journal & Messenger*
Cincinnati Daily Times
Cincinnati Volksfreund
Circleville Union
The Circleville Watchman
Daily Morning Cleveland Herald
Cleveland Plain Dealer
The (Cleveland) *Daily National
    Democrat*

The (Columbus) *Crisis.* The most valuable single newspaper source on the
    peace movement. Owing to its complete devotion to the cause and its
    practice of clipping and reprinting news articles and editorials on this
    subject from papers all over the Middle West it is a storehouse of infor-
    mation.

Daily (Columbus) *Ohio State Jour-
    nal*
The Daily (Columbus) *Ohio States-
    man*
Conneaut Reporter
The Coshocton Democrat
Dayton Daily Empire
Weekly Dayton Journal
Dayton Daily Journal

The (Findlay) *Hancock Jefferso-
    nian*
(Jefferson) *Ashtabula Sentinel*
The (Painesville) *Press and Ad-
    vertiser*
Painesville Telegraph
The (Salem) *Anti-Slavery Bugle*
Daily Toledo Blade
Washington Herald
Xenia Torch-Light

c. Indiana

(Connersville) *Fayette and Union
    Telegraph*
The Connersville Telegraph
Evansville Journal
Daily Fort Wayne Sentinel
The Fort Wayne Sentinel
The (Indianapolis) *Indiana State
    Guard*
The Indianapolis Daily Journal
(Indianapolis) *Daily State Sentinel*

The Lafayette Daily Courier
(Ligonier) *Noble County Herald*
The (Madison) *Daily Evening
    Courier*
The New Albany Daily Ledger
The (Paoli) *American Eagle*
(Richmond) *Broad Axe of Free-
    dom*
The (Richmond) *Quaker City
    Telegram*

d. Illinois
    Because of the lack of anything approaching a complete repository of Illi-
nois newspapers for this period, use of such papers as were available to the
author has been supplemented by extensive reference to the excerpts from
newspapers of the state made under the direction of Dr. A. C. Cole in the
preparation of his volume in the *Centennial History of Illinois.* These are
deposited in the Illinois Historical Survey, Urbana, Illinois.

Aurora Beacon
Belleville Advocate
Belleville Democrat
Bloomington Times
Cairo Morning News
Cairo Daily Democrat
Cairo Weekly Democrat
Canton Weekly Register
Canton Weekly Republican
Carthage Republican
(Champaign) *Central Illinois Gazette*
Chicago Evening Journal
Chicago Morning Post
The Daily Chicago Post
The Chicago Times
Chicago Daily Tribune
Galena Daily Advertiser
Galena Daily Democrat
Galena Weekly Democrat
Jacksonville Journal
The Joliet Republican

e. Michigan
Detroit Advertiser and Tribune
Detroit Daily Advertiser

f. Wisconsin
(Alma) *Buffalo County Journal*
The Appleton Crescent
The Appleton Motor
Baraboo Republic
Beaver Dam Argus
The Beloit Journal and Courier
The (Boscobel) *National Broad-Axe*
Brodhead Weekly Reporter
Delevan Patriot
Dodgeville Chronicle
The Elkhorn Independent
Fond du Lac Weekly Commonwealth
Galesville Transcript
(Grand Rapids) *Wood County Reporter*
Green Bay Advocate

g. Iowa
Burlington Daily Hawk-Eye
Charles City Republican Intelligencer

Joliet Signal
Jonesboro Weekly Gazette
Ottawa Free Trader
The (Paris) *Prairie Beacon*
The (Petersburg) *Menard Index*
Quincy Daily Whig-Republican
Weekly Quincy Whig-Republican
Rock Island Weekly Argus
Rockford Democrat
(Rockford) *Rock River Democrat*
Rockford Register
Rockford Republican
Rushville Times
(Springfield) *Illinois Daily State Journal*
The Weekly (Springfield) *Illinois State Journal*
(Springfield) *Illinois State Register*
(Urbana) *Champaign County Democrat*
The Prairie Farmer. Chicago

The Detroit Free Press

The (Green) *Bay City Press*
Janesville Daily Gazette
The Kenosha Democrat
The Kenosha Telegraph
La Crosse Weekly Appeal
La Crosse Democrat
La Crosse Weekly Mirror
Daily (Madison) *Argus & Democrat*
The (Madison) *Wisconsin Patriot*
(Madison) *Wisconsin State Journal*
The Manitowoc Pilot
Daily Milwaukee News
The Milwaukee Sentinel
The (Milwaukee) *Evening Wisconsin*
Weekly Racine Advocate
The Racine Democrat

Davenport Weekly Democrat and News
Davenport Daily Gazette

(Davenport) *Daily Democrat &
News*

(Dubuque) *Herald*

h. Minnesota

*Mankato Independent
The Mankato Union
Saint Anthony Weekly Express
St. Paul Daily Pioneer*

The Daily (St. Paul) *Pioneer and
Democrat
Saint Paul Press
Saint Paul Daily Union*

i. Missouri

Daily (St. Louis) *Missouri Democrat*

Daily (St. Louis) *Missouri Republican*

4. Pamphlets

Basset, George W. *A Discourse on the Wickedness and Folly of the Present
War. Delivered in the Court House at Ottawa, Ill., On Sabbath, Aug. 11,
1861*

Bassett, George W. *A Northern Plea for the Right of Secession.* Ottawa, Ill.:
Office of the *Free Trader,* 1861

Harrison, Richard A. *Oration of the Hon. Richard A. Harrison, Delivered
at Pleasant Valley, Madison County, Ohio, on the Fourth of July, A.D.
1863.* Published by the Citizens before Whom It Was Delivered. London, Ohio: Madison County Union Print., 1863

K.G.C. *A Full Exposure of the Southern Traitors; The Knights of the
Golden Circle. Their Startling Schemes Frustrated. From Original Docu-
ments Never Before Published.* (*The Five Cent Monthly.*) Boston: E. H.
Bullard & Co., 1860–1 (?)

Leland, Charles Godfrey. *Ye Book of Copperheads.* Philadelphia: Frederick
Leypoldt, 1863

*Madison Y. Johnson vs. J. Russel Jones, John C. Hawkins, Oliver P. Hop-
kins, Elihu B. Washburne and Bradner Smith; Appeal from Jo Daviess
County; Abstract, Brief; Argument of Plaintiff with Opinion and Judgement of Court.* (*State of Illinois, Supreme Court, April term, A.D. 1866.*)
Dubuque: Herald Steam Printing House, 1869

Pomfrey, J. W. (Gov.-Gen. of the K.G.C. of the state of Ky., Capt.-Gen. for
Kenton County), *A True Disclosure and Exposition of the Knights of
the Golden Circle Including the Secret Signs, Grips, and Charges, of
the Three Degrees, as Practiced by the Order.* Cincinnati: Printed for
the author, c. 1861

a. Democratic

*Address of Democratic Members of Congress to the Democracy of the United
States.* Washington: L. Towers & Co., printers (1862)

*Address of the New Jersey Democratic State Central Committee to the
Voters of the State.* Trenton, 1862

*Address to the People by the Democracy of Wisconsin, Adopted in State
Convention at Milwaukee, Sept. 3d, 1862*

*An Address to the People of the United States, and Particularly to the Peo-
ple of the States Which Adhere to the Federal Government.* Washington, July 1864

Allen, William, *Speech of Hon. William Allen of Ohio, on the State of the*

Union, Delivered in the House of Representatives, February 7, 1861. Washington: McGill & Witherow, printers, 1861

Allen, William J. *Speech of Hon. William J. Allen, of Illinois, upon the President's Message, Delivered in the House of Representatives, January 27, 1864.* Washington: Office of "The Constitutional Union," 1864

Black, Jeremiah S. *The Doctrine of the Democratic and Abolition Parties Contrasted—Negro Equality—The Conflict between "Higher Law" and the Law of the Land: Speech of Hon. Jeremiah S. Black, at the Hall of the Keystone Club, in Philadelphia, October 24, 1864.* Philadelphia: The *Age* office, (1864)

Cincinnati Convention, October 18, 1864, for the Organization of a Peace Party upon State-Rights, Jeffersonian, Democratic Principles and for the Promotion of Peace and Independent Nominations for President and Vice-President of the United States

Corruptions and Frauds of Lincoln's Administration. Document No. 14. Sold at 13 Park Row, and at all Democratic Newspaper Offices. (New York, 1864)

Cox, Samuel Sullivan. *Free Debate in Congress Threatened—Abolition Leaders and Their Revolutionary Schemes Unmasked: Speech of Hon. Samuel S. Cox, of Ohio, Delivered in the House of Representatives, April 6, 1864.* Washington: Constitutional Union Office, 1864

Cox, Samuel Sullivan. *Puritanism in Politics: Speech of Hon. S. S. Cox, of Ohio, before the Democratic Union Association, Jan. 13, 1863.* New York: Van Evrie, Horton & Co., (1863)

Cox, Samuel Sullivan, *Reply of Hon. S. S. Cox, of Ohio, in Reply to Messrs. Hutchins and Stanton. Delivered in the House of Representatives, February 9, 1861.* Washington: Lemuel Towers, printer, 1861

Democratic Loyal League of New York. *The Real Motives of the Rebellion. The Slaveholders' Conspiracy, Depicted by Southern Loyalists in Its Treason against Democratic Principles, as Well as against the National Union; Showing a Contest of Slavery and Nobility versus Free Government: Address of the Democratic League to the "Loyal Leagues" and Loyal Men throughout the Land.* New York, 1864

Dix, John Adams. *Letter from John A. Dix to the War Democracy of Wisconsin.* New York, 1863

Douglas, Stephen Arnold. *Remarks of Hon. Stephen A. Douglas, in the Senate of the United States, March 6, 1861, on the Resolution of Mr. Dixon to Print the Inaugural Address of President Lincoln.* n.d.p.

Douglas, Stephen Arnold. *Speech of Senator Douglas, before the Legislature of Illinois, April 25, 1861. In Compliance with a Joint Resolution of the two Houses.* n.d.p.

Douglas, Stephen Arnold. *Speech of Hon. S. A. Douglas, of Illinois, on the State of the Union. Delivered in the Senate, January 3, 1861.* Washington: 1861

For Peace and Peaceable Separation: Citizen's Democratic Address to the People of the State of Ohio, and the People of the Several States of the West and North. Cincinnati: The author, 1863

Holman, William S. *Speech of William S. Holman, of Indiana, on the State of the Union, Delivered in the House of Representatives, January 16, 1861.* Washington: McGill & Witherow, printers, 1861

Jenkinson, Isaac. *The Peace Party and Its Policy: Speech of Isaac Jenkinson, at Fort Wayne, Indiana, March 16, 1863.* Fort Wayne: R. C. F. Rayhouser, printer, (1863)

Kendall, Amos. *Letters Exposing the Mismanagement of Public Affairs by Abraham Lincoln, and the Political Combinations to Secure His Re-election.* Washington: Constitutional Union Office, 1864

Knapp, A. L. *The Constitution and the Union, Maintain the One to Preserve the Other: Speech of Hon. A. L. Knapp, of Illinois, on the Policy and Object of War. Delivered in the House of Representatives, June 5, 1862*

The Lincoln Catechism, Wherein the Eccentricities and Beauties of Despotism are Fully Set Forth: A Guide to the Presidential Election of 1864. New York: J. F. Feeks, (1864?)

Der Lincoln Katechismus worin die Schönheiten und Exzentrizitäten des Despotismus vollständig dargestellt sind: ein Wegweiser zur Präsidentenwahl vom 1864. New York: J. F. Feeks, (1864)

McArthur, Arthur. *Address by the Loyal Democracy of Wisconsin, to the People of the State.* Reported by Arthur McArthur, and Adopted in Convention at Janesville, September 17, 1863. Milwaukee: Daily Wisconsin Steam Press Establishment, 1863

McClelland, Robert. *Letter on the Crisis.* n.p.d.

McClernand, John Alexander. *Speech of Hon. John A. McClernand, of Illinois, on the State of the Union: Delivered in the House of Representatives, January 14, 1861.* Washington: Printed at the Congressional Globe Office, 1861

Morrison, William R. *Speech Delivered by Col. W. R. Morrison, at Edwardsville, Madison County, Ill., October 13, 1863.* St. Louis: George Knapp & Co., printers, 1863

Mr. Lincoln's Arbitrary Arrests: the Acts Which the Baltimore Platform Approves. Document No. 13. (New York: Democratic National Committee, 1864)

O'Melveny, H. K. S. *Speech of Hon. H. K. S. O'Melveny on the Causes of the War and Mode of Adjustment. Delivered at Vandalia, Illinois, August 29, 1862.* Chicago: Chicago Times Book & Job Establishment, 1862

Papers from the Society for the Diffusion of Political Knowledge, No. 1: The Constitution. Addresses of Prof. Morse, Mr. Geo. Tichnor Curtis, and Mr. S. J. Tilden, at the Organization

Parker, Joel. *Our National Troubles—Their Cause and Remedy: Speech of Governor Parker at Freehold, N.J., Aug. 20, 1864*

Pendleton, George H. *The Resolution to Expel Mr. Long, of Ohio: Speech of Hon. Geo. H. Pendleton, of Ohio, Delivered in the House of Representatives, April 11, 1864.* n.p.d.

Pendleton, George H. *Speech of Hon. George H. Pendleton, of Ohio, on the State of the Union, Delivered in the House of Representatives, January 18, 1861.* Washington: Lemuel Towers, printer, 1861

Pendleton, George H. *Speech of Hon. George H. Pendleton, of Ohio, in the House of Representatives, December 10, 1861.* n.p.d.

Proceedings of the Democratic State Convention Held at Columbus, Ohio, Friday, July 4, 1862. Containing the Speeches of Hon. Samuel Medary, Hon. C. L. Vallandigham, Hon. Rufus P. Ranney, and Hon. Allen G. Thurman. The Address and Platform, Balloting for Candidates, and Names of Delegates in Attendance. Dayton: Dayton *Empire* Press, 1862

Proceedings of the Great Peace Convention, Held in the City of New York, June 3d, 1863: Speeches, Addresses, Resolutions, and Letters from Leading Men, Abridged from the Elaborate Report Published in the New York "Daily News," June 4th, 1863

Pugh, George E. *Speech of Hon. George E. Pugh, of Ohio, on the State of the Union, Delivered in the Senate of the United States, December 20, 1860.* Washington: L. Towers, printer, 1860

Reception of M. Y. Johnson and D. Sheean, Esqs., at Galena, Illinois, on Their Return, Honorably Discharged from the Bastiles Fort La Fayette, and Delaware: The Speeches Delivered on the Occasion, and an Account of Preliminary Proceedings. Galena: Office of the *Democrat,* 1863

Reed, Henry. *The Secession of the Whole South an Existing Fact. A Peaceable Separation the True Course. Its Effect on Peace and Trade between the Sections.* Cincinnati: Office of the Cincinnati Daily Press, 1861

Republican Opinions about Lincoln. Democratic National Committee, Document No. 18. n.p., (1864)

Robinson, John Bell. *An Address to the "People" of the Several Sovereign States of the United States, on the Frauds on Their Elective Franchise, under Official Orders, and the Danger of the People Being Reduced to Mere Serfs to a Tyrant Despot, under the Pretext of Negro Freedom, Military Necessity, Union and Liberty.* n.p.d.

Turpie, David. *Speech of Mr. Turpie, Delivered in the Senate of the United States, Feb. 7, 1863.* Papers from the Society for the Diffusion of Political Knowledge, No. 2

Vallandigham, Clement Laird. *"After Some Time Be Past": Speech of Hon. C. L. Vallandigham, of Ohio, on Executive Usurpation, in the House of Representatives, July 10, 1861*

Vallandigham, Clement Laird. *The Great Civil War in America: Speech of Hon. Clement Laird Vallandigham of Ohio, in the House of Representatives, January 14, 1863*

Vallandigham, Clement Laird. *Speech of Hon. C. L. Vallandigham, of Ohio, Delivered in the House of Representatives, February 20, 1861.* Washington: Henry Polkinhorn, printer, 1861

Voorhees, Daniel W. *Speech of Hon. D. W. Voorhees, of Indiana, Delivered in the House of Representatives, March 9, 1864.* Washington: Constitutional Union Office, 1864

Voorhees, Daniel W. *Speech of Hon. D. W. Voorhees, of Indiana, Delivered in the House of Representatives, May 21, 1862.* Washington: Towers, printers, 1862

Wall, James W. *Speeches for the Times by Hon. James W. Wall of New Jersey, with a Sketch of His Personal and Political History.* New York: J. Walter & Co., 1864

Wilkinson, Morton S. *Speech of Hon. Morton S. Wilkinson, of Minnesota, on the Constitution as It Is; Delivered in the Senate of the United States, March 2, 1861.* Washington, 1861

Wood, Benjamin. *Peace: Speech of Benjamin Wood, of New York, in the House of Representatives, February 27th, 1863*

Wood, Benjamin. *Speech of Benjamin Wood, of New York, on the State of the Union, in the House of Representatives, May 16, 1862.* Washington: McGill, Witherow & Co., printers, 1862

b. Republican

Arthur, Timothy Shay. *Growler's Income Tax.* Loyal Publication Society pamphlet, No. 57. New York: Francis & Loutrel, printers, (1863?)

Ashley, James M. *The Liberation and Restoration of the South: Speech of Hon. J. M. Ashley, of Ohio, in the House of Representatives of the United States on the 30th Day of March 1864.* Washington: H. Polkinhorn, printer, 1864

Ashley, James M. *Speech of Hon. James M. Ashley, of Ohio, Delivered in the House of Representatives, January 17, 1861.* Washington: H. Polkinhorn, printer, 1861

Bingham, John A. *Speech of Hon. John A. Bingham, of Ohio, in the House of Representatives, January 22, 1861.* Washington: Office of the *Congressional Globe,* 1861

Blake, Harrison G. *Speech of Hon. Harrison G. Blake, of Ohio, Delivered in the House of Representatives, February 19, 1861.* Washington: Printed at the National Republican Office, 1861

Brough, John. *The Defenders of the Country and Its Enemies; the Chicago Platform Dissected: Speech of Governor Brough Delivered at Circleville, Ohio, Sept. 3.* From the Cincinnati Gazette, September 5, 1864. Cincinnati: Gazette Co., 1864

Chandler, William Eaton. *The Soldier's Right to Vote: Who Opposes It? Who Favors It? or the Record of the Record of the M'Clellan Copperheads against Allowing the Soldier Who Fights the Right to Vote While Fighting.* Prepared for the Union Congressional Committee. Washington: Lemuel Towers, printer, 1864

Coddington, David S. *The Crisis and the Man: Address on the Presidential Crisis Delivered before the Union War Democracy at the Cooper Institute, New York, Nov. 1, 1864.* New York: Wm. Oland Bourne, 1865

The Chicago Copperhead Convention: the Treasonable and Revolutionary Utterances of the Men Who Composed It: Extracts from All the Notable Speeches Delivered in and out of the National "Democratic" Convention—a Surrender to The Rebels Advocated—a Disgraceful and Pusillanimous Peace Demanded—the Federal Government Shamefully Vilified and Not a Word Said Against the Crime of Treason and Rebellion. Washington: Congressional Union Committee, 1864

Conkling, Henry. *An Inside View of the Rebellion, and American Citizens' Text-Book.* Chicago: Tribune Book and Job Printing Establishment, 1864

Cook, William A. *Opinions and Practice of the Founders of the Republic in Relation to Arbitrary Arrests, Imprisonment of Tories, Writ of Habeas Corpus, Seizure of Arms and of Private Papers, Domiciliary Visits, Con-*

fiscation of Real and Personal Estate, etc., etc., or the Administration of Abraham Lincoln Sustained by the Sages and Heroes of the Revolution. Washington: William H. Moore, printer, 1864

The Copperhead Catechism for the Instruction of Such Politicians as Are of Tender Years, Carefully Compiled by Learned and Designing Men. Authorized and with Admonitions by Fernando the Gothamite, High Priest of the Order of Copperheads. New York: Sinclair Tousey, 1864

Copperhead Conspiracy in the North-West: an Expose of the Treasonable Order of the "Sons of Liberty"—Vallandigham, Supreme Commander. (New York?) Union Congressional Committee, (1864)

Corwin, Thomas. *Speech of Hon. Thomas Corwin, of Ohio, Delivered in the House of Representatives, Jan. 21, 1861.* Washington: Henry Polkinhorn, 1861

Davis, Henry Winter. *Speech of Hon. H. Winter Davis, of Maryland, on the Resolution Offered by Mr. Colfax Proposing the Expulsion of Mr. Long, Delivered in the House of Representatives, April 11, 1864.* Washington: L. Towers, printer, (1864)

Defrees, John D. *Remarks Made before the Indiana Union Club of Washington, D.C., Monday Evening, August 1, 1864.* Washington: L. Towers, printer, 1864

The Echo from the Army: What Our Soldiers Say about the Copperheads (Loyal Reprints, No. 1). New York: Wm. C. Bryant & Co., printers, 1863

Funk, Isaac. *Scene in the Illinois Legislature: Speech of a Brave Old Patriot; Terrible Philippic against Traitors.* Philadelphia: Henry B. Ashmeal, 1863

George H. Pendleton, the Copperhead Candidate for Vice-President: His Hostility to the American Republic Illustrated by His Record as a Representative in the Congress of the United States from the State of Ohio. Washington: Union Congressional Committee, 1864

The Great Northern Conspiracy of the "S.O.L." "Resistance to Tyrants Is Obedience to God." n.p.d.

The Great Surrender to the Rebels in Arms: the Armistice, Sept. 2, 1864. Union Executive Congressional Committee. Washington: McGill & Witherow, 1864

Gurley, John A. *Speech of Hon. Jno. A. Gurley, of Ohio, on the State of the Union, Delivered in the House of Representatives, January 16th, 1861.* Washington: McGill & Witherow, 1861

Gurley, John A. *Speech of Hon. J. A. Gurley, of Ohio, Delivered in the House of Representatives, January 29, 1862.* Washington: McGill & Witherow, printers, 1862

Holt, Joseph. *Report of the Judge Advocate General on "The Order of American Knights," alias "The Sons of Liberty"; a Western Conspiracy in Aid of the Southern Rebellion.* Washington: Union Congressional Committee, 1864

Hutchins, John. *Speech of Hon. John Hutchins, of Ohio, in the House of Representatives, February 9, 1861.* Washington: McGill & Witherow, printers, 1861

Kellogg, William. *Speech of Hon. Wm. Kellogg, of Illinois, in Favor of the*

Union, Delivered in the House of Representatives, February 8, 1861. Printed by Lemuel Towers

Lieber, Francis. *Lincoln or McClellan: Appeal to the Germans in America.* Translated from the German by T. C. No. 67. New York: Loyal Publication Society, (1864)

Logan, John Alexander. *Rede des General-Majors John A. Logan, bei seiner Rückkehr nach Illinois nach der Einnahme von Vicksburg (Loyal Bekanntmachungen der National Union's Association von Ohio, No. IV).* Cincinnati: Office of the *Cincinnati Union,* 1863

Logan, John Alexander. *Speech of Major-General John A. Logan on Return to Illinois after Capture of Vicksburg. Reported by "Mack," of the Cincinnati Commercial.* Loyal Publications of National Union Association of Ohio, No. 4. Cincinnati: Caleb Clark, printer, 1863. (publ. Aug. 1863)

Loyal Publication Society. *Proceedings at the First Anniversary Meeting of the Loyal Publication Society, February 13, 1864.* New York: Loyal Publication Society, 1864

The Next Presidential Election: Mr. Lincoln—The Presidency—Action of Legislatures—One Term Principle—Patronage—Prolonging the War —Inability and Vascillation (sic)*—"Honest Old Abe"—Military Commander as a Candidate—The Candidate Wanted.* With extract from *Wilkes' Spirit of the Times.* n.p.d.

Orth, Godlove S. *Shall Sympathizers with Treason Hold Seats in Congress? Speech of Hon. Godlove S. Orth, of Ind., on the Resolution to Expel Mr. Long, Delivered in the House of Representatives, April 14, 1864.* Washington: Printed by L. Towers for the Union Congressional Committee, 1864

Perry, Aaron Fyfe. *Speech of Aaron F. Perry, Esq., Delivered before the National Union Association at Mozart Hall, Cincinnati, Sept. 20, 1864.* (Cincinnati: National Union Association of Ohio, 1864)

Pomeroy, Samuel C. *Speech of Hon. S. C. Pomeroy, on the Platform and Party of the Future, and National Freedom Secured by an Amended Constitution, Delivered in the Senate of the United States, March 10, 1864.* Washington: McGill & Witherow, 1864

Reasons Why the Radical Union Delegation from Missouri to the Baltimore Convention Should Be Admitted. Published on Behalf of the Delegation. Washington: Gibson Bros., printers, 1864

Schenck, Robert C. *No Compromise with Treason: Remarks of Mr. Schenck, of Ohio, in Reply to Mr. Fernando Wood, of New York, in the Debate on the Resolution to Expel, Mr. Long, Delivered in the House of Representatives, April 11, 1864.* Washington: L. Towers, for the Union Congressional Committee, 1864

Seward, William Henry. *Speech of William H. Seward, in the Senate of the United States, January 12, 1861.* Washington: Office of the *Congressional Globe,* 1861

Seward, William Henry. *Speech of William H. Seward in the Senate of the United States, on Presenting the New York Petition, January 31, 1861.* Washington: Office of the *Congressional Globe,* 1861

Sherman, John. *Speech of Hon. John Sherman, of Ohio, Delivered in the House of Representatives, January 18, 1861.* Washington, 1861

Sherman, John. *Valandigham's* (sic) *Record Reviewed; a Political Traitor Unmasked: Speech by Hon. John Sherman, U.S. Senator from Ohio, Delivered at Delaware, Ohio, July 28th, 1863.* Dayton: Daily Journal, printer, (1863)

Stirring Appeals from Honored Veterans: Democratic Statesmen and Generals to the Loyal Sons of the Union—Views of Gens. Grant, Sherman, Dix, Wool, Butler, Edward Everett, John A. Griswold, and Others. Union Campaign Documents, No. 8. Albany: Weed, Parsons & Co., printers, 1864

Swinton, William. *A Few Plain Words with the Rank and File of the Union Armies.* (Washington): Union Congressional Committee (1864)

Swinton, William. *The Military and Naval Situation and the Glorious Achievements of Our Soldiers and Sailors.* Washington: Union Congressional Committee, 1864

The Votes of the Copperheads in the Congress of the United States. (Washington): Union Congressional Committee, (1864)

Wade, Benjamin Franklin. *Speech of Hon. B. F. Wade, of Ohio, on the State of the Union, Delivered in the Senate of the United States, Dec. 17, 1860.* Washington: McGill & Witherow, printers, 1860

What Genuine Democrats Think of the Rebellion. New York: National Union Executive Committee (1864)

Wilson, Thomas L. *A Brief History of the Cruelties and Atrocities of the Rebellion, Compiled from the Most Authentic Sources.* Washington: Union Congressional Committee, 1864

Yates, Richard. *Message of His Excellency, Richard Yates, Governor of Illinois, to the General Assembly, January 5, 1863.* Springfield; Baker & Phillips, printers, 1863

Yates, Richard. *Speech of Governor Yates at the Great War Meeting at Chicago, August 1, 1861.* Taken from *Chicago Tribune*

5. Books and Articles

(Allen, T. F.). "John Morgan Raid in Ohio," *Ohio Archaeological and Historical Publications*, XVII, (1908), 48–59

Ayer, I. Winslow. *The Great Northwestern Conspiracy in All its Startling Details; the People's Union Book; The Plot to Plunder and Burn Chicago—Release of all Rebel Prisoners—Seizure of Arsenals—Raids from Canada—Plot to Burn New York—Piracy on the Lakes—Parts for the Sons of Liberty—Trail of Chicago Conspiracy—Inside Views of the Temples of the Sons of Liberty—Names of Prominent Members.* Chicago: Rounds & James, 1865

Ayer, I. Winslow. *The Great Treason Plot in the North during the War. Most Dangerous, Perfidious, Extensive and Startling Plot Ever Devised: Imminent Hidden Perils of the Republic. Astounding Developments Never Before Published.* Chicago: U.S. Publishing Co., 1895

Baker, William Washington. *Memoirs of Service with John Yates Beall, C.S.N.* Richmond: Richmond Press, 1910

Beck, E. W. H. "Letters of a Civil War Surgeon," *Indiana Magazine of History*, XXVII (June 1931), 132–63

Birdsall, D. C. "McClellan and the Peace Party," *The Century Illustrated Monthly Magazine*, XXIX, new ser. XVII, (Feb. 1890), 638–9

Bright, Jesse D. "Some Letters of Jesse D. Bright to William H. English (1842–1863)," *Indiana Magazine of History*, XXX (Dec. 1934), 370–92

Burnett, H. L. *Reply of the Judge Advocate, H. L. Burnett, to the Pleas of the Counsel for the Accused, to the Jurisdiction of the Military Commission, Convened by Major-General Hooker, Commanding Northern Department, in case of United States vs. Charles Walsh, Buckner S. Morris, Vincent Marmaduke, R. T. Semmes, Charles Travis Daniel, George E. Cantril, G. St. Leger Grenfell, Benjamin M. Anderson, Charged with conspiring to release the Rebel prisoners at Camp Douglas, Chicago, Illinois, and to lay Waste and Destroy that City.* Cincinnati: Moore, Wilstach & Baldwin, 1865

Carr, Clark E. "Why Lincoln Was Not Renominated by Acclamation," *The Century Illustrated Monthly Magazine*, LXXIII, new ser. LI, (Feb. 1907), 503–6

Castleman, John B. *Active Service.* Louisville, Ky.: Courier-Journal Job Printing Co., publishers, 1917

Chittenden, Lucius Eugene. *A Report of the Debates and Proceedings in the Secret Sessions of the Conference Convention, for Proposing Amendments to the Constitution of the United States, Held at Washington, D.C., in February, A. D. 1861.* New York: D. Appleton & Co., 1864

Coffin, Charles Carleton. *My Days and Nights on the Battlefield.* 2nd ed. Boston: Ticknor & Fields, 1864

Cook, Charles N., and Ball, Lafayette. "Letters of Privates Cook and Ball," *Indiana Magazine of History*, XXVII (Sept. 1931), 243–68

Cook, Frederick Francis. *Bygone Days in Chicago & Recollections of the "Garden City" of the Sixties.* Chicago: A. C. McClurg & Co., 1910

"Correspondence of New York Editors with Governor Bradford," *Maryland Historical Magazine*, III (June 1908), 176–8

Davis, Jefferson. *The Rise and Fall of the Confederate Government.* 2 vols. New York: D. Appleton & Co., 1881

Dean, Henry Clay. *Crimes of the Civil War and Curse of the Funding System.* Baltimore: Wm. T. Smithson, 1868

De Bow's Review of the Southern and Western States

Doolittle, James R. "Speech Delivered by Senator James R. Doolittle, Springfield, Illinois, October 4, 1864," The Illinois State Historical Society, *Journal* (Oct. 1909), pp. 29–37

Drell, Muriel Bernitt, ed. "Letters by Richard Smith of the Cincinnati Gazette," *The Mississippi Valley Historical Review*, XXVI (March 1940), 535–54

Duke, Basil W. *Reminiscences of General Basil W. Duke, C.S.A.*, Garden City, N.Y.: Doubleday, Page & Co., 1911

Early, Gen. Jubal A. "The Story of the Attempted Formation of a N.W. Confederacy," Southern Historical Society, *Papers*, X (April, 1882), 154–8

Fergus, Robert, comp. *Chicago River-and-Harbor Convention; an Account of Its Origin and Proceedings. . . .* Fergus Historical Series, No. 18. Chicago: Fergus Printing Co., 1882

Harrington, Fred Harvey, ed. "A Peace Mission of 1863," *The American Historical Review*, XLVI (Oct. 1940), 76–86

Hines, Thomas H. "The Northwestern Conspiracy," *The Southern Bivouac: a Monthly Literary and Historical Magazine,* conducted by Basil W. Duke and R. W. Knott. New ser., II (June 1886–May 1887), pp. 437–45, 500–10, 567–74, 699–704

Johns, Jane Martin. *Personal Recollections of Early Decatur, Abraham Lincoln, Richard J. Oglesby and the Civil War.* Decatur, Ill.: Decatur Chapter of the Daughters of the American Revolution, 1912

Julian, George W. *Political Recollections, 1840 to 1872.* Chicago: Jansen, McClurg & Co., 1884

Keefe, Colonel Thomas H. "How the Northwest Was Saved: a Chapter from the Secret Service Records of the Civil War," *Everybody's Magazine,* II (Jan. 1900), pp. 82–91

Klaus, Samuel, ed. *The Milligan Case.* American Trials. New York: A. A. Knopf, 1929

Koerner, Gustave. *Memoirs of Gustave Koerner, 1809–1896: Life Sketches Written at the Suggestion of His Children.* 2 vols. Edited by Thomas J. McCormack. Cedar Rapids, Iowa: Torch Press, 1909

Leland, Charles G. "The Knights of the Golden Circle," *The Continental Monthly: Devoted to Literature and National Policy,* I (May 1862), 573–7

Mahoney, Dennis A. *The Four Acts of Despotism: Comprising I. The Tax Bill, with All Amendments; II. The Finance Bill; III. The Conscription Act: IV. The Indemnity Bill; with Introductions and Comments.* New York: Van Evrie, Horton & Co., 1863

Mahoney, Dennis A. *The Prisoner of State.* New York: Carleton, publ., 1863

McPherson, Edward, ed. *The Political History of the United States of America during the Great Rebellion, Including a Classified Summary of the Legislation of the Second Session of the Thirty-Sixth Congress, the Three Sessions of the Thirty-Seventh Congress, the First Session of the Thirty-Eighth Congress, with the Votes Thereon, and the Important Executive, Judicial, and Politico-Military Facts of That Eventful Period; Together with the Organization, Legislation, and General Proceedings of the Rebel Administration; and an Appendix Containing the Principal Political Facts of the Campaign of 1864, a Chapter on the Church and the Rebellion, and the Proceedings of the Second Session of the Thirty-Eighth Congress.* 4th ed. Washington, D.C.: J. J. Chapman, 1882

"A Memorable Speech at Springfield and a By-Stander's Account of It," The Illinois State Historical Society, *Journal,* II (Jan. 1910), 40–3

Official Proceedings of the Democratic National Convention, Held in 1864 at Chicago. Chicago: Times Steam Book & Job Printing House, 1864

Pease, Theodore Calvin, and Randall, James Garfield, eds. *The Diary of Orville Hickman Browning.* Vol. I, 1850–1864. Springfield: Illinois State Historical Library, 1925

Pierce, Edward L. *Memoir and Letters of Charles Sumner.* 4 Vols. Boston: Roberts Bros., 1877–93

Pierce, Franklin K. "Some Papers of Franklin Pierce, 1852–1862," *The American Historical Review,* X, 110–27, 350–70

Pitman, Benn, ed. *The Trials for Treason at Indianapolis, Disclosing the Plans for Establishing a North-Western Confederacy: Being the Offi-*

cial Record of the Trials before the Military Commission Convened by Special Orders No. 129, Headquarters District of Indiana. Cincinnati: Moore, Wilstach & Baldwin, 1865

Pritchett, John Perry. "Michigan Democracy in the Civil War," *Michigan History Magazine*, XI (Jan. 1927), 92–110

Robertson, John Cox. "Journal of Melville Cox Robertson," *Indiana Magazine of History*, XXVIII (June 1932), 116–37

Sheppley, Helen Edith. "Camp Butler in the Civil War Days," The Illinois State Historical Society, *Journal*, XXV (Jan. 1933), 285–317

Stidger, Felix G. *Treason History of the Order of Sons of Liberty, Formerly Circle of Honor, Succeeded by Knights of the Golden Circle, Afterward Order of American Knights. The Most Gigantic Treasonable Conspiracy the World Has Ever Known.* Chicago: The author, 1903

Thompson, Taylor. "The Northwestern Confederacy," *Confederate Veteran*, XXIV, 87–8

Thorndike, Rachel Sherman, ed. *The Sherman Letters; Correspondence between General and Senator Sherman from 1837 to 1891.* New York: Charles Scribner's Sons, 1894. Needs to be checked at every point against originals in the W. T. Sherman MSS. in the Library of Congress. The editor carefully deleted evidences of opposition to Lincoln and of sharp political practices. In some cases the meaning is completely reversed.

Thwaites, Reuben Gold, Tilton, Asa Currier, and Merk, Frederick, eds. *Civil War Messages and Proclamations of Wisconsin War Governors.* Madison: Wisconsin History Commission, 1912

The Trial of Hon. Clement L. Vallandigham, by a Military Commission: and the Proceedings under His Application for a Writ of Habeas Corpus in the Circuit Court of the United States for the Southern District of Ohio. Cincinnati: Rickey & Carroll, 1863

The Tribune Almanac and Political Register, 1855–68

Vallandigham, Clement L. *Speeches, Arguments, Addresses, and Letters of Clement L. Vallandigham.* New York: J. Walter & Co., 1864

Vallandigham, Clement L. "Three Vallandigham Letters, 1865," *Ohio Archaeological and Historical Quarterly*, XLIII (Jan. 1934), 461–4

Welles, Gideon (1802–78). *Diary of Gideon Welles, Secretary of the Navy under Lincoln and Johnson.* With an introduction by John T. Morse, Jr. Boston & New York: Houghton Mifflin & Co., 1911. 3 Vols.

Winterbotham, William Wrigley. "Memoirs of a Civil War Sleuth," *The Wisconsin Magazine of History*, XIX (Dec. 1935), 131–60

Woodward, George W. "The Union and the States by a Jeffersonian Jurist," Edited by Philip G. Auchampaugh, *Tyler's Quarterly Historical and Genealogical Magazine*, XII (Jan. 1931), 177–81

Wright, Crafts J., ed. *Official Journal of the Conference Convention Held at Washington City, February, 1861.* Washington: McGill & Witherow, printers, 1861

Young, John Edward. "An Illinois Farmer during the Civil War: Extracts from the Journal of John Edward Young, 1859–66," The Illinois State Historical Society, *Journal*, XXVI (Apr.–July 1933), 70–135

B. SECONDARY WORKS

Abrams, Ray H. "The Copperhead Newspapers and the Negro," *The Journal of Negro History*, XX (Apr. 1935), 131–52

Abrams, Ray H. "The *Jeffersonian,* Copperhead Newspaper," *The Pennsylvania Magazine of History and Biography*, LVII (July 1933), 260–83

Adams, William Forbes. *Ireland and Irish Emigration to the New World from 1815 to the Famine.* New Haven: Yale University Press, 1932

Allen, Mary Bernard. "Joseph Holt, Judge Advocate General (1862–75): a Study in the Treatment of Political Prisoners by the United States Government during the Civil War," in The University of Chicago *Abstracts of Theses.* Humanistic Series, VI, 179–86. Chicago: University of Chicago Press, 1929

Ambler, Charles Henry. *A History of Transportation in the Ohio Valley, with Special Reference to Its Waterways, Trade, and Commerce from the Earliest Period to the Present Time.* Glendale, Cal.: Arthur H. Clark, Co., 1932

Anderson, Russell Howard. *Agriculture in Illinois during the Civil War Period, 1850–1870.* Abstract of Thesis, University of Illinois, 1929. Urbana, Ill., 1929

Antevs, Ernst. *The Last Glaciation, with Special Reference to the Ice Retreat in Northeastern North America.* New York: American Geographical Society, 1928

Antevs, Ernst. "Maps of the Pleistocene Glaciations," The Geological Society of America. *Bulletin,* XL (Dec. 1929), 631–720

Baldwin, Eugene F. "The Dream of the South: the Story of Illinois during the Civil War," The Illinois State Historical Society, *Transactions,* 1911

Barnhart, John D. "Sources of Southern Migration into the Old Northwest," *The Mississippi Valley Historical Review*, XXII (June 1933), 49–62

Barnhart, John D. "Southern Contributions to the Social Order of the Old Northwest," The *North Carolina Historical Review* (July 1940)

Barnhart, John D. "The Southern Element in the Leadership of the Old Northwest," *The Journal of Southern History*, I (May 1935), 186–97

Benton, Elbert J. *The Movement for Peace without a Victory during the Civil War.* Collections of the Western Reserve Historical Society, Publication No. 99. Cleveland, 1918

Boggess, Arthur Clinton. *The Settlement of Illinois, 1778–1830.* Chicago Historical Society's Collections, Vol. V. Chicago: Chicago Historical Society, 1908

Bovey, Wilfrid. "Confederate Agents in Canada during the American Civil War," *The Canadian Historical Review*, II (March 1921), 46–57

Bowman, Isaiah. *Forest Physiography: Physiography of the United States and Principles of Soils in Relation to Forestry.* New York: J. Wiley & Sons, 1911

Boyer, Margrette. "Morgan's Raid in Indiana," *Indiana Magazine of History,* VIII (Dec. 1912), 149–65

Bridges, C. A. "The Knights of the Golden Circle: a Filibustering Fantasy," *The Southwestern Historical Quarterly*, XLIV (Jan. 1941), 287–302

Briggs, John Ely. "The Enlistment of Iowa Troops during the Civil War," *The Iowa Journal of History*, XV (July 1917), 323–92

Bross, William. *Biographical Sketch of the Late Gen. B. J. Sweet. History of Camp Douglas.* Chicago: Jansen, McClurg & Co., 1878

Brummer, Sidney David. *Political History of New York State during the Period of the Civil War.* Studies in History, Economics, and Public Law Edited by the Faculty of Political Science of Columbia University, Vol. XXXIX, No. 2. New York: Columbia University, Longmans, Green & Co., agents, 1911

Buck, Solon J. "The New England Element in Illinois Politics before 1833," The Mississippi Valley Historical Association, *Proceedings,* 1912–13, pp. 49–61

Burley, Augustus Harris. *The Cairo Expedition: Illinois' First Response in the Late Civil War: the Expeditions from Chicago to Cairo.* Chicago: Fergus Printing Co., 1892

Callahan, J. M. "The Northern Lake Frontier during the Civil War," (with remarks of Gen. H. B. Carrington), The American Historical Association, *Annual Report,* 1896, i, pp. 335–9

Canup, Charles. "Conscription and Draft in Indiana during the Civil War," *Indiana Magazine of History,* X (June 1914), 70–83

Chaddock, Robert Emmett, *Ohio before 1850: a Study of the Early Influence of Pennsylvania and Southern Populations in Ohio.* Studies in History, Economics, and Public Law Edited by the Faculty of Political Science of Columbia University, Vol. XXXI, No. 2. New York: Columbia University Press, 1908

Channing, Edward. *A History of the United States.* 6 vols. New York: Macmillan Co., 1927–30

"The Chicago Conspiracy," *The Atlantic Monthly. A Magazine of Literature, Science, Art and Politics,* XVI (July 1865), 108–20

Church, Charles A. *History of the Republican Party in Illinois, 1854–1912: with a Review of the Aggressions of the Slave Owner.* Rockford, Ill.: Press of Wilson Bros. Co., printers, 1912

Clark, Charles Branch, "Politics in Maryland during the Civil War," *Maryland Historical Magazine,* XXXVI (Sept., Dec. 1941), 239–62, 381–93

Clark, Dan Elbert. *History of Senatorial Elections in Iowa: a Study in American Politics.* Iowa City: State Historical Society, 1912

Cochran, William C. "The Dream of a Northwestern Confederacy," The State Historical Society of Wisconsin, *Proceedings,* 1916, pp. 213–53. Madison, 1917

Cole, Arthur Charles. *The Era of the Civil War, 1848–1870,* Vol. III of *The Centennial History of Illinois.* Edited by Clarence Walford Alvord. 5 vols. Chicago: A. C. McClurg & Co., 1922

Cole, Arthur C. "Lincoln and the Presidential Election of 1864," The Illinois State Historical Society, *Transactions,* 1917, pp. 130–40

Cole, Arthur C. "President Lincoln and the Illinois Radical Republicans," *The Mississippi Valley Historical Review,* IV (March 1918), 417–36

Cole, Cyrenus. *A History of the People of Iowa.* Cedar Rapids, Iowa: Torch Press, 1921

Coleman, Charles H., and Spence, Paul H. "The Charleston Riot, March 28, 1864," The Illinois State Historical Society, *Journal,* XXXIII (March 1940), 7–56

Coleman, Charles H. "The Use of the Term Copperhead during the Civil War," *The Mississippi Valley Historical Review*, XXV (Sept. 1938), 263–4

Colgrove, Kenneth W. "The Delegates to Congress from the Territory of Iowa," *The Iowa Journal of History*, VII (Apr. 1909), 230–65

Cooley, Verna, "Illinois and the Underground Railroad to Canada," The Illinois State Historical Society, *Transactions*, 1917, pp. 76–98

Coulter, E. Merton. *The Civil War and Readjustment in Kentucky*. Chapel Hill: University of North Carolina Press, 1926

Coulter, E. Merton. "The Commercial Intercourse with the Confederacy in the Mississippi Valley, 1861–1865," *The Mississippi Valley Historical Review*, V (March 1919), 377–95

Coulter, E. Merton, "The Effects of Secession upon the Commerce of the Mississippi Valley," *The Mississippi Valley Historical Review*, III (Dec. 1916), 275–300

Crandall, Andrew Wallace. *The Early History of the Republican Party, 1854–1856*. Boston: Richard G. Badger, 1930

Crenshaw, Ollinger, "The Knights of the Golden Circle," *The American Historical Review*, XLVII (Oct. 1941), 23–50

Craven, Avery Odell. *Soil Exhaustion as a Factor in the Agricultural History of Virginia and Maryland, 1606–1860*. University of Illinois Studies in the Social Sciences, Vol. XIII, No. 1. Urbana: University of Illinois, 1925

Davis, Stanton Ling. *Pennsylvania Politics, 1860–63*. Cleveland: The Bookstore, Western Reserve University, 1935

Dewey, David Rich. *Financial History of the United States*. New York, London: Longmans, Green & Co., 1903

Dodd, William E. "The Fight for the Northwest, 1860," *The American Historical Review*, XVI (July 1911), 774–88

Dodd, William E. *Lincoln or Lee: Comparison and Contrast of the Two Greatest Leaders in the War between the States; the Narrow and Accidental Margin of Success*. New York & London: Century Co., 1927

Dudley, Harold M. "The Election of 1864," *The Mississippi Valley Historical Review*, XVIII (March 1932), 500–18

Dunning, William A. "Disloyalty in Two Wars," *The American Historical Review*, XXIV (July 1919), 625–30

Dunning, William A. "The Second Birth of the Republican Party," *The American Historical Review*, XVI (Oct. 1910), 56–63

Ellis, Mrs. L. E. "The Chicago Times during the Civil War," The Illinois State Historical Society, *Transactions*, 1932, pp. 135–82

Ellison, Joseph. *California and the Nation, 1850–1869: a Study of the Relations of a Frontier Community with the Federal Government*. Berkeley: University of California Press, 1927

Ewbank, Louis B. "Morgan's Raid in Indiana," The Indiana State Historical Society *Publications*, VII, no. 2

Fahrney, Ralph Ray. *Horace Greeley and the Tribune in the Civil War*. Cedar Rapids, Iowa: Torch Press, 1936

Faust, Albert Bernhardt. *The German Element in the United States, with Special Reference to Its Political, Moral, Social, and Educational Influence*. 2 vols. New York: Steuben Society of America, 1927

Fesler, Mayo. "Secret Political Societies in the North during the Civil War," *Indiana Magazine of History*, XIV (Sept. 1918), 183–286

Fish, Carl Russell. "The Decision of the Ohio Valley," The American Historical Association, *Report*, 1910, pp. 153–64

Fishback, Mason McCloud. "Illinois Legislation on Slavery and Free Negroes, 1818–1865," The Illinois State Historical Society, *Transactions*, 1904, pp. 414–32

Fite, Emerson David. *The Presidential Campaign of 1860.* New York: Macmillan Co., 1911

Fite, Emerson David. *Social and Industrial Conditions in the North during the Civil War.* New York: Macmillan Co., 1910

Fleming, Walter L. "The Peace Movement in Alabama during the Civil War," *The South Atlantic Quarterly*, II (Apr., Oct. 1903), 114–24, 246–60

Folwell, William Watts. *A History of Minnesota.* 4 vols. St. Paul: Minnesota Historical Society, 1921

Foulke, William Dudley. *Life of Oliver P. Morton; Including His Important Speeches.* 2 vols. Indianapolis & Kansas City: Bowen-Merrill Co., 1899

Friedel, Frank. "The Loyal Publication Society: a Pro-Union Propaganda Agency," *The Mississippi Valley Historical Review*, XXVI (Dec. 1939), 359–76

Fuller, George N. "Settlement of Michigan Territory," *The Mississippi Valley Historical Review*, II (June 1915), 25–55

Gates, Paul Wallace. *The Illinois Central Railroad and Its Colonization Work.* Harvard Economic Studies, Vol. XLII. Cambridge: Harvard University Press, 1934

Geikie, James. *The Great Ice Age and Its Relation to the Antiquity of Man.* 3rd ed., largely rewritten. London: E. Stanford, 1894

Glover, Gilbert Graffenried. *Immediate Pre-Civil War Compromise Efforts.* Contribution to Education Published under the Direction of George Peabody College for Teachers, No. 131. Nashville: George Peabody College for Teachers, 1934

Goodwin, Cardinal. "The American Occupation of Iowa, 1833 to 1860," *The Iowa Journal of History and Politics*, XVIII (Jan. 1919), 83–102

Goodwin, Cardinal. "The Movement of American Settlers into Wisconsin and Minnesota," *The Iowa Journal of History and Politics*, XVII (July 1919), 406–28

Goodwin, Cardinal. *The Trans-Mississippi West (1803–1853): a History of Its Acquisition and Settlement.* New York & London: Appleton, 1922

Green, Anna M. "Civil War Public Opinion of General Grant," The Illinois State Historical Society, *Journal*, XXII (Apr. 1929), 1–64

Greene, Evarts B. "Sectional Forces in the History of Illinois," The Illinois State Historical Society, *Transactions*, 1903, pp. 75–83

Greene, Evarts B. "Some Aspects of Politics in the Middle West, 1860–72," The State Historical Society of Wisconsin, *Proceedings*, 1911, pp. 60–76

Hamilton, E. Bently. "The Union League: Its Origin and Achievements in the Civil War," The Illinois State Historical Society, *Transactions*, 1921, pp. 110–15

Hamilton, J. G. de Roulhac. "The Heroes of America," Southern History Association, *Publications*, XI (Washington, Jan. 1907), 10–19

Harbison, Winfred A. "The Elections of 1862 as a Vote of Want of Confidence in President Lincoln," *Michigan Academy of Science, Arts, and Letters, Papers,* XIV (1930), 499–513

Harbison, Winfred A. "Indiana Republicans and the Re-election of President Lincoln," *Indiana Magazine of History,* XXXIV (March 1938), 42–64

Harbison, Winfred A. *The Opposition to President Lincoln within the Republican Party.* Urbana, Ill., 1930

Harbison, Winfred A., ed. "Zachariah Chandler's Part in the Re-election of Abraham Lincoln," *The Mississippi Valley Historical Review,* XXII (Sept. 1935), 267–76

Harris, N. Dwight. *The History of Negro Servitude in Illinois.* Chicago: A. C. McClurg & Co., 1904

Headley, John William. *Confederate Operations in Canada and New York.* New York & Washington: Neale Publishing Co., 1906

Hesseltine, William Best. *Civil War Prisons: a Study in War Psychology.* Columbus: Ohio State University Press, 1930

Hicks, John D. "The Organization of the Volunteer Army in 1861 with Special Reference to Minnesota," *Minnesota History Bulletin,* II (Feb. 1918), 324–368

Hill, Benjamin Harvey, Jr. *Senator Benjamin H. Hill of Georgia. His Life, Speeches, and Writings.* . . . Atlanta: T. H. P. Bloodworth, 1893

Hofer, J. M. "Development of the Peace Movement in Illinois during the Civil War," The Illinois State Historical Society, *Journal,* XXIV (Apr. 1931), 110–28

Holt, Edgar Allan. *Party Politics in Ohio, 1840–50.* Ohio Historical Collections, Vol. I, Columbus: Ohio State Archaeological and Historical Society, 1931

Holt, Robert D. "The Political Career of William A. Richardson," The Illinois State Historical Society, *Journal,* XXVI (Oct. 1933), 222–69

Hubbart, Henry Clyde. *The Older Middle West, 1840–1880: Its Social, Economic, and Political Life and Sectional Tendencies before, during, and after the Civil War.* The American Historical Association. New York: D. Appleton-Century Co., 1936

Hubbart, Henry Clyde. " 'Pro-Southern' Influences in the Free West, 1840–1865," *The Mississippi Valley Historical Review,* XX (June 1933), 45–62

Hutchinson, William T. *Cyrus Hall McCormick: Harvest, 1856–1884.* New York & London: D. Appleton-Century Co., 1935

Johnson, Allen. "Illinois as a Constituency in 1850," *The Iowa Journal of History and Politics,* III (July 1905), 399–421

Johnson, Allen. *Stephen A. Douglas: a Study in American Politics.* New York: Macmillan Co., 1908

Johnson, Peter Leo. "Port Washington Draft Riot of 1862," *Mid-America,* XII, n.s. I (Jan. 1930), 212–22

Jordan, Henry D. "Daniel Wolsey Voorhees," *The Mississippi Valley Historical Review,* VI (March 1920), 532–55

Jordan, Wayne. "The Hopkinsville Rebellion," *Ohio State Archaeological and Historical Quarterly,* XLVII (Oct. 1938), 319–54

Joyner, Fred B. "William Cortenus Schenk, Pioneer and Statesman of Ohio," *Ohio State Archaeological and Historical Quarterly* (Oct. 1938)

Kellar, Herbert A. "The Reaper as a Factor in the Development of the Agriculture of Illinois, 1834–1865," The Illinois State Historical Society, *Transactions*, 1927, pp. 105–14

Kenworthy, Leonard S. *The Tall Sycamore of the Wabash, Daniel Wolsey Voorhees*. Boston: Bruce Humphries, 1936

Kimball, E. L. "Richard Yates: His Record as Civil War Governor of Illinois," The Illinois State Historical Society, *Journal*, XXIII (Apr. 1930), 1–83

Kirkland, Edward Chase. *The Peacemakers of 1864*. New York: Macmillan Co., 1927

Knapp, Charles Merriam. *New Jersey Politics during the Period of the Civil War and Reconstruction*. Geneva, N. Y.: W. F. Humphrey, 1924

Kohlmeier, Albert L. "Commerce and Union Settlement in the Old Northwest in 1860," The Illinois State Historical Society, *Transactions*, 1923, pp. 154–161

Kohlmeier, Albert L. *The Old Northwest as the Keystone of the Arch of American Federal Union: a Study in Commerce and Politics*. Bloomington, Ind.: Principia Press, 1938

Knox, Clinton Everett. "The Possibilities of Compromise in the Senate Committee of Thirteen and the Responsibility for Failure," *The Journal of Negro History*, XVII (Oct. 1932), 437–65

Lane, J. Robert. *A Political History of Connecticut during the Civil War*. Washington, D.C.: Catholic University of America, 1941

Laughlin, Sceva Bright. *Missouri Politics during the Civil War*. Salem, Ore.: S. B. Laughlin, 1930

Lee, Judson Fiske. "Transportation, a Factor in the Development of Northern Illinois Previous to 1860," *The Illinois State Historical Society, Journal* (Apr. 1917), 17–86

Long, Byron E. "Joshua Reed Giddings: A Champion of Political Freedom," *Ohio Archaeological and Historical Publications*, XXVIII (1919), 1–47

Lonn, Ella. *Desertion during the Civil War*. The American Historical Association. New York & London: D. Appleton & Co., 1928

Lowrey, Lawrence Tyndale. *Northern Opinion of Approaching Secession, October, 1859–November, 1860*. Smith College Studies in History, Vol. III, No. 4. Northampton, Mass.: Smith College, 1918

Lynch, William O. "The Flow of Colonists to and from Indiana before the Civil War," *Indiana Magazine of History*, XI (March 1915), 1–8

Lyons, Adelide Avery. "Religious Defense of Slavery in the North," Trinity College Historical Society, *Historical Papers*, XIII (Durham, N.C., 1919), 5–34

Marshall, John A. *American Bastile: a History of Illegal Arrests and Imprisonments of American Citizens during the Late Civil War*. Philadelphia: T. W. Hartley, 1869

Martin, Bessie. *Desertion of Alabama Troops from the Confederate Army: a Study in Sectionalism*. Columbia University Studies, No. 378. New York: Columbia University Press, 1932

Mathews, Lois Kimball. *The Expansion of New England: the Spread of New England Settlement and Institutions to the Mississippi River, 1620–1865*. Boston & New York: Houghton Mifflin Co., 1909

Matthews, Albert, "Origin of Butternut and Copperhead," The Colonial Society of Massachusetts, *Publications*, XX (Apr. 1918), 205–37

Matthews, Albert. "A Last Word on 'Copperhead,'" *The Nation: A Weekly Journal Devoted to Politics, Literature, Science, Drama, Music, Art, Finance Founded 1865*, CVI (June 29, 1918), 758. (Letter to the editor, Boston, Apr. 6)

Matthews, Sidney T. "Control of the Baltimore Press during the Civil War," *Maryland Historical Magazine*, XXXVI (June 1941), 150–70

McFarland, R. W. "The Morgan Raid in Ohio," *Ohio Archaeological and Historical Publications*, XVII (1908), 243–46

McHarry, Jessie, "John Reynolds," The Illinois State Historical Society, *Journal*, VI (Apr. 1913), 7–57

Milton, George Fort. *The Eve of Conflict: Stephen A. Douglas and the Needless War*. Boston & New York: Houghton Mifflin Co., 1934

Minahan, Mary Canisius. "James A. McMaster: a Pioneer Catholic Journalist," The American Catholic Historical Society, *Records*, XLVII (June 1936), 87–131

Mitchell, Robert Stewart, *Horatio Seymour of New York*. Cambridge, Mass.: Harvard University Press, 1938

Moore, Albert Burton. *Conscription and Conflict in the Confederacy*. New York: Macmillan Co., 1924

Morrow, Curtis Hugh. "Politico-Military Secret Societies of the Northwest," *Social Science*, IV (Nov. 1928–Aug. 1929), 9–31, 222–42, 348–61, 463–76, V (Nov. 1929), 73–84

Murphey, Hermon King. "The Northern Railroads and the Civil War," *The Mississippi Valley Historical Review*, V (Dec. 1918), 324–38

Murphy, Charles B. "Samuel J. Tilden and the Civil War," *The South Atlantic Quarterly*, XXXIII (July 1934), 261–71

Myers, William Starr. *A Study in Personality: General George Brinton McClellan*. New York & London: D. Appleton-Century Co., 1934

Nevins, Allan, *Fremont, the West's Greatest Adventurer*. New York & London: Harper & Bros., 1928

Nicolay, John G., and Hay, John, eds. *Abraham Lincoln: Complete Works, Comprising His Speeches, Letters, State Papers, and Miscellaneous Writings*. 2 vols. New York: Century Co., c. 1894

Nichols, Roy Franklin. *Franklin Pierce, Young Hickory of the Granite Hills*. Philadelphia: University of Pennsylvania Press, 1931

Oliver, John W. "Draft Riots in Wisconsin during the Civil War," *The Wisconsin Magazine of History*, II (March 1919), 334–37

Owsley, Frank Lawrence. "Defeatism in the Confederacy," *The North Carolina Historical Review*, III (July 1926), 446–56

Owsley, Frank Lawrence. *State Rights in the Confederacy*. Chicago: University of Chicago Press, c. 1925

Parish, John Carl. *George Wallace Jones*. Iowa Biographical Series. Edited by Benjamin F. Shambaugh. Iowa City: The State Historical Society of Iowa, 1912

Paxson, Frederic L. "The Railways of the Old Northwest before the Civil War," The Wisconsin Academy of Sciences, Arts, and Letters. *Transactions*, XVII (1912), 243–74

Pelzer, Louis. "The Disintegration and Organization of Political Parties in

Iowa, 1852–1860," The Mississippi Valley Historical Association, *Proceedings,* V (1911–1912), 158–66

Pelzer, Louis. "The History and Principles of the Democratic Party of the Territory of Iowa," *The Iowa Journal of History and Politics,* VI (1908), 3–54, 163–246, VII (1909), 179–229

Pennell, William W., and Vance, J. R. "Holmes County Rebellion—Fort Fizzle," *Ohio Archaeological and Historical Quarterly,* XL (Jan. 1931), 23–51

Plumb, Ralph G. *Badger Politics, 1836–1930.* Manitowoc, Wis.: Brandt Printing & Binding Co., 1930

Pooley, William Vipond. *The Settlement of Illinois from 1830 to 1850.* Bulletin of the University of Wisconsin, No. 220, History Series, Vol. I, No. 4. Madison, 1908

Porter, George Henry. *Ohio Politics during the Civil War Period.* Studies in History, Economics, and Public Law Edited by the Faculty of Political Science of Columbia University, Vol. XL, No. 2. New York: Columbia University Press, 1911

Potter, David M. "Horace Greeley and Peaceable Secession," *The Journal of Southern History,* VII (May 1941), 145–59

Power, Richard Lyle. "Wet Lands and the Hoosier Stereotype," *The Mississippi Valley Historical Review,* XXII (June, 1935), 33–48

Pratt, Harry E. "The Repudiation of Lincoln's War Policy in 1862—Stuart-Swett Congressional Campaign," The Illinois State Historical Society. *Journal,* XXIV (Apr. 1931), 129–40

Putnam, James William. *The Illinois and Lake Michigan Canal: a Study in Economic History.* Chicago Historical Society Collections, Vol. X. Chicago: University of Chicago Press, 1918

Radcliffe, George L. P. *Governor Thomas Hicks of Maryland and the Civil War.* Johns Hopkins University Studies in Historical and Political Science, Ser. XIX, No. 11. Baltimore: Johns Hopkins Press, 1901

Ramey, Homer A. "Fort Fizzle," The Historical Society of Northwestern Ohio, *Quarterly Bulletin,* XIII (Jan. 1941), 1–7

Randall, James Garfield. *The Civil War and Reconstruction.* New York: D. C. Heath & Co., c. 1937

Randall, James Garfield. *Constitutional Problems under Lincoln.* New York & London: D. Appleton & Co., 1926

Raney, William F. "Recruiting and Crimping in Canada for the Northern Forces, 1861–1865," *The Mississippi Valley Historical Review,* X (June 1923), 21–33

Rhodes, James Ford. *History of the United States from the Compromise of 1850 to the End of the Roosevelt Administration.* 9 vols. New York: Macmillan Co., 1928

Robeson, George F. "Henry Clay Dean," *Palimpsest,* V (Sept. 1924), 321–33

Rogers, Adolph. "North Carolina and Indiana; a Tie that Binds": *Indiana Magazine of History,* V (June 1909), 49–56

Ross, Earle D. "Northern Sectionalism in the Civil War Era," *The Iowa Journal of History and Politics,* XXX (Oct. 1932), 455–512

Russ, William A., Jr. "Franklin Weirick: 'Copperhead' of Central Pennsylvania," *Pennsylvania History,* V (Oct. 1938), 245–56

Russell, R. R. "A Revaluation of the Period before the Civil War: Railroads," *The Mississippi Valley Historical Review*, XV (Dec. 1928), 341–54

Ryan, Daniel J. *The Civil War Literature of Ohio: a Bibliography with Explanatory and Historical Notes.* Cleveland: Burrows Bros. Co., 1911

Sanger, Donald Bridgman. "The Chicago Times and the Civil War," *The Mississippi Valley Historical Review*, XVII (March 1931), 557–80

Schafer, Joseph. *Four Wisconsin Counties, Prairie and Forest.* Wisconsin Domesday Book, General Studies, Vol. II. Madison: State Historical Society of Wisconsin, 1927

Schafer, Joseph. "Peopling the Middle West," *The Wisconsin Magazine of History*, XXI (Sept. 1937), 85–106

Schafer, Joseph. "Who Elected Lincoln?" *The American Historical Review*, XLVII (Oct. 1941), 51–63

Schmidt, Louis B. "History of Congressional Elections in Iowa," *The Iowa Journal of History and Politics*, X (Oct. 1912), 463–502

Scott, Franklin D. "The Political Career of William R. Morrison," The Illinois State Historical Society, *Transactions*, 1926, pp. 134–71

Scrugham, Mary. *The Peaceable Americans of 1860–1861: a Study in Public Opinion.* Studies in History, Economics, and Public Law Edited by the Faculty of Political Science of Columbia University, XCVI, No. 3. New York, 1921

Sellers, James L. "James R. Doolittle," *The Wisconsin Magazine of History*, XVII (1933), 168–78, 277–306, 393–401, XVIII (1940), 20–41, 178–87

Sellers, James L. "Republicanism and State Rights in Wisconsin," *The Mississippi Valley Historical Review*, XVII (Sept. 1930), 213–29

Sellery, George Clark. *Lincoln's Suspension of Habeas Corpus as Viewed by Congress.* University of Wisconsin, *Bulletin*, History Series, I, 213–86

Shannon, Fred Albert. *The Organization and Administration of the Union Army, 1861–1865.* 2 vols. Cleveland: Arthur H. Clark Co., 1928

Sharp, Walter Rice. "Henry S. Lane and the Formation of the Republican Party in Indiana," *The Mississippi Valley Historical Review*, VII (Sept. 1920), 93–112

Sherwood, Henry Noble. "The Movement in Ohio to Deport the Negro," The Historical and Philosophical Society of Ohio, *Quarterly Publication*, VII (June & Sept. 1912), 53–78

Shilling, David Carl. "The Relation of Southern Ohio to the South during the Decade preceding the Civil War," The Historical and Philosophical Society of Ohio. *Publication*, VIII (Jan.–Mar. 1913), 1–28

Shippee, Lester Burrell. "Social and Economic Effects of the Civil War with Special Reference to Minnesota," *Minnesota History Bulletin*, II (May, 1918), 389–412

Smith, Donnal V. "Salmon P. Chase and the Election of 1860," *Ohio Archaeological and Historical Publications*, XXXIX (1930), 515–607, 769–844

Smith, Edward Conrad. *The Borderland in the Civil War.* New York: Macmillan Co., 1927

Smith, Guy Harold. "The Settlement and Distribution of the Population in Wisconsin," Wisconsin Academy of Sciences, Arts, and Letters, *Transactions*, XXIV (1929), 53–107

Smith, Theodore Clarke. *The Liberty and Free Soil Parties in the Northwest.*

Toppan Prize Essay of 1896. Harvard Historical Studies, VI. New York: Longmans, Green & Co., 1897

Smith, William Ernest. *The Frances Preston Blair Family in Politics.* 2 vols. New York: Macmillan Co., 1933

Snepp, Daniel W. "Evansville's Channels of Trade and the Secession Movement, 1850–1865," The Indiana Historical Society, *Publications,* VIII (Indianapolis, 1928), 325–91

Stevens, J. Harold. "The Influence of New England in Michigan," *Michigan History Magazine,* XIX (autumn, 1935), 321–53

Stiles, C. C. "The Skunk River War (or Tally War), Keokuk County, August, 1863," *Annals of Iowa,* 3rd Ser., XIX, 614–31

Streeter, Floyd Benjamin. *Political Parties in Michigan, 1837–1860: an Historical Study of Political Issues and Parties in Michigan from the Admission of the State to the Civil War.* Michigan Historical Publications, University Series, Vol. IV. Lansing: Michigan Historical Commission, 1918

Sweet, William Warren. *The Methodist Episcopal Church and the Civil War.* Cincinnati: Methodist Book Concern Press, 1912

Tasher, Lucy L. "The Missouri Democrat and the Civil War," *The Missouri Historical Review,* XXXI (July 1937), 402–19

Tatum, Georgia Lee. *Disloyalty in the Confederacy.* Chapel Hill: University of North Carolina Press, 1934

Turner, Frederick Jackson. *The United States, 1830–1850: the Nation and Its Sections.* With an introduction by Avery Craven. New York: Henry Holt & Co., c. 1935

Upham, Cyril B. "Historical Survey of the Militia in Iowa, 1838–1865," *The Iowa Journal of History and Politics,* XVII (July 1919), 299–405

Vallandigham, Edward N. "Clement L. Vallandigham, 'Copperhead,'" *Putnam's Monthly: a Magazine of Literature, Art and Life,* II (Aug. 1907), 590–9

Vander Velde, Lewis G. *The Presbyterian Churches and the Federal Union, 1861–69.* Harvard Historical Studies. . . . Vol. XXXIII. Cambridge, Mass.: Harvard University Press, 1932

Van Fossan, W. H. "Clement L. Vallandigham," *Ohio Archaeological and Historical Publications,* XXIII (1914), 256–67

Ware, Edith Ellen. *Political Opinion in Massachusetts during the Civil War and Reconstruction.* Studies in History, Economics, and Public Law Edited by the Faculty of Political Science of Columbia University, LXXIV, No. 2. New York: Columbia University, 1916

Way, R. B. "The Commerce of the Lower Mississippi in the Period 1830–1860," *The Mississippi Valley Historical Association. Proceedings,* X (July 1920). 57–68

Weber, L. J. "Morgan's Raid," *Ohio Archaeological and Historical Publications,* XVIII (1909), 79–104

Weeden, William B. *War Government, Federal and State in Massachusetts, New York, Pennsylvania, and Indiana, 1861–1865.* Boston & New York: Houghton Mifflin & Co., 1906

White, Horace. *The Life of Lyman Trumbull.* Boston and New York: Houghton Mifflin Co., 1913

Williams, Harry. "Benjamin F. Wade and the Atrocity Propaganda of the Civil

War," *Ohio Archaeological and Historical Quarterly,* XLVIII (Jan. 1939), 33–43

Williams, T. Harry. *Lincoln and the Radicals.* Madison: University of Wisconsin Press, 1941

Wilson, Buford, "Southern Illinois during the Civil War," The Illinois State Historical Society, *Transactions,* 1911, pp. 93–106

Wilson, Charles R. "Cincinnati's Reputation during the Civil War," *The Journal of Southern History,* II (Nov. 1936), 468–79

Wilson, Charles R. "Cincinnati a Southern Outpost in 1860–61?" *The Mississippi Valley Historical Review,* XXIV (March 1938), 473–82

Wilson, Charles R. "McClellan's Changing Views on the Peace Plank of 1864," *The American Historical Review,* XXXVIII (Apr. 1933), 498–505

Wilson, Charles J. [sic. R.]. "The Negro in Early Ohio," *Ohio Archaeological and Historical Publications,* XXXIX (1930), 717–68

Wilson, Charles R. "New Light on the Lincoln-Blair-Fremont 'Bargain' of 1864," *The American Historical Review,* XLII (Oct. 1936), 71–8

Wilson, Charles R., ed. "The Original Chase Organization Meeting and *The Next Presidential Election,*" *The Mississippi Valley Historical Review,* XXIII (June 1936), 61–79

Wittke, Carl. *We Who Built America: the Saga of the Immigrant.* New York: Prentice-Hall, Inc., 1939

Woodburn, James Albert. "Party Politics in Indiana during the Civil War," The American Historical Association, *Annual Report,* 1902, I, 223–52

Wright, Edward N. *Conscientious Objectors in the Civil War.* Philadelphia: University of Pennsylvania Press, 1934

Zimmerman, Charles, A.M. "The Origin and Rise of the Republican Party in Indiana from 1854 to 1860," *Indiana Magazine of History,* XIII (Sept., Dec. 1917), 211–69, 349–412

Index